D1032085

2-97

CHAN KOM

A Maya Village

CHAN KOM

A Maya Village

BY

ROBERT REDFIELD

AND

ALFONSO VILLA ROJAS

LIBRARY
SEMINOLE JR. COLLEGE
Rec. MAY 23 1972
SANFORD, FLORIDA

Phoenix Books

THE UNIVERSITY OF CHICAGO PRESS

CHICAGO & LONDON

This book is also available in a clothbound edition from
THE UNIVERSITY OF CHICAGO PRESS
It includes appendixes and a bibliography

THE UNIVERSITY OF CHICAGO PRESS, CHICAGO & LONDON
The University of Toronto Press, Toronto 5, Canada

First published in 1934 by the Carnegie Institution of Washington
First Phoenix edition 1962
Third Impression 1967
Printed in the United States of America

CONTENTS

v

LIST OF ILLUSTRATIONS

VII

TEXT-FIGURES

TABLES

PREFACE

A first acquaintance with the peninsula of Yucatan indicates the presence of one underlying folk culture common to all the communities of the region, from the most isolated village of what was formerly the Territory of Quintana Roo to the capital city of Merida. The local differences in Yucatan that do strike the attention are those apparently due to the different degrees to which various communities have been exposed to what we often speak of as "civilization"—schools, roads and economic exploitation. The towns and villages are in varying stages of a process of transition as a result of these influences.

When, therefore, in 1930, Carnegie Institution of Washington made provision for ethnological and sociological investigation in Yucatan, these facts guided the formation of a plan of research involving, first, the study of a community in which the folk culture is fairly complete and, second, the study of other communities where that culture is in disorganization or conversion into something else. After the first part of this plan had been well advanced, a beginning was made with the second part. Now, at the time when these words are written, some work, at least, has been carried on by the authors and their associates in Merida, in the railroad town of Dzitas and in certain villages in Quintana Roo. Although the present volume is presented as a simple ethnographic description, the work has been done with a view to a future comparative study of these different communities.

This book is an account of the basic folk culture as it manifests itself in one particular village in eastern Yucatan. Though that village is composed of persons of Maya blood and speech, and in this sense justifies the sub-title of this report, their culture can not be called, strictly speaking, Indian, any more than it can be called Spanish. Many of the customs described in these pages could be as well or better reported from towns on the railroad or even from neighborhoods in the city. In Yucatan, culture elements of European derivation have penetrated to the uttermost forest hinterland, while Indian practices and ceremonies are carried on by people who dwell in the capital. Nevertheless, taken as a whole, the culture of the village is notably different from that of the city. It is the folk culture and the village community that concern us, while it is the differences from the town and the city that constitute the larger problem to which this first report is a contribution.

The reader should know something of the immediate circumstances under which the work was done, and of the workers who did it. Alfonso Villa was born and brought up in Merida. In 1927 he left the third year of the preparatory school of that city to take charge of the Chan Kom school. The University of Chicago gave me leave of absence to permit me to go to Yucatan and undertake the investigation for Carnegie Institution of Washington. In the winter of 1930, I made Villa's acquaintance, and paid a short visit to Chan Kom. I spent the first five months of 1931 in Yucatan; half of my time was devoted to the study of Chan Kom.

During this period, and for several months thereafter, Villa also devoted time remaining to him after the discharge of his duties as teacher to the study of the community. He remained in Chan Kom, with occasional short periods of absence, until December 1931. In February 1933, I spent three weeks with Eustaquio Ceme of Chan Kom, going over a provisional draft of this manuscript and checking and revising it. Villa spent some days in May at the same task. The writing of the ethnological text was done by me, but Villa has read it all with care, has suggested many small changes, and has given it his approval. I will add that while I speak Spanish, my knowledge of Maya is confined to a vocabulary, simple conversational phrases, and a reading knowledge with the aid of a dictionary. Villa has obtained a good conversational ability in the language.

The support and sympathy and sound advice of Dr. A. V. Kidder, Chairman of the Division of Historical Research of Carnegie Institution, has carried the authors along through their work. At Chichen Itza, Dr. Sylvanus G. Morley and his staff gave much practical help. Miss Katheryn MacKay, during the period when she was Staff Nurse at Carnegie Headquarters at Chichen, was of great assistance. Indeed, she brought about the collaboration between Villa and me. It was her work in the free clinic that gained us the goodwill of the Indians of the villages near Chichen. Miss MacKay has generously allowed us to publish materials she collected on birth customs. Mr. Ralph L. Roys gave many hours of his time and lent his ability to the translation of the Maya prayers and to a general checking of the text. Dr. Manuel Andrade and Mr. Alfredo Barrera Vasquez also gave invaluable advice with regard to Maya passages. We have included data on physical type furnished by Dr. Morris Steggerda, who spent pleasant days with the authors in Chan Kom; and we have summarized medical data secured in the village by Dr. George C. Shattuck and his associates. Father T. L. Riggs assisted in the identification of elements of Catholic ritual and liturgy; we are very grateful to him. My wife, Margaret Park Redfield, has participated in the planning of the work and in the preparation of the report; she has been my associate in the comparative study of Dzitas, begun in 1933. Mrs. Florence Ziegler Ljunggren during the field season of 1931 gave very efficient assistance, drawing maps and preparing tables. Dr. Alfred M. Tozzer, Dr. Kidder and Mrs. Josephine Hallinan have read all or part of the manuscript, and have made useful suggestions. Of the many men and women in Chan Kom who gave generously of their time and knowledge and patience, Sr. Don Eustaquio Ceme is to be specially mentioned. Our debt to him is very great. We particularly acknowledge the permission he has given us to publish the autobiographic document that appears in Chapter XIII. Dr. Steggerda, Miss MacKay and Mr. Fernando Barbachano gave permission to publish photographs.

In the spelling of Maya words, there is here followed an orthography much used in Yucatan, in which the glottalized consonants corresponding, respectively, to t, p, c, tz and ch are written th, pp, k, dz and ch̃. Spanish words are printed in italics and Maya words in Roman characters.

ROBERT REDFIELD

University of Chicago

CHAN KOM—A MAYA VILLAGE

Chapter I

THE VILLAGE OF CHAN KOM

This book describes the mode of life in a peasant village. A large part of the population of the peninsula of Yucatan dwells in such villages. These villages are small communities of illiterate agriculturalists, carrying on a homogeneous culture transmitted by oral tradition. They differ from the communities of the preliterate tribesman in that they are politically and economically dependent upon the towns and cities of modern literate civilization and that the villagers are well aware of the townsman and city dweller and in part define their position in the world in terms of these. The peasant is a rustic, and he knows it.

Of those people of Yucatan who do not live in peasant villages, a few in the extreme southern part of the peninsula are truly primitive. The Lacandones (on the borders of Chiapas) are people of this sort. They live apart from modern governmental controls; they make little use of money; literacy has neither practical nor prestige value.

About ninety thousand people live in Merida, the capital of the state of Yucatan. This is the one city of the peninsula. Like other provincial Mexican cities, there is little industry, and the city resembles an overgrown town. But the size of the population, the relatively high mobility, the abundance and importance of impersonal contacts and of formal institutional controls make it much like any North American or European city.

Besides the primitive tribal settlement, the peasant village and the city, one may distinguish the town, intermediate between the city and the village on this rough scale of community types. The town in Yucatan is, in most cases, on the railroad. There are many mixed-bloods in the population, whereas the peasant village is almost entirely Indian. Not all the people are agriculturalists; some are tradesmen and artisans. Labor, generally, is more specialized, professionalized and secularized. There is more literacy and more practical need for it. Class distinctions are present, and these are in part based on degree of sophistication, or participation in the life of a wider world, and tend to be associated with racial differences or with distinctions in costume.

GRADIENTS OF CIVILIZATION IN YUCATAN

The peninsula of Yucatan is physiographically simple: a low, level limestone shelf, without watercourse of any size, and diversified only by countless small irregular hillocks and corresponding depressions.[1] But differences in rainfall make

---

[1] There are hills in the southwest and extreme south.

great differences in vegetation and hence in the suitability of the land for occupation. As one goes east and south, rainfall increases and scrubby bush gives way to higher, denser bush, and then to tropical rain forest. The old boundary line between Yucatan and Quintana Roo[1] marked a rough division between the semiarid bush, or jungle, and the rainier forest. Only in the northwestern part of the peninsula can be grown henequen, the one money crop that has made Yucatan so dependent upon the markets of the world. Here, in the northwest where henequen is grown, are large estates and big landowners; here dwell most of the population; here are the railways, the newspapers and the books. As one goes east and south from Merida, in the extreme northwest corner, the center of political and social influence, the population grows scantier, the railways and the towns come to an end, the villages become fewer and the proportion of Indian blood and custom increases. The gradients of population, economic development and Spanish-American civilization run southeastward, diminishing, until the outermost hinterland is reached in the south central part of what was, until recently, the Territory of Quintana Roo. This hinterland is inhabited by a few thousand Indians whose customs are much like those of the villages of Yucatan, but who maintain a tribal organization largely apart from and unfriendly to modern governmental control. In fact, these Indians are not quite peasant villagers, as are most of the people of Yucatan, but tend to fall into the category of primitive tribesmen. Two extractive industries, chicle and logwood, bring these forest Indians into limited contact with the economy of the wider world.

THE INTERMEDIATE VILLAGES

The village of Chan Kom lies in the north central part of the peninsula, in a position geographically and socially intermediate between the villages of the henequen area to the northwest and the settlements in the tropical forests to the south. It is situated in that zone that lies between the rail termini and the tropical rain forests. This zone is too far southeast for henequen production and too far northwest for chicle exploitation; therefore the Indians within it work only for themselves. They raise corn which they themselves consume or sell or barter for manufactured articles. Very few are laborers for hire. In their independence of the larger hacienda, in their relative remoteness, and in the recency of their incorporation into the Yucatecan state, the villages in this area, of which Chan Kom is one, differ from the villages northwest of them.

On the other hand, the Indians of this area differ from those of Quintana Roo in the kind and degree of adjustment they have made to the modern world. The Quintana Roo Indians are still politically independent; their organization is local and tribal; and schools have only a recent and precarious foothold among them. The Indians of the Chan Kom area, however, are integral parts of the State of Yucatan. This is the outermost region in which governmental and educational controls function effectively. The interests of the villagers here are not wholly turned in upon themselves, but are directed northwestward, toward the towns from

---

[1] Abolished in January 1932, when Quintana Roo was divided and the north half made a part of the state of Yucatan and the south half a part of the state of Campeche.

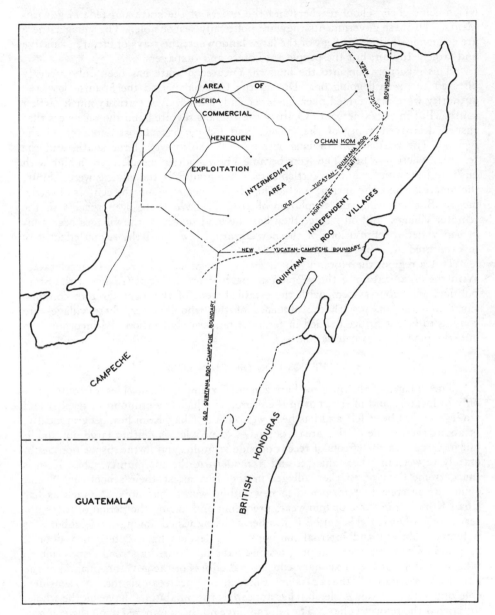

FIG. 1—Peninsula of Yucatan, showing location of Chan Kom.

which come their school teachers and the orders of the state and federal governments. To these governments they are politically responsible. The villagers here are economically independent of the large landowner; the ways of life are primitive and largely Indian; but the people are voters and taxpayers.

This incorporation into the modern Yucatecan state has been only recently effected and is still going on. During the Colonial period the Spanish law and authority were maintained over this area and, indeed, over territory much farther south. But in the Nineteenth Century the Indians revolted and the race wars that ensued destroyed many of the villages and for periods almost depopulated the region. The recalcitrant Indians withdrew to the forests of the south, and the territory where now lies Chan Kom became a new frontier, a region grown high with bush, to be rewon for human settlement. Then gradually the villages were rebuilt; the cenotes, where the ancient pueblos had been, became again the centers of settlement. But only since the revolution of 1910–21 have there been schools in the remoter villages, and only since then has the land tenure of the villages been confirmed under the provisions of the new agrarian laws, and the region effectively incorporated into the state of Yucatan.[1]

It is a region, therefore, in which social change has been recently accelerated. With the organization of the people into participant divisions (Ligas) of the State political and labor system, with the establishment of the local agrarian commissions, and especially with the influence of the schoolteacher, these villages are coming to face a future defined in terms of modern civilization and incorporation into the modern Mexican nation.

THE POSITION OF CHAN KOM

The villages of this intermediate zone differ among themselves, of course, not only in location and in size, but in the degree to which the stimulus of teacher and tradesman has been felt and has been welcomed. Chan Kom lies, geographically, in about the middle of this area; its size—250 people—is neither large nor small; but in respect to the effects of recent outside stimulus and in the disposition deliberately to welcome these changes and to modernize the community, Chan Kom is the extreme deviate. Other villages in the area assist their schoolteacher and evince an interest in reform and in new public works, but none so much as has Chan Kom in the three or four years preceding and during the period of these observations. During this period it has been distinguished among its neighbors for industry, sobriety and internal harmony. Its leaders have determined upon a program of improvement and progress and have manifested a strong disposition to take advantage of the missionary educational efforts of the government and of the advice and assistance of the occasional American or Yucatecan visitor. No considerable opposition to this leadership has appeared; the inhabitants have, on the whole, supported the reform policy. The reforms have not been imposed upon the community from outside; they have arisen out of the conviction of the village leaders and

---

[1] The map (p. 5) indicates how the legal confirmation of the communal lands (ejidos) began in Yucatan first in the cases of villages and towns near the railroads, and only later, in 1920–24, reached the region between Valladolid and Sotuta, where Chan Kom is situated.

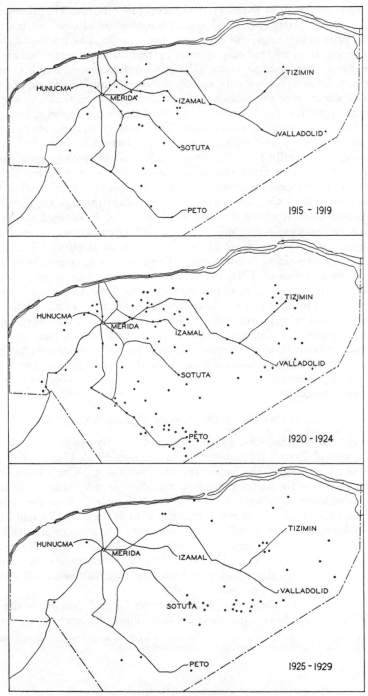

Fig. 2—Maps showing outward spread of *ejido* grants during three five-year periods.

have been put into effect by the efforts of the people themselves. The principal of these reforms involves matters of public hygiene, construction of new and more modern public and private buildings, and support of the school. The traditional social and religious life has been affected only indirectly; there has been no frontal attack upon it. The shaman continues to function; he is still quite essential and his prestige has suffered very little, and then only among the more traveled and experienced few.

The explanation of the fact that Chan Kom has, more than any other Maya village in the region, defined "progress" for itself lies in a complex of circumstances that can be only imperfectly understood. One of these circumstances is certainly the unusual sympathy and guidance the people have had from certain of their schoolteachers, especially from the junior author of this monograph. Another is the particular attention given the village by Americans at Chichen Itza, where the Carnegie Institution maintains its center for archæological work. Contacts with the Americans at Chichen began to be significant through the distribution of medicines and medical advice from the clinic there, and extended to the visits of scientific investigators in the village.[1] A third circumstance is, probably, the chance occurrence in the village of Maya with unusual gifts of leadership and temperamental disposition to enterprise. These factors have interacted upon one another. The presence of Villa, the teacher, drew the Americans at Chichen to Chan Kom; on the other hand, Villa's contacts with these Americans increased and partly shaped his interest in the village where he worked. Villa's advice and help supported the leadership native in the village. And the traditional Maya institution of *fagina*, whereby membership in the community is conditional upon faithful performance of labor tasks for purposes decided by the local leaders, has gradually eliminated those families who were least disposed to cooperate in the program of reform and improvement, and attracted to the village new families to whom the reforms were congenial.

THE LOCATION OF CHAN KOM: COMMUNICATIONS

The state of Yucatan (disregarding the part recently assigned to it by the partition of Quintana Roo) is for administrative purposes divided into sixteen *partidos;* each is named after the most important town within it. Chan Kom lies in the southwestern part of the southeasternmost *partido*, that of Valladolid. It is situated about 50 kilometers southwest of the town of Valladolid, where the railroad terminates, and about 14 kilometers south (and a little east) of Chichen Itza.

Chan Kom lies in a world of oral and face-to-face communication; a man speaks to his neighbor and, with small exception, to no one else. News comes to the village only as people come. The lanes of transportation and of communication are one and the same: the webbing of footpaths that link one bush village with another and all of them to the towns.

From the city and the towns two roads enter Chan Kom: one is the old path from Valladolid southeastward through Cuncunul, the seat of the municipal

[1] Such visitors include: A. V. Kidder (archæologist); George Shattuck and J. H. Sandground (tropical medicine); Manuel Andrade (linguistics); Morris Steggerda (physical anthropology); A. T. Hansen (sociology).

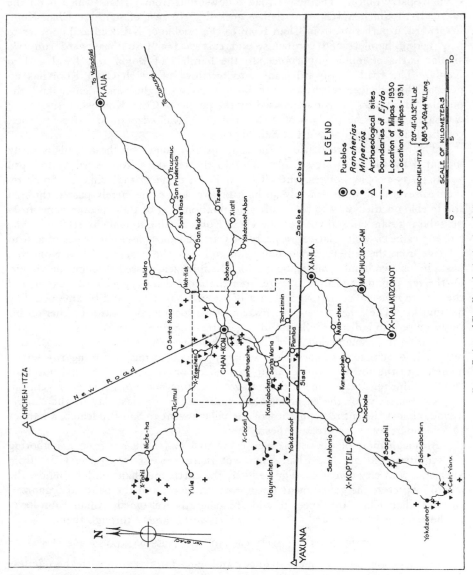

FIG. 3—Environs of Chan Kom, showing location of milpas.

government to which Chan Kom belongs, and through Kaua, where is located the Civil Registry office. The newer road follows that from Dzitas (which is on the railroad) to Chichen Itza, and thence goes slightly east of south to Chan Kom. Westward, a path runs from Chan Kom to the pueblo of X-Cocail and another to neighboring hamlets and cornfields; and eastward and southeastward run two similar paths of minor importance, to the hamlets of Bojon and Tzeal and to Xanla. The road southward leads into territory of which Chan Kom has no personal knowledge; southward the bush becomes higher and denser and the population scarcer. This road is used by the people of Chan Kom when they have occasion to visit the pueblos of X-Kopteil or X-Kalakdzonot, or to go to their cornfields in the neighborhood of Sahcabchen.

The nature and frequence of the comings and goings by these roads is fairly indicated by the following sample. During the ten days from April 21 to April 30, 1931, 35 people, not residents of Chan Kom, came to that village. Some remained several days, others only an hour or two, and some merely passed through the pueblo on their way to some other destination. 23 of these people came from neighboring hamlets and villages like Chan Kom; 8 came to make purchases in the store, 3 came to visit relatives, a party of 5 arrived to remove the bones of a dead relative from the cemetery, one man came to invite the people of Chan Kom to a fiesta in his own hamlet, and 3, bound for Muchucuxca, passed through the village. Of the remaining 12 visitors, 4 were from the more distant pueblo of Tekom; 2 of these were masons, come to work on a house in Chan Kom, and 2 came peddling hammocks. The other 8 were *mestizos* and townspeople; one was a teacher on his way to a post in a distant village and 7 were traveling merchants.

During this same period, 28 of the Chan Kom people left the village; most soon returned;[1] 9 went to their cornfields, 7 to visit friends or relatives in nearby settlements, 4 to the town of Valladolid to buy goods or to attend to official business, and 8 to Chichen Itza—some of these to get medicine, some to sell eggs or venison, and some merely for the excursion. In addition, on the last day of the sample period, almost the entire population of the village went to San Prudencio, a hamlet 10 kilometers away, to attend a fiesta there.

Although most of the people who come to Chan Kom are from neighboring communities that are like Chan Kom, yet there are not infrequent visits from townsmen and city dwellers. The peddler, the cattle merchant on his rounds, the school inspector, the government forester or surveyor, and the political organizer, all visit Chan Kom, are expected, and are generally welcomed. Chan Kom looks to these for its contacts and knows the wider world largely through them.

THE SPATIAL LIMITS OF THE NATIVE'S WORLD

Of these contacts, the most frequent and most intimate are with the hamlets that lie within 10 kilometers of Chan Kom. Chan Kom is larger than any of the other settlements in this area, and for them it is a center of influence. The area extends northward to include Nicteha and Yula, westward to X-Cocail, southward

---

[1] Trips made to cornfields, on routes not passing through other settlements, are not included in this enumeration.

to Santa Maria and Pamba and eastward and northeastward to Tzeal, Zucmuc and San Prudencio.[1] This is the region of frequent personal contact: if a boy from Chan Kom does not find a wife in Chan Kom itself, he is likely to find her in one of these hamlets; people have relatives in them, the fiestas there are well attended from Chan Kom, and their inhabitants buy goods in the Chan Kom store, make use of the Chan Kom midwife and bury their dead in the village cemetery.

South of Chan Kom, and more remote from it, lie the pueblos of X-Kopteil and X-Kalakdzonot. These villages use the Chan Kom cemetery too, having none of their own, but they lie in a zone of less frequent and less intimate contact; in it falls also, probably, Kaua. The fiestas of these villages are attended by the people of Chan Kom, but the villages are visited on few other occasions. Still more distant from Chan Kom are other villages, where occasional visiting takes place. But X-Kopteil and Tekom have, ordinarily, separate political and social worlds, whereas the public affairs of the nearer and smaller hamlets tend to be the public affairs of Chan Kom too, and the men of the hamlets not infrequently look to Chan Kom for leadership. Among the more distant settlements there is often rivalry and sometimes open conflict, as in the disputes between Ebtun and Chan Kom (p. 29) and between Ticimul and Kaua. Yet there does exist a larger polity, a consciousness of common interests that may, in emergencies, be fanned into a flame of regional patriotism. The list of villages (p. 221) that fought together against "the Liberals," during the revolution of 1917, defines for us this world of wider political union: Piste, Tinum, Ebtun, Cuncunul and Tekom. The area bounded by these pueblos embraces the "folk state" of the Chan Kom region. Contacts with the towns—Valladolid and Dzitas—are much more frequent than with Ebtun and Piste, but they are contacts of buying and selling, or of official business, with the *Liga*, or with the officers of the state government. The Chan Kom people do not have friends in Valladolid; they are not at home there. Merida is of course still more remote; most of the women and some of the men of Chan Kom have never been there, though all speak of it and know something about it. The world of interest and activity includes the nearest towns, but the world of intimacy and sentimental attachment is only the local region of neighboring villages.

The area within which lie the villages with which the loyalties of Chan Kom were bound during the period of revolutionary disorder of 15 years ago (indicated by the widest boundary on the map on page 10 includes almost all the communities with which the adults of Chan Kom have personal knowledge. Such personal knowledge extends only a little way beyond the limits of this area: northeast to Popola and other villages just beyond Valladolid, and south no farther than Tixcacalcupul. One man has been to Santa Cruz del Bravo. Even the traveling merchants, whose range of activity is wider than that of the villagers themselves, go no farther south than X-Kopteil or X-Kalakdzonot; a few reach Kancabdzonot. Then they turn north again. Only one, a hammock-seller, continues west to Sotuta, Ticul and Oxkutzcab.

---

[1] These places are all *rancherias* (hamlets) with the exception of X-Cocail and Xanla and, these latter two, though pueblos (villages), are small and unimportant.

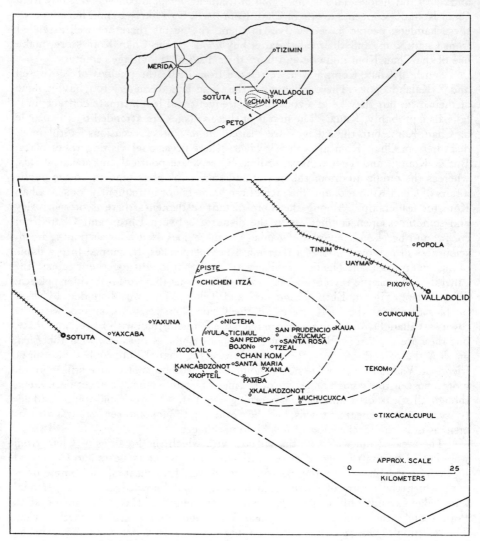

FIG. 4—Western part of *partido* of Valladolid, showing extent of the world of social participation of Chan Kom.

Westward the personal knowledge of the men of Chan Kom goes a greater distance beyond the present area of interest and activity. During the revolutionary period, the men of Chan Kom joined the men of Yaxcaba in military engagements, at that village, with the troops of the reactionary government. So the older men know Yaxcaba and some are acquainted with Sotuta. But today, although there are in Chan Kom one or two families from Yaxcaba, except these families none from Chan Kom ever goes to Yaxcaba, and the feeling plainly is that these westerns are not "our people." The attachments of Chan Kom do not go west of X-Cocail and Piste. This is partly a result of the fact that Chan Kom was colonized from the Valladolid region and of the fact that commercial and governmental contacts are with Valladolid. But the present situation may also preserve the political alignments of the Sixteenth and Seventeenth Centuries. For then Yaxcaba belonged to the territory of one ruling family (the Cocoms), while the site of Chan Kom lay on the western edge of Cupul territory. (See Chapter II.)

Within this area of personal knowledge travel is, of course, on foot. The people of Chan Kom use the railroad only to go to Merida. Not all the men of the village have been to Merida, but many have; the dozen most traveled men have been there on the average of six or seven times. In most cases these visits are made in discharge of official duties as representatives of the village government. A few men, and one or two women, have stayed in Merida for weeks or months; one woman was born there. A very few people have taken the railroad beyond Merida; one man has been to Campeche; only four or five have ever seen the sea.

By reputation and report, the people of Chan Kom know of Mexico City and, although the governor of the state is the person whom they petition for special assistance, they are quite aware of belonging to the Mexican nation. The state of mind can be referred to by no term more affirmative than "awareness"; no patriotic activity ever asserts nationality. The new schoolbuilding is named for Plutarco Elias Calles, but no real nationalistic feeling animated the choice. Except for Mexico, it is the United States that engages attention. The interest in this country, general throughout the peninsula, is reinforced at Chan Kom, due to contacts with the Americans at Chichen Itza. The United States is known as a distant country of great wealth and fabulous powers; it is the distant star to which the reform sentiment in Chan Kom has hitched the wagon of progress. But it is doubtful if anyone in Chan Kom has seriously conceived of himself as ever going there.

THE TEMPORAL LIMITS OF THE NATIVE'S WORLD

As life in Chan Kom is lived without books, continuity with the past is made by oral tradition alone and history extends backward only to the time of the fathers of the older men now living. These older men participated in the events of the revolutionary period of 1917–21 and they frequently recall them in anecdote and conversation. Although henequen is not grown commercially in the area, there were once cattle estates. During the early days of this period peonage was abolished, and the period before this event recalled as "the times of slavery" by these men. They remember life in the villages to which they were bound, the names and personalities of their masters and punishment by the lash.

Before the time of the fathers of the men now living, there are only myths, the stories, moral or merely fantastic, of the acts and happenings of supernatural races, unconnected with the Maya of today. "A long time ago, in the time of my grandfather, there lived in these parts a race of little people," a typical story begins. The "time of my grandfather" is a time of magical and mysterious events.

The stories of this remote period center around what are known as the Good Times. Then lived a race of men known as the Itza—a different race from that which dwells in the land today—who had mysterious wisdom and supernatural power. Then nature cooperated with man; stones did his bidding, and at his whistle leaped into place. These ancient people built the great structures at Chichen and Coba, and fashioned the elevated stone roads (sacbe). The bush was burned without felling, firewood came to the hearth at man's mere bidding, and the corn cooked itself. No one was wicked, and all were wise.

The climax of these stories is the destruction or banishment of the Itza as a result of some mistake or impiety: the secret whistle is forgotten; the stone is carried on the shoulder; a tower is built to reach the house of God. Destruction follows, by flood or banishment, and the Good Times are over. In some stories two old races enter into these episodes: The Itza, who were wise and who still dwell beneath the floors of the ruined cities and will some day return to their ancient cities, and the ppuzob, a race of hunchback dwarfs, who were all drowned.

Now man lives in the Bad Times; he must toil for his living and his mind is dark. But once it was otherwise: man had wisdom and all nature did as man wished. If only the sources of secret knowledge had not been stopped! [1]

But in Chan Kom today, the striking fact in connection with the temporal viewpoint of the native mind is the disposition for it to be prospective rather than retrospective. The older men still know and tell these stories of the lost paradise, but the progressive influences of recent years have aroused in many of them the feeling that a future of dignity, importance and wealth lies before them, not behind them.

The village leader[2] has pictured a Chan Kom millennium, when everyone will live in a masonry house and own cattle and a phonograph; when a village cooperative will market fruit and corn by means of a collectively owned automobile truck, when all necessary domestic industries will be performed in Chan Kom itself so that specialized labor will not have to be brought in from outside, when Chan Kom will be the head of its own *municipio*, and when the Americans will drive to Chan Kom by automobile to admire and further dignify the paramount community

[1] The functions of these stories are to explain by pointing out the loss of supernatural power, the discrepancy between the grandeur of the old buildings and the humbleness of life today, and to justify arduous toil. To what extent these legends of the Good Times preserve the vestiges of historical reminiscence it is not possible to say. The ancient race is known as the Itza; the building of the now-ruined cities is attributed to these people; it is known that before the clay effigies (incense-burners?) sometimes found in the bush, "our grandfathers used to burn incense to make them come alive;" stories are told of a serpent named Xkukican who once dwelt at Chichen and demanded human sacrifice; the shaman at Chan Kom says that in the old days they killed men for the gods and took the viscera from their bodies. On the other hand, there is much in these stories that suggests the Biblical story of the Fall from Paradise.

[2] The career of this man is described in Chapter XIII.

of Yucatan. "We are going to make a pueblo like a pueblo of the famous Americans; all will be workers, even the women, just like ants; and if more land will be needed, the government will give it to us." This image he has conveyed, in varying degrees of brilliance, to others of the village, and it is the stimulus for the industry and persistence which in some degree is bringing the ideal to realization.

POPULATION

Chan Kom is a village of young people. In May 1930,[1] the population consisted of 251 individuals, 131 males and 120 females, of whom 22.2 per cent were under 5 years of age, 83 per cent were under 30, and only 7.2 per cent were 45 years of age or older.

Table 1 compares this distribution with the percentages of the population in these same age-groups in the United States and in Campeche, a Mexican state similar to Yucatan.[2]

TABLE 1—*Percentage of population in certain age-groups*

Age	Chan Kom	Campeche	United States
Under 5..........	20.2	14.7	11.0
Under 30.........	83.0	67.2	58.0
Over 45..........	7.2	13.3	20.8

The high proportion of persons in the lower age-groups, characteristic of primitive groups with high birth rates and high death rates, is further emphasized in the case of Chan Kom, by reason of the fact that the inhabitants are the pioneering founders of a new settlement; presumably it was the young, not the aged, who emigrated. The complete age distribution is given in table 2.

POPULATION CHANGES

There has been no other census of Chan Kom with which to make comparison. The village is new; 20 years ago it consisted of about a dozen huts. During the 18 months from February 1, 1930, to August 1, 1931, there were twenty-one births (an annual rate of 56 per mille), and ten deaths (an annual rate of 26.4 per mille), indicating an unusually high rate of natural increase (29.6). There were three marriages (an annual rate of 80 per 10,000 population).

[1] The enumeration, made in connection with the national census of that year, was accomplished by the junior author of this monograph. As Villa had personal knowledge of most of the individuals recorded, the data are dependable. However, the ages reported are in most cases estimates. The people of the village have only uncertain ideas as to their own ages and even as to the ages of their own children, and sometimes they give figures for themselves and for their own children that are irreconcilable. In making his estimates, Villa took into account the individual's statement, the probable age of his children and the facts that the age of marriage does not vary much and that the first child is born soon thereafter. We were later able to secure birth records (made in the offices of the *Registro Civil*) for 22 children and 5 adults. With regard to the 22 children, the figures given in the census are correct to the nearest birthday in twelve cases, one year too high in four cases, one year too low in four cases, and two years too low in four cases. With regard to the five adults, in age from 17 to 39 years, the census figures are wrong by one year in three instances, by two years in one case, and by three years in the last instance. The average per cent of error in estimating the ages of these five adults is seven. The total amount of over-estimate is the same as the total amount of under-estimate. It is therefore not probable that errors in estimating age seriously affect the frequency distributions given in the accompanying table.

[2] The figures for Campeche are for 1921. The summary of the 1921 census of Yucatan has not been published and at the time of writing the 1930 figures are not available.

During the same period two families changed their residence from other settlements to Chan Kom, while five families moved away.[1] The village loses more inhabitants by emigration than it gains by immigration, chiefly because the demands upon the inhabitants to work on public improvements (*fagina*) are unusually exacting.

VITALITY

If the number of births (21) that took place during the eighteen-month period is typical, an annual rate is indicated of 400 births per 1000 married women of child-bearing age. No still-births occurred, and the midwife says she never attended such a case.

Fourteen of the married women, between the ages of 20 and 40, averaging 23 years of age, have had 52 children; this is an average of 3.7 children apiece. Of these 52 children, 34, or 66 per cent, survive. The average age of 23 mothers at the birth of the first child was 16 years. Of the 25 married women for whom data were secured, all but one had the first child within the first two years of marriage; and she is childless, though married 7 years.

TABLE 2—*Sex and age groups in Chan Kom*

Age	Males		Females		Both	
	Number	Per cent	Number	Per cent	Number	Per cent
Under 5.......	27	10.7	24	9.5	51	20.2
5–9...........	25	9.9	14	5.6	39	15.5
10–14.........	17	6.8	16	6.3	33	13.1
15–19.........	14	5.6	14	5.6	28	11.2
20–24.........	13	5.2	20	8.0	33	13.2
25–29.........	14	5.6	10	4.0	24	9.6
30–34.........	1	0.4	5	2.0	6	2.4
35–39.........	4	1.6	6	2.4	10	4.0
40–44.........	6	2.4	3	1.2	9	3.6
45–49.........	4	1.6	2	0.8	6	2.4
50–54.........	2	0.8	3	1.2	5	2.0
55–59.........	2	0.8	0	0	2	0.8
60–64.........	0	0	1	0.4	1	0.4
65–69.........	2	0.8	1	0.4	3	1.2
70–74.........	0	0	1	0.4	1	0.4
Total......	131	52.2	120	47.8	251	100

All of the 10 deaths were of children under 6 years of age, and 4 of these children were less than 2 weeks old. An epidemic of whooping-cough was responsible for three deaths; two or three were caused by intestinal infections, and two were of recently born infants with cardiac deficiencies. (This statement is based on laymen's diagnoses.) The adults of Chan Kom are in most cases in good health and there are very few old people.

[1] The two new families came from Yaxcaba and Xanla, respectively. Four of the departing families moved to Santa Maria and one to Valladolid. There were also transfers of legal domicile, involving the duty of *fagina* (see p. 78) to the *comisaría* of Chan Kom, of persons not actually resident in Chan Kom. Seven families living in Ticimul, Ebtun, Santa Maria or Yula came to depend upon Chan Kom, while five families, living chiefly in Ticimul, ceased to owe their *fagina* to Chan Kom.

In April 1929, Shattuck and his associates made medical examinations of 379 individuals from Chan Kom and neighboring settlements.[1] The morbidity characteristics observed in this group are similar to those found in other Maya populations of the Peninsula. Except for influenza, which was epidemic at the time when the observations were made, gastro-intestinal disorders were found to be greatly in excess of all other diseases. But no case of amebic dysentery was recognized or suspected. Malaria was probably present, but no clear-cut case was recognized. No cases of syphilis were identified, and only one case suggested gonorrhea. There were many cases of a trachoma-like disease of the eyelids. There were a few instances of hookworm, arthritis, tuberculosis, chronic bronchitis, pellagra, scurvy and scabies. None of these ailments presented a conspicuous incidence.

RACE AND NATIVITY

The people are apparently racially homogeneous. They conform to the Maya Indian type general in Yucatan.[2] In no individual is White admixture apparent, and with one exception all bear Maya, not Spanish, surnames. On the other hand it is probable that some White blood has entered into the population. These people have been in contact with White persons for four hundred years. One Chan Kom woman was born in Merida, and two or three persons come from villages with large *mestizo* elements. One of these describes his father as "an important man with a book whom everyone had to obey."

Few of the adults of Chan Kom were born in the village, but almost all were born within forty miles of it. With very few exceptions, the people come from villages in the southeastern part of the *Partido* of Valladolid. They have always dwelt, therefore, in communities much like that which they now inhabit. They come from villages, not towns,[3] but these villages are near the towns and some are close to the railroad. Ebtun is the parent community of Chan Kom; it has contributed the largest share to the present population. (The Pixoy people in fact moved to Ebtun before coming to Chan Kom.) Other considerable increments come from Pixoy, Tinum and Uayma. These villages are all north of Chan Kom, near Valladolid. The settlement of Chan Kom represents a reoccupation, from the north, of territory depopulated during the latter part of the Nineteenth Century.

LANGUAGE

Maya is the general language of communication among the people of the village. Those who know Spanish use it almost exclusively in talking with persons from outside of the community, or in conversations with the teacher. Nevertheless,

[1] *The Peninsula of Yucatan—Medical, Biological, Meteorological and Sociological Studies*, by George Cheever Shattuck and collaborators, Carnegie Inst. Wash. Pub. No. 431, 1933.

[2] Dr. Morris Steggerda made measurements on 27 males and 14 females in Chan Kom. This small series indicates a physical type slightly shorter and heavier than the general average for the entire region. As compared with a weighted average derived from Dr. Steggerda's entire series and from Starr's and Williams' published results, the males measured in Chan Kom have a mean stature of 154.22 ±0.51 while the mean for the general Maya population of Yucatan is 155.21; the females have a mean stature of 142.36 ±0.80. The mean weight of the Chan Kom males is 54.57 ±0.57, as compared with 53.54 ±0.45 for Dr. Steggerda's entire series; with respect to mean weight of females the corresponding pair of figures is 50.21 ±1.23 and 48.37 ±0.60. The mean cephalic index of the Chan Kom males is 84.91 ±0.21, as compared with 85.38 for the weighted average derived from all comparable series; for the females the corresponding figures are 87.64 ±0.57 and 86.31.

[3] Except the woman who comes from Merida.

Spanish enjoys the superior prestige; some parents make an effort to speak it in their homes; and many people who do not speak it feel themselves therefore inferior.

In the census, 35 persons, or 14 per cent of the population, are reported as speaking Spanish. Of these 35, 26 are males, and all but one of the females (and she is the woman from Merida) are under 21 years of age and have learned their Spanish in the Chan Kom school. On the other hand, about half of the Spanish-speaking males knew Spanish before they came to Chan Kom. With respect to

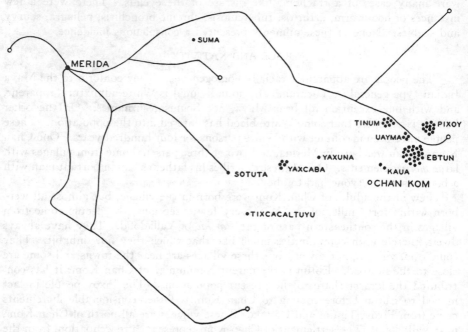

Fig. 5—Pueblos of origin of sixty-one adults of Chan Kom.

those families that include Spanish-speaking persons, where there are children of school age or over, in five cases the man speaks Spanish, the wife does not, and one or more of the children do; in one case the man speaks Spanish and none of the children do; and in one case both parents speak Spanish but no child does; and in only two cases one child speaks Spanish while the parents do not. With respect to families having no children of school age or over, there are four cases where both spouses speak Spanish, but ten cases where only the man speaks Spanish. There is no household where an adult female is the only Spanish-speaking member of the group.

━ Thus it appears that the social superiority and the opportunity for wider experience traditionally enjoyed by men is expressed and also reinforced by their linguistic superiority over women. On the other hand, although on account of the recent extension of rural education in Yucatan more young people speak Spanish than do old people, there are as yet few households where the children enjoy a linguistic superiority over their parents and few situations where parents are obliged to use their children in order to communicate with the wider world.

LITERACY

Because schools are recent in this part of Yucatan, it is the young people rather than the old who know how to read and write. Of the 53 persons from 10 to 18 years of age, 35 (69 per cent) were reported by the census as knowing how to read and write. Of the 107 persons over 18 years of age, 28 (26 per cent) were reported as literate. 63 persons out of 160, 10 years of age or over, or 39 per cent, were reported as literate; of the females of this age group 27 per cent are literate and 49 per cent of the males.

This statistical statement does not, however, adequately represent the facts. Most of the people whom the schools have taught to read and write seldom or never do so. In many cases the literacy means an ability to pronounce Spanish words without much understanding of their meaning. Indeed 16 of the persons reported in the census as literate are also described as not knowing how to speak Spanish. As no instruction is given in reading or writing Maya, this means either that these persons do in fact have some knowledge of Spanish or that—and this is the larger share of the truth—their reading knowledge of Spanish is a superficial ability, an accomplishment, not an instrument of communication.

The actual uses of literacy are so few as to be easily mentioned. The *comisario*, or some other literate man, reads the official communications occasionally sent to the village by the national or the state government, by the *Liga* or by the Agrarian Commission. One or two men are able to compose replies without the aid of the teacher. Two kinds of books exist and are consulted. One is the church calendar; to this recourse is had when a name is sought for a new-born infant. The other is the booklet of Catholic prayers, in print or in manuscript; there are several of these and they are studied by those *maestros cantores* who happen to be literate, that they may perfect their knowledge of the ritual used at novenas (see p. 151). There is one man (and probably no other) who owns and occasionally reads a Spanish New Testament (see p. 229). This man has also come very recently to read the Merida newspaper, which is occasionally sent to Chan Kom for the teacher; sometimes he explains to others of the village items that have interested him.

Chapter II

HISTORY

THE PRE-HISPANIC PERIOD

Concerning the first founding of a settlement at Chan Kom[1] and as to the participation of its inhabitants in the life of pre-hispanic times, we can only speculate. Although the present population of the village are colonists at this site, or the children of colonists, people have probably lived around the cenote at Chan Kom for many centuries, not continuously, but at various periods. Because the sources of water supply in Yucatan are limited to these natural wells (cenotes), formed by the collapse of the limestone shelf of which the peninsula is composed, the possible sites for human settlement are few and communities are likely to be built and rebuilt on the same spot. Pieces of worked stone that are still to be found at Chan Kom indicate that here once stood the masonry buildings of a pre-hispanic city. Fragments of ancient pedestals and broken columns have been recently incorporated into the new masonry buildings of the present village. Outside of the village, in the bush, or in the cornfields, are many low mounds, in most cases bordered with walls of uncut stones. Fragments of old pottery are not uncommonly found in excavations made in house-lots, and pieces of obsidian are still to be encountered in the plaza.

Chan Kom lies between two of the most extensive and archæologically impressive sites of ancient civilization in the northern part of the peninsula. It is situated about 20 kilometers south of Chichen Itza and about 90 kilometers west of Coba. One of the many artificial raised roadways (sacbe) that radiate from Coba, passes within 8 kilometers of Chan Kom on its way to its terminus at Yaxuna, a third nearby site of archæological interest. There are traces of a lesser sacbe running between Chan Kom and Xanla.

It is probable that the region where Chan Kom now lies was colonized from the south, and that Coba, Yaxuna and Chichen Itza were all founded before the cities of the so-called Old Empire of the Maya (occupying eastern Chiapas and Tabasco, northern Guatemala, western British Honduras, and the westernmost part of Honduras) were abandoned, as they soon after came to be. A stela at Coba bears the Maya date 9.9.0.0.0; if the Goodman-Thompson-Martinez correlation is accepted, this date corresponds to 613 A.D.[2] At about this same time it is probable[3] that Yaxuna was founded and the causeway built that connects Coba and Yaxuna and passes so close to Chan Kom. The founding of Chichen Itza occurred soon after this. The native history, embodied in a manuscript brought to light in the Nineteenth Century and known as the Chilam Balam of Chumayel, refers to the

---

[1] The name Chan Kom means "little ravine" or "little depression." As there are no watercourses in Yucatan, there are really no ravines, and a "kom," such as that, not far from the cenote, from which Chan Kom takes its name, is a roughly bowl-shaped depression.
[2] By the Spinden correlation, it is 260 years earlier.
[3] Gann and Thompson, *The History of the Maya*, 74.

settlement of Chichen Itza in a certain katun 6 Ahau that is probably 9.14.0.0.0, or by the correlation here adopted, 712 A.D. The only definite date inscribed on a monument at Chichen occurs on a reused lintel; it is 10.2.10.0.0, or 879 A.D.

For the period of perhaps about eleven hundred years that elapsed from the founding of these cities in the Chan Kom region, to the first coming of the Spaniards, the ancient Maya chronicles give us in briefest outline a story of the migrations of various tribal groups within the peninsula, of the occupation and reoccupation of its cities and of tribal wars. These chronicles—the Books of Chilam Balam—reduced to writing the oral traditions of certain of the chiefly families: the Chilam Balam of Chumayel records the traditions of the Itza, and the Chilam Balam of Mani and of Tizimin those of the Xiu, principal rivals of the Itza. These documents give accounts, of doubtful historicity, of the abandonment of Chichen by the Itza, its occupation and abandonment by the Xius, and its later reoccupation by the Itza. The sources then recount the founding of Uxmal (west of the present Sotuta) by the Xiu and the formation of a military league consisting of the Xiu, of the Cocoms of Mayapan (situated between the present Merida and Muna), and of the Itza of Chichen. During this period Yucatan, and especially Mayapan and Chichen, were brought under Nahua influence; Chichen underwent an architectural renaissance with which is associated, as leader and organizer, a Nahua chieftain known among the Maya as Kukulcan. For about two hundred years after this time (the middle of the Thirteenth Century) the league appears to have functioned and Chichen flourished. But in the middle of the Fifteenth Century a war broke out between the Xiu and certain other Yucatecan peoples, on the one hand, and the Cocoms and Nahua allies, on the other. This war culminated in the destruction of Mayapan and the rout of the Cocoms. It also brought about the permanent dissolution of centralized authority among the Maya. The Itza abandoned Chichen Itza for the Peten region of Guatemala and the Xiu withdrew to Mani (east of the present Ticul).

THE SPANISH CONQUEST

When the Spaniards entered the peninsula in 1527, it is probable that Coba had been abandoned and that Chichen was much reduced in importance, or was in desuetude. Just what tribal group was in control of Chichen at the time of the arrival of the Spaniards is uncertain. The Xiu were established at Mani, the Chel at Itzmal (Izamal), and the Cocoms at Sotuta. At some time between 1530 and 1540 we are told that the Xiu, desiring to make certain human sacrifices to the rain gods at the sacred cenote at Chichen, asked permission of the Cocoms to pass through Cocom territory in order to visit that city. However, during the Sixteenth and Seventeenth Centuries, and even earlier, it is the Cupul family that is most often referred to as in control of the region around Chichen and in the neighborhood of Valladolid. Cogolludo (Book IV, Chapter 5) refers to the Cupuls as "the people of the territory of the town of Valladolid," and says that while at Chichen in 1528, the elder Montejo was murderously attacked by a *cacique* named Cupul. According to Cogolludo, the instructions given in 1539 by the elder Montejo to his son, making plans for the campaign which was about to effect the subjugation of the peninsula, directed him to conquer, among other "provinces," that of the "Kupules." A survey made in 1545 shows Chichen as lying in Cupul territory.

It is probable that the first Spaniard passed by or near the cenote at Chan Kom in 1528 when the elder Montejo, after effecting a landing on the peninsula on the northeast coast, and fighting a battle with the Indians at Ake (probably the present Akedzonot, east of Tizimin), went southwest to Chichen Itza (according to Cogolludo). This route must have taken him near Chan Kom. The Spaniards, under the elder Montejo, remained for a time at Chichen, while another party sought vainly for gold in the neighborhood of Bakhalal (Bacalar). To both parties the Indians were hostile; Montejo was beseiged at Chichen and finally forced into a battle which cost him 150 men; and in 1535 the Spaniards withdrew from Yucatan to Campeche and Tabasco. A second attempt to subjugate Yucatan was successful. The elder Montejo and his son pressed inland, this time from the west coast. In 1541 the ruling Xiu of Mani voluntarily submitted to the Spaniards, and an army of recalcitrants, among whom were the Cocoms, was decisively defeated not long after. The following year saw the founding of Merida, the fall of Sotuta, last stronghold of the Cocoms, and the presence of a military expedition in the "province" of Choaca, in the northeast corner of the peninsula. In 1545 Valladolid was founded (at a first site of uncertain location, "six leagues from the sea"), and a church was established. From that time Spanish and Catholic rule was firm in Yucatan.

AFTER THE CONQUEST

Nevertheless, during the Sixteenth Century and into the Seventeenth, the prestige of the Cupul family in the territory centering at the present town of Valladolid (the old Zaci) persisted, so far as was compatible with Spanish authority. At this time, and before the Conquest, no single head chieftain (halach uinic) appears to have ruled the entire region, but various branches of the family controlled its various parts. The *Relaciónes de Yucatán* (II, 53)[1] speak of one Namon Cupul, living at Ekbalam and ruling also over Tahcabo and Nabalam. Nadzul Cupul exerted his authority over several places around Zaci (pp. 43, 129, 140); this man may have been not merely a batab (village chief) but a true halach uinic. The *Relación* of Tikuch (p. 116) says that Nadzbon Cupul was lord of the entire province; as far north as Tecay (near Tizimin) they paid him tribute, and it is said that he lived at Chichen Itza (p. 150). Various Cupuls are reported as batabs or *gobernadores* of Cuncunul and Tixcacal in documents[2] of the year 1600, and in that year the chieftains of Sotuta visited Nachi Cupul in Ticinmul.

In none of the Sixteenth and Seventeenth Century documents available to us appears the name of Chan Kom, but most of the other place names figuring on present-day maps of the region in which Chan Kom lies occur frequently in these documents;[3] among these are Yaxcaba, Kancabdzonot, Kaua, Cuncunul, Tekom, Tixcacal (Tixcacalcupul, or Tixcacaput), Tinum; also Ticinmul (Ticimul) which

---

[1] Mr. Ralph L. Roys has kindly made these references to the *Relaciónes* available to us and given us his valuable commentary.
[2] *Copia de los Documentos de Tierras de Sotuta*, Berendt Linguistic Collection, No. 50, p. 192.
[3] Loc. cit. pp. 193, 197; *Títulos de Ebtun*, p. 50; Books of Chilam Balam.

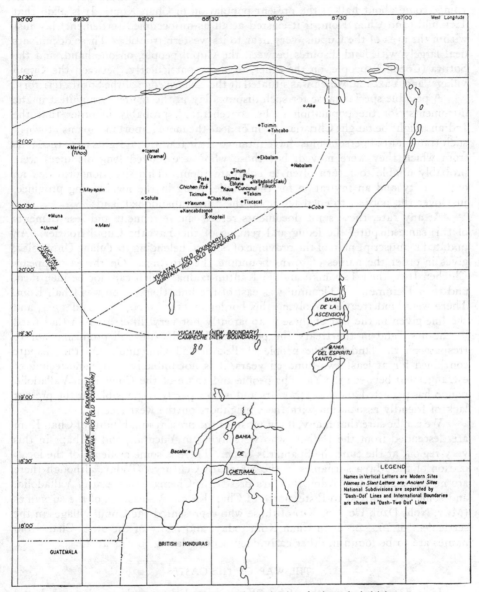

FIG. 6—Peninsula of Yucatan, northern part; showing locations of ancient and colonial sites.

at present is a little hamlet 5 kilometers north of Chan Kom, and Ebtun, from which village come about half of the present population of Chan Kom. It is plain that Ticinmul (and Chan Kom, if it existed at all as an occupied settlement) lay just within the area of the Cupuls, very near to its western frontier. These documents deal largely with land disputes between the Cupul people, on one hand, and the Sotuta (Cocom?) people, on the other, or more particularly, between the Cupul villages and Yaxcaba, which was situated at the eastern edge of the Sotuta territory.

A possible special cause for such disputes lay in the tendency manifest in the documents[1] for the population to be concentrated, probably in order that the Indians might be taught Christianity, in or near the more important Spanish towns;[2] such transplanted persons must have retained their traditional rights over the lands from which they were moved, but those who were moved long distances were probably unable to return often to cultivate them. This situation provided an opportunity and an invitation for the people living in the neighboring province, just over the border, to encroach upon these half-abandoned lands.

At any rate, these same documents record the settlement and resettlements of this same dispute, the fixing and refixing of the Yaxcaba-Cupul frontier. An undated manuscript map of the province of Sotuta, belonging to Tulane University, gives in order the names of towns bounding the province. On the east appears Chichen Itza, then Tapomku and Ti Kantun-tzalna, which can not be identified, and then Ticinmul. If Ticinmul was east of the line, then so too was Chan Kom. There were land treaties involving this border in 1545, 1600, 1700 and 1764; and the line given in the last of these is apparently not very different from that fixed in the first, and in the treaty the people of Yaxcaba are still promising not to trespass on the lands of the people of Tekom and Cuncunul. As this dispute continued for at least two hundred years, it is not unlikely that some feeling of estrangement between the Yaxcaba people and those of the Chan Kom-Valladolid region has persisted another 150 years and is now partly responsible for the present lack of friendly association with these neighbors on the west (see p. 11).

We can be sure that many, if not most, of the present inhabitants of Chan Kom are descended from the Indians who were living in Yucatan, and perhaps in this very region, at the time the Spaniards came. There is some evidence of the localization of the Maya surnames in the Sixteenth Century. Today, although there are no Cupuls in Chan Kom, they are present in Chemax, just east of Valladolid, and some have moved to Piste, north of Chan Kom. At least six of the surnames (May, Noh, Dzul, Uc, Un, Ku) of those who represented the Cupul villages in the settlement of 1600 occur in Chan Kom today, and many of the other Chan Kom names are to be found in other early documents relating to this area.

THE WAR OF THE CASTES

It is not known whether Chan Kom existed during this early period and participated, as a minor village, in the land disputes mentioned, or whether its

---

[1] *Ibid.* Mr. Roys originated this suggestion, which seems to us likely.
[2] The *Títulos de Ebtun* indicate a concentration of population, drawn from the west, into Tekom and Tixcacalcupul.

founding as a colonial or post-colonial settlement dates from the Eighteenth or even the late Nineteenth Century; at any rate the village has no extended history of continuous occupation. For that matter, few, if any, of the villages in the southeastern part of the state of Yucatan have histories of undisturbed occupation. In the Sixteenth Century epidemics decimated or even obliterated villages and caused remnants of village populations to migrate. A more important cause of depopulation lies in Indian uprisings since the Conquest. The subjugation of the eastern and southeastern Indians has never been complete. From time to time there have been bloody insurrections. One took place in 1761. Another, known as the War of the Castes, began in 1847 and can not be said to have come to a definite and conclusive end, although real military operations ceased in the seventies. During part of the period between the outbreak of this race war and the beginning of the Twentieth Century much of the southeastern part of the (then) state of Yucatan was uninhabited. It was a wild frontier, that had to be rewon for human habitation by pioneers and colonists from the villages farther north. "When my father was five years old," said a man of Chan Kom, "there were only three or four houses [at Chan Kom]. No one lived in Ticimul, or in Ticinkakab, or in X-Kopteil, or in Xanla, because Chan Kom was the last settlement here."

The War of the Castes flared up from the smoldering embers of racial hatred, kept alive in the Indians by their long mistreatment by the Whites. It was made possible by the arming of the Indians as soldiers in a Mexican revolution. The insurrectionary movement began among some of the eastern tribes of Quintana Roo and spread to those of the south. During colonial times the Spaniards had built a string of towns down into the tropical peripheries of their realm; these included Saban and Tituc; the southernmost was Bacalar. In the first year of this rebellion, the whole territory south of Valladolid was in the hands of the Indians; Mexican and Yucatecan military expeditions regained towns and villages only to lose them again. In January of 1848 the Indians occupied and destroyed Pixoy, attacked Uayma and occupied Ebtun. Three months later the Whites evacuated Valladolid. Meantime, in the same year, Bacalar had fallen to the Indians; and although the Mexicans recaptured it, they were beseiged for years and were compelled to abandon the town in 1858. The Indian uprising spread northwestward almost to Merida, and there was checked, because the season for planting had come and the Indians deserted their battalions to return to their cornfields.

One result of this Indian uprising was to emphasize the difference between the Quintana Roo Indians and those of Yucatan. The present inhabitants of Chan Kom and its neighboring settlements are descendants of Indians who remained near or with the Whites during the war; the Quintana Roo Indians are the sons of recalcitrants in whom the hostility to the Whites has never fully subsided. The southernmost tribes of the Territory made a formal peace with the Mexicans in 1853, but the eastern tribes never did so; merely, the Mexican troops withdrew and the Indians reoccupied the land. Saban, Tituc and the other Spanish towns were never rebuilt; they are today the dwelling-place of the owl and the temporary camp of the chiclero.

COLONIZATION

The founding of the present settlement of Chan Kom took place in response to the stimulus of agricultural necessity. It illustrates a cycle of events that takes place over and over again in eastern Yucatan and that may be stated in general terms. The soil is made ready for cultivation by cutting and burning the bush. This method and the scantiness of the humus make it impossible to raise corn on the same tract for more than two or three consecutive years and require that the land lie fallow for many years before it is again tilled. This fact in turn causes the agriculturalist, especially as his village grows in size, to go farther and farther in search of good land. At last his cornfields are so remote from his village that he remains at his fields during periods of agricultural labor; his wife accompanies him, with her pots and metate; the place has become a *milperío*. Others from his village, or from others, join the pioneers; a community spirit grows up at the new site. If there is a convenient water supply, the necessity for return to the parent village is reduced. The temporary shelters are made more permanent; the inhabitants return to the parent community only to perform their public work-contribution (*guardia*) or to attend a fiesta. The parent community recognizes some individual as the spokesman for the daughter-settlement; this latter is now a *ranchería*. But, finally, the distance from the parent settlement being considerable, and the loyalties coming to be attached to the new site where the labor and the love are spent, it grows increasingly irksome to return periodically to labor in the parent, and now somewhat alien, community. The parent community, however, tries to enforce the obligation of *guardia;* disaffection sets in and ill feeling grows between parent community and colony. Then perhaps actual conflict results. Commonly the *ranchería* seeks, and sometimes attains, political independence and local sovereignity; it becomes a pueblo (village) itself. And, if it flourishes, it may in turn establish *milperío* colonies of its own.

Into the region devastated and depopulated by the War of the Castes ventured, in search of fertile land, three pioneering agriculturalists from the village of Ebtun. It was some time in the 1880's that they set up their huts around the cenote at Chan Kom. Then there was nothing else at this *milperío* but the stone walls used as ramparts by the Indians in the war recently ended, and the fragments of carved stones from a much more ancient epoch. A man from Chan Kom tells the story:

Now you are going to see how Chan Kom was made.

All at once my papa was very poor, because for a long time he had been *comisario* of Pixoy, since those called Ceme come from Pixoy. Then my papa and also my uncles, Don Fano and Don Pil, moved to Ebtun. My father was a tall man and knew many things; he knew more than the batabs; he spoke good Spanish because he worked for a man called Don Pedro Lopez.

All at once he and my uncles came here to make milpa, because it was high ground and good. When they came they met here Don Asunción Pat, the father of Don Tino, and also Don Concho Uc, Don Dono Uc, Don Manuel Uc, because the Ucs came here before us. But before the Ucs came, there lived here three men: one was called Andres May, the other José May, and the other Tiburcio Caamal, who were from Ebtun.

When my father came I was the same size as Quinto [five years old]. Then there were only three or four houses. No one lived in Ticimul or in Ticinkakab, or in X-Kopteil, or in Xanla, because Chan Kom was the last settlement here.

This man's story continues in the paragraphs below. It mentions the three important series of events in the history of the village: (1) the Revolution, which brought liberty to the Indians and induced a mobility which favored colonization of new and independent Indian villages and which carried schools and political propaganda to the Indians; (2) the attack of the "Liberal" troops upon the Indians at Yaxcaba, resulting in the participation of Chan Kom in this local war and the addition of colonists from the Yaxcaba region to the population of Chan Kom; and (3) the growth of illwill between Chan Kom and Ebtun along with the growth of Chan Kom, resulting in the separation of Chan Kom as an independent pueblo.

All at once liberty for the Indians came, I think in 1910 or in 1914, when Alvarado[1] was here, who knows? All at once some people came who freed those in the haciendas. Don Polin, Don Julio Yam, Don Feliciano, Don Leandro, Don Trano, who worked in the hacienda San José, belonging to Don Claudio Cetina, which is near Tinum, came here. Then there were more of us, but we owed our service to Ebtun.

All at once Socialism began. That was when Don Juan Fernandez, who spread propaganda for the *Liga*, came. Then Don Juan told us that it would be good to have a school because there were many of us.

All at once Don Juan got us the school and, as he was a very good man, he stayed as teacher. This teacher always went on the hunts, but his wife looked after the children.

All at once we went to Don Felipe Carrillo,[2] because we had no furniture in the school. Then Don Felipe was disturbed and told us that there was only furniture in the pueblos; that is if we wanted to turn our little settlement into a pueblo, then they would give us furniture. But we said we didn't want to.

All at once those of Ebtun began to malign us, and then Don Fano, Don Tino, Don Elut and Don Guillermo, we thought it would be better to change into a pueblo here. Then we thought we would work to attain this, even if it should cost the value of a horse apiece.

All at once there took place a dispute in Sotuta and Yaxcaba and many from Yaxcaba came to live here. That was when Don Bus came. All at once the Liberals met poor Don Bus in the street and gave him a beating.

Also the Maestra Dala came, and many others.

All at once the Engineer came from Merida and saw that there were many of us. Then, when a short time had passed, the Engineer returned to lay out the streets and make the plan for the *ejido*.

Then those of Ebtun and those who lived in the neighboring *rancherías* were annoyed, and said that they ought to attack Chan Kom and burn all the houses. They never did it.

Then when we were a pueblo here, we began to work hard to surpass the other pueblos.

THE REVOLUTION OF 1910–21

By the year 1918 there were over a hundred persons at Chan Kom. The settlement, a thriving *ranchería*, had already a reputation for kindliness and hospitality; merchants, reluctant to spend the night at more turbulent villages, found safe lodging there. The first school was established in Chan Kom in 1910,

[1] Salvador Alvarado, initiator of the Revolution in Yucatan, governor from 1915 to 1918.
[2] Felipe Carrillo Puerto, leader of the social revolution, and principal governor of Yucatan (after Alvarado), until January 1924.

before the Revolution, due to an interest taken in the settlement by Don Epigmenio Gonzales, the *Comandante Militar* of Valladolid. The leaders of Chan Kom built a large hut, of wattle wall and palm-leaf roof, to house the school. People from Santa Maria, Yokdzonot and other neighboring settlements sent their children to this school, and the importance of Chan Kom in the region was thus increased.

The Revolutionary disorders of the ensuing period, which resulted in removing the old landed aristocracy from political control in Yucatan, as in the rest of Mexico, gave further impetus to the growth of Chan Kom. In the first place the safe and solid character of the community attracted to it refugees from disordered communities, and in the second place Chan Kom participated in a military action with such distinction as to win for it a status among such older villages as Ebtun, Cuncunul and Piste. Certain people of Yaxcaba, taking advantage of the tumultuous times and acting in the name of political parties of the period, set about robbing and pillaging and destroyed humble settlements whose inhabitants were guilty merely of a reputation for allegiance to the other political party. The settlements west and southwest of Chan Kom were particularly hard hit. Kancabdzonot, X-Kopteil and Yaxuna were attacked, and many of their inhabitants slain with machetes or thrown into the cenotes. At last one Juan Hu, a man of Chan Kom, was cut down in his own milpa. Then the leaders of Chan Kom summoned the men of Ebtun, Piste, Tinum and Cuncunul and a gathering was held at Chan Kom which further raised the prestige of that village. Headed by the Chan Kom leader, this augmented party of men went to Yaxcaba in pursuit of the malefactors. These latter had, however, fled. The pursuers burned the house of one of the enemies' leaders, and returned satisfied. On their way they met many refugees, hiding in the bush. To them the men of Chan Kom offered shelter and protection; many came for temporary aid and a few families took up their residence at Chan Kom. A man of one of these families, a native of Yaxcaba, tells the story as follows:

It was in the year that Felipe Carrillo Puerto died (1924) that I left Yaxcaba; the cause lay in politics; they were killing many people; it was the Liberals who did it. The Liberals came with wagons and carried off corn, pigs, chickens—they robbed everybody. Nobody stayed in Yaxcaba. A great crowd of people set off together. Cleofas Yama was among them; the leader was Clotilde Com. We rested that night at Kancabdzonot. There were about a hundred and thirty of us. Then all at once Rosa Pat came bringing a paper written by one Baak, who was the leader of the evil-doers. He was in Santa Elena. On the paper he wrote that we should go back to our village, that there was nothing bad there now, that it was all over. But Don Clotilde said that that was no good, that they would only seize us and beat us. Then all at once Don Eustaquio and some others came to Kancabdzonot, and said: "Men, come to Chan Kom, because there is nothing bad going on there, there are no factions." Right away the people got up and traveled to Chan Kom. The people of Chan Kom were good people; they brought everyone *nixtamal* (boiled corn), so he could make his dinner. Each man got an *almud* or, if he had children, perhaps an *almud* and a half of *nixtamal*.

Then, after a week, there arrived a paper from the colonel, who was in Valladolid, saying the people from Yaxcaba should appear there and make themselves right with the law. So we went, some of us at one time, and some at another. The Colonel said: "Are you going to stay in Chan Kom? In that case take this paper; you were of Sotuta [the *partido*]; now you are of Valladolid; show it when you get your things in Yaxcaba." Then Don Eus said, "Now there is liberty; if you want to go back to your village, all right; if you want to stay here, all right. But here there is no politics," said Don Eus.

I went back [to Yaxcaba] just to get three pigs, two little ones and one sow, but *Dios mio*, when I got there what was left? Even the hammocks cut to pieces with machetes and all the water-jugs broken. They had even carted away to Sotuta the doors of the houses. There were three hundred men, but well armed; they had a cannon and two machine guns, and fifty cavalry.

Chan Kom was a *ranchería* then. Where the house of Don Fano is now, there was only bush, and where the house of Don Eus is now, there was a hill, just rocks, and where the house of Don Elut is there was nothing but bush, and around the cenote there were great trees.

CHAN KOM BECOMES A PUEBLO

The ties that had to be broken before Chan Kom could become an independent village (pueblo) were with the village of Ebtun. About one-third of the present families of Chan Kom have come from Ebtun, but these are the largest and the most influential families; leadership in Chan Kom has always resided with the Ebtun colonists. The men who held the first public offices in Chan Kom had previously held offices in Ebtun; there was a schism in Ebtun while Chan Kom was still an unimportant *ranchería*. But now as the new settlement grew, one Ebtun faction, with its cornfields at Chan Kom, returned less and less often to Ebtun. The duty of *guardia* at the parent village, almost 30 miles away, had become intolerable. When the new school[1] was built in 1917, the men gathered there in the evening to discuss their growing quarrel with Ebtun. Then followed the early years of the Revolution and, under the influence first of Alvarado and then of Carrillo, the villages of this marginal area were helped to assert their independence and to participate in the new socialist state. The grant of communal lands to Yucatecan villages, under the provisions of the new lands laws, became a sort of accolade, a symbol of new status; formal delivery of the *ejidos* was performed with ceremony and rejoicing. Only if a settlement manifested an intention to welcome the new era and become a pueblo, would the reform government help. "Only in the pueblos," the Chan Kom leaders heard Felipe Carrillo say, "is there furniture in the schools."

The difficulties with Ebtun could be resolved, the aid of the governor could be had, if Chan Kom would become a pueblo. The leaders' determination became fixed on this immediate and practical program.

Then we set out for Merida. There, in the office of the Government, was Don Benjamin Carrillo. We explained to him that we wanted to make a pueblo. We explained to him that we did not want to have to make our dry tortillas to carry nine leagues to Ebtun so as to make our *guardia* there. He said, "All right; it is the Socialist Party that makes pueblos. It is not the party that destroys pueblos, but the party that builds them. Wait till my brother Felipe comes."

So we waited, and Don Felipe came, and we began to explain it to him: that we had done everything in Ebtun, that we had built the church and the *cuartel*, and that now we wanted to make a pueblo in Chan Kom; and would he not please give his approval.

[1] The school persisted, in spite of vicissitudes. There were 8 successive teachers in 7 years; 3 were removed because of drunkenness and immorality; 2 resigned after brief stays; 3 were conscientious, helpful and well liked.

Directly he said that the authorities would not approve a pueblo unless first it gave lands to the pueblo. If you take *ejidos*, even though they be the lands of the dzules,[1] then it will be all right. You can not make a pueblo unless you take your *ejidos*."

"All right," we said, "we will take our *ejidos*."

Then he said we had to install our *Liga*.

"All right," we said, "we all agree to that."

Then we said: "We all agree. Please give us some drums and some cornets and a flag of the *Liga*."

Immediately Don Felipe ordered Don Benjamin, who was the boss of the store-room to give us two drums and two cornets and a flag of the *Liga*. And he explained to us that we must elect a president, and a secretary, and a treasurer, and a claims agent, and a representative.

When we got to Chan Kom, we played the drums and the cornets, and we summoned all the people, and we elected the officers of the *Liga*.

The Government sent to Chan Kom agents to perfect the organization of the new *Liga Local*. The agents instructed the village leaders as to what they should do, and these in turn transmitted these ideas to their people:

Then we drew up a petition to the government, and they gave us a few tools. That helped to make improvements in this little village. Then we were told in the assembly that we should persuade our fellow villagers to build pretty stone houses. Whereupon they began to take this into consideration and began to ask me whether what I said was true, whether this would get to be a well-populated village. "We see only woods around us. There are no other villages near."

And I said to them: "You may be quite sure that we are going to build up a village with the help of your children who are studying there in our village: it is with them, indeed, that we are going to people a real pueblo. Because, my companions, they will trust my words more than you, for they are reading about the good things they are going to do."

Whereupon they said, "Very well. We also believe what you tell us. We are going to do these things little by little."

"Good!" I said. "It is not only I, but even those who come here to visit us that are going to tell you that we are doing right, because I am seeing and reading in books these good ideas."[2]

To become a pueblo meant two things: To take on the appearance of a Spanish-American town, and to secure legal confirmation of the communal lands. The people of Chan Kom cleared the land around their cenote of trees, and laid it off in the form of a square plaza; streets were marked off, bounding square blocks of house sites, and some of the people moved their huts down to the street line. Around the new plaza the first masonry houses were built and, not far from the schoolbuilding, a rectangular masonry structure to serve as public building (*cuartel*).

In this same year (1923) the first petitions were sent asking that Chan Kom be granted its own *ejidos*. The petitions claimed for Chan Kom a population of 217, alleged the difficulty of carrying out *guardia* to a pueblo nine leagues away, and urged the petitioners' character as loyal socialists. Action on the petitions was delayed due to the governmental upsets following upon the shooting of Felipe

---

[1] One not an Indian. See p. 101.
[2] From a text taken down in Maya by Dr. Manuel Andrade.

Carrillo, but when in 1924 order was restored under Iturralde, Chan Kom renewed its efforts. This time the Government sent a representative, who reported favorably. A temporary, and then a final survey of the proposed *ejido* was made. The engineer who made the final survey in June 1925 described what he found at Chan Kom in his official report. While the men of Chan Kom saw their visions of the pueblo they wished to become, the townsman's eyes beheld something very different:

The 2400 hectares of land granted to the village are rugged and very stony. When rains fall regularly there can be produced 2250 litres of maize per hectare on this land, which can be cultivated twice consecutively every 10 years. In small portions of the *ejido*, at the most a hectare in size, in the stony land of which it is composed, they cultivate pineapple, sugar cane, and bananas, also with good results when, as said before, the rains are not scanty. The village devotes itself to produce of this kind and obtains very good harvests; but most of the time they are not able to take advantage of them because they lack the necessary tools. Thus, in order to grind sugar cane, they use an apparatus made of wood, and for the cooking of the juice, copper boilers of very small capacity, which they lend to one another, since there are very few in the village. To granulate the sugar they use a sort of basket made of vines which they get from the fields, and in these they place the sugar with the molasses and then place earth on top, and something heavy, so that the syrup, the residue of the sugar, runs off through the little crevices in the baskets—an entirely primitive process.

All these deficiencies in the exploitations of their crops are so great, added to the very low prices paid for the molasses, the residue of the sugar, by the *rematador* of the tax on alcohol (who is the one distiller in the whole Department of Valladolid) bring it about that plantations of sugar cane are only half exploited or are never begun at all, because 50 per cent of the small cultivators have very small resources and therefore they attempt only to get out the juice without turning it into sugar and to sell it to the distiller, the one purchaser in this Department, who pays very low prices. As said before, pineapples and bananas are other products of the *ejidos*; from these they can get almost no income, because of the great distance which separates them from the railroad, a distance of at least 50 kilometers on the worst sort of roads, over which their produce is carried on their own backs or on beasts of burden. This brings it about that the income from these products is very scanty, since the price paid for them in the city of Valladolid is very low, and so they are mostly cultivated for their own use.

This village is one advanced in civilization, though in the middle of the bush; it is the last large settlement of the Department of Valladolid before entering the territory of Quintana Roo.

On August 16, 1926, the pueblo obtained actual possession of its *ejidos*.

The success of Chan Kom served to increase the resentment of Ebtun, and acts of violence occurred. Chan Kom was one of the first of the frontier villages to take to cattle raising; men of Ebtun are said to have killed cattle of Chan Kom and to have destroyed cornfields. In 1928 the people of Chan Kom became convinced that Ebtun had conceived a plan to attack and sack Chan Kom. At any rate, men from Ebtun lay in the bush around Chan Kom; for a week Chan Kom was in a state of siege. Through the intermediacy of a leader from a third village, however, the siege was lifted without bloodshed. In later years the enmity with Ebtun yielded to common aims and interests; there is, apparently, only goodwill between the two pueblos now.

Since the close of this episode, the history of Chan Kom has been one of peace and prosperity. More streets were opened and more masonry houses built; the cattle industry, in spite of setbacks, grew; the school throve. With the material gains went an intensification of the reform spirit. The sale of liquor was prohibited; and even the sale and discharge of fireworks rockets.[1] *Fagina* (compulsory labor for public purposes) became a more exacting duty; by means of this institution a new *cuartel* and a new school were built, and a wagon-road was laid out through the bush to connect the village with Chichen Itza. "The road to the light," people called it. More and more the interests of the people turned toward Chichen Itza, as Villa, the teacher, drew their curiosity and then their sympathy to the Americans, Yucatecans and Mexicans there; visitors from Chichen were asked to make addresses in Chan Kom on topics of progress and social betterment.

To lay out the line of the new road, the men of Chan Kom built a tower of poles, 50 feet high; and from the platform surmounting this tower they were able, for the first time, to gaze over miles and miles of level bush, to look down upon the settlements of their less progressive neighbors, and to descry, far on the horizon, the white triangular outline of the Castillo at Chichen, a building erected by unclaimed ancestors as a temple-base for vanished shrines. But to these watchers it was not a symbol of a forgotten past, but a guide to the future.

[1] Used for festal purposes.   Objected to as wasteful and dangerous.   Later their use was resumed.

Chapter III

TOOLS AND TECHNIQUES

The transitional character of the Chan Kom community is expressed in its changing architecture. The visitor's first impression is of a village that is being remade and of a people who have formed a civic plan. These villagers are building themselves a new village. The old houses of poles and thatch still stand on the hummocks that formed the natural house sites (Plate 1a), but along the rectangular plaza, that has not yet been cleared of boulders and rubble, are rising the masonry houses of those who begin to turn their backs on the old ways (Plate 1, and b c, and Plate 2). At each of the four corners of the plaza stands a short piece of heavy wall, whitewashed and painted with a street number; it marks the angle of the street intersection and is a pledge of the building some day to be erected there.

Ever since the Sixteenth Century the plaza and the rectilinear street have been symbols of the European civilization.[1] Those Indian communities that enter into the larger social and political order adopt the architecture of the Spaniard. The usual Indian settlement of the remoter parts of Yucatan is a scattering of huts, built of poles, mud and thatch, and distributed without order or symmetry. But the determination of the inhabitants of Chan Kom to make their *ranchería* a pueblo carried with it the necessity to lay out regular streets at right angles to the plaza and to build houses of rubble masonry (*mampostería*). So the lines of the streets were fixed and the worst of the stony hummocks leveled. People built straight stone walls along the lines of their properties, and most of the inhabitants moved their houses so that they stood close upon the thoroughfare, each one in line with all the others (Plate 3a). The one mason in the community began the construction of stone houses, and as he worked he taught the trade to other men. Masonry houses of Spanish style began to take the place of the thatched Maya huts, first around the plaza and then on the side streets. A new public building (*cuartel*) was built of *mampostería*, and plans made for a new school (Plate 3b). "Now Chan Kom has become a pueblo," people said.

Nevertheless, with the exception of this architectural transformation, the changes that are going on in Chan Kom find few evidences in the material culture. The incorporation of European elements into the body of tools and techniques which the Indian had, took place centuries ago, and this early readjustment to the environment has since encountered little to disturb it. The extra margin of wealth, with which to buy goods from the outside, remains about the same; many of the articles of practical use are locally made by traditional techniques; and some of

[1] "Item, una de las cosas que ha impedido e impide la policia temporal y espiritual de los naturales de las dichas provincias, es el vivir apartados unos de otros por los montes. Por este mando, que todos los naturales de esta dicha provincia se junten en sus pueblos, y hagan casas juntas, trazadas en forma de pueblos todos los de una parcialidad y cabecera en un lugar comodo y conveniente, y hagan sus casas de piedras, y de obra duradera, cada vecino casa de por si, dentro de la traza que se le diere, y no siembren milpas algunas dentro del pueblo, sino todo este muy limpio y no haya arboledas, sino que todo lo corten, sino fuere algunos arboles de fruta, pena, etc." Cogolludo, Bk. I, p. 474.

these techniques have acquired the inviolability conferred by sacred sanction. The iron handmill tends to reduce the importance of the grinding stone; factory-made hats are commoner than they once were; some young men wear long blue trousers instead of the older short trunks and apron, and people bring in lamps and chairs and phonographs. Such are the small changes of which the present generation is aware. The older generation knew its changes too (though probably not so many of them)—changes represented by survivals of older artifacts: an old style bag that preceded the *sabucan*, a kind of pot no longer made, a loin cloth still worn by one old man in the community. On the whole it is probable that the practical problems of life are solved today much as they were centuries ago.

Culture remains fairly homogeneous. The tools of life are almost equally available to all. By working a little harder, one may acquire a masonry house or another cow. One man may own more than another, but he owns the same kind of thing. One woman may wear clothing of better quality than her neighbor, but she wears the same kind of garment. The old peasant costume has been modified only to the small extent that elements from the city have become part of the man's holiday attire. A man dresses somewhat differently on Sunday from the way he dresses on a week day, but one man dresses like another. And all share a common fund of knowledge as to how to kill a deer, to raise a crop, or to build a house.

Those kinds of practical knowledge which are the oldest, generally speaking, are those which are the least specialized and the least subject to change. The fashion in gasoline lamps may change in a few days. Cattle raising experiences its vicissitudes, hog raising has recently become unpopular. People are willing to uproot an unprofitable fruit tree in order to plant a better. Some men know about carpentering and sugar-making, while others do not. But all the women cook the same foods in the same manner,[1] and all the men hunt, keep bees, and raise corn in the same ways; these ways change little and are interwoven with religious and magical ideas.

From the dependence upon maize there is in Chan Kom no escape. To live is to "make milpa"; there is no other way. "How do people live," asked one of Chan Kom who for the first time visited the seacoast, "here where there are no milpas?" There are few opportunities for a man to sell his labor, and these are only to work in the fields of another instead of his own.[2] If a man is to be fed, he must make the land produce corn—this rocky shelf that is dry and almost bare of soil and yet is everywhere overgrown with a dense and thorny bush. How to accomplish this is therefore a knowledge that all men have and that they learn following their fathers to the milpa, almost as they learn to speak, hardly knowing that they learn it.

The fundamental tools of life lie rooted in the oldest folkways; we know they have not changed essentially in four hundred years; they are probably very much older. And as they are old, and yet not sure in their results, from the vagaries of

[1] With small exceptions, to be mentioned later.
[2] To some degree an exception is presented by the mason, who is, but only in part, relieved from agriculture.

PLATE 1

a, House and house-plot, old style.

b, The house of poles and thatch.

c, Building a masonry house to take the place of the old house.

PLATE 2

a, House interior, old style.

b, House interior, new style.

the winds and the uncertainty of the rain, they are not purely practical acts, but are also conventional gestures, expressive of desire for a good harvest, or of thanks that it has been achieved. Agricultural toil is arduous, but so inevitable and little questioned that there is small bitterness in its ardors; and it is so interwoven with non-practical customs, that it is also, in a sense, prayer.[1]

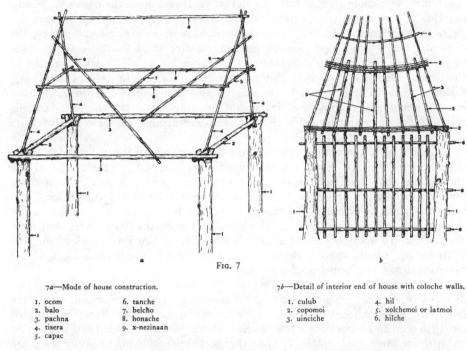

FIG. 7

7a—Mode of house construction.

1. ocom	6. tanche
2. balo	7. belcho
3. pachna	8. honache
4. tisera	9. x-nezinaan
5. capac	

7b—Detail of interior end of house with coloche walls.

1. culub	4. hil
2. copomoi	5. xolchemoi or latmoi
3. uinciche	6. hilche

HOUSES

The masonry house is an innovation and a luxury for the progressive and the ambitious; the thatched house is a necessity for everybody. The masonry house is built by individual initiative, in some cases with the remunerated aid of others; the Indian hut (at least until recent years in Chan Kom) was built by communal labor.[2] The masonry house follows the Spanish pattern common all over Mexico. It is rectangular, with a flat, very slightly sloping roof supported on round beams; the walls are of broken stone laid in mortar; the floor is cement; the doors and windows—often barred with iron—are furnished with iron hinges and wickets; there is but one room.

[1] This latter aspect of the agricultural life will not be described in this chapter, although to set out separately the practical techniques does some injustice to the facts.

[2] That is, by *fagina*. See p. 78. At the time of writing (1931) ten of thirty-four households have masonry houses and five more are under construction.

The Maya house of poles, mud and thatch is found all over Yucatan; its construction differs from place to place only in details. In Chan Kom the mode of construction is as follows (Plate 4 and text-fig. 7*a*).

Two pairs of stout forked posts (ocom) are driven into the ground (in large buildings three pairs are used). The forks stand in the same plane as is occupied by the long dimension of the house; in them rest two horizontal beams (balo). At right angles with these, and resting upon them, are two long straight beams (pachna). Two more slender forked poles (tisera)[1] rest upon the balo and, bound together at their upper ends, support the central roof beam (honache). Across the tisera, at their midpoints, are fastened two slender horizontal pieces (capac); the ends of these in turn support two long poles (tanche) which lie above and parallel to the pachna. Across the midpoint of the tanche lies a pole (belcħo) parallel to the capac. Rigidity is given to this framework by an oblique pole (x-nezinaan), fastened to tisera and to pachna (in some houses there are two of these, crossing each other). In some buildings, instead of the x-nezinaan, the xolmuch is used; this is a forked beam, placed with its forked end against the balo and with its upper end lashed to the honache.

Upon this framework are fastened smaller poles to form the walls and to make the supports for the palm-leaf thatch. Into the ground, between the ocom and in a curved line at the ends of the structure, are driven posts (culub). To these are bound two bunches of withes (copomoi); to these latter are fastened long thin radiating poles (uinciche). To the uinciche are bound, at right angles, many slender parallel withes (hil),[2] upon which are later hung the palm leaves that form the thatch. In many houses added rigidity is given to this framework of the roof by inserting, evenly spaced, three thicker poles (xolchemoi or latmoi), that are fastened to the two bunches of copomoi.

The wall is made in one of two ways. The sketch shows the technique known as cololche (fig. 7*b*). Slender vertical poles (cololche) are interwoven with three horizontal poles (hilche) that are in turn bound to the culub. Sometimes added strength is given by inserting a few heavier vertical posts (mulche),[3] and by binding them to the interlacing poles. In the other technique (chuyche) heavier posts are placed close together and driven a short distance into the ground. Heavy withes (bahche or copoche) are bound ("sewed," they say) to the outside of this fence; and there is no interweaving. If the walls are to receive a mud plaster, then (in both kinds of wall) a number of slender horizontal withes (chacanche)[3] are fastened to the interior to support this plaster.[4]

"You look for a place which is very good for leveling the ground to make a house. After getting the place ready, you look for the most important beams, which are the *horcon* (ocom). Then you look for the balos, the pachna, then the belcħo, then the *tijeras*, then the *cabellete* (honache). These are the principal beams."

---

[1] From Spanish *tijera*—scissors.
[2] Only one of many is shown in the sketch.
[3] Not shown in the sketch.
[4] The names given in this note are those used by the people who came originally from Pixoy, Ebtun and other neighboring villages. It is apparent that there are local variations in these names, especially in the terms for the lesser parts of the house. People from Suma and those from Yaxcaba give different names in some instances. The new house ceremony is discussed on p. 146.

"Then you look for the uinciche, then you look for the hil, then you look for the vines (ak). When you find some vines, you cut them and begin to scrape them to get off all the little twigs. There is a vine called anicab which can be used dry, but the others can not be used dry.

"The anicab is used when it is dry by wetting it in water. The others can not be; they are breakable. They are only used green.

"You have to cut them in the middle and begin to tie them.

"You begin to cut the palm leaves even if they are dry. You can dry them if they are not dry. You get up there and begin to put them in place. After tying them and covering the whole slope of the roof with palm leaves, you cover the top ridge with palm leaves. This is called pach-hol [this means thatching the ridge pole]. After finishing all this, you cut the *bajereque* [coloche]—these are the poles which are put so [vertical], for the walls. After getting together all the poles, you begin to put them in their places, fastening them with vines. After this, if you are very poor you make the door to the house with vines, which door we call in Maya x-macak, vine cover. That is the door of sticks and vine. And if you wish, you look for the very red earth and you mix it with *zacate*. Mostly you find red earth (chac kancab), where ants live. You can use the ant hills. You collect the earth and wet it and you make the mixture for the plaster. After doing all this you can go to your house with a feeling of security.

"*Sascab* is a soft white stone which is found on top of the ground. It is used to make the walls of masonry houses.

"The principal beams are of a wood which is called chacte. Yaxek is another kind. It is a very hard wood. If the house burns, the beams do not burn. Oxcitinche is used for the forked posts (ocom); dzudzuc is also used. These four woods are the only ones which can be used for posts, because other woods can not be put in the ground, as they don't last many years, and when you put up a house, it is for your life. The pachna are mostly of zac-cuyziche which is used for upper beams which are not put in the ground.

"Or else you look for another kind, iciche. In this house the belcho and the *tijeras* are of iciche. Mostly those which are used above are of two or three sorts—zac-cuyziche, iciche, chactecoc, or chimtok. The uinciche are of elemuy, the hil is also of elemuy, or if not, we use dzudzuc." [1]

The house-group includes lesser structures: commonly a fowlhouse (zooy) rectangular in form and made of slender poles driven into the ground and bound together with liana (Plate 4*b*). A similar structure (*chiquero*) may be built for the pigs. Most men keep their corn in the milpas, but in a few instances a granary (chil), like that made in the fields, is built in the owner's yard (Plate 4*c*).

The hollowed logs and tray-like gardens (caanche), elevated on poles to keep them from the pigs, are common adjuncts to the dwelling, and only less commonly a number of bee-hives (described on p. 48), covered with a roof of thatch, stand at the far end of the yard.

DOMESTIC EQUIPMENT
(Plate 5*a*)

The activities of the house center around the hearth, merely three stones, on which rests the pot or griddle. The hearth (koben) has given its name to the kitchen; the three stones that compose it bear no special names. Beside the hearth stands the *banqueta*,[2] a low, round, wooden table (sometimes with a smaller circular

[1] Told by a man from Piste.
[2] No Maya name in use.

extension) on which the tortillas are patted out. Although the metal hand-mill is in general use, most families retain the metate for making the meal fine. A woman does not kneel when she grinds; she stands at the *banco*,[1] a narrow sloping table cut from a large log, and having low walls on its long sides. On this table stand the metate (ca) and its tapering handstone (u-kab-ca, "hand of the metate"), and on it the meal collects as it is ground. The *banco* may be placed in the yard, where one invariably finds the *batea*,[1] an oval wooden tray, supported on four legs, on which clothes are washed (Plate 6*b*).

The calabash (luch) and the gourd (lec) are more important than the pot (cum). The ordinary vessel, made by cutting a globular gourd transversely, bears the generic name (lec). From this (except in houses where purchased china or metal-ware is used) one drinks and eats. When larger gourds are cut through from the stem-end, another sort of vessel (x-hau lec) results. Another gourd vessel, similar to the ordinary lec, but oval in outline, is huaz; perforated it serves as a strainer (chachab). An oval gourd, with a small opening at the stem-end, and stood on end, is homa; this vessel is used in offering food ceremonially, and also in cupping. Large gourds of this shape are used to hold fresh tortillas (lec-i-uah).

Small homa are used to hold balche in the ceremonies. The gourd that is constricted in the middle (chu) is especially prized; this is the water bottle of the Maya. Gourd vessels are suspended from circular carriers (cħuyub) made of rings of the bark of the habin tree, over which are wound strips of *guano* palm (xaan); into these strips designs are woven with dyed henequen fibers.

Of pottery (Plate 5*b*) the two forms in most frequent use are the ppul, a narrow-mouthed, wide-bodied jug in which women carry water from the cenote, and the kat, a large, wide-mouthed jar for the storage of water (and sometimes balche). The small shallow bowl (lac) is sometimes employed in daily use and is also used to hold offerings of food on the occasion of *rezos* (ritual Catholic prayers).[2] The incenseburner (ppulut) is a small, perforated vessel with an incurved rim, supported on a spreading base.[3]

A narrow-mouthed jar, about 15 inches high, is known as *botijuela*, or botix. It is made of a very heavy ware, different from that of other pottery vessels. Some are corrugated. It has a pointed bottom and will not stand on a surface. It is not bought nor made any more. People do not remember when it was possible to procure them, but a considerable number still exist and are used chiefly to store honey.[4]

There used to be also a flat, wide, shallow bowl with an outcurved rim; the rim was notched, apparently, or dentate, and there were four small, evenly spaced holes in the rim. This vessel was known as ocliz lac (or as kix lac?). It was used chiefly or solely to hold the cooked turkey carried to the house of the girl's parents on the occasion when the agreement for marriage was solemnized.

---

[1] No Maya name in use.

[2] On *Todos Muertos* a larger size (about 6 inches in diameter) is used for the souls of the adult dead, and a smaller size for the offerings for the souls of dead children.

[3] The shallow circular vessel with the sharply incurved rim (*apaste*), used in some neighboring villages (as for example, Piste), is not used in Chan Kom.

[4] Dr. A. V. Kidder suggests that the botix is a Spanish olive or oil jar.

Baskets (Plate 5c) fall into three classes. The xux is a basket about 20 inches high and 18 wide, made of dried vine stems woven over sets of five vertically placed pieces. This basket is used in harvesting corn, the ears are thrown into it and by it carried to the granary.[1] Xac is a shallow basket with a flaring rim, about 24 inches wide and 10 deep, made by means of the same technique as the foregoing, but of the stiff integument of the central rib of the mature palm frond. This basket is one of general household utility; it is used, for example, as a sewing basket. The third basket, baaz, is substantially the Mexican *petaca*, and is made in various sizes, of strips torn from the palm fronds when they are still young and have not yet unfolded. The strips are plaited into a top and bottom that fit closely together, making two layers to this covering—"clothes kept in it do not become damp."

"Peten" is the name given to a flat, circular tray, about 18 inches in diameter, made of bark of the hol tree stretched over a withe bent into a circle. This is suspended from the ceiling by three cords and on it food is kept from harm, or strips of meat are hung from it and dried over the fire (Plate 6a).

Many of the standard articles of domestic equipment are commercial products of iron. The griddle (xamach) is of iron, a commercial product. This and the metal pots (cum) now generally used for cooking, and the metal pails (choy)[2] used in drawing water, apparently bear the names of the old articles which they have displaced (Plate 6c). Knives and the machete (mazcab) are, of course, of iron. The wooden chocolate pot and beater is called by its Spanish name (*batidor*).

Light is supplied by a candle or by a simple metal lamp (*quinque*) in which kerosene is burned. Many homes have only the light from the hearth fire.

Matches are in general use. Flint and steel are known, but no longer used. Occasionally, when a man is away from the village, a fire is lighted with the fire-drill (haxab kak). A pointed stick of hard wood, either puc ak or chacah, is rotated with the palms of the hands in the stump of a dry squash stem until the heat ignites the tinder.

Of the larger furniture, the hammock (kaan) deserves first mention. If the house is small and the family large, these may at night be swung across one another at different levels. By day, the gesture of hospitality is to lower the hammock, tied up out of the way, for the guest to sit on. Practically all houses have one or more small benches (kanche), blocks of wood, 4 or 5 inches high, hollowed out beneath; and most have one or more small home-made tables; chairs are less common. Shelves of poles at one end of the palm hut, or wooden gasoline boxes, serve to store articles; many people have metal-bound trunks, equipped with lock and key.

FOOD AND COOKERY

A considerable variety of dishes are known and are prepared occasionally, especially for fiestas, but the daily fare is very simple. Essentially, people live on maize cakes and maize gruel, together with chile as an essential condiment and a moderate quantity of beans. Quite as often as not the meal consists simply of

---

[1] Corn on the ear is often measured in terms of this basket, "un canastro."
[2] The Motul dictionary gives choy as the word for "bark pail," which is still occasionally made and used in *rancherías* around Chan Kom. It is also the name of the tree from which this bark is taken.

boiled corn meal made into toasted cakes (*tortillas*; uah) or prepared as a thin mush; in some houses beans may not be cooked even if beans are available in abundance. So far as meat enters into the diet, it is chiefly the product of the hunt. The average inhabitant eats venison, wild pig, or agouti about once a week. Beef is eaten perhaps two or three times a year; it is much preferred to game or wild fowl. Pork is not esteemed and even when an occasional hog is slaughtered, the meat is not easily disposed of. Greenstuffs are eaten, not as vegetables, separately cooked, but as flavorings and condiments. Much pains are taken in raising them in the little gardens, but the quantity consumed is small. Chile pepper is eaten at nearly every meal; the tortilla is dipped in the ground pod. Beans are regularly boiled in *epazote* (*Chenopodium*). Tomatoes, cabbage and onions are frequently used, and very small quantities of coriander and mint.

Wheat flour is used only by the baker. When he bakes, people who can afford it buy his bread; most families eat wheat bread once in a while; it is not a regular article of diet for anyone. Hardly any rice is eaten; of course rice, like wheat, is not produced locally. When in season, people eat the starchy tubers: cassava, yam, *jicama* (chicam), sweet potatoes, and also the Lima bean (ib). Eggs are eaten not uncommonly; domestic fowl (hens, turkey) are festal foods only.

Atole (corn gruel) is the usual morning beverage; coffee is commonly taken in the evening. Chocolate is drunk less often, but occasionally, especially on fiesta days. It is beaten up in the wooden vessel with the wooden beater and sweetened either with sugar or honey. Milk is not used.[1] Carbonated beverages are sold in the stores and occasionally drunk. Beer or spirituous liquors are not sold, and during the present period very rarely drunk in Chan Kom.[2] Balche, the old ceremonial beer, fermented from the bark of the *Lonchocarpus* tree, is used in many of the non-Catholic ceremonies; it is not otherwise used. "Four pieces of bark, about a foot long, are pounded with sticks and placed in a jar with two *jicaras* of water and a cup of honey. It is left three days and then tasted. If it is not good, more honey is added and it is allowed to stand till it comes out yellow, good." Corn beer is not made.

In the morning, on arising at dawn, most people drink a bowl of *atole*; but some take coffee, or, less commonly, chocolate, with a few of yesterday's tortillas toasted on the griddle. Fresh tortillas are made for the midday meal—generally taken an hour or so before noon—and others are made in the late afternoon. If there are beans, or starchy tubers, they are eaten at these meals. Later in the evening, before going to their hammocks, people drink coffee (sometimes chocolate), with bread, if there is bread or money to buy it.

The maize which forms the basis of this simple fare, as it has formed that of all Mexican cookery for thousands of years, is (except for a few dishes) boiled in lime to soften it. A little lime[3] is stirred into a little boiling water. Then the maize is put in and cooked a few minutes and allowed to stand, usually over night. The

---

[1] Canned milk is sometimes used.
[2] This is not typical for the region.
[3] The lime is the same used in making mortar; it is made by burning limestone in a slow fire.

grains so softened are then washed in several waters, until the water remains clear. The boiled corn, with the grains swollen and soft (*nixtamal*; kuum), is not eaten as it is, but is ground on the metate. The resulting meal (*masa*; zacan) is made into tortillas (uah); these are patted out on pieces of banana leaf and cooked on the hot iron griddle. A half-cooked tortilla, laid for a moment in the ashes, expands into a crisp hollow breadstuff (opp).

The simplest preparation of maize is zaca.[1] Shelled corn is cooked without lime and ground, and the resulting meal is made into balls. A little is stirred into water. Zaca is not part of secular cookery, but it is the form in which maize is customarily offered to non-Christian gods and spirits.

For *pozole*[2] (keyem) the meal is prepared as for tortillas, except that usually the grains are washed when half-cooked, and then cooked again in clear water until soft. The ground meal is carried by the laborer to his milpa; he mixes some of this dough with cold water and drinks the mixture. *Pozole* is a staple food when away from home; it is an occasional but not a usual part of the domestic cookery.

Atole (za) is corn-meal gruel. It is usually made of the same meal of which tortillas are made; a little is dropped into boiling water and cooked about 15 minutes. Salt is usually added, occasionally sugar or honey.[3] Other *atoles*, less commonly prepared, are made differently. *Atole* is sometimes made of maize put into cold water without lime and brought to a boil; this corn (chacbil-ixim) is then ground and made into a gruel. Another *atole* is made of cheche-ixim—raw corn ground just as it comes from the ear. These two varieties are regarded as beneficial for slight sicknesses. Still another variety is made from chambixim (chambel-ixim?), corn uncooked but allowed to soak in water without lime for three days before grinding. Two kinds of *atoles* are made of new corn; these are seasonal dishes, very much relished. For one of these, called iz ul, the fresh ripe corn is ground, mixed with water and cooked in a pot with sugar and salt. In making ahza, the fresh corn is broken with the hand stone on the metate, but not ground. It is then put into a pot and a little hot water added with salt, being stirred meanwhile, then a little cold water is added and it is stirred again; when it bubbles it is taken off and allowed to stand till morning. Next day the liquid is squeezed from the grains by hand, the grains are then ground and after a little cold water has been added to the meal it is strained through a cloth; what remains is boiled into a porridge. Sugar is added, as well as the liquid previously squeezed from the grains and once more it is put on to cook until thick.[4]

Tamales are made of a dough prepared from carefully washed and ground *nixtamal*. This is strained and cooked till thick. Lard is mixed with this dough and bits of meat are put into it. Then square pats of this dough are laid in banana

[1] "*Zaca:* atol en lengua mexicana, hecho de agua y maiz; bebese frio, sin cozer ni calentar, ya entrado el día; es bevida fresca y sustenta; algunas veces mezclan cacao en ella." Motul Dictionary.

[2] In speaking Spanish, people use "pozole" for either zaca or keyem.

[3] "Primeramente se pone el maiz para cocerse, y despues se saca del agua; despues se lava el nixtamal; y despues se muele; despues se pone otra vez en el fuego para cocerse con sal, unos quince minutos. Es el atole mas comun, que se come de ordinario." Motul Dictionary.

[4] "Primeramente es el elote nuevo. Se desgranan, se muelen. Despues de moler, se cuela—en colador de alambre fino o con tela. Despues de colarlo, se pone en el fuego para cocerlo. Se puede poner sal o dulce, al gusto."

leaves; kol, the broth from chicken boiled with seasonings, is poured over the pats of dough, then they are tied in the leaves and boiled for an hour or two. In Chan Kom, *tamales* fulfill a festal function that is secular rather than sacred. They are not made in connection with the pagan ceremonies, nor are they made for the *novenas;* they have a limited use for birthday parties and for a few other occasions that are apparently not part of the older tradition.

One form in which maize is eaten does not require the preliminary softening of the grains in lime water. This is *pinole* (kah), a drink that not infrequently takes the place of *atole* or chocolate, especially on cold mornings or evenings. The maize is toasted on the griddle, cinnamon, aniseed, and often pepper are added, and the whole ground together to form the basis of a beverage boiled like coffee, or sometimes beaten like chocolate.[1]

A drink known as x-taan[2] chucua used to be made as a part of the gifts offered to a girl's parents when the agreement for marriage was solemnized.[3] Powdered cacao was beaten into water with a little corn meal, strained and mixed with tabasco pepper and cinnamon.

Maize is also made into a variety of sacred breadstuffs, prepared and consumed only as a part of non-Catholic ceremonies. Chief among these are the tuti-uah large breads made of the ordinary corn meal combined with ground squash seed (zicil). These assume a great number of special shapes and sizes, each appropriate to a special ritual, and bear many special names.[4] After baking, these breads are mixed with the broth prepared from the consecrated turkeys and hens.

Chachacuah is made on the fiesta of *Todos Muertos*, or on other festal occasions. The usual maize dough for tortillas is colored red with arnotto, and large tortillas made of it are wrapped around boiled fowl.

Beans are prepared for eating simply by boiling, with *epazote* to flavor them, until they are soft. Lima beans (ib) are usually ground to paste and mixed with ground squash seeds. A dish called toczel is made by putting cooked Lima beans and ground squash seeds together in a pot; two heated stones are dropped in and the beans thus dried, while they are stirred with a stick to keep them from burning.[5] So prepared they may be kept a week or more.

Meat of all sorts is usually boiled. Zac hanal is the name given to boiled fowl as most commonly prepared: cooked with onion, garlic and saffron. Box hanal is made by boiling the fowl in a sauce made of the peppers known as x-nuc ic. Only those peppers are used that have fallen off the plant to the ground (known as maazte ic). The seeds are removed and the peppers toasted in a pot. Then they are soaked for four days, the water being changed three times, and are ground in a meal to

---

[1] "Se agarra el maiz, y se pone en los comales para que se medio quema. Despues se saca y se muele. Se derrete entre el agua, frio o caliente. Para dar mas gusto, se pone pimienta de tabasco, o canela, o azucar."

"Se pone el maiz en un comal para tostarse. Despues se saca del comal, se le pone canela, anis en grano, pimienta de tabasco—un puño de los tres. Despues se muele. Se prepara con agua caliente como café, o batido como chocolate. Se toma en la mañana en lugar de chocolate. Se toma mucho en el invierno en lugar de chocolate, porque es una cosa calentando."

[2] "X-tanpam" is a young woman. Motul Dictionary.

[3] See p. 194.

[4] The detailed descriptions of these sacred breads appear in the accounts of the ceremonies in which they are employed. See pp. 129, 136, 141.

[5] "Se hacen de ibes bien cocidas y de pepitas molidas. En una pasta se revuelve, se l'echan piedras calientes hasta que salen bien tostadas, secas. Esto se aguantan muchos días."

PLATE 3

a, Street corner, off the plaza.

b, New masonry buildings on the plaza. The half-finished school and the *cuartel*.

PLATE 4

a, House framework.

b, Fowl pen.

c, Granary.

which enough water is added to permit the fowl to be cooked in the mixture. *Epazote*, onion and other condiments are added. Dzanchac is the name given to meat (of any sort) first cooked in the earth oven and then boiled with vegetables and seasonings; it is chechac when the meat is not first cooked in the earth oven. Venison and other meat are sometimes dried over the fire; often the peten[1] is used for this purpose.

The earth oven is one of three cooking techniques in use. (The others are boiling in the pot and toasting on the griddle.) It is used chiefly, but not quite entirely, in festal cookery. Preparation of the earth oven (pib tah) is an invariable part of the more important ceremonies. A rectangular pit is dug about a meter long, half as wide, and half as deep. Into it firewood is heaped and kindled and on the wood are placed pieces of stone. When the wood is burned out, the largest of the hot stones are removed and the smaller raked into an even floor. On these are placed grass and twigs and then the food to be cooked, wrapped in banana or bob leaves. Squashes, sweet potatoes, cassava, yam and *jicama* are cooked in the oven, occasionally meat, and often maize meal mixed with beans (buul-i-uah). Over the food leaves, usually muloch and yam, are placed, and the heat is sealed in with earth. It takes about an hour or an hour and a half for the food to cook.[2]

CLOTHING

On ordinary days a man wears short white trousers (culex) and a shirt (*camiseta*);[3] the former is always home-made, the latter may be bought ready-made. Around the waist is wound a rectangle of cotton cloth, usually blue striped. This garment (*delantal*, or descriptively, baktan nok, "around-the-front-garment") is tucked in the short trousers and hangs loose to the knees like an apron. Some men wear cloth belts (*ciñidor;* kaxnak nok) made, by the women, of purchased cloth. The old loin cloth (uith) is not now worn in Chan Kom, but is still used by some old men in nearby villages. Of sandals (*alpargatas;* xanab) two sorts are recognized: tabil xanab, sewed sandals fastened with thongs or rope (Plate 7*a*) and babil xanab, which have leather thongs and are cobbled with nails. The former is made locally. Sandal ties are distinguished according to the direction in which the cords are wound: noh hax ("twisted to the right") and dzic hax ("twisted to the left"). Noh-hax is preferred, because with cords so wound one may drive away a x-tabai (see p. 122).

The straw hat (ppoc) is commonly a city-made article, but another kind (hithbil ppoc) is locally made by hand; strips of palm leaf being sewed together with henequen fiber.

Women wear a skirt (pic) and the long loose blouse (*huipil;* ipil) (Plate 7*b*); both garments are home-made of factory-made textiles. Much of the colored ornament on the *huipiles* is now bought by the meter. But most of the women embroider,

---

[1] See p. 37.

[2] This statement as to food and cookery describes what is known and practiced by the people of Chan Kom generally. A very few women, more acquainted with city ways, know how to make dishes that are more characteristic of the city, such as *puchero*, *pavo relleno*, *escabeche de pavo* and *empanadas*.

[3] The loose blouse, *guayabera* (no Maya name), long white trousers (*calzones*), and red silk neckerchief are commonly worn as festal attire; these are bought ready-made.

table cloths and towels as well as *huipiles*, using commercial embroidery cotton. Cross-stitch (xocbil-chuy, "counted stitch") is less commonly used than the ordinary embroidery. The curvilinear, floral designs are drawn free hand on the cloth.

The *rebozos*,[1] of a great variety of colors, are bought in Valladolid, as are the soft-soled shoes worn for dancing. Small gold earrings (*aretes;* tup) are almost universal; married women of course wear their rings and gold chains on festal occasions. Some young women use a commercial scent. It is remembered that they made a perfume from a flower called payluch. Young women today sometimes fold their clothes away with the pods of the vanilla (zizbic) and of the zac-cuyzil-che; these impart a pleasant odor to the garments.

HANDICRAFTS[2]

No pottery is made in Chan Kom. Aside from the embroidery done by the women and the simple techniques used in the manufacture of baskets and gourd-carriers (Plate 7c) the only handicrafts practiced are those involving henequen fiber. Several families grow patches of henequen in the village. The leaves are placed on an inclined board (pacche), locked in with a large peg, and the fiber is rubbed out with a slender stick (*burriquete;* u kab pacche), triangular in outline (Plate 8a). The fibers are dried and twisted into cord by rolling them on the thigh. Hammocks are made of these cords; also carrying-bags (*sabucan;* no Maya name). Many people make simple carrying straps (*mecapal,* taantab), which are used to support burdens, on top of which small children often ride, fastened securely with handkerchiefs.

Not in Chan Kom itself, but in several of the neighboring *rancherías* (notably Noh-kak) small quantities of cotton (tanam) are grown. The fiber is spun (kuch) into thread by means of a spindle (pecheech) weighted with a wooden whorl cut integrally with the spindle-stick. The spindle-dish is an ordinary gourd vessel set in a base (lococ) of beeswax and weighted by the addition of two rows of the small fruits of the chac-molon-che, fastened around the rim with beeswax. The homespun thread is used principally for mending garments and for wicks for wax candles. Weaving, on looms with back-straps, was common in neighboring villages 75 years ago, but is now entirely, or almost entirely, extinct.

AGRICULTURE

The agricultural cycle swings around the entire year; there is no season when some men are not engaged in their milpas; but the rhythm is marked by four chief tasks: felling the bush, burning, planting and harvesting.

Although the small amount of land legally owned, by village or by individual, in this part of the State (p. 64) leaves plenty of unappropriated territory in which to make milpa, the choice of the site is not an easy matter. Some lands are more fertile than others and on some, it is believed, more rain is apt to fall. One may ask Divine assistance in making the choice; one is certainly guided by practical

---

[1] No Maya name.
[2] The division of labor in respect to the various kinds of technical knowledge is discussed in Chapter IV.

considerations of the convenience of the location and especially by the character of the soil. Yellow soil (kan luum) is not good for milpas; black soil (ek luum) is. Places where the trees are large and abundant, particularly uaxin and kanpokolche are selected. Especially where palms grow, the stony floor is apt to be better covered with pockets of soil. These places are "cacab"—"very good land," the agriculturalist will say, with real enthusiasm. "But where the aloe (c͟heleem) grows, there the land is poor." This is "very thin red land" (hayam kan luum).

When the site has been selected, the land to be cleared is measured[1] in *mecates* (kaan), each a square, 20 meters to a side.[2] The *mecates* are measured with a stick, or with a piece of string.[3] The *milpero* takes a meter as the distance from the tip of his middle finger to the outer margin of his breastbone.[4] Around the contemplated field a narrow little path is cut and a stone or a little heap of stones is placed to mark each *mecate* corner (xuuk). The *milpero* sights down these markers to make sure that they are aligned.

The bush is felled with the small steel ax used throughout Yucatan. Everything is cut down except a few of the largest trees; these are left "because a little shade is good for the growing corn in a time of drought, and because too much ash would result if they should be burned." Small growth is cut at the roots; larger trees a foot or two above ground.

Most of the land around Chan Kom produces two harvests (in two successive years), a few good lands produce three successive crops, and a very few distant lands (as, for example, at X-Ceh-yaax) produce four harvests. Some poor lands yield only one harvest. The corn stalks left standing into the second year are called *caña rosa* (zakab). These, and whatever bush has sprung up again, must be cut (*chapear*; pac zakab) and burned before the second sowing. Sometimes some of the larger trees left standing the first time are felled now. The first harvest (c͟hacben) is the best, the second harvest (zakab) is about three-fourths of the first, and the third (x-lak zakab) is about half of the first. After the one, two or three successive harvests which the land allows, it must be left fallow for a number of years. This period of time is not fixed, but before maize is again planted there at least 7 years elapse, and if sugar-cane is to be planted at least twelve. Lands may be left fallow for greater periods; if left longer, the next harvest is greater. During the first two or three years the idle milpa is called col zakab hubche, but after the old stalks have fallen, it is simply hubche. Sometimes land is cleared in one year and not fired until the next (x-lak c͟hacben).[5]

Usually a man clears off the second growth (pac; *chapear*) from his old milpa, and also fells bush (cah col; *tumbar*) for a new milpa; so that his harvest each year comes in part from c͟hacben and in part from zakab.[6]

[1] One does not measure more land than one is sure one is going to clear, so as not to offend the deities that protect the trees (p. 132).
[2] Sometimes the *mecates* are made 21 meters to a side, "because of what the birds take."
[3] "Kaan. Medida de un cordel con que los indios miden sus milpas, llamado mecate entre españoles." Motul Dictionary.
[4] This distance from the fingertip to the middle of the breastbone is a *vara*. In somewhat more sophisticated villages meter-rods are used. In measuring (cloth, for example) four other linear measures are used: the span (*cuarta*; naab); the distance from the end of the thumb to the end of the index finger (*jeme*; chinaab); the width of the closed fist with the thumb extended (*coto*; kok); and the cubit (*codo*: cuc). The cubit is regarded as half a *vara*.
[5] "If there is much cold weather during the time of clearing it is a sign that the sun will dry out the milpa and that the firing will go well." Then the *milpero* is encouraged to burn his milpa.
[6] The sizes of milpas and amounts of harvests in accompanying table (p. 53) include all lands under cultivation, of whatever class.

Most of the felling of the bush for new milpas takes place in the autumn and early winter. At least three months is allowed to elapse before the milpa is burned. This is a critical juncture, and one calling for the exercise of judgment by the agriculturalist. If he fires his milpa too soon, it may still be too green to burn properly; and if he waits too long, the rains may come and make necessary a second clearing of the land before it can be burned.[1] The burning usually begins early in March, is at its height in April, and continues into the first part of May. The act of kindling the milpa is partly ceremonial and is accompanied by propitiatory offerings (p. 134). The firing is usually done on a day when the wind is in the south or east. Two or more men set the dry bush on fire; some run along the east side and some along the south side, pausing at intervals to kindle the field with a torch, and whistling for the winds to come (Plate 8*b*). This torch (tahche) is a pole of catzim wood, about 4 feet long and much split at the end with a machete.

As there are cattle in the bush, a man usually fences (zupp) his milpa. He does this by setting forked poles upright along the margins of his field and felling the standing brush so that the boughs are held in these forks. Sometimes these small trees are cut only half through; therefore when the rains come, the leaves again come out and make the fence more difficult to penetrate. The stone wall (cot) is largely reserved for yards and lots in the village, where more permanent fences are needed.

The sowing begins with the rains, in the latter part of May or in the first days of June. Occasionally a man plants his corn in the dry ground before the first rain has softened the earth. Planting is done with the aid of a pointed stick, about 5 feet long. The stick (xul), which is not fire-hardened, is nowadays almost invariably equipped with an iron point, but if such be lacking a man may use a sharpened stick of catzim wood, stopping from time to time to give it a new point with his machete. With this stick small holes, about 3 inches deep, are driven in the ground. The holes are more or less regularly spaced, but are rarely in rows, and are about a meter apart—a little more for x-nuc-nal, a little less for x-thup-nal. The seed-grain is carried in a fiber-bag (*sabucan*) swung over the shoulder. Into each hole four to six grains of corn are tossed. In addition, an indefinite number of squash and of bean (or ib) seeds may go into each hole, for it is customary to mix squash, or squash and one of the beans, with the maize kernels before beginning the sowing. The seed corn is taken from the harvest of the preceding year. Some of the largest ears are selected for the purpose, and the small grains at the ends of the ear are not used.

After the seed is once planted, no practical care is taken of the growing maize except that the second growth is once cleared off (pac) with a small hooked knife called loob.[2] This clearing has to be done early if much time has elapsed between the burning and the sowing, for in that case, even though the rains have not yet come, the second growth sprouts again before the maize has secured a start. If the wild animals are causing much damage in the fields, remedial steps may be taken,

---

[1] It is in attempt to solve this problem that the calendrical divination known as xoc kin is used.
[2] "Lob, tah, t: escardar la milpa y limpiar caminos con aquel palo que suele tener un hierro en la punta." Motul Dictionary.

either by practical action or by asking the guardian spirits of the milpas to make their protection more effective (p. 134).

When the ears are ripe, in October or November, most agriculturalists, but not all, bend over (*doblar;* uadz) the stalks, without breaking them, making the ends of the ears point downward so that the birds will find it more difficult to eat the grains. But the stalks must not be bent so low that the terrestrial animals can easily pull down the ears. At this time some men cut a clear space around the milpa, so that the animals will be more reluctant to enter the milpa from the bush, and that the owner, carrying his gun, may reach the milpa without being heard by marauding animals.

When once the maize is ripe and dry, there is no great hurry about removing the ears from the stalks. The harvest (*pizca;* hoch) begins in November and continues during the next months, as convenience dictates. In fact, the maize keeps better if left for a while on the stalks to dry thoroughly; and March, when no rain falls, is the most favorable month for harvesting x-nuc-nal. In Chan Kom the ears are usually taken from the stalks with the husks (holoch) still on (hek che) and are stored in this form (ina), standing upright in rectangular storage-houses (chil) (Plate 4c). The ears are set close together so that the animals and insects can reach easily only the outer ears. From time to time, as the needs of the household dictate, the owner goes to the field to get maize, bringing it in on horse or burro in bags, or on his own shoulders in bag or basket (xux; *canastro*). Rarely in Chan Kom, but commonly in some of the towns in the region, the corn is taken from the husks as it is harvested (hetz dzil), and the kernels then and there removed from the ear. The husks are cut open with a sharpened stick or a pointed instrument made of a deer's antler or a deer's tibia. The grains are knocked from the ears (ppuch) by placing them in elevated racks (caanche) and hitting them with sticks. The same is done on a smaller scale in the house by using a hammock, or a basket. In this case the harvest is brought to the village in the form of grain and is stored in round thatched granaries (chil) in the house. When only the stalks are left in the field, cattle may be let in to feed.

Corn is grown by everyone, and only a minority grow anything else. Most commonly a white variety (zac ixim)[1] is grown, but a yellow maize (kan ixim) is not uncommon; the white variety is sometimes preferred for local consumption and is more easily sold. Less common and less favored varieties are chob, a kind with purple and white kernels, and an all-red variety, chac chob. The preferred white variety requires a better soil than the yellow; the latter gets along with less moisture. The yellow and the white differ in flavor; the little grown colored varieties taste like the white. Both yellow corn and white occur in early and late varieties, but most of the early corn is of the yellow variety. Early corn (x-thup-nal, or mehen-nal) yields its harvest in from 10 to 15 weeks; late corn (x-nuc-nal) requires up to four and a half months. X-thup-nal produces small ears and if watered may be grown in small quantities in the yards at any time of year; but it requires good soil.[2]

---

[1] The word ixim is the general word for corn, when speaking of it as a product for the market; but when it is thought of as growing in the milpa, and always in ritual prayers, it is referred to as *gracia.*
[2] See p. 137 for the religious restriction upon the planting of x-thup-nal.

Of the other crops, squash and beans are most often sown. Squash is planted with and among the corn. The common squash (kum) contains the small soft seeds (mehen zicil) that are ground to form a flavoring for *atole* and for the ceremonial breads (tuti-uah). Another not quite so common squash is white with yellowish stripes; this contains the large seeds (topp) that are soaked and peeled to be used in making a sweet, or that are toasted on the griddle and eaten as zicil topp.

Chile peppers are generally grown in the milpa, in separate patches. Varieties are zucure ic (*escurre*)—a small hot pepper occurring in both green and white varieties—x-kat ic, *pico paloma*, and *habanero* (which are all hot peppers), x-tza and zac ic, also max ic, which occurs in a large and in a small variety. Some of the peppers, especially *habanero* and x-kat ic, are grown in the house yards.

Various kinds of beans are planted with the corn. The common black bean may be descriptively referred to as x-col-i-buul ("milpa bean"). Instead of this, one may plant the Lima bean (ib), or a bean called peron (*espelón*), or a quick-maturing bean called mehen buul. Another kind, tzama, is grown in separate fields, apart from the corn; it matures in August.

Of the root and tuber crops, the commonest are *jícama* (xicam) and sweet potatoes (*camotes; iz*). Four kinds of *camotes* are recognized: white (zac iz), purple (morado iz), yellow (x-ya iz) and an uncommon variety called chacal-haaz. Some men grow yams (varieties are buc macal and cucut macal) and some cassava (chin). The root crops are planted separately, although occasionally *jícama* is planted with the corn.

A very few of the men of Chan Kom grow sugar cane; some years ago more was grown than at present. In recent years[1] one or two grow tobacco (kutz), the leaves being dried in the houses. A few have also added the castor-oil bush. Pineapple (*piña*)[2], on the other hand, is a crop that enjoys a waning popularity. In earlier years planting of pineapples in the milpas was not uncommon, but that is rare now, although several men have pineapple patches in the village. Occasionally an agriculturalist plants peanuts,[3] out in the milpa; a few men grow watermelons (*sandía*)[4], and one or two grow lentils (*lentejas*).[4] Henequen (ci) is grown by a few in empty lots in the village, and most people have a few growing gourd vines (lec).

Chay (*chaya*) is grown, by a very few, in corners of the yards, but other vegetables and condiments are grown in specially prepared gardens. Formerly (and characteristically in Maya villages) these gardens were planted in the split halves of hollow logs, raised from the ground on poles (Plate 8c); but this device (caanche) tends now to be supplanted by gardens made on the ground, because increasing care is being taken to wall the yards so that the pigs may not get in. For these gardens the earth must be collected. In them are planted onions, coriander, *epazote* (*Chenopodium*), cabbage, tomatoes, mint and balm-gentle. In succeeding years the same garden is planted again; only a little fresh black earth being put on top.

---

[1] The suggestion to add tobacco to the crops came from a man of Yaxcaba.
[2] No Maya name.
[3] The Spanish (Nahuatl) word *cacahuate* is used; the term x-caliz cacao is remembered, but not generally used.
[4] No Maya name.

Much attention is given to fruit trees; seedlings are cared for and transplanted, and grafting is understood and practiced. Papayas (put) are the commonest; these are easily grown and nearly every yard contains a few. Oranges (pakal), both sour (meek) and sweet (c̅huhuc pakal), limes,[1] and grapefruit[1] are not uncommon, and there are also several kinds of bananas (haaz), custard apples (two varieties: chac op and yaax op), guavas (pichi), pomegranates,[1] guanabanas (pox), hog plums (abal)—of which there are three varieties: tuxilo abal, kan abal and tuzpana abal—chirimoyas (pox), soursops (tzutzulpox) and guayos (uayam).[2]

CATTLE AND POULTRY

The techniques employed in the care of cattle and poultry are simple, few and familiar. Hogs and cattle are acquired as investments, not as sources of food (p. 58); cows are not milked, and cattle not often butchered. Most people own hogs, but they are given no care whatever. Cattle are allowed to roam at will in the bush. Milpa owners fence their fields to keep them out, and not infrequently they stray off and are lost. During the dry season they are watered at the cenote; during the wet season, when water is available in the bush, they are often not seen for weeks or even months. Occasionally cattle are rounded up, abrasions are treated with creolin, and the increase branded with purchased branding irons. Gelding is rarely done.[3]

Every family raises chickens. Each household owns, on an average, thirty hens. The meat is a favorite festal food and the eggs are ready currency. Chickens are fed small quantities of maize, and at night are shut in the small fowlpens away from carnivores and blood-sucking bats. There is little knowledge, either magical or rational, as to their care. When they fall sick during the hot season, the fowl are bathed in an infusion of chacah leaves, or are given this to drink. At long intervals the poultry suffer from an epizoötic known as x-cim-caxil ("fowl's death") for which no remedy is known.

Setting hens are established in a corner of the dwelling on nests fashioned of banana bark or palmleaf. The chicks are fed on meal or ground tortilla. Caponizing is practiced; the wound is sewed with thread and on it ashes are rubbed. "Then one puts a little salt on the bird's beak; otherwise it would not fatten properly." Pugnacious cockerels are discouraged from fighting by a feather thrust through their nostrils.

Turkeys are kept in smaller numbers; being hard to raise, they are unpopular. But they are essential as sacred offerings and festal food. Ducks are kept by a very few; their meat is not relished and their eggs are not accepted in the store.

[1] No Maya name.

[2] Of all the fruit trees, native and introduced, papaya is the one about which cluster many magical beliefs and practices. Most of the papaya trees in Chan Kom have had two thin sticks driven through the trunk at the base. This is called "caponizing the tree" and is thought to increase the yield. Very commonly a large gourd of the water-bottle type (chu), or even a glass bottle, is tied around the tree just before the flowers appear, to suggest that the fruits grow large (Plate 8d). (Gourd vessels are similarly tied on gourd vines.) There is a feeling that the papaya should not be spoken of as "put," but euphemistically as "boy" (xipal). "If you speak frequently of the tree as 'put,' the fruits remain 'bird papaya' "—that is, small and inedible, like the wild variety.

If a fruit tree of any sort does not bear, it is customary on Saint John's Day to get some man or boy named Juan to beat the tree with a vine whip. If, in the second year it still fails to bear, such a person is again called upon to deal the tree several vertical slashes with a machete.

If onions, garlic or jícamas are not growing as they should, almost all the leaves are removed when the moon is full. The plant is thought to grow properly thereafter.

[3] Sicknesses of cattle are treated magically; see p. 172.

HUNTING

Hunting (Plate 9*a*) is usually a cooperative enterprise (ppuh ceh). One man engages the interest of a few others; he sometimes whistles as a signal, and any others who wish to do so join the group. When they have reached a likely region, they surround a tract of land (often a grassy place where a village stood—lab-cah) and boys, or men who lack guns (ppuhob), drive the game forward on one side of the enclosed square toward the armed men (pah ppuhob) waiting on the side away from the wind. Dogs accompany the hunters, following game driven to earth, or pursuing deer. If a deer or wild boar is killed, the man who shoots it receives one leg, the hide, the head, the belly and the liver;[1] the remaining meat is equally divided among other members of the party. In the case of other game, including birds, the successful hunter receives all the kill, but commonly offers cooked morsels to the others.

Sometimes a man goes alone to hunt. Then he usually lies in wait at a water hole, or at a x-mabche tree, the fallen fruit of which is much eaten by deer. In the season when the young deer are born, some men imitate the call of the fawn by the use of a wooden whistle or by making the sound through their noses. Occasionally a man hunts at night, using a carbide head lamp. The watch-towers used in parts of Yucatan are seldom employed in Chan Kom. Birds are trapped with several sorts of nooses, baited with corn.

Aside from the deer (ceh) and peccary (citam), other animals hunted and eaten are Mexican agouti (haleb), wild turkey (cutz), Yucatan tinamou (nom), spotted agouti (tzub), squirrel (cuuc), *pisote* (chic), gopher (ba), quail or grouse (bech), curassow (kambul), the white-winged dove (zac pacal), *chachalaca* (bach), the cox, the white-fronted dove (tzutzuy), the red-billed pigeon, (x-cucutcib) and the chibilub.

The single-barreled shotgun is the only weapon used; blowguns or bows are not employed.

BEES AND BEE-KEEPING

Most of the men of the village keep bees. The hive is a hollowed section cut from a tree known as yaxnic, from 50 to 60 centimeters in length and from 20 to 25 centimeters in diameter. The ends are closed with circular stoppers of wood, held in place with dried mud. A small entrance hole is made in the center of a small square or circular depression cut in the center of the side of the hive; over the entrance hole a small cross is cut.[2]

A number of such hives, in some cases as many as several score are grouped together on racks built of poles (Plate 9*b*). Two such racks are inclined so as to support one another, and over them is built a palm-thatched shelter, made much as dwellings are, but without walls. Commonly a wooden cross is laid on top of the racks. These racks are set up in a corner of the house-lot, usually distant from the house. They are not put in the maize fields, nor anywhere outside of the villages. In almost every case they are set running east and west.[3]

---

[1] These parts are first offered to the supernatural protectors of the deer (p. 117).

[2] "To show the bees where the door is." "To give good luck to the hive." "To show which is right side up when you move the hive."

[3] They say that in this position the hives are less likely to get wet when it rains. It may be that there was originally some idea of orientation with respect to the points of the compass; such ideas are still rather strong in the religious symbolism.

PLATE 5

a, Grinding corn on the metate.

b, Ppul, botix, kat and ppulut.

c, Xux, baaz and xac.

PLATE 6

b, Washing clothes on the *batea*.

c, The old-style bark pail.   Furnished by Fernando Barbachano.
(*Photograph not taken in Chan Kom.*)

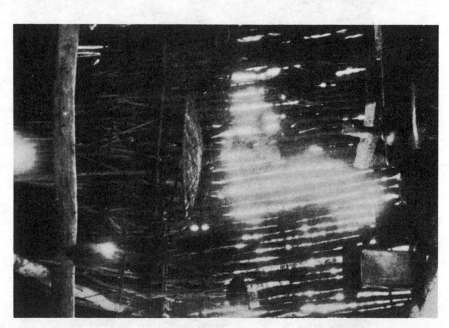

a, Peten.

The honey is taken from the hives four times a year: in March, April, May and November. Both stoppers are removed, and about one-third of the accumulated comb removed from each end (Plate 9c). Beyond this, no practical attention is given to the hives. As the colonies increase, the owner transfers some bees to a new and empty hive.

The honey is strained into a jar through a perforated wooden disk (chichipche). Honey is principally used to sweeten *atole* (corn gruel) and chocolate, to eat with yams and sweet potatoes, and to make balche, and it is occasionally used in making candy of squash rind. However, as a sweetener, honey is now in large part displaced by cane sugar, though much is still so used, and for balche it is essential. Honey is regarded as a food suitable for the sick; it is given to mothers after childbirth.

The wax is clarified by melting it and putting it in cold water, when the good wax comes to the top. Beeswax is chiefly used in making ceremonial candles.[1] Wax candles are made just as are those of paraffin; about fifty wicks are suspended from a horizontal wooden ring and as this is revolved melted wax is poured over the wicks until the desired diameter is obtained. Wax candles are used (along with paraffin candles) for novenas. Black wax candles are sometimes burned at the funerals of adult dead and at that part of the All Souls' Day ceremonies when the adult dead are commemorated.

Beeswax is accredited a slightly supernatural character. Figures are made of it, in black magic, and there is a belief that children who play with it become somnambulists.

The bees that occupy the hives just described are known as colelcab ("lady bee").[2] They furnish almost all of the honey and wax consumed. Occasionally swarms of these go off into the bush, but essentially this is a domesticated insect, living for generations under human care. A man wishing to begin keeping bees, secures some from the hive of a neighbor, not from the bush. There are, however, a number of wild, honey-producing hymenoptera that are known and utilized by the Maya. Five varieties have been mentioned in Chan Kom: kantzac, xik, ehol, yaxich and niitcab; the quoted accounts given below describe some of their characteristics.[3] Apparently the kantzac is the only kind that stings. The first four build their combs in natural cavities, trees usually, but also in caves in the case of ehol and yaxich. Niitcab builds a mud house in the branches of trees.

The honey of all of these insects is taken and used, when found in the bush. Occasionally, moreover, a man will put some of any of the first four kinds into a hive, such as he uses for the domesticated bee, and hang the hive under the palm-leaf eaves of his house. He never puts the wild bees on the racks with the domesticated bees, and such hives of wild bees apparently do not multiply or become of real importance.

"The kantzac is yellow; these bees make a noise when they go in and out. The xic is small; their houses are very fine, as if of silk. These don't make much commotion; just

---

[1] Wax candles are either yellow or black. Some hives produce wax of a darker color than do others. Sometimes yellow wax is darkened by allowing it to burn slightly.

[2] *Melipona fulvipes* Quer.

[3] It will be noted that the accounts present one apparent inconsistency: as to whether the wild honey is boiled.

one goes out, in a minute another goes out, another comes back, so. You have to look pretty carefully for the hole. They are black, and their wings—just a little bit of their wings—are white. But they are richer than the kantzac. Sometimes of the kantzac almost the majority are lazy; but almost all of the xic have honey. If you get a hundred of the kantzac houses, in half of them there is no honey except just a little; but the xic make as much as three meters of honey in the tree. But among the kantzac there are many who just want to be there inside their hives. The xic don't sting, or it isn't much, their sting; it doesn't hurt. When you take the honey from the kantzac, many of them have to die.[1]

"The ehol has wings that are half yellow and black; all of them work; it is richer than the xic, just like the hives of the house.[2] The honey of all these bees is good; you don't have to boil it. Yaxich is a different kind; their houses are very fine, and their honey is very delicious; it has no bad taste. They are very small like gnats; they don't give much honey, only one bottle. The kantzac gives up to five bottles, the ehol up to two bottles. The yaxich have green eyes. Ehol and yaxich sometimes make their little houses in caves or in trees; the others only in trees. Niitcab is another kind; they are very fine. They are also called limoncab, because they smell like limes. They don't make much honey, and besides it isn't good honey. These bees are very intelligent; when one is breaking open their house, immediately they go into the room where the honey is and they put a little of their saliva on it, or they urinate on it, and so give it a bad flavor. To fool them, the man must first urinate on the tree, then he will take out good honey; that is the secret."[3]

"The beehives placed together we call cab. Bees of the house can not be obtained, they can only be bought.[4] You look for certain kinds of wood which have a hole inside. You cut the wood, so, in pieces. After cutting it in pieces, you clean it very well. When, at the time of cutting the honey combs (*castra;* puzcab) you get hold of the young bees, quite little ones, you put them into a beehive, without anything in it, and you shake into it a few of the big ones. When you have succeeded in getting one hive of bees by doing this, you may from time to time succeed in getting another one. When the beehives, which have bees inside, are opened, you shake in the little ones.

"In taking out the honey, you should not remove all the honey that the hive holds.

"The house bees do not sting, but there is a kind in the bush, called kantzac, which do sting. There are three other kinds of wild bees, which do not sting: ehol, xic and yaxich. The yaxich is very tiny, it has green eyes. Wild honey is a little sour. You take it out, so, and put it on the fire to boil. After boiling it well, this gets rid of all the sourness. You keep on taking off the foam, and there remains a honey like the honey of the house bees, which is not boiled. The house bees are called colelcab.

"You put all the wax together, melt it, the wax comes out very fine, you put it in cold water, and then take out the true wax. The wax which is no good stays underneath. It comes out very, very yellow. You take it out, and throw away the remains. You take some wicks and make candles. They are used for the *santos*, to have novenas."[5]

The domesticated bees and the hives they occupy enter prominently into the religious beliefs and practices. Bees are handled with some circumspection; in removing the honey, care is taken not to injure or kill any of the insects. If a bee becomes honey-soaked, it is dried and freed; if one is killed, it is buried in a bit of leaf. This is because the bees are under the protection of certain deities, who watch over them and become angered if their wards are not treated properly (p. 116).

[1] That is, one kills them, brushing them from face and arms.
[2] *I. e.* the domesticated bees.
[3] Told by a man in Chan Kom.
[4] *I. e.* you buy them from your neighbor; you can not find them in the bush.
[5] Told by a man of Piste.

CHAPTER IV

ECONOMICS

The ways of life, both practical and religious, rest upon the growing of maize. Maize is the people's food, their work and their prayer—it fills the days and the talk.

But the value of the harvest is fixed not merely by the immediate food needs of the village. Twice as much maize must be grown as the population will consume; half is converted, in the towns, into other goods. People take the road to the market, as well as the road to the milpa. As maize is regularly sold that other goods may be bought, maize becomes a measure of other values; goods and labor are sold in terms of maize; it is like money. But the value of maize is fixed outside of Chan Kom, in remote markets of the towns and city. To changes in this market price everyone in Chan Kom is attentive. "What is maize worth?" is one of the first questions asked of a man returning from Valladolid. If the price goes up, so do the spirits of the people. If it goes down, the traveling merchants sell little in Chan Kom, local economic enterprise languishes, the scheduled fiesta is canceled or a more modest program of entertainment is substituted.

Moreover, the price of maize influences the extent of agricultural activity. All men grow maize; to abandon one's milpa is to forsake the very roots of life; tradition and religion conspire with economic necessity to make agriculture inevitable. But just how much maize is grown depends not merely on the local needs, but on the worth of corn in the city market. When the price of maize is low, people do not sell their surplus corn, and as it is not customary to accumulate maize reserves additional to what is needed for the current year, the agriculturalist reduces the size of his field, or even does not sow at all, but lives on what is left in his granary from the previous year.

QUANTITY OF MAIZE PRODUCTION

Table 3 (p. 53) shows the amount of land planted[1] by fifty-four agriculturalists of Chan Kom during two successive years, 1930 and 1931, and the amount of maize and of other crops harvested from each tract in 1931. Data for the table were secured from the men themselves in the course of general meetings at which the matter was discussed and attempts made to eliminate errors. The table is probably very nearly correct. In Chan Kom a man does not count the hours of his day, or the years of his life, but he does count the units of his fields and the loads of his harvest. Furthermore these quantities are much talked about and tend to be notorious.

The table includes information as to the fields and crops of all of the agriculturalists in Chan Kom who "made milpa" in these two years. For five or six men the data were not actually secured; the table has been completed by assigning to them average amounts for the period.

[1] Including both fields newly cleared and those cleared in a previous year and sowed for a second or a third time.

51

In 1930 every man and grown boy in the village, except one, planted and harvested corn. In 1931 the amount of land planted diminished by almost one-third, and five men did not make milpa at all. This was because the price of corn fell after the harvest of 1930;[1] therefore the people did not sell their surplus corn, and so reduced the amount of planting for the following year. Four of the men who did not plant at all lived on their accumulated stores of maize; and one man hired himself out to his neighbors. Another, the mason, earned enough money at his trade to make it possible to reduce his field to twelve *mecates*—a very small size.

The unit of land measure is the *mecate* (about one twenty-fifth of a hectare, see p. 43). The unit of harvest is a volume measure of shelled maize, the *carga* (about 42 kilos or 12 *almudes*). The average milpa size in 1930 was 72 *mecates;* in 1931 it was 62 *mecates.* In 1930 two-thirds of the milpas were from 30 to 60 *mecates* in area; eight were over 100 *mecates*, and one was 700 *mecates.* The owner of this last large tract had, of course, to hire help to fell bush, plant and harvest. Such large scale production is very unusual.

The total harvest (2962 *cargas*) indicated in the table for the year 1931 does not represent quite the total yield from the land planted the previous year, because there are always a few tracts, or parts of tracts, that are not harvested in the year when the corn ripens; the owner simply leaves the ears on their stalks and harvests them the following season. This in part accounts for the fact that the apparent average yield per *mecate* indicated by the table is 0.8 *carga*, although people think in terms of an expected average yield of a *carga* from each *mecate*. Another reason for the lower indicated yield lies in the fact that some of the land planted had also been planted the previous year, and on such lands the yield is low (see p. 43). The lowest yield reported was 0.5 *carga* to a *mecate*, the highest, 1.4 *carga*. The average yield for each agriculturalist was 57 *cargas*. The small milpas have a somewhat larger yield, in proportion to area, than the large ones. If 42 kilos are allowed to each *carga*, 498 kilos of corn were realized for each man, woman and child in Chan Kom.

It will be noticed that while almost every man planted maize, only 9 are reported as planting beans; 3, sweet potatoes; 14, *jícamas;* 12, squashes; and 5, chili peppers.[2] The people who do not plant these minor crops buy the commodity from their neighbors who do.

THE MAN-LAND RATIO

Ordinarily a man plants for a second time land cleared and planted the year before, and he also fells bush and plants in a new milpa. The second crop on the same land is about three-fourths of the first, and the third crop (if there is one) is about one-half. Figures were not obtained as to what proportion of the land under cultivation during these two years (1930 and 1931) was cleared in the same year in which it was planted, and what proportion was being sowed for a second or even third successive year. From statements made, however, it is probable that a small

---

[1] Maize may be worth as little as one peso a *carga*, and sometimes rises to eight or nine pesos.
[2] Other minor crops—yams, lentils, sugar cane, tobacco—are not given in the table.

TABLE 3—*Number of mecates under cultivation by each of the fifty-four agriculturalists of Chan Kom, during 1930 and 1931, and number of cargas of maize and other crops harvested in 1931*

	Number of *mecates* under cultivation		No. of *cargas* of corn harvested 1931	Number of *cargas* of other products harvested				
	1930	1931		Beans	Sweet potatoes	*Jícamas*	Squash seeds	Chili
1........	90	50	120	..	..	2	3	..
2........	50	30	60	..	2	½	½	..
3........	40	80	50	½	..	½	1	1
4........	30	12	24*	..	..	..	..	..
5–7......	150	250	220	9	..	1	..	..
8–11......	170	150	150	..	..	..	1	..
12......	12	62*	10	..	..	..	..	..
13......	200	100	100	2	..	..	8	..
14, 15......	130	..	67	1	..	1	1	..
16......	60	45	60	..	..	..	..	..
17......	700	..	350	12	..	..	..	..
18......	180	150	100	..	..	1	..	1
19......	..	150	..	½	..	½	½	..
20......	35	60	40	1	..	1	1	..
21......	100	44	100	..	..	..	..	..
22......	60	62*	50	..	..	..	..	..
23......	70	62*	50	..	..	..	..	..
24......	60	60	50	..	..	..	..	..
25......	72*	50	57*	..	..	..	..	..
26......	40	62*	40	..	..	..	..	..
27......	60	50	50	..	..	1	½	..
28......	60	50	50	..	..	..	..	..
29......	60	60	70	..	..	..	..	..
30......	15	80	10	..	..	..	..	..
31......	35	..	30	..	..	..	..	..
32......	45	33	50	..	..	..	..	..
33......	69	62*	55	..	..	..	..	..
34......	40	60	45	..	..	..	..	..
35......	80	100	80	..	..	..	..	..
36......	40	40	40	..	..	½	..	1
37......	80	..	60	..	..	..	..	..
38......	40	48	40	..	..	1	..	..
39......	60	60	53	..	..	1	..	..
40......	60	75	58	..	..	1	½	1
41......	75	60	70	..	..	..	..	..
42......	130	100	60	..	..	..	..	..
43......	24	..	23	..	..	..	..	..
44......	72*	100	57*	..	..	..	..	..
45......	50	60	12	..	..	..	..	..
46......	72*	30	57*	..	..	..	..	..
47......	15	..	15	..	..	..	..	..
48......	120	40	100	..	..	..	..	..
49......	40	..	30	..	..	..	..	..
50......	30	62*	30	..	..	..	7	1
51......	40	60	32*	..	..	..	..	..
52......	72*	25	57*	3	1	1	..	..
53......	30	62*	30	2	4	..	3	..
54......	..	50	..	..	..	..	..	..
	3761	2846	2962	31	7	13	27	5

The amounts marked with an asterisk (*) were not actually determined, but were estimated by assuming that the size of the tract or of the crop was the average size for that year.

Where more than one number occurs in one place in the first column, the cornfields referred to in the opposite data were worked collectively by a group of kinsmen (see p. 56).

minority of lands are sowed only once and a similar, or perhaps slightly larger, minority are sowed for three successive years. In other words, land cultivated by the people of Chan Kom is, on the average, planted 2 successive years. It is then left for 7 years before being again reduced to cultivation. If this estimate be adopted, it follows that each year, for each of the 250 inhabitants of Chan Kom, about 6 *mecates* of land are cleared anew, and about 12 sown; and that about 42 *mecates* of tillable land must always be available for each inhabitant, at the standard of living and with the techniques of maintenance now prevailing.

OTHER FOOD PRODUCTION

Production of consumable goods other than maize plays a relatively small part in the local economy. About a dozen men own cattle, but during a year and a half only two or three steers were sold outside the village and as many were slaughtered for food. Poultry are raised by all the families. The flesh of fowl is consumed largely on festal occasions. Some eggs are eaten locally, but many are sold out of the community. The yield of fruit trees is consumed locally. The proceeds of the hunt and the products of the small vegetable and condiment gardens contribute small quotas to the total production.

FIREWOOD AND BUILDING MATERIALS

Firewood is available in the immediate neighborhood of the village. Two or three hours of work every two days suffice to supply an ordinary household. It is often the boys of the family who perform this task. The bush also supplies building materials; labor is the only expenditure, but this is a heavy one.

The building of a house of poles and thatch requires several kinds of wood (p. 35), a certain variety of palm leaf for thatching, red clay for the walls, and a little lime for whitewash. The hard wood used for the corner posts (*horcones*) and for the two transverse beams (balo) that support the walls is obtainable not nearer than 4 or 5 kilometers from the village. To secure the proper palm leaves for the roof, a man must go about as far; one man, on the average, cuts and carries about a hundred leaves a day. The materials for the other parts are nearer at hand. Small trees are close by, and the red clay (pahluum) can be obtained almost anywhere.

The following is an estimate of the number of man-days required to build a house of this type. In fact, such houses are built by groups of men working together, either by customary cooperative labor, or (in recent years) for hire.

	No. of days
Cutting and hauling the six principal posts and beams...	6
Cutting and hauling the other poles and vines........	5
Collecting 4000 palm leaves.......................	40
Constructing the framework.......................	20
Thatching...	10
Covering the walls with clay.......................	3
Making the doors..................................	2
Total.....................................	86

PLATE 7

a   b

c

a, Sandals; *b*, Huipil; *c*, Making gourd-carriers.
(*a, taken by Morris Steggerda; b, taken by Miss Katheryn MacKay*)

PLATE 8

a, Using the pacche.

c, Caanche.

b, Firing the milpa.

d, A papaya treated magically to cause it to produce good fruit.

A house of rubble masonry (*mampostería*), such as people are building in Chan Kom nowadays, is much more of an undertaking.   There is more large lumber (about 22 beams are needed to support the flat roof); it is necessary to haul decomposed limestone (*Sascab*) and to burn limestone to make lime for the mortar; and the actual mason's work, in breaking up limestone and setting it in the mortar to form the walls, is slow and laborious; one average lime-burning supplies just about enough lime for such a house.   The lime-burning is made on the outskirts of the village where plenty of suitable firewood may be found[1] (Plate 10*a*), and after the lime is burned it must be carried to the village.   One man can carry ten *cargas* of lime a day; for every *carga* of lime two of *sascab* are needed.   At the present time three pits (*sascaberas*) are in use, each about one kilometer from the village.   A man can dig and carry on his back seven *cargas* a day; if he uses a donkey, the rate of production is somewhat increased.

There follows an estimate[2] of the number of man-days required to build a masonry house consisting of one rectangular room 7 meters long, 5 wide and 6 high, with walls one-half a meter thick.

		No. of man-days
Preparation of 250 *cargas* of lime:		
	Cutting wood	7
	Breaking limestone	7
	Preparation of lime-burning	1
	Hauling lime	25
	Total	40
Sascab:		
	Digging out 500 *cargas* of *sascab* and hauling to the place of building	72
Building:		
	Cutting and preparing beams (one each day)	22
	Work of mason	215
	Carpenter work (roof, doors)	30
	Total	267
	Grand Total	379

PRODUCTION AND CONSUMPTION GROUPS

In the very large majority of instances, land is cleared, planted and harvested by a man on his own account (with or without help secured by hire or work-exchange) and the maize utilized by his immediate household group. This group, as will be seen in the discussion in another chapter (page 89), consists in most cases of a man, his wife and his children. This is the normal pattern. A woman must have a man to "make milpa" for her. In Chan Kom one or two widows are supported by the agricultural activities of half-grown or grown sons. If a boy marries and his widowed mother has not re-married, she usually continues to live with him and to receive his support. In three Chan Kom households there is not now, or

[1] See the account of lime-burning methods and of masonry techniques, of present-day Maya, by Earl H. Morris, *The Temple of the Warriors*, Carnegie Inst. Wash. Pub. No. 406, vol. I, p. 220 ff, 1931.
[2] This estimate was arrived at by observing the construction of a house of this sort on which four to six men were employed at various times, and recording the time spent by each on the various activities. One man did all the mason's work, with the assistance of a boy, in two-thirds of the time we have allowed for one man working alone.

was not in years just past, even a half-grown boy to make milpa. In two of these cases the widows were left enough money by their husbands to enable them to hire men to make milpa for them. The third widow, till her boys grew up, was supported by gifts of maize from her deceased husband's brother. The deceased man's brother is the person first looked to for assistance by the widow, but the aid is not always forthcoming.

In 36 out of 42 cases, milpas were made by individual laborers and the harvests consumed as the individual property of these single agriculturalists in individual small-family households. In two cases, however, the milpas were maintained by patrilineal extended domestic families (p. 89). The father and his married sons cleared, sowed and harvested the fields together, with no division of any kind. Each of these two large-family groups maintained a single granary and a single kitchen. In the remaining four exceptions, groups of relatives together cleared, sowed and harvested a common tract, but within each tract the separate milpas of each individual laborer were marked off, and the harvests were kept separate and consumed in the individual small-family households of the separate men. The groups who followed this practice were: a man, his unmarried son, his three married nephews (sons of his brother), and his son-in-law; a father and his married son; a man and his son-in-law; a man and his stepson.[1] It may be said in summary that although the prevailing institution is an economically and agriculturally independent small parental family, there are exceptional patrilineal extended families, the members of which dwell together, work collectively, and share capital and income without dividing it; in addition, there is a tendency for small groups consisting of a man and some of his younger male relatives to help one another closely in agricultural pursuits, while maintaining separate harvests and households.

CONSUMPTION: A FAMILY BUDGET

The average family, of two adults and two or three children, requires about half a *carga* of maize for its domestic consumption every week. Ordinarily, in Chan Kom, the maize is put into granaries built in the fields, if not actually left on the stalks, and the man of the household makes a trip to his milpa every week, or two weeks, or three, to secure another short supply for his kitchen. From time to time he uses small quantities of maize for purposes of barter at the local store or in buying goods or services from his neighbors; and moreover, when the market price of maize is high, or when he is in need of cash, he sells some of his accumulated harvest in the town (Valladolid). The economic equilibrium is based upon an agricultural endeavor which produces about twice as much maize as is locally consumed; the excess is taken by the townsman in exchange, principally, for manufactured goods.[2] A man in average circumstances uses about three suits of

---

[1] Of course a man's unmarried son customarily helps his father in the fields; the "individual laborer," referred to in this paragraph, often has this help.

[2] In preceding paragraphs it was stated that the average yield of maize for each agriculturalist was, in 1931, 57 *cargas*. Here it is stated that the average agriculturalist's domestic consumption needs require 26 *cargas* a year and that about as many *cargas* are converted into other goods quickly consumed. The figure, 57 *cargas*, may be a little higher than the average yield over a period of years. But some maize goes into capital investment (cattle and gold chains), and some goes into the birds and the rodents.

work clothes a year and two suits of Sunday clothes. Both are made of factory-woven textiles. A woman uses two ordinary dresses, one dress of better quality (these include both skirt and *huipil*), a *rebozo*, a pair of shoes, some earrings, ribbons and rings. Each child needs about six sets of clothing. In addition there are many small occasional purchases to be made, of gunpowder, spices, candles, perfume, thread, medicine, and matches, and of minor foodstuffs not locally produced, such as sugar, coffee and salt; and a man must pay his small taxes. The following annual budget was secured, by estimate, from observation of and consultation with a married man with two small children in about the middle range of wealth in Chan Kom:

A. *Produced by the man himself, or produced by others in the same village, and by him purchased or bartered.* Approximate value in pesos

24 *cargas* of maize @ 5 pesos[1] a *carga*..............	120.00
24 kilos of beans @ 40 centavos a kilo.............	9.60
12 kilos of chili @ 25 centavos a kilo..............	3.00
Occasional eggs and chickens (15 fowl at 1 peso apiece; 100 eggs @ 4 centavos each)...................	19.00
Occasional wild and cultivated fruits and roots......	13.00
Occasional meat, 50 centavos a month.............	6.00
Firewood, one *tercio* every 2 days, 185 *tercios* @ 5 centavos a *tercio*............................	9.15
Total................................	179.75

B. *Purchased, with currency, either in the village or town:*

	Cost
Salt, 12 kilos @ 10 centavos a kilo..................	1.20
Sugar, 12 kilos @ 30 centavos...................	3.60
Coffee and bread................................	10.00
Three suits of men's work clothes @ 1.90..........	5.70
Three suits of men's better clothing @ 5.00........	15.00
Men's hat and sandals............................	10.00
Two ordinary sets of woman's clothing............	4.20
One set of fine woman's clothing..................	12.00
Rebozos for the woman..........................	5.00
Shoes for the woman............................	3.00
Earrings, ribbons and rings......................	3.00
Children's clothing, 12 sets @ 1.00..............	12.00
Gunpowder, spices, perfume, candles, etc...........	10.00
Total................................	94.70

WEALTH AND ITS DISTRIBUTION

Low as is this standard of living, there is within it room for very marked variation as one family is compared with another. Some people have sugar in their maize gruel every day and eat bread and drink chocolate several mornings in each week; while others know sugar, bread and chocolate as rare luxuries. Some enjoy a diet varied with beans and starchy root crops; while others subsist for days on tortillas alone. It is difficult not to attribute most of these differences to corresponding individual differences in ability and initiative. Given average health, one man

[1] The value (5 pesos a *carga*) is in the middle part of the range of price fluctuation.

may plant and harvest as much maize and as many kinds of crops as another. The essential techniques of maintenance are known to everybody, and one man has as good a chance to secure good land as another. To these statements some exceptions should be made. The techniques of sugar production are better understood by some men than by others. One or two men have accumulated sufficient capital to enable them to hire field laborers and grow corn on a larger scale. But it is probable that these men began at no economic advantage over their neighbors. This community is, in many respects, one of pioneers; industry and perseverance, not inherited wealth or privilege, are the outstanding advantages. Certainly there are evidences of lack of ambition in many houses. In some homes, the family will sit down to many successive meals of tortillas alone, while beans, ready for the pot, are spoiling in a basket in the corner.

If there is an excess of production over the current consumption needs, a man may put it into a masonry house, or into a few tools or small household furnishings, but the important goods for the storage of wealth are a man's cattle and his wife's gold chains. Cattle-raising is a relatively recent activity in these southeastern villages, but there are perhaps two score head of cattle in Chan Kom. They are raised partly as a means to store and to multiply wealth, and partly because to own cattle is to gain prestige; a man's wealth is thus made manifest and, furthermore, he may enter a bull in one of the rustic bull-fights that distinguish the fiestas of the region. The chains a woman wears around her neck are a part of her marriage portion; but to them her husband may make later additions, and accordingly his status and hers are raised. These chains are the principal and often the only form of wealth; if a man must pledge his credit, he may deposit one of these chains with his creditor.

Some men store up savings in the form of money, usually buried in some part of the house lot. Or, if piety or desire for conspicuous leadership takes hold of a man, he may become the sponsor of a local fiesta in honor of a *santo*, and spend all his year's savings at one stroke.

TRADE

The permanent institutions that link Chan Kom with the wider economy are the town market, the traveling merchant and the village store. Trade is carried on constantly by these three means. The second two, being immediately at hand, provide most of the buying and selling. A man makes purchases in Valladolid when some other errand calls him there, or he goes there to make those most important purchases that are necessary once a year, like the buying of clothes for his family or, once in many years, for the buying of a bridal costume. Some families probably never make purchases in the town, except when a son is to be married.[1] There are no special market days in the towns or villages of the neighborhood. The annual fiesta, an occasional political demonstration, or political or governmental business may bring the villagers to the town, but no one goes there often or reg-

---

[1] The bridegroom's family buys the bridal costume.

ularly except the boy whose father keeps the local store. He goes every two or three weeks to buy supplies.

The traveling merchants make their regular rounds; their errands and their personalities are familiar to the people of Chan Kom, to whom they bring diversion and news, as well as opportunities to trade. Often they stay for the night with some man of the village. Most of them are people of mixed blood, but they all speak Maya. They carry their goods on mule or burro, and on their return to the town their mounts are hung with the poultry they have taken in trade. Such men carry a miscellaneous store of manufactured goods: cotton cloth to be made into garments; strips of embroidery; mirrors, combs and cheap jewelry. Some bring bread, some candy. In Lent dried fish is carried to the villages, and there are even occasions when ice (to cool drinks served at fiestas) is sold in villages a full day's ride from Valladolid. There are occasional tinsmiths and vendors of patent medicines. Another group of men deal in livestock, some in poultry, some in hogs and some in cattle and horses. These men buy, sell or trade. Months go by in Chan Kom without a single sale of cattle, and then some first sale, or some adventitious event,[1] will arouse a perfect fever of buying and selling.

Until the autumn of 1931, no outsider was permitted by the people of Chan Kom to maintain a store in the village. In November of that year one of the most trusted of the traveling merchants received permission to open a store on the plaza. Before that time there were two stores in Chan Kom, kept by villagers. In one of these the stock in trade was so minute, and the sales so infrequent, that it can be disregarded. Table 4 (p. 60) records the purchases made in the other store over a typical period of ten days. It will be seen that the principal commodities are salt, sugar, cocoa, candles, soap, thread and cloth, and that about five pesos a day is spent in the store by all the 250 inhabitants together. A rough estimate suggests that on the average about ten pesos a day is paid by the village to the traveling merchants, and not more than a peso a day (on the average) is expended directly in the stores and the markets of the towns.[2]

There is also trade, although but little, between Chan Kom and neighboring villages. Rarely and irregularly some one comes from a neighboring hamlet to sell bananas or henequen fiber, or some man of Chan Kom goes to a *ranchería* to buy sugar cane, or a hog, perhaps. The large Indian village of Tekom specializes in hammock production, and its hammock vendors are periodic visitors to Chan Kom. On the other hand, one man of Chan Kom makes a regular business of buying eggs from his neighbors and selling them, at a profit, to the archæologists at Chichen Itza.

Commercial dealings between neighbors are common. One man sells another a cow and bargains for a price; another trades his cornet for a hog; the man who knows how to bake bread sells it through the local store; the barber has a price, and so do the midwife and the shaman. But the midwife's price and that of the shaman do not fluctuate as does the value of maize; they are matters of tradition; part of

[1] Such as the epizoötic among the hogs, which set everyone to exchanging hogs for cattle.
[2] This estimate does not include the occasional large expenditures, such as those for cattle and gold chains.

their recompense is in food or in rum, and especially in respect. Some men make it a practice to give occasional presents to the midwife; then they feel freer to call upon her. With these traditional professionals we pass out of purely economic valuation into the sphere of ritual and sacred prerogative.

TABLE 4—*Amounts (in pesos) expended in the principal store, over a period of ten days, (Feb. 23-Mar. 4) according to commodities.*

Commodities	Mon.	Tues.	Wed.	Thurs.	Fri.	Sat.	Sun.	Mon.	Tues.	Wed.	Total
Sugar	0.30	0.80	0.79	0.55	0.29	0.50	1.19	1.24	0.40	0.50	6.56
Bread	.53	.76	1.06	.56	.30	.46	.55	.99	.55	.41	6.17
Cocoa	.15	.40	.40	.15	.25	.20	.15	.25	.05	.25	2.25
Coffee	.14	.13	.61	.15	.15	.10	.32	.13	.05	.13	1.91
Salt	.27	.25	.08	.05	.08	.15	.11	.37	.27	.....	1.63
Spaghetti	.04	.....	.10	.....	.....	.15	.....	.15	.....	.....	.44
Corn	.12	.....	.....	.....	.....	.....	.10	.....	.....	.....	.22
Pepper	.....	.08	.10	.09	.05	.....	.....	.19	.03	.....	.54
Garlic	.....	.....	.05	.....	.....	.....	.....	.....	.....	.05	.10
Flour	.....	.....	.04	.....	.....	.....	.....	.....	.....	.....	.04
Eggs	.....	.....	.12	.32	.....	.....	.....	.....	.....	.....	.44
Lard	.....	.....	.....	.....	.....	.....	.....	.....	.40	.35	.75
Milk (canned)	.....	.....	.....	.....	.....	.....	1.25	.....	.....	.60	1.85
Pop	.15	.15	.....	.20	.15	.....	.....	.....	.....	.....	.65
Cloves	.....	.....	.02	.06	.03	.....	.....	.....	.....	.03	.14
Limes	.....	.....	.....	.....	.....	.....	.25	.....	.....	.25	.50
Tobacco	.12	.02	.05	.....	.07	.03	.09	.....	.....	.03	.41
Cigarettes	.....	.20	.45	.30	.....	.10	.....	.....	.....	.....	1.05
Matches	.....	.....	.10	.....	.....	.....	.03	.05	.....	.05	.23
Candles	.15	.47	.36	.51	.10	.22	.52	.20	.19	.28	3.00
Soap	.60	.15	.10	.25	.40	.20	.50	.20	.15	.35	2.90
Blueing	.05	.05	.....	.....	.05	.05	.....	.....	.....	.05	.25
Coal oil	.....	.45	.19	.10	.25	.25	.05	.15	.....	.05	1.49
Mentholatum	.....	.....	.40	.....	.....	.....	.....	.....	.....	.....	.40
Bicarbonate (as medicine)	.03	.02	.....	.....	.....	.....	.03	.....	.02	.....	.10
Balsam (patent medicine)	.....	.....	.....	.....	.50	.....	.....	.....	.50	.....	1.00
"Florida Water" (toilet water)	.....	.....	.....	.....	.....	.....	.30	.....	.....	.....	.30
Chalk	.02	.....	.05	.....	.....	.....	.....	.....	.....	.....	.07
Pencils	.07	.14	.....	.....	.....	.....	.07	.07	.....	.....	.35
Note books	.....	.30	.10	.....	.....	.....	.....	.....	.....	.....	.40
Office paper	.....	.....	.....	.....	.....	.....	.....	.45	.....	.....	.45
Envelopes	.....	.15	.....	.....	.....	.....	.....	.....	.....	.....	.15
Thread	.35	.25	.05	.15	.40	.15	.90	.25	.15	.20	2.85
Thread—fine	.....	.05	.....	.06	.....	.....	.....	.03	.....	.....	.14
Cloth	.25	1.25	.....	.87	1.10	.....	.....	.50	.25	.50	4.72
Rebozo	.....	.....	.....	.....	.....	.....	.....	.....	1.75	.....	1.75
Combs	.....	.....	.....	.08	.....	.....	.....	.....	.....	.....	.08
Ribbons	.06	.....	.07	.....	.....	.....	.....	.....	.....	.....	.13
Ornaments	.....	.....	.....	.....	.....	.....	.05	.....	.....	.....	.05
Rubber strips for sling-shots	.....	.....	.....	.....	.....	.....	.26	.....	.....	.....	.26
Leather	.50	.30	.....	.....	.....	.....	.....	.....	.....	.....	.80
Gunpowder	.....	.....	.....	.....	.05	.....	.30	.10	.....	.....	.45
Shot	.....	.....	.10	.....	.10	.....	.15	.....	.10	.10	.55
Cartridges	.05	.10	.....	.....	.05	.05	.05	.05	.05	.....	.40
Total	P3.95	6.47	5.39	4.37	4.45	2.61	7.22	5.37	4.91	4.18	48.92

MONEY

Everyone understands the general nature of money, knows how to count currency, and uses silver, copper and—once in a while—gold coins. In making purchases in the towns and in the local sales for larger amounts (chiefly cattle), Mexican national currency is used. In the minor transactions, however, and therefore in payment of most purchases, money plays a secondary rôle. In the stores most purchases are made with eggs. During the period of observation, eggs were worth four centavos apiece, but their local value varies with their price in the town market. Copper centavos serve as small change. About one-fifth of all small local purchases are made with maize and a smaller fraction in real money. The traveling merchants are paid chiefly in poultry, but partly in money. The amount of money in circulation depends on the time of the year and the value of maize; just after the annual harvest has been sold, there is more; on the other hand, if people have withheld their surplus maize from the market for a better price, most purchases must be made with eggs, maize or hens.

There is no banking, and no lending of money at interest.

WAGES

Although in most instances a man is supported by his own agricultural labor, there are cases every year of employment for wages in the fields. A few men plant more corn than they alone can care for; also, there are the widows with money; and there are one or two men too old to work effectively. The egg-merchant hires men to make milpa for him, and this he did even in a year when the price of maize was so low that it would have been cheaper for him to buy the grain for his kitchen. The men who are hired are usually from other villages, but occasionally one man from Chan Kom hires another to help him. The wage earners are men who, through accident or indolence, lack enough maize for their own needs. The laborer is paid by piece, not by time. The rate of pay varies with the current market price of maize. In 1931 the rate was three *almudes* of maize for felling bush on one ordinary *mecate* of land, and four *almudes* if the bush was unusually high. For clearing second growth the pay was two *almudes* a *mecate*, and for harvesting the rate was one *cuartillo* of maize for every *canastro* (basket) of maize on the ear harvested.[1] The daily wage for assistance in building was one peso.

In earlier days, before the founding of Chan Kom, some of the older men of the village were employed on large estates, either as peons or as earners of actual money. Today there are few opportunities for the villagers to find employment outside the village, and there is little inclination to do so. The archæological excavations at Chichen hire a number of laborers from neighboring villages, but communities nearer than Chan Kom supply the need. During the period of observation one boy in Chan Kom sought and found employment in a store in Valladolid, but in ten days he was back again in the village. And one girl found employment as a domestic servant with a mixed-blood family in a larger village.

PERSONAL PROPERTY AND INHERITANCE

A man owns whatever he has made himself, or bought with his own money or goods. A woman's clothing and other personal effects are hers by gift from her husband, and the personal articles of a child are also individually owned.[2] If a woman—

[1] At this time an *almud* of maize was worth twenty *centavos*.

[2] In the extended domestic families described elsewhere (p. 56 and p. 89), clothing is owned individually, although bought out of general family funds; these funds, and the stores of maize, are controlled by the patriarchal family head.

wife or daughter—makes and sells gourd-carriers or other articles of handicraft, the proceeds are hers.

But the woman's ownership of articles of clothing or household furniture is conditional upon her good behavior. All the contents of the house, even including her personal wardrobe, are marital property, in the sense that the husband has provided them, and in that he is not required to share them with his wife if the marriage is broken through her fault. If she leaves her husband for no good cause —if she leaves him without making known any serious dereliction on his part, or if she becomes enamored of another man and goes off with him—she may take with her only what her husband allows her to take. She must return to him the chain that was given in the muhul, and the *terno* (p. 193). If she goes off with another man, she may not take any of the children with her; but if she simply returns to her parents' house, she may be allowed to take some of the children.

On the other hand, if a husband does not wish to live longer with his wife, even though it be because he prefers to live with another woman, and if his wife has not taken up with another man, then all the property is divided equally between them—cattle, maize, milpa and chains and rings bought for the wife after the marriage. The woman keeps her personal clothes and the chain of the muhul. If there are small children, then the wife may have the house if she wishes, including the minor furnishings, and may continue to live there with the children. But if there are no small children and the woman is able to return to her parents' house, then she can not claim the house, and the man may live there and bring his new woman there if he chooses. In the case of a separation by mutual consent, or at the initiative of the man, the children are divided between husband and wife, the boys going to the husband, and the girls to the wife. Furthermore, if there are small children the division of the property is so modified that each child is provided for. If, for example, there are several boys and no girls, the husband gets the larger share of the property. But if the husband has taken up with a new woman, he can not claim any of the children, and the wife takes of the marital property enough beyond her half to provide for the small children she has yet to raise.

If the man treats the wife badly, the woman may bring a complaint before the *comisario* (and then to the *municipio*) and prove mistreatment; then she may take the initiative in leaving the house and may take her share of the property and the children. If the husband has another woman, but does not bring her into the house, provided he continues to treat his wife well, she may not leave him without losing rights to the property. But adultery, when it does occur, is rare, occasional and surreptitious.

If either husband or wife dies, and the other spouse is living, the property is not divided, whether the children be young and unmarried, or be married and living elsewhere. The marital property is maintained as a whole by a widow, who continues to provide as best she can for the children not yet grown. If a woman remains a widow and her son marries after his father's death, in most cases he continues living with his mother; and he may not claim a separate share in the property left by his father. The property is divided only (with exception to be noted) when the widow dies and all the children are married. A widow picks out some relative to whom are to be entrusted the young unmarried children and the property received from her deceased husband. Commonly she picks out a dependable married son, or, if such is lacking, a reliable brother of her deceased husband, or of herself. After her death, her property and the responsibility for the care of the young children pass to this person. When all the children are grown and married, whether this condition exists at the death of the widow or comes about later, then the property is divided in equal parts, daughters sharing equally with sons.

If the widow takes another husband (married legally or not), the children may still make no claim for shares in their father's estate, provided the new husband treats the stepchildren well and is not consuming the estate. But if he begins to misuse the property left, the children may present their complaint and bring about the division of the property. If a man marries a second time, the children have no claim upon his estate until his death. And in this case the entire property is kept by the second wife, if she is legally married to the man, or if there are young children by this second marriage, until her death, when it is equally divided among all the children of the man. But if this second woman is not the legal wife of the man, or if she has no children by the man, and she is wasting the property, the children may bring a complaint to compel division of the property. Thus, when Anastacia Dzul refused to hand over a part to her dead husband's son, on the ground that he was married and able to take care of himself, the son brought a complaint before the authorities of the *municipio* in order to force his stepmother to turn over to him three cows and a milpa from his father's estate. He showed that his mother's new husband was consuming the property. The text of the resulting settlement follows:

In the village of Chan Kom, *municipio* of Cuncunul, Valladolid, on the second of July 1925, at four o'clock in the afternoon there appeared before the *comisaría* in my charge, Santiago Yam, Tranquilino Yam and María Isidora Yam, all children of the deceased, Marcelino Yam, making known that they are the legitimate heirs of the deceased; likewise María Hilaria Pat, the widow, made known her right to a part of the goods in view of the fact that she had lived and served some years at his side; both parties entered into arrangements making known the part to fall to the share of each. Finally they reached a friendly agreement that: of the 150 *mecates* of cleared land 50 were to go to Sra. Pat and 25 to each one of the four children; the allotment of a horse remaining pending a second meeting was fixed for the tenth so as to arrange this definitely. It was likewise agreed that of the 120 *canastros* of maize, more or less, 30 fall to Sra. Pat and the remainder to the four children; with this the meeting ended, and this document was caused to be signed by the authorities and the parties concerned.

(It was later agreed that the widow was to keep the horse. Only the crop, or the labor expended, is property in the case of the land, of course. See following section.)

The case of Marcelino Yam illustrates these rules. His wife, mother of his three small children, died. The two sons married by haan cab (p. 87) and went to live with their respective mothers-in-law. The daughter also married. Marcelino found another woman in Santa María: María Hila ria Pat. This woman refused to live in Chan Kom. Marcelino accordingly moved to Sa nta María, taking with him his household furnishings. Then Marcelino died. The married children then brought an action which resulted in a settlement by agreement, wh ereby a share of the property went to María Hilaria, because sh e had lived with Marcelino for some years (without giving birth to children), and the rest was divided among the three children. If María had had a child by Marcelino, this child would have shared equally with the others. And if María had lived in Chan Kom, with young children, especially if she had legally married Marcelino, she could have kept all the property until her death or remarriage.

LAND

In the current ideas of land tenure notions of individual ownership and special rights are constantly struggling to assert themselves against a theory of collective ownership and equal opportunity. It is not clear to the writers to what extent the ideas of collective ownership are in the folkways. According to Federal and State laws, the village lands are owned by the village, and an individual villager has merely a right of temporary tillage or occupancy. Outside of the villages, lands are owned by the Federal government. People are aware of these laws, and to some uncertain extent these recent statutory regulations conform to customary rights and obligations. But frequent land disputes occur. In certain of these disputes one local community claims special rights in lands theoretically open to cultivation equally to all persons. In other quarrels that arise inside the village, an individual claims ownership of his house-lot, by trying to sell it for his own benefit, while the village authorities deny him that right on the ground that the lands of the village (*ejidos*) are owned collectively.

Outside of the *ejido* (particularly at San Pedro and X-Kopchen) there are a number of tracts of agricultural land owned by individuals of Chan Kom. These lands are bought and sold like any other property, and there is documentary record of title. But the agricultural techniques, which depend in turn on the natural conditions, are not such as to favor a feeling for individual ownership. Land is cultivated only one or two years in seven; during most of the time any piece of land outside of the village is overgrown with bush. The milpas must be constantly moved from one site to another. What a man owns, and feels he owns, therefore, is the temporary results of his labor: the clearing, the planting, and the harvesting, not the land itself. Once the field has gone back to bush, he has no better right to till that piece of land again than has another man. But a cleared field, or a standing crop, is commonly sold. In 1931 a cleared field was worth 40 *centavos* a *mecate;* a field of sprouting corn was worth eighty; and a field ready for harvest up to one peso and twenty-five *centavos* a *mecate.*

The *ejidos* of Chan Kom consist of 2400 hectares of land surrounding the village.[1] These lands belong to the village collectively. The individual agriculturalists have equal rights to find their milpa sites within them. The *ejidos* merely

---

[1] The laws provide that the size of the *ejidos* be in proportion to the number of agriculturalists in the village and the quality of the land. Chan Kom was granted 24 hectares for each of one hundred (liberally estimated) agriculturalists.

PLATE 9

c, Taking honey from the hives. (Taken in Piste by Miss Katheryn MacKay)

a, Hunting party. (Taken by Morris Steggerda)

b, Beehives.

PLATE 10

a, Burning limestone to make lime.

b, *Fagina*: work on the new school building.

give the people of Chan Kom an exclusive right within this area as against other villages. Before the *ejidos* were granted, Chan Kom had no legal basis for resisting the encroachment of agriculturalists from other settlements.

From the map (fig. 3) it will appear, however, that most of the milpas made by the men of Chan Kom are outside of the *ejidos*. There is not, in fact, enough land inside the *ejidos* to supply good milpas for all,[1] and better crops can be secured by going farther away. The average distance of the milpas from the village is 9 kilometers, and some milpas are 30 kilometers away. The milpas made outside of the *ejidos* are (mostly) on land owned by the Federal Government. In this land any agriculturalist from any village may make milpa. People feel that they have an unrestricted right to make milpas in the uninhabited bush; they have always done so. When, as occasionally happens, the Federal forestry inspector reports the practice and the authorities require the agriculturalist to pay, as the law provides, one peso for each 25 *mecates* of land cultivated, the agriculturalist feels a sense of injury.

Nevertheless settlements assert special rights in these Federal lands, and thus conflicts arise between one hamlet or village and another. Men from one village who have long made their milpas in the general neighborhood of some cenote sometimes resent it if people from other villages make milpas in the vicinity. Especially do they feel it wrong if the lands immediately about the settlement are trespassed upon. The recent agrarian laws provide a way to protect these nearest lands: the settlement petitions to become a pueblo and to receive its *ejidos*.[2] These laws, it has been discovered, also provide a way for a village to secure control of even the more distant lands under the color of law. When men have for some time made their milpas in distant fertile lands, and they wish to keep other men from making milpa there,[3] they sometimes apply for *ejidos*, asserting that what is in reality a temporary *milperío* is an old and independent settlement. The law provides that *ejidos* may be granted if there are twenty agriculturalists in a settlement. To make this appearance, men temporarily move their families and domestic paraphernalia, and even their poultry, to the camp in the bush, so that when the representative of the government comes to inspect the settlement and take a census, he finds what is apparently a thriving hamlet. There are even cases where hamlets help one another with the temporary loan of population. If the deception is successful and the grant of *ejidos* secured, the village is of course a pueblo only on the map, not in reality. The men go back to their real village, with their poultry, their metates, and their wives, but they have now a legal claim of right as against any trespasser.

Within the village it is the house-lots that are the subjects of dispute. The house-lots compose what is known as the *fundo legal*, a rectangle of 15 hectares lying inside the *ejidos*. The *fundo legal* is the village-site itself, early settled in fact around the cenote and confirmed by law when the *ejidos* were granted. At this time the

---

[1] By no means all of the 2400 hectares in the *ejidos* are tillable.

[2] This explains why (as appears from the map) eight men of Chan Kom made milpas at Uaymilchen in 1930, but none made milpa there in 1931. At the end of 1930 *ejidos*, including these lands, were granted to X-Cocail.

[3] Another motive for taking the steps here described lies in the desire of schismatic colonists to free themselves from the obligation of *fagina* to the parent village. See p. 24.

boundaries of the house-lots were drawn, parallel and at right angles to the lines of the streets. Some moving of houses was necessary to fit the houses into the new lots; many men moved their houses down to the street lines, and some began to erect new houses of masonry. The best house-lots—those facing the plaza and near the cenote—were assigned in public meeting to the men already living there; these men were the village leaders, and in most cases the village pioneers. Many more house-lots were laid out than were actually needed at the time; people who now come to take up their residence in Chan Kom may receive, without charge, one of these unoccupied house-lots.

According to law, and probably also according to the customs that prevailed before the laws were effective, the individual's right with respect to the house-lot exists only so long as he is a member of the community. If he withdraws, the ownership reverts to the village and the authorities may assign the lot to some other member of the community. Nevertheless, in the several cases when men have in recent years abandoned Chan Kom for some other place of residence, they have tried to sell their house-lots. These persons entered into negotiations with outsiders to sell their lots and were very much displeased when the village authorities insisted that they lacked the right to do so. In one of these cases it was decided in a meeting of the men of the village, that the village could sell the abandoned house-site to some new settler who might care to pay for a better house-site than those remaining for free distribution at the outskirts of the village, and that the money would go for public improvements. On the other hand, the village authorities raised no objection when one villager sold a part of his house-site to another villager. The essential fact probably is that although the house-sites are both legally and traditionally communal property, recently the idea has arisen that a man who leaves the village having contributed to public improvements should in fairness be allowed to sell his house-lot and pocket the proceeds. As between one villager and another, these house-sites and their boundaries furnish endless discussion and frequent dispute; the original location of sites is recalled and questioned, and encroachments upon a neighbor's land are vigorously resented.

The house itself, if made of poles and thatch in the old Maya style, is treated in the same manner as the land on which it stands, for the reason that such houses are built—or were until very recently—by the cooperative labor of all the men of the community. The owner does the larger share of the work, but it is part of public duty to help him build it. Therefore on leaving the village, a man may not sell his house. When Don Tacio was about to move from Chan Kom, he prepared to sell his house to another villager, intending to pocket the proceeds. But the village authorities said that if the house were to be sold, Don Tacio could keep only half of what was realized; the other half must go to the village treasury. The masonry houses that people are building nowadays are constructed by individual initiative and often with the hired help of a mason; these houses will probably be regarded as fully saleable by their individual owners, but so far no such sale has occurred.

Fruit trees are owned by the person who plants them, whether or not he is also owner of the land on which they grow. In the early days of the settlement before the clearing around the cenote was divided into house-lots, each settler put his house where it suited him, and planted his trees wherever he found it convenient. Later, when the streets were laid out and the boundaries of the house-lots were fixed, the rights of the planters of the trees in this property continued to be recognized, although these trees were in many cases scattered through the village and on the house-lots of other men. The owner of a fruit tree growing on the land of another harvests the fruit and disposes of it as he wishes, and he may sell the tree itself, even to a third person. When Don Tacio, in the case mentioned in the previous paragraph, was about to give up his residence in Chan Kom, although objection was made to his intention to sell his house, his sale of fruit trees apart from his land was taken as a matter of course. Public opinion condemns occasional instances where the owner of the lot has taken fruit from the tree of another growing on his land without permission of the owner of the tree.

In the facts that have been set forth in this chapter lies much of the justification for the assertion that Chan Kom is like peasant villages everywhere, rather than like the truly primitive community of tribesmen: in the economic dependence, established through the store and the peddler, upon the market of the town and the factory of the city; in the production of an important money-crop; in the great development of inter- and intra-community trade; in the recognition of impersonal statutory law imposed from outside the community; in the circulation of national money; and in the tendency toward the pecuniary valuation of all goods, even land.

CHAPTER V

THE DIVISION OF LABOR

In all essential respects the division of labor in Chan Kom is like that found everywhere in cultures that are primitive and relatively immobile. As between the sexes, the conventional allocation of function is definite and rigid. Between one individual and another of the same sex differences in function are small. The fundamental techniques of maintenance are known and practiced by all; there is no man who is not a farmer, and no woman who is not a housekeeper and cook. The professionalization of practical functions has only rudimentary development; even new practical techniques, such as the mason's art, spread quickly to all the population and are soon practiced by all. The barber and the baker are only part-time professionals; their specialities do not interfere with their agriculture and their hunting. As the economic organization is simple, no member of the community lives by trade; there are almost no commercial specialists.[1] Furthermore, the professions that do exist are, chiefly, sacred rather than secular; these are the activities of the shamans, of the chanters of ritual prayer, and of the marriage-negotiator; these specialties depend on esoteric knowledge that is not easily gained and on special qualities of personality; on these functionaries the community is dependent; for these reasons such specialties are not easily assumed or laid down.

BETWEEN THE SEXES

As in so many other places, in Chan Kom a woman's sphere is about the home and her activities are always private; whereas a man is occupied in the field and forest and his activities are often public. The cultural patterns characteristic of Chan Kom, however, appear from a definition of the precise ways in which these general rules operate, the exceptions to those rules and the manner of reconciling conflicting patterns of thought and practice.

The man does all the agricultural labor.[2] He fells the bush, burns, sows, weeds and harvests; and he brings the maize from the granary to his house. Nevertheless, if a man spends extended periods at his milpa, he often takes his wife with him; and if such an event falls in harvest time, she not uncommonly helps him gather ripened ears, putting them into a fiber-bag (*sabucan*). The little gardens in the house-yards, whether made as caanches (p. 35) or on the ground, are prepared by the men of the family; persons of either sex may plant them; but their subsequent care is in the hands of the women, who water them and weed them. Men do all the hunting and take all care of the cattle; but women take primary (but not exclusive) care of the poultry. The bees are cared for by the men; they build the hives, make new

---

[1] The storekeepers spend most of their time on agriculture and kindred tasks. The egg-merchant has specialized his work to a greater degree; he spends two days a week in trade. And recently a man from Chan Kom entered into partnership with a peddler from the towns.

[2] One case is reported of a woman in a neighboring settlement who for a time lived alone and made milpa. But this woman came from the city and her agricultural labors were the subject of much comment.

colonies, and take the honey from the hives; but once the honey is in the house a woman may boil it to clarify it. All building operations, whether on houses of the old type or of the new masonry kind, are performed by the men, down to the thatching of the roofs and the whitewashing of the walls. Women do the cooking, make and wash the garments for members of the family of both sexes, and embroider. Men and boys fetch the firewood, and women and girls the water. Men scrape the fiber out of the henequen leaves; but both sexes participate in the making of bags, hammocks and carrying-straps out of this fiber. The making of baskets is a technique exclusively practiced by men, but candles, like hammocks and bags, are made by persons of either sex.[1] Gourd-carriers (chuyub) are made, nearly always, by women.

In all secular offices, and in all ritual functions that are public rather than domestic, it is the men who figure, and not the women. Offices in the local government are held only by men (but the teacher—who is not a native, but is imported from the town—may be a woman). Public meetings are composed of men only, and at public secular celebrations—dedications of new public buildings, for example—women are never active participants. Men, not women, play musical instruments and take part in card games and the few forms of competitive play, but both sexes tell stories for entertainment and both dance.

The marriage-negotiator, if a public functionary, it is felt must be a man; and all of the h-mens (shaman-priests) are men.[2] On the other hand the midwives have no male competitors.

The allocation of specialized and conspicuous function in connection with religious ritual is obedient to two principles: *one*, the worship of the pagan rain and maize gods tends to fall into the hands of the men, while the Catholic rituals are more often in charge of the women; and, *two*, public or community rituals are led by men, but domestic rituals by women. In various circumstances where the two principles conflict, one or the other dominates. Thus, in the important public fiestas in honor of a village *santo* (p. 153), the men organize and take charge of the fiesta, whereas in minor domestic offerings of first fruits to pagan gods, women may take the initiative. On the other hand, in therapeutic rituals taking place in the family circle, but involving the assistance of a shaman, who is in every case a man, this specialist takes charge, and not the women of the houses. The family has simply called a doctor.

In the more important and therefore more communal religious ceremonies offered to the pagan deities, the two principles are in accord. In such rituals only the men participate, and in the most important (the rain ceremony; cha-chaac), the presence of women is out of the question, and sexual intercourse before the ceremony is proscribed for the men. It is probably the association of the bees with these pagan gods and rituals that makes the care of the apiaries, although a domestic operation, a matter for the man. On the other hand, in the strictly domestic

---

[1] In villages (of which Chan Kom is not one), where pottery is made, both men and women are potters.

[2] A woman living in a *rancheria* learned some of the h-men's prayers and techniques and—there being no h-men near by—began to practice, and even to make u hanli col (p. 134). But leading h-mens of the region put a stop to this. (The more important ceremonies of the h-men are taboo to women.)

ritual offered in Catholic forms (novenas; *rezos*), the women take as much part as the men. Nevertheless, the person who recites the ritual prayers at the more important domestic ceremonies of this Catholic sort is in most cases not a casual participant, but a specialist called in just to do this, and such permanent professionals (*maestros cantores*) are always men. This is, no doubt, a provision in harmony with the pattern of the Catholic church service, in which women constitute the greater part of the congregation, while a male priest leads the ritual.

Of course, not all of these restrictions of activity to one sex or the other, here stated so categorically, have behind them the same kind of depth of attitude. It would cause little or no comment if a man should make a gourd-carrier, although men rarely or never do make them. But a man would be astonished if asked to wash clothes or to grind corn on the metate. A man always has a woman to do these things for him. There are no adult bachelors; between one marriage and the next, or in other emergency, some kinswoman will wash and cook for a man. These ideas as to the division of labor and notions of family life are two halves of a single whole: a man must have a woman because these tasks must be done by a woman; and it is felt that these tasks must be done by a woman, because there is always a woman there to do them.

Therefore for a man to wash clothes or to cook, or for a woman to go hunting or to act as a mason's helper, is something not thought of at all, or, if thought of, considered as involving a distinct impropriety. It is more than mere convenient usage, as is the case with the allocation of chuyub manufacture to the women. On the other hand, even deeper levels of condemnation would attend the suggestion (should some outsider make it) that a woman act as ritual assistant (idzac) in a first-fruit ceremony offered to the pagan gods. This would be dangerous and morally wrong.

There are also situations where two categories with respect to the division of labor between the sexes intersect and conflict, and such situations often provide exceptions to general principles, or special cases that modify the rule. If no man or boy is available to send for firewood, the women of the house will fetch it. The drawing of water from the cenote is woman's occupation; one may watch the well from dawn to dark and see only women and girls going and returning, and pausing at the rim to fill their buckets and to exchange remarks. The rim of the cenote is a woman's precinct; this is the principal place where women meet throughout the ordinary day, filled with domestic tasks that otherwise keep each to her house; here gossip is born; the Chan Kom equivalent of "a little bird told me" is, "I heard it at the rim of the cenote." For no domestic purposes does a man go to the cenote to fetch water, and even the watering of cattle is women's work. But as the care of the cattle is in other respects a man's task, the men often help with the watering, and for an hour the cenote may become a man's place. And when water must be used in the ritual foods offered to the pagan gods at the ceremonies which women may not attend, this water is drawn at the cenote by a man.

There are similar exceptions to the general feeling that all cookery is woman's work. No man would use the metate, but a man is not averse to turning the newer iron handmill occasionally, perhaps because it is machinery. And when the sacred breadstuffs are to be prepared for the gods of the rain and of the milpas, in connection with ceremonies which women may not attend, the principle that women are cooks admits of important exception. For the men pluck the consecrated fowl, make and bake the ritual breads, while, indoors, and some distance off, the women have already ground the maize from which the cakes are made, and they will later boil the fowl into broth to be placed on the altar. The ritual breads, together with squash and starchy roots that are offered on these altars, are baked in earth-ovens made near the altar, and as the earth-oven is used principally on such occasions, it is one technique of cookery carried on primarily by men. In quite another, and secular context, cooking may be done by men: baking of bread in masonry ovens of Spanish type is a man's trade in the city and the towns and, in Chan Kom too, all such baking is done by men. Tortillas are made domestically on the griddle by the women of each household; wheat bread is baked in ovens, for sale, by men specialists.

WITH RESPECT TO AGE

There are no defined age-groups, each with its appropriate special functions. As tradition and technique still pass by word of mouth, and the young do not as yet have special advantage through literacy or knowledge of Spanish (p. 17), Chan Kom is no exception to the general rule among primitive peoples that specialized activities, particularly those attended with prestige or involving the exercise of esoteric knowledge, are carried on by the older people. No young person is shaman, midwife or marriage-negotiator. There is not the same reluctance, however, for a young man to act as *maestro cantor* (reciter of Catholic prayers); some of these are in their early twenties. There are, after all, only a few people in Chan Kom over forty-five. The elective offices, that change frequently, must be discharged in many cases by young men.

Children begin early to take up the easier tasks that their parents are discharging. Boys and girls of 6 or 7 years of age carry their smaller brothers and sisters around and, when of this age or even younger, the boys fetch firewood and the girls begin to carry water. A boy follows his father to the milpa as soon as he can keep up with him on the path, and takes part almost from the first in the work of the field; by the time a boy is 12 or 13 years old he generally is making a small separate milpa of his own; and some boys begin even younger.

THE SECULAR PROFESSIONALS

As has already been indicated, the significant specialization of practical activities does not exist within the village of Chan Kom, but concerns that wider economy, including the towns, the capital city, and even the factories and markets of the world, with which Chan Kom is bound. The secular professionals on whom the people of Chan Kom depend are not themselves people of Chan Kom; they are the merchants, peddlers, professional musicians, migratory artisans and cattle-traders who come to the village or whom the villagers go to find in Valladolid. Among the people of Chan Kom themselves the specialization of secular labor is slight; of course there are differences in interest and ability; but only in a few cases do such differences become the basis for real professional specialization. Everybody, substantially, knows how to make candles, to make cinches and carrying-straps, just as every man knows how to make milpa and every woman to sew. With the manufacture of gourd-carriers, hammocks and bags (*sabucanes*), the case is different, for only a minority can make these articles. Those who do make them, however, make them largely for themselves; to some small extent the makers sell them to their neighbors, but many such objects are bought from traveling vendors. Barbering is more nearly a professional specialty; several men make claim to know the art, but one man does most of the haircutting for his neighbors at ten *centavos* for each such service. This man learned what he knows merely by observing the barbers in the town. Baking is still more of a specialty, partly because it requires the capital investment of an oven. Four or five men in Chan Kom have learned to bake wheat bread—they learned from bakers of the towns who came to Chan Kom to work for a time in the local store, or for social purposes; but only one man in Chan Kom bakes bread now,[1] and this he does infrequently and irregularly, selling the bread through the store, and he must compete with the traveling vendors of bread. For a brief time, when the village was beginning to build houses of rubble-work and plaster, the mason's art was a true profession. Only one man knew the art; he had learned it in the towns and there practiced the specialty as a full-time trade. Therefore, when the first masonry houses were built, this man devoted his time to the work, laboring for hire or by work-exchange and doing very little work in his milpa; and his neighbors who wanted masonry houses either called upon him or brought in masons from other villages or towns. But as the new houses were constructed, and the other men of the village acted as helpers to this first mason, the knowledge spread until most men in Chan Kom knew how to put up a masonry wall. The simple techniques of carpentering door-frames and ceiling-beams similarly spread from certain men of Cuncunul who were adept at this; and the art of making fiber bags came to Chan Kom from Yaxcaba and Chichimila—places which used to be known for this work.

MIDWIFE AND KAX BAAC

The midwife (*partera*[2]) is truly a professional. Her knowledge is specialized and requires a period of training to acquire. She is a village institution; if a man's wife is in labor, he sends for Doña Leandra without hesitation. Some men occasionally make presents to her, that they may feel that her services are willing and painstaking. She charges a fixed fee of one *peso* for each delivery (whether the child be boy or girl). This fee is customary, and does not vary from midwife to midwife. The midwife of Chan Kom serves the neighboring hamlets too. In 1931, when Doña Leandra removed her residence from Chan Kom, another woman

---

[1] A second oven was built, but bread-making in it soon suspended.
[2] In speaking Maya this Spanish word is used; or else the midwife is referred to as x-ilah-kohan ("she who visits the sick woman"), or as x-hiikab ("she who does massage").

assumed the practice of midwifery. This woman had learned the art from Doña Leandra, but she would not venture to practice while Doña Leandra was available. Probably most midwives in these villages have in training some assistant-disciple.

The knowledge of the kax baac ("bone tyer") includes that of setting fractures and of massaging for sprains and displaced muscles. The treatment of dislocations and sprains is known as chen zahi. Though a kax baac is strictly one who can set broken bones, the term is loosely used for those who know only chen zayi. Many men have some knowledge of these arts; an occasional man enjoys a professional reputation in the field and practices his calling for a fee. There is no real kax baac in Chan Kom; in case of fractures, a specialist is called from another village. The kax baac may be also a h-men, or he may not.

THE SACRED PROFESSIONALS; THE MAESTROS CANTORES

In that important class of religious ceremonies, Catholic in form, which are known as novenas or *rezos* (p. 148), the essential ritual is the recitation of memorized prayers from the Catholic liturgy. Many men and women can repeat some of these prayers and, although they are in Spanish or in Latin, those who can recite them are in many cases people who speak only Maya. But there are certain men in the community who devote themselves to the memorizing of such prayers, and who, by reciting them at these ceremonies, practice a sacred profession: that of *maestro cantor*. Some of these men can repeat, in a low, rapid gabble for as much as an hour, Latin and Spanish prayers with little or no repetition.

The *maestro cantor* is called in to officiate at practically all novenas and *rezos* [1] (p. 151). On All Souls' Day these professionals are kept busy, hour after hour, going from one house to another to recite the ritual. They make no charge for their services, but they are accorded the highest respect when they appear professionally, and the best part of the food distributed at the end of the ceremony is reserved for them.

There is a feeling among the people that not every one can become a *maestro cantor*, but only those whom God has called to the rôle. Of the five or six *maestros cantores* in Chan Kom, the two who are men of advanced years enjoy the greatest prestige. These men profess not to remember where they first learned the prayers; one of them, when a youth, was a house-boy in the home of a priest in Valladolid and probably first learned them there. This man has transmitted the calling to his son. Several of these men are illiterate as well as ignorant of Spanish, and have learned the prayers by rote from repeated hearing of them, but one or two reinforce their stock of texts by studying the little printed pamphlets of Catholic prayers that circulate in Yucatan.

THE CASAMENTERO

One man in Chan Kom discharges the professional functions of marriage-negotiator (*casamentero;* no Maya name). These functions depend upon the

---

[1] Perhaps it should be stated that these men never administer sacrament; their functions are not confused with those of the priest in the town or city.

customs of betrothal: the parents of the boy take the initiative and ceremoniously make request of the girl's parents for their daughter in marriage for the petitioners' son; and this ceremonious petition is repeated, usually three additional times (p. 193). It is felt, however, that the request should not be made directly by the boy's parents or by them alone. It is a delicate matter, involving the forging of new kinship bonds between two family groups and the negotiations to fix the muhul (bride-gift). The *casamentero* is the public functionary who may be called upon to act as representative of the petitioners and as go-between in the negotiations. In some neighboring villages, and in the towns where this mode of betrothal is practiced, there is no *casamentero*, and parents ask the aid of any trusted person, or even carry on the negotiations themselves; and this last manner of procedure is followed occasionally in Chan Kom. There is no obloquy incurred by dispensing with his services, but what would be regarded as "the best marriages" are made by calling in the *casamentero*.

The *casamentero* must be an older man, one who enjoys public esteem by reason of his virtuous habits, his moral example, and his knowledge of Biblical lore and of the lives of the saints. Not many in Chan Kom have more than an inkling of such lore, and to have it is to have spiritual worth. A man of the village stated that the success of a marriage increases in proportion to the knowledge the *casamentero* has of such matters. In Chan Kom the man who is now *casamentero* is also a leading *maestro cantor*, and the man who takes his place, if the other is unable to function, is another *maestro cantor;* the two offices, obviously, are likely to be filled by the same individual.

The *casamentero* accompanies the boy's parents to the girl's home and as their spokesman asks for the girl's hand. He stresses the virtues of the boy on whose behalf he has come, and minimizes his defects. He urges upon his hearers acceptance of the valuables—gold chains, silk *huipil* (p. 193)—which the boy's parents are prepared to offer, and, if the other couple are disposed to be exacting, he drives a bargain with them. Not uncommonly he acts as a witness to the church marriage. He is likely to assume some later responsibility for the success of the marriage; commonly before they marry, he advises the boy and girl as to their duties and responsibilities, and if discords arise between them after marriage, he will often intercede to repair the breach. For his services he collects no fee, but the bridegroom maintains an attitude of respectful obligation to him and not uncommonly gives him some assistance in working his milpa.

THE H-MENS

By far the most distinct and important professionals in the village are those known as *h-menes* (h-menob),[1] who discharge the functions of priest and of shaman. For all the important ceremonies dealing with the pagan gods, for the exorcistic rites, and in connection with the ritual curing of disease, their services are indispensable and allow of no substitution. Their knowledge is very special; it is acquired

[1] From the root *men*, to know, and the prefix indicating substantive of importance or of masculine sex.

only after long novitiate periods; and there is a clear break between their knowledge and that of the laymen. As this knowledge is esoteric, involving the occult and the holy, the h-mens are persons set apart, a little uncanny. At the same time the special respect accorded them, mixed with a touch of dread, is modified by other feelings induced by the prestige of the modern, the rational, the "civilized." The influence of the schools and of the political propagandist, and the respect nowadays accorded rational medicine and hygiene, tend to qualify the status of the h-men and make him, while still a person apart, no longer a person above. The state of intoxication in which, traditionally, the h-men maintains himself while officiating, conflicts with the ideals and practices of abstinence current in Chan Kom. When the drunken shaman turns his crystals in the candlelight and reads in them the will of the gods, the devotees who attend the ceremony hasten to perform the orders of which the h-men is mouthpiece, but their obedience does not move in unmixed reverence. There is also distaste, even disgust, and—sometimes—distrust. The attitude toward the h-men of those most affected by modernizing influences varies with the mood and the emergency. A man who when sick will call the shaman to perform the rituals of contrition offered to offended spirits, when well will decry the h-men and oppose his leadership. "Really," writes the village political leader in his autobiography (p. 227), adopting the jargon of the propagandist, "the h-mens are the exploiters of the working man. . . , the worst enemies of all the workers of the world." Nevertheless, when these lines were written their author had just employed several shamans to undo the black magic other shamans had worked to his ill.

The h-men leads in the Maya ceremonies; he recites the prayers, offers the food to the gods, and directs his lay assistants. He diagnoses illness, predicts its outcome, and effects cures, partly by performing propitiatory, expiatory or exorcistic ceremonies, partly by administering herbal medicine, and partly by bleeding and cupping. The priestly and therapeutic functions are thus closely interrelated. Their exercise involves the use of special paraphernalia: the crystals of divination (zaztun; p. 170); rattlesnake fangs or obsidian or glass blades with which the patients are bled; and certain small gourd vessels of special shape (homa) which are used only to hold the sacred liquor (balche) in the ceremonies.

The h-mens take no part in rituals involving the recitation of Catholic prayers. The maestros cantores are not h-mens, and the h-mens are not maestros cantores. Nor do the h-mens have any concern with the ritual or practical acts attending childbirth.

Three terms are in use which distinguish among the functions of the priest (h-men), the herbalist (dzadzac) and the sorcerer (pulyah). The h-mens are, probably without exception, herbalists too. But there are also herbalists who are not h-mens: they do not perform the religious ceremonies or in other ways act as intermediaries between man and god. And while the priestly functions are appropriate to men only, those of the herbalist are sometimes carried on by women (x-dzadzac). Commonly a h-men's wife is an herbalist.

But the functions of the priest (h-men) and of the performer of black magic (pulyah) are fundamentally incompatible. The h-men is uncanny, and suspected witchcraft is often attributed to him, just as h-mens are easily suspected of being *uayes* (p. 178). But sorcery is a black art, while the priestly office is a sacred calling. For a h-men to get a reputation as a sorcerer is to lose his reputation as a h-men. If such rumors spread about a h-men, he is less sought after to perform the ceremonies. One h-men of great fame suffered such a darkening of his reputation: it was said of him that he had begun to engage in sorcery; it was told that he was practicing his art in order to make money; and when finally he went blind, his misfortune was explained by reference not to his great success as a h-men, but by saying that this was his punishment for taking up sorcery. The older people say that when a h-men begins to act as pulyah, "the yuntzilob (agricultural deities) will not accept him." As a sign of this, the ritual breads come out of the earth-oven underdone.

The pulyah of greatest reputation are not h-mens. And some of them are women. Furthermore, the most powerful and most feared of them do not reside in the villages, but in the neighboring towns, and are not Mayas, but *mestizos*.

In Chan Kom, during most of the period of these observations, there were two h-mens.[1] For the less important ceremonies and for the curing of sickness, where the case is not desperate, these local practitioners are called upon. But if the stubborn illness does not yield, or the reluctant rain does not fall, a h-men of greater prestige, from some other village, is called. There are great differences in the reputations of these men; in the case of a few their fame extends over an area including several score of settlements. The two h-mens of Chan Kom, being professionals of only moderate repute, spend only small parts of their time in the exercise of their calling and make milpa like any other man. But there are h-mens who apparently devote themselves to their special vocation and subsist without planting maize. The h-men's fee is in money and rum, and the amount varies with the magnitude of the service rendered and the dignity of the practitioner. Thus, for performing an exorcistic ceremony to cure a sick child, a minor h-men charged 30 *centavos* and drank two bottles of *anis* (p. 173) while a shaman of renown sold only his advice and some glass blades for bloodletting for the sum of 45 pesos (p. 227).

There is a tendency for this calling to descend from father to son. One of the h-mens of Chan Kom learned his art from his father, and another, in a neighboring village, comes from a family of which the men are reputed to have been h-mens from remote times. On the other hand, there are cases where persons of seclusive or mystical temperament seek out famous shamans and become their apprentices. Another Chan Kom shaman in this way learned his vocation from a famous shaman in the village where he was born (Tixcacaltuyu).

The period of training lasts one year, during which the novice is the apprentice and assistant of the established h-men, attending his master at the ceremonies he performs, while the master teaches him the prayers, his knowledge of the plants, and the ways of diagnosing and of curing disease. At the end of the year, the master gives his disciple some of his zaztuns (crystals of divination) and there is held a ceremony of initiation and dedication. This ceremony is called u lohol u kub kubah ti yuntzilob yetel ti yum hahal *Dios* ("his redemption, the delivery of himself

[1] Shortly afterward, both removed to other and neighboring villages.

to the yuntzils[1] and to the Lord God"). The ceremony is conducted by the master h-men. He erects an altar and has ritual breads made in the earth-oven (p. 125). The initiate brings a turkey. He and his wife kneel at the altar, the new h-men lifting up the turkey as an offering to the yuntzilob while the old h-men recites prayers. The wife kneels too, because at future ceremonies she will in some cases direct the women in the preparation of the broth (kol; p. 129). Both the h-men and his wife wear on their heads a sort of crown made of vines encircling the head and also crossing it, once longitudinally and once transversely. To the vines are fastened *Plumeria* flowers (nicte).

After the ceremony has been performed, the new h-men is free to practice. The master receives nothing for the training he has given, but he may call upon his disciple to treat him or to aid him in his profession. H-mens do not charge one another; they treat one another free.

Friends of the candidate may bring to this ceremony an *almud* of maize and a hen. If they do this, during the following year they may call upon the new h-men without having to pay him for his services.

COOPERATIVE LABOR AND WORK-EXCHANGE

The specializations of function which have been described in this chapter bring it about that one individual depends upon another, and so help to weave the fabric of Chan Kom society. This dependence upon the labor of another results also from institutions which do not involve specialization of function: labor is not only divided; it is also pooled and exchanged.

Communal labor—by which is here meant compulsory cooperative labor by the whole community—exists as an important institution; it will be discussed in the next section. Such communal labor is expended chiefly on public works. A man's cornfield and his garden-plot are the results of his private initiative and the fruits of his own personal toil. In the great majority of cases a man clears, plants and harvests his milpa without help, unless it be that of his small son. In a very few cases, however, a group of friends or of relatives help one another in the work on the individual milpas. This is by the principle of work-exchange. Thus, one man helped first his father's brother and then the son of another paternal uncle with the harvesting, expecting his uncle and his cousin to help him with his harvest; and two brothers and the husband of their sister similarly exchanged services in the milpa. But the work-exchange plays a much smaller part in agricultural labor than it does in house-building. According to custom now disappearing, house-construction was by communal labor, and probably the sentiments that attended such collective toil are manifest today in the frequent cases of work-exchange in connection with the construction of masonry houses. A few masonry houses in Chan Kom have been built by the owner alone, but most have been built by cooperating groups of men who have constructed, in turn, a house for each member of the group. In part, these groups have been composed of relatives and in part of neighbors. An uncle and four nephews built five masonry houses in succession,

[1] P. 113.

one for each member of the group. The work was intermittent; while it was going on one of the nephews helped his father-in-law to build his house, expecting the older man to return help when the younger should build a second smaller masonry structure on his own lot. Meanwhile this son-in-law and his father-in-law were earning labor-credit from a neighbor, who was not a relative, by helping in the construction of his house. Before the fifth house of the group first mentioned was complete, the same uncle and two of the nephews began to help another uncle, brother of the first, with his masonry house; each expecting a return of labor some day when he should need it. Apparently no exact record is kept of the time spent by one man on the house or in the field of another; but such matters are public knowledge, and public opinion reminds a delinquent if he has not given an approximate return.

Besides these frequent instances of the exchange of labor in house-construction, there are also cases of simultaneous cooperative labor, also voluntarily entered into, by groups of men upon single projects in which they all share equally. Lime-burnings are often made this way; for example, the mason and two of his neighbors, no kin of his, pooled their efforts to make a lime-burning, and then divided the lime equally among them. Four neighbors, who lived in a part of the village distant from the cenote, together opened a well for their common use.

COMMUNAL LABOR; FAGINA

"*Fagina*" is the name given to the labor which every man in the village must perform for the public good without receiving remuneration. The custom is clearly defined and the part played by the institution in the social mechanics of the village is of great importance. The duties discharged in accordance with it are of two sorts: regular public service in rotation and occasional special labor in which all adult males simultaneously participate. The former variety, known as *guardia*, provides the personnel for the village administration. The obligation of *guardia* falls upon every male member of the community as soon as he leaves school. Men about forty-five years of age or over are exempt, also those who have been *comisario*, or president of the *Liga*. At the beginning of each calendrical year the *comisario* makes out a list of all the boys and men who are subject to *fagina;* to each he assigns one week of duty as member of a body of four men always on duty in the public building (*cuartel*). These four are the *guardia;* each is a *policia*. That one of the four who has received the most education is called *sargento;* he is charged with receiving official letters or orders which may come to the village and with communicating matters of interest to the *comisario*. The *sargentos* appointed for all the weeks of the year[1] constitute the deliberative body of the village. When a matter comes up for discussion, a meeting of *sargentos* is held, presided over by the *comisario*, and the question is decided by this assemblage.

The four men constituting the *guardia* perform any public service, under the direction of the *comisario*; they run errands, provide an escort for returning visitors, arrest and incarcerate deliquents, go from door to door announcing decisions made

[1] There are about fifteen *sargentos* in Chan Kom; each man serves several weeks of *guardia* a year.

at public meetings and perform tasks in connection with public improvements. They may be called upon to walk the 50 kilometers to Valladolid in order to deliver some official communication. During the period of service, the *policía* swing their hammocks in the *cuartel*, and there they remain, except when duty calls them out, or when, for brief periods, they go home to eat. It is their special duty, from the vantage point of the *cuartel*, to watch for visitors to the village and to notify the *comisario* of such arrivals. There are days at the height of the agricultural season, when the milpas engage the attention of nearly everyone and when the *policía* are the only men in the village.

Guardia maintains the persisting machinery of local government and does the continual small labors for the public good. Special *fagina*, which falls occasionally and simultaneously on all men, accomplishes the exceptional, the extra task. *Fagina* is a work-drive, a collective spurt. *Guardia* maintains the overhead of village business; *fagina* provides for expansion. Under the stimulus of village leadership and progressive ideas, Chan Kom has been expanding rapidly during the years of these observations, and therefore there has been a great deal of *fagina*. By this institution the plaza and the streets have been laid out, school gardens have been prepared, and there have been successively constructed the *cuartel*, a new school (Plate 10*b*), a basketball field, and 12 kilometers of roadway. Until recent years all private houses were built by *fagina*, but this custom is disappearing with the introduction of the masonry house.

The performance of *fagina* is attended with the impressiveness of collective determination and the stimulus of a situation where all men work shoulder to shoulder on one common task. When *fagina* has been decided upon, all the men meet at the *cuartel*, and first taking note of any absentees, that derelictions may not go unpunished, they go off together, with their tools, to the place where the task is to be done. At the meeting the night before when *fagina* was decided upon, there have been speeches exhorting the people to special effort that Chan Kom may grow in power and prestige; these words are still in their ears as they go out to do the work, and perhaps the *comisario*, who is with them as their leader, urges them on with fresh exhortations. During the work there is plenty of opportunity to talk and to joke; *fagina* is permeated by a cheerful enthusiasm.

This willingness and enthusiasm depend, of course, upon the sanction of public opinion; *fagina* could not go on if the public will opposed it. There are, in fact, always some individuals who find *fagina* too great a burden to be borne cheerfully, or to be borne at all. But the institution of *fagina* is so interrelated with other institutions as to bend such individuals into conformity, or, if they will not bend, to exclude them from the community entirely. *Fagina* is a duty that can not be escaped while a man lives in Chan Kom. It is an essential condition of citizenship. It can not be avoided by mere absence from the village. If a man is in his milpa, word is sent him (by *policía*) to remind him that his task at the village is soon to be performed.[1] Failure to perform *fagina* is punished by arrest and imprisonment,

[1] This is a frequent cause for the secession of *milperío* colonies from their parent village (see p. 24). When the *milpero* remains for long periods at his distant milpa, return to the village to perform *fagina* is irksome. The burden can be avoided if the *milperío* can become an independent pueblo.

and sometimes by the imposition of extra tasks. A man may not take up residence in Chan Kom without agreeing to participate in the *fagina* program then current. On the other hand, if an old resident is not faithful in the performance of his *fagina*, he is notified that he will have to discharge these duties or leave the village. There are even cases where a strong *comisario* imposes extra tasks upon such suspect citizens as a test of their willingness. If a man, discontented with the burden of *fagina*, elects to move his residence from Chan Kom, he may not go with *fagina* unfulfilled, and the authorities of other villages, to which he applies for admission, will cooperate with Chan Kom by denying him admission as a resident until he has been discharged from Chan Kom.

OCCUPATIONAL DIVISION OF TIME

Some idea of the ways in which a Chan Kom man spends his time may be had from table 5. The subjects of these records are two young married men, each with two children, occupying intermediate positions of wealth and social prominence.

TABLE 5—*Division of time, by days, among various occupations in the cases of two men of Chan Kom*

	1st Man 1930, No. Days	1st Man 1931, No. Days	2d Man 1931, No. Days
Agriculture:			
Felling bush	21	10	6
Sowing	5	7	7
Clearing second growth	3	9	31
Fencing milpa	8	4	9
Doblando	4	1	13
Harvesting	11	14	18
Fetching corn from milpa	15	6	11
Shelling corn for sale or selling it	0	14	22
Other agricultural tasks	0	2	5
Helping friend or relative in milpa	6	1	0
Total	73	68	122
Cattle:			
Hunting for cattle in the bush	19	10	1
Slaughtering	1	0	0
Total	20	10	1
Housebuilding:			
On own house	13	25	16
Helping friend or relative	25	38	0
Total	38	63	16
Small Domestic Tasks:			
Minor labors in house or yard	6	5	23
Handicrafts (string, hammocks)	0	3	1
Total	6	8	24
Hunting	14	14	6
To Towns on Private Business	3	9	11
Public Service:			
Guardia or *fagina*	48	74	35
Discharging official duties in village	3	0	3
To towns on official business	11	0	0
Total	62	74	38
Fiestas:			
In village	12	7	8
Domestic	1	0	0
Other villages	7	5	7
Political demonstration in town	3	0	0
Total	23	12	15
Idle	8	11	18
No Record	118	111	114
Total	365	365	365

The activities of one of these men are reported for the greater part of two consecutive years; those of the other, for most of the second of the same pair of years. The first man was president of *Liga Socialista* during the first year; the second man was head of the Local Agrarian Committee during the second year.

The one predominant and inescapable task is agriculture; a man spends from a quarter to a half of his days in its pursuit.[1] Felling bush, sowing, weeding and harvesting each requires a week of labor, or several weeks. Another important element in the agricultural toil, that does not appear from the table, is the mere going and coming on the trail to the milpa; in many cases it takes a man a day to reach his milpa and another day to return; and such trips, either to bring the workman to the site of his work, or to fetch the ripened corn that it may be cooked and eaten, consume many days of every man's time every year. Although the close association of village life is the predominant experience for everyone, it is probably true that during a third of every man's time (and during a smaller proportion in the case of a woman) a Chan Kom individual is alone, or in a small family group, camping in his milpa or walking through the silent bush.

Public service, chiefly in the form of *fagina*, demanded, during the period of these observations, a sixth to a quarter of a man's time. This is much more than is usual in neighboring villages.[2] The table shows that although all men are supposed to contribute equally to *fagina*, in fact there is some variation. The most public-spirited do more than the others; and if a man holds public office, he must go to the town on public business or devote some of his hours at home to it. During these particular years of observation, when the building of masonry houses swept the village like a wave, individuals caught up by it spent as much as one-quarter of their active hours in building. But the second man represented in these tables only lately turned to architectural improvements, and therefore only 5 per cent of his time was so taken up. The men who have cattle have to devote a score of days or more to them, chiefly by using up days on end looking for the cattle in the bush, that they may not stray away from the neighborhood, die of thirst, do injury to a milpa, or be stolen. Hunting expeditions consume another 10 or 20 days, and about as many go to small tasks around the house, and about a score to attending fiestas, either in other villages and towns or in Chan Kom. Only one or two local religious ceremonies require a full day or more; most take place in the afternoon hours after a man has already put in some hours at work.

A woman's activities are, of course, less varied. Occasionally she accompanies her husband to the milpa or on his rarer trips to town. While she is in the village her domestic duties at one season are like those at another season; only the periods of fiesta and ceremony interrupt the uniformity of her days.

THE YEARLY ROUND

Festal days and work days in Chan Kom are determined partly by the fixed days of the Catholic calendar and partly by the shifting seasons. The calendar

[1] With the occasional exceptions mentioned on p. 52.
[2] And since the period of observation, *fagina* has much decreased in Chan Kom.

maintains a day, week and month count which everyone observes, marking the Sundays, the period of Lent, the days on which to worship this saint or that, on which to tell fortunes,[1] on which to plant bananas. But the agricultural year underlies and controls the emphases of the church calendar. Only those Catholic feasts are observed which nature permits or recommends the people to observe, and there are other and most important feasts which are independent of the Catholic lists of days, but obey only the growing corn. The life cycle of the maize plant, that every year sees repeated, fixes the annual rhythm of life for all the individuals of Chan Kom and for the community itself. The activities of the people, indeed their moods, change as the maize plant changes; and the maize, in turn, changes with the alternating seasons, wet and dry. But some of the duties that the maize imposes, such as felling bush for new milpas, may be discharged at any time over a period of months, while others, like sowing and gathering the new corn, must be performed quickly and within a few days. These latter occasions, therefore, mark most sharply the rhythms of the communal life, because at these times the annual cycles of the activities of the individuals coincide with one another; the whole village acts together. When one man is felling bush another may be building a house, but when one man sows, most of the others sow also; and the gathering of the new ears takes place, for all milpas, within a period of a few days. The same unifying effect of common concerns appears in the contrast between the two chief critical periods in the agricultural year. These are the period just before the burning, when a man struggles in the conflict between two contrary impulses— to wait until the felled bush is thoroughly dry before firing it, or to fire it now before the rains come and make it impossible to fire it at all—and, second, the occasional periods of drought. The crisis in respect to burning must be faced separately by each agriculturalist, because different men fell bush at different times and different milpas dry differently. Therefore this is a problem to be met separately by each man, by means of individual prayers and offerings. But drought is a danger of another sort; it descends simultaneously and more or less equally upon all men; it threatens the security of everyone. Therefore it occasions the most important communal religious ceremony.

Sowing might similarly involve communal ceremonies, because the period of planting is so short, but for the facts that milpas are separately and individually sown and that they are situated at such distances from one another. When men plant, they all plant at the same time; but they are separated from one another and are busy with practical activities. The gathering of new corn, however, provides the opportunity for communal festivity. For eleven months the people have been living on dry corn. Then the milky ears ripen in all the milpas within a few days; this does not require the separate labors of each agriculturalist in his milpa as does sowing; it merely invites him to bring a few of the fresh ears to his house and there, with his neighbors (who tomorrow will return the courtesy) to enjoy, in security and relaxation and the company of his fellows, the flavor of the new corn.

[1] St. John's Day, August 24.

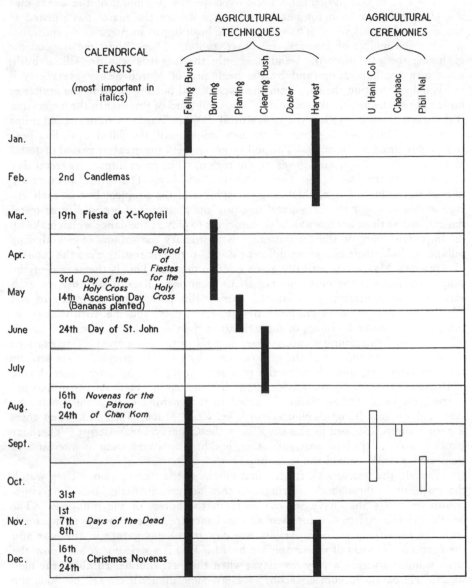

Fig. 8—Chart showing yearly round in Chan Kom.

The periods indicated for the seasonal agricultural activities are not average periods, but the extreme spans.
The dates given for the cha-chaac ceremony and for u hanli col are those when these ceremonies were actually performed during the period of observation. The cha-chaac can be performed at any time a drought threatens between seed time and harvest, and u hanli col at any time of year (but especially from July to October).

The end of one agricultural cycle overlaps the beginning of the next: men are already felling bush for next year's milpa before the maize has ripened in the milpa made this year. The felling of the bush begins in August and continues till after the middle of January (see chart, p. 83). Then "the time is good for gathering the ears of corn," [1] and it is only the laggards who are felling bush; most men are harvesting, and by the beginning of March nearly everybody is in his milpa, twisting the ears from their stalks and putting them in the granaries built right at the fields. By the middle or second third of this month the harvesting is done and there is a lull in the agricultural duties. The corn from the old milpa is in and nothing can be done on the new milpa until the felled bush has been thoroughly dried for burning. This lull coincides with the greatest period of festal activity in the villages and towns of the region. The most important festal day of the year is the Day of the Cross, the third of May. Then ritual prayers are offered to the Holy Cross, chief religious symbol of the people. But as each village wishes to honor the Cross, and to enjoy the pleasures of hospitality at festal dances, and as there are few available musicians to play at the dance which make up an important part of the festivities, it is customary for groups of neighboring villages to hold their fiestas on different days, so that it results that the months of April and May are practically given over to fiestas. This is the season of the year when there is the most moving about from one village to another, as each successive fiesta attracts its visitors. During this period the stringency of toil relaxes; many of the days are given over to festal play, and the work that is accomplished is house-building, or *fagina*, rather than agricultural labor.

Yet one agricultural concern does intrude into this period of relaxation: the matter of the burning of the milpas. One by one the agriculturalists perform this necessary act, guided as to the precise moment by the progressive drying of the felled trees or by the advice of the h-men (see p. 132). As the milpas are burned, the heat of these flames is added to the growing heat of the advancing year and the sky becomes clouded with smoke. "Muan, April 22d, when there is a ring around the sun in the sky," says the Chumayel manuscript. The heat grows in volume till it almost suffocates, building up a crescendo of interest and then anxiety. When will the rains begin?

Eagerly the people look for the first omens of the coming rain. They watch the bush, until through the drying branches flit certain little birds—the chuctzimin (p. 208)—that have set out to fetch the horses of the rain-gods. The people scan the eastern sky, for there all the chaacs are gathered, ready to ride forth with the fructifying waters. At last one day the clouds gather in the east and the first low thunders of the season are heard. This is a welcome sound; now the rains will come within a very few days; when this first thunder rumbles, the men shout, "He cutalo le yum chaacob!" ("Here come the lords chaac!"). Soon the gathering clouds sweep westward, spreading across the heavens; the chaacs are riding the sky and the first rains fall.

[1] Quoted from Roys' translation of the Chumayel manuscript: "The count of the uinals in one year. Yaax, Jan. 12. The time is good for gathering the ears of corn."

The first rainfall marks a sharp transition in the cadence of the year; the heat breaks or is at least refreshed with verdure and water-pool, and the men are released once more to activity. Within a few days all have departed to plant their milpas, and the village is drowsy and silent. The first rains come at the end of May or at the beginning of June. The successive events in the agricultural year take place earlier or later, depending on the time of arrival and on the volume of these rains. If, after the planting, the rains fall in abundance, the men are called once more into the fields to clear the weeds from the sprouting plants. By the middle of July the corn has grown clear of the second growth; there is another lull. The fields no longer demand practical attention, but they are more and more the objects of anxiety as the ears form and as the rains decrease. Now comes the danger of drought. In this pause, therefore, are apt to be performed the private agricultural ceremonies in propitiation of the gods that watch over the fields; the man who has let several years go by without offering to the gods the prayers and sacred breads of the "dinner of the milpa" ceremony, turns to the h-men for help as he sees the shallow water-holes going dry and the maize leaves turning yellow. And in this same period, if the drought is prolonged, is it likely that the rain (cha-chaac) ceremony is performed (p. 138), although it may be celebrated at any time between planting and harvest.

The fiesta of the patron saint of the village, San Diego, also falls in this period (on August 24), and the dignity and importance given to its celebration vary with the amount of ready money on hand and with the amount of concern felt for the safety of the crop.

By the end of August some men have already begun the felling of bush for future milpa, but the approaching event, once drought has been averted, is the ripening of the new ears. Late August and early September constitute a third period of agricultural idleness, but if the rains have kept up, or have fallen again, anxiety relaxes and it is a season of pleasurable anticipation. The milpas ripen in a sort of race; the man who first makes roasted ears for his neighbors feels a certain prideful exultation as he shares the succulent maize. The other milpas ripen immediately thereafter, and for a week or more almost nothing is done in the village, except as concerns the preparation of maize gruel and new roasted ears, the exchange of hospitality, the delightful gorging of sweet food, and the offering in a lighthearted and confident spirit of the first fruits of the milpa to the generous gods.

This is the climax of the year. Effort has resulted in successful accomplishment and thankful rejoicing has been expressed. Now the corn will stay safely where it is, except as the birds and the rodents, or occasional marauding cattle, take their toll. In October and November some men bend down (*doblar*) the maturing ears,[1] and immediately thereafter the harvest begins, to continue, in interrupted and desultory fashion, for several months. In these autumn and winter months there are other annual fiestas, of less importance than the celebration of the new corn, but still of individual and communal consequence. October 31

---

[1] "Teyaxkin, November 13, the corn stalks are bent double," says the Chumayel.

and November 1 are the Days of the Dead; for these two days, and for the two days a week later constituting the octave of the feast, people give themselves up to festivity, the women are busy preparing the food for the departed and the *maestros cantores* are occupied in the recitation of prayers. And again, on the nine nights preceding Christmas, there are prayers in many houses in honor of the Child God. These nights of prayer in November and December, Candlemas and the Day of the Holy Cross, are the days in the Catholic calendar which are observed in Chan Kom by the recitation of ritual prayer and the distribution of festal food. The calendar is frequently consulted and the Fridays in Lent are recognized, but observed only by a disposition on the part of some to leave their work and spend the day in hunting or in rest and conversation. Sundays are treated similarly; a man is more apt to go hunting on Sunday than on any other one day of the week, and it is common for men to put on their best clothes on Sunday and pass the day in talk and small relaxing occupations. But the same men will on other Sundays work in their milpas, and there appears to be no defined attitude with regard to the appropriateness of the day for rest or play.

Chapter VI

FAMILY, VILLAGE AND STATE

In reviewing kinship and the family as they exist in Chan Kom today there becomes apparent a sort of theoretical organization from which actual cases depart, sometimes very widely. This theoretical organization was more nearly true in fact a generation ago than it is today. It is made known to us from the statements of the older people as to what "ought to be" the situation, from the few conservative extended domestic families that exist in the village today and from the symbolism of the familial and marriage rituals.

In this theoretical system, every small parental family lies within two great families. Behind each spouse is the control and support of his or her kin. Marriages are arranged by the parents: the father and mother get their son a wife. The new husband becomes obligated to his parents-in-law. Until recent years marriage was by "haan-cab" ("work of the son-in-law"), the youth going to live with and to serve his prospective parents-in-law for a year, before receiving his bride. On the other hand, when the marriage is consummated, the new couple lives—in this theoretical system—with the parents of the husband and the wife becomes subject to the control and direction of her mother-in-law. Thus, in effect, every young married person is responsible and respectful to three pairs of older persons: his parents, his godparents and his parents-in-law. Older people direct younger persons and receive respect from them. Fathers control sons, older brothers control younger brothers. Women are always under the protection and subjection of a man: father, brother or husband. In every small family the husband gives orders to the wife; in every great family there is a responsible male head.

In actuality, however, this ideal organization is far from realized, although the familial attitudes involved in it are present in less systematic and consistent form. The settlement is one of pioneers, who have in many cases left their kinsmen behind them. This fact, the growing mobility, and other factors have brought it about that many parental families are complete within themselves, the spouses living with very little social connection with or dependence upon their kin. Haan-cab is no longer practiced and it is even exceptional for a young married man to bring his mother-in-law an occasional present of firewood. Many, perhaps most, young people begin married life in a separate home of their own. Although the subordination of women to men is general, there are marked individual variations with respect to the influence of parental ties beyond marriage. A realistic statement of the actual situation requires a consideration of particular cases.

FAMILY AND HOUSEHOLD

The small family in Chan Kom is much as it is with us, consisting of the mating couple and their children. Even where the great family organization is

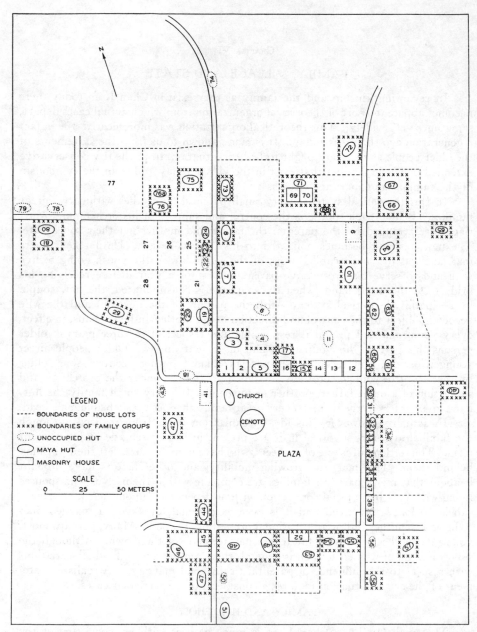

FIG. 9—Map showing housing of families.

significant, the ties that are emphasized are those between husband and wife. Both spouses enter into marriage fairly free from ties to the kinship groups in which they were brought up. The functioning social group is (with exception to be noted) the small parental ("biological") family; technical and moral instruction is transmitted within it; and there is no other institution, not even the school, that seriously competes with it in the discharge of these functions. The small parental family is in general the economic unit. The man produces the food and, together with his wife and children, consumes it.

In general, the household and the parental family coincide; the household contains a married couple and their children and in some cases unmarried relatives of the one spouse or the other, two-thirds of the Chan Kom households being of this sort. The other one-third provide exceptions: ten of them to the general statement made as to households, in that they contain more than one family; and two of them to the generalization with respect to the family, in that they house families of a notably different sort.

Of the ten multiple family households, three house the families of two married brothers. In one case a married brother and a married sister share a house. In four cases one or more married sons remain under the parental roof. In one case a married daughter and her husband live with her parents; in another a married uncle and his brother's married son share a house. In all these cases the households are composite, but the families are separate.[1] Each couple keeps its property separately, although each may contribute to a common table.

There are also two cases of polygynous families. These were recently formed in violation of custom. In both cases a single household is maintained. The two women share the domestic duties, and on trips to the milpa the husband takes along sometimes one woman and sometimes the other. In neither case are there children by the second wife, and the latter takes no part in the care of the children of the other. Her social position is distinctly subordinate. There has been no ceremony to sanction the second mating, and the theoretical morals of the people provide for monogamy only. In one case (and probably also in the other) the husband appears with the first wife on public occasions; if visitors come, he summons her and the second woman is ignored before outsiders, except members of the community and such associates as the writers of these pages.

The exceptions just stated affect the make-up of the household, but they leave the family in its prevailing form. The other and more important exception, already referred to (p. 56) arises from the existence of two extended domestic families. One of these has been undergoing dissolution during the period of observations; the other remains a completely functioning institution. This latter consists of a man, his wife, seven unmarried children, three married sons and the wives and children of these last. These nineteen persons constitute one intimate household and a single social-economic group. The father and his sons,

[1] With the possible qualification introduced on the following page.

married and single, work together in clearing, sowing and harvesting an undivided milpa, and no individual lands or crops are recognized. When more corn is
needed for tortillas, one of the men fetches it from the milpa; in the evening all
members of the group help in shelling it, when it is placed in a single basket. All
of the women of the group prepare the meals together and all eat together. The
cattle are owned collectively also.

The parental couple direct and control this familial commune.[1] The father
decides what agricultural tasks are to be performed; and he must be consulted before any crops or cattle are sold. His wife allocates the domestic duties among her
daughters-in-law—this one to grind, that one to make tortillas. All of the domestic
work of the sort stipulated is done by the girl indicated, with one limitation: the
girl who does the washing, although she washes the clothes of the other women
and of the children, does not wash the clothes of the other women's husbands;
this each wife does for her husband. The family funds are kept by the older
woman; the sons or their wives ask her for small sums for personal purposes, and
she knows if the need really exists and acts accordingly.

The other extended domestic family is similar, except that it is an older
man's married nephews (sons of his deceased brother) who live with him and his
unmarried children. This man's present wife is the mother of only one of the
children in the house. Her authority does not appear to be as great as that of
the older woman in the former family, but the uncle's control over his married
nephews is great and the family properties were long maintained undivided.
However, this family has been recently breaking-up; two of the married nephews
have set up independent family households. To do this they were helped by their
uncle, who aided them in building their houses. They are still very intimate
with him, and the group of nephews, cousins and uncle-father still help one another
in their various tasks.

Varying degrees of parental control are exerted over the married sons in the
multiple family households mentioned in a previous paragraph. Indeed, some of

[1] The expansion of the house-group in response to the development of the extended domestic family is illustrated by the history of
house-building in this family (fig. 10). The patriarch arrived in Chan Kom in 1906. He then built a house of poles and thatch (No. 1)
which served both as sleeping-room and as kitchen. When the streets were laid out he built another thatched house (No. 2) along the street,
and shortly afterward a separate cook-house (No. 3). By this time he had a number of children, some of whom slept in the cook-house.
In 1928, by which time he had nine children, two of whom were married, he built a masonry house (No. 4) on the corner and then a new
and better kitchen (No. 5). Accustomed to the thatched houses, the family continued to sleep in these, part in No. 2 and part in No. 5—
for No. 3 was abandoned—and an addition (No. 6), to house the grinding apparatus, was made to the new kitchen (No. 5). Now the older
couple and their unmarried children sleep in No. 2. Another masonry room (No. 7) is being built, and these individuals plan to move there.
In No. 4 sleep the two oldest married sons and their wives; the youngest, for the present, sleeps in the kitchen.

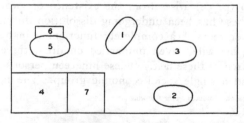

Fig. 10—House group of extended domestic family

these households, where separate kitchens are maintained, but the families sleep under a single roof, appear to illustrate other stages in the break-up of extended domestic families.

It is probable that the extended domestic family was once more common and is now yielding to the small parental family in response to technical and economic changes. It is noteworthy that the two men who maintain these large families are the two most prominent of the older men in the village, pioneers in the founding of the community and distinguished by wealth, property and moral character. The composition of the households is summarized in table 6:

TABLE 6—*Composition of households*

Single family households:	
Couple (with or without children)..................	24
Couple; mother of man living with them...........	2
Couple; man's paternal aunt living with them......	1
Couple; man's unmarried sister living with them.....	1●
Couple; and secondary wife......................	2
Widow with unmarried children..................	3
Total...........................	33
Multiple family households (each family a separate economic unit):	
Two married brothers living together..............	3
Married brother and married sister................	1
Couple living with husband's parents..............	4
Couple living with wife's parents.................	1
Couple living with man's paternal uncle and wife.....	1
Total...........................	10
Extended domestic families (more than one couple constituting a single economic and social unit):	
Man and married sons.........................	1
Man and married nephews (brother's sons).........	1
Total...........................	2
Average number of persons per small parental family.....	5.1
Average number of persons per household..............	5.6

KINSHIP AND THE GREAT FAMILY

There are great differences among married individuals as to the extent to which they feel themselves bound to kinsmen who are not members of the small family household. In some cases, married sons and daughters go hardly any oftener into the houses of their parents than they go into the houses of their other neighbors; and many parents, who live in Chan Kom near their married children, pay small attention to them. But in some cases children have built their houses on the same house-lots with their parents, the familial ties persist after marriage, and the great family maintains some cohesiveness. Such a group, in fact, is only less of a social unit than the two extended domestic families. The fact that estates are usually kept intact until the death of the surviving parent (p. 62) helps to preserve the control of widows and widowers over married children. But some small parental families in Chan Kom have no relatives in the village, and many others act as if they had not.

Two principal great-family groups are, indeed, recognizable in the village. One of these is composed of one of the extended domestic families and the patriarch's other married relatives who maintain separate small families. Thirteen of the forty-five households in Chan Kom consist of a brother, sister, son, daughter, niece, nephew or grandnephew of this man. When he gives a domestic feast or ceremony, many of these kinsmen with their spouses come to his house. When disputes occur in the village, involving a member of this great family, there is a disposition for its members to stand together, especially in opposition to the other functioning great family. This latter is composed of three married brothers and their widowed mother, and the married son of one brother, all forming four small families living in adjacent houses. The older people in these two great families were among the pioneers in Chan Kom and are persons of consequence in the village. A third surname is borne by kinsmen in ten small families, but these relatives have little or no cohesiveness and are humbler folk.

The essentially bilateral character of kinship is evidenced by the facts that in family gatherings and deliberations it is as much a person's mother's relatives as it is his father's who participate, and that any first cousin, no matter how related to a man, is regarded as an unsuitable wife, while more distant relatives of all sorts are eligible. Nevertheless, the transmission of the surname from father to children does put some emphasis on this tie, particularly as marriage does not affect a woman's possession of her father's name. The great-families manifesting group-consciousness are composed of individuals with the same surname. Moreover, there is disposition to emphasize the inter-family bonds between males, rather than females, and the man is the head of the family. There are no great family groups based on an association of married sisters, and no extended family including an older couple and the married sons of the wife, or her married nephews— and such groups are hardly conceivable in Chan Kom. Furthermore, unattached females go to live with a married son or brother, not with a female relative. A man may be expected to support his own adult unmarried female relatives, but not his wife's. A young couple, if they do not set up an independent household, go to live with the bridegroom's parents. This patrilocal tendency is manifest in half a dozen cases, and the feeling certainly is that this is proper and to be expected. The only case of residence with the wife's parents is that of the illegitimate son of a man now dead; the newly married couple had no property and were given the only shelter available, with the girl's parents. There is also a case where a man of property has partitioned his large house-lot for the benefit of his married daughters; but these, though living near him, maintain separate households with their husbands.

The essential fact is the feeling that of every group of kin, whether small family or great, there should be a male head. A man is responsible for his kinsmen, especially if they be close to him in blood, female, unmarried and younger than he. Women and children are under the control and protection of an older man. Widows are expected to re-marry, unless advanced in years.

KINSHIP TERMS

The terms in use in Chan Kom today are the following:

1. *mama.* Mother.
2. *tata.* Father.

These terms are also used, with awareness that the use is extended, by both men and women, to mother- and father-in-law, respectively, in cases where there is considerable intimacy and mutual regard between the parents-in-law and their children-in-law.

3. *hijo.* Son.
4. *hija.* Daughter.

Although these terms are known, and occasionally used, the term "pal" is much more frequently used by a parent to refer to or to address his child. The term means, however, "boy" (or girl) and is also widely used for any boy or girl.

5. coolel⎫ Two equivalent terms, of which the former is more common, for either
6. chich ⎬ maternal or paternal grandmother.
7. ca coolel. Great-grandmother (any).
8. *señor.* Grandfather, either paternal or maternal.
9. ca *señor.* Great-grandfather (any).
10. abil (uabil). Grandchild (of either sex and through either line).
11. ca uabil. Great-grandchild (any).
12. mahan *tata* ("substitute father"). Stepfather.
13. mahan *mama.* Stepmother.

But the terms *padrastro* and *madrastra* are in wide use too. For stepson and stepdaughter *ahijado* and *ahijada* are used. One case is given of the use of the term mahan lak ("substitute brother") for a man's mother's first husband's son.

The parent and child terms, as well as all the other terms for relatives by consanguinity, are used for both full-blood and half-blood relationships.

14. lak. Brother or sister, either older or younger. Not often used.
15. zucuun. Older brother.

The term is also very commonly used for a wife's brother, older than the speaker (and probably older than the wife); for a husband's brother, older than the speaker (and older than the husband); for the son of any aunt or uncle, older than the speaker; and for the sister's husband, older than the speaker. There is also one case where the term was applied to a wife's father's brother's son.

16. idzin (uidzin). Younger brother and younger sister.

The term is also very commonly used for one's younger brother's wife (at least where younger than speaker—and all cases available are of this sort). But it is not applied to the wife of an older brother, even if she is younger than the speaker. It is also applied to a younger sister's husband, at least where he is younger than the speaker.

17. cic. Older sister.

The term is also applied to husband's older sister; to wife's older sister (where older than speaker), to an older brother's wife (where she is older than speaker), and to a wife's older brother's wife (where she is older than speaker).

18. *tio.* Father's brother, mother's brother, father's sister's husband, and mother's sister's husband.
19. *tia.* Father's sister, mother's sister, mother's brother's wife, and father's brother's wife.
20. *sobrino.* Brother's son, sister's son, husband's brother's son, wife's brother's son, husband's sister's son, wife's sister's son.

21. *sobrina.* Brother's daughter, sister's daughter, husband's brother's daughter, wife's brother's daughter, husband's sister's daughter, wife's sister's daughter.
22. atan (uatan). Wife.
    But much more commonly a man refers to his wife as "in *familia.*"
23. icham (uicham). Husband.
    The word is not often used by a wife in speaking of her husband. She generally says simply "leti" ("that one").
24. *suegro.* Used for husband's or wife's father, in cases where "tata" is not used.
25. *suegra.* Used for husband's or wife's mother, in cases where "mama" is not used.
26. haan. Daughter's husband.
27. ilib (uilib). Son's wife.
28. *cuñado.* Wife's brother, in cases where zucuun is not used; sister's husband, in cases where zucuun is not used.
29. *cuñada.* Recognized as an alternate term for brother's wife. But where such is younger than speaker, uidzin is ordinarily used; where she is older, cic. Also: husband's younger sister, younger than speaker. Where she is older, cic is used.

A teknonymic form of address ("tata-Bina," for the father of a girl named Bina; "mama-As," for the mother of Asunción, etc.) is used, of both men and women, not in speaking directly to the person so designated, but in referring to him in speaking with others, when the speaker wishes to refer to him with some degree of respect. It is not used between spouses in addressing one another. The oldest child still living with the parent referred to lends his or her name to the term.[1]

OLDER BROTHERS

The terms zucuun, idzin and cic have their equivalents in Spanish discourse in the terms *hermano, hermanito, hermana* and *hermanita* (except that the Maya term idzin includes younger siblings of either sex); and the Spanish terms, when used by persons speaking that language, are often used in the extended meanings indicated above for the Maya terms. The use of these terms expresses the importance of age-distinctions within the same generation, especially as between actual brothers. Among actual brothers the terms zucuun and idzin are exactly complementary: one whom I call zucuun always calls me idzin, and vice versa. The brothers constitute a series, according to order of birth, down to the youngest (thup), and each owes a certain amount of respect and obedience to those older than he. The extended use of the term zucuun for older brothers-in-law and for older cousins expresses a diminished form of the same respect relationship. But the term is used only for those cousins who are distinctly older than the speaker. Cousins of approximately the same age address one another by personal names. Some of these would explain that the other was his *primo*, although this last term is not in common use. Zucuun (or *hermano*) is therefore a term indicating respect toward an older male relative of the same generation as one's self.[2] Thus in one case where there were close personal ties, a younger man used the term for his wife's father's brother's son.

[1] Thus for example, there are frequent cases of the use of this teknonymous term by women in speaking of their husband's sister's husbands.

[2] As *tio* is used for many older persons of the paternal generation, or of older persons unrelated to the speaker.

The complementary term, idzin, is not used as generally in the extended senses. That is, while among brothers, one whom I call zucuun always calls me idzin, among cousins one called zucuun does not call the other idzin. Nevertheless, there is a disposition to make the age-distinction in speaking to or of younger male cousins. One man, speaking Spanish, referred to male cousins and to his paternal uncle's son-in-law, all younger than himself, as "*sobrinos*." (These men all called him "zucuun.") After reflection, he said they were not "*sobrinos*," but "*primos*." If these men had been older than he, he would not have used the word "*sobrino*" in speaking of them.

The age distinction is not so important among women, and the term cic is not commonly used for older female cousins or by a man for his older female cousins. But the term is used for older sisters-in-law.

With reference primarily to the actual brother, and only in a diminished significance with respect to cousins, a man owes to his zucuun respect and obedience. "When an idzin asks you to do something, it is a favor asked; when a zucuun asks it, it is an order." If a serious matter arises, a man will go to his father or to his uncle; for lesser matters, or if the older people are not available, he will go to his zucuun. Thus, to cite only one example, when two young men of the village were in doubt whether or not to believe missionary teaching that dancing was wrong, they went for advice, in the absence of older brothers, to their oldest male cousin (whom they called zucuun).

The zucuun (blood brothers) share in the control exerted over a woman by her parents. They often participate, with the parents, in the conferences which deal with the question as to whether a suit for the hand of the younger sister should be entertained. But the younger brothers do not participate. After the marriage is arranged, there is often an expectation that the zucuun give clothes to their sister. The zucuun similarly stand ready to support their younger sister in connection with marital difficulties. Thus, when a man left his wife and ran off with a younger woman, the wife's older brothers (her father being dead) called upon the older male relatives of the husband to take steps to bring back or punish the delinquent.

MARRIAGE: CHOICE OF SPOUSE

Marriage is the state expected by and of all adults, and in fact almost all adults are married. In 1930, of 110 persons 18 years of age or over, 8 were not married. 4 were elderly widows, 1 was a boy soon to be married, 1 was a girl not long divorced, 1 was a lame girl of 18 whose infirmity made her an undesirable wife, and the last was a woman of 60. The case of this woman, the only really unmarried person in Chan Kom, is explained by her homosexual disposition.

Both sexes marry soon after puberty. The average age at marriage of 25 women was 14.9 years; 4 married at 13, 8 at 14, 8 at 15, 2 at 16, and 1 each at 18, 19, and 20. The average age of 23 mothers at the birth of the first child was 16 years. The average age at marriage of 16 men was 17.4 years; 7 married at 16, and only 1 at more than 20.

Marriage is an arrangement between two pairs of parents providing for the adult life of their children. The initiative is taken by the boy's parents. In selecting his wife, they look for a young, healthy and industrious girl. Girls with light complexion are more sought after than those with dark, but considerations of health are much more important than those of beauty. Very fat girls are not desirable; they are thought to age rapidly. But thin ones are less recommended, because these do not give promise of health. Parents in selecting a wife for their son are attentive to the vigor of the candidate's older married sisters, especially during periods of lactation; for it is concluded that the younger sister will respond similarly to the demands of motherhood. "It would be a great waste of money to marry my son to Ana, because her sister always gets thin when she is nursing a child."

If the girl's family are well-to-do, so much the better. Stories as to the girl's premarital sexual experiences receive attention; virginity is not necessarily demanded, but if gossip insists loudly as to a girl's early intercourse, she is not, to the negotiating parents, a desirable wife for their son. Still, this can be overlooked. But a premarital pregnancy is more serious; it is doubtful if a young man, marrying for the first time, would take a wife bringing with her the child of a previous casual union.[1]

The only restriction on choice of spouse based on kinship is the feeling that relatives as near or nearer than first cousins (no matter through what line related) should not marry. One case of cousin marriage occurred within recent years in Chan Kom, when the son and daughter of two brothers were married. The couple were soon separated, although other reasons than the kinship bar were given for the separation. On the other hand, in speaking of the unsuitability of cousin marriages, people refer to the unfortunate outcome of this instance. Sentiment is certainly against such marriages. Indeed, the *casamentero* had to overcome objection in bringing about an agreement to marry between a man and the daughter of his paternal uncle's son. There appears to be no objection to marriage between unrelated persons of the same surname and several such cases are reported.

Among the recorded marriages there are four cases of consecutive marriage to two sisters. In one of these cases a brother of the husband was married to a third sister. No feeling that such second marriages are especially suitable appears to exist. On the other hand, there is no feeling that they are less propitious than any other kind of marriage, in spite of the fact that it is said that men who have had sexual intercourse with or have married their wife's sisters meet with unhappy fates. One story is that the souls of such men become the little whirlwinds that send the dust rotating, and another is that the death agonies of these men are fearful and end only when someone draws a bucketful of water from the cenote into which their souls must pass on their way to hell (metnal). But when, just after these stories were told, it was pointed out that men present had married their deceased wife's sisters, there was only merriment and no embarrassment. The stories sanction no attitude or custom.

[1] P. 97.

Whether a man's wife is taken from his own village or from another depends simply on where he and his parents happen to find a suitable girl. Two-thirds of the marriages of the old people, entered into before the settling of Chan Kom, were inter-village marriages. Of 9 boys who have grown up in Chan Kom and married, 5 found their wives in neighboring settlements and 4 in Chan Kom.

Relationships between the sexes are not in the least romantically conceived. There are no obvious conventional patterns of courtship, and many marriages take place without any courtship whatsoever. There are no lovesongs, no serenades, and no love stories. Caresses, either in word or act, between husband and wife are not to be observed. Extra-marital relationships are either occasional, clandestine and carried on without the connivance of third parties; or else they result in more permanent attachments amounting to a new assortment of partners. Married men do not also have mistresses. A man has a woman—or, in the two exceptional cases, he has two—and this woman is his wife because she lives with him and serves him, and also because, in many cases, she has been formally married to him. Mutual economic support is the essence of the relationship; in addition each spouse gives the other varying degrees of advice and sympathy; and he expects sexual fidelity of her; she does not expect it quite so much of him. He provides her with food and other necessaries and she cooks and washes for him. To live with a man, to make his tortillas and to wash his clothes is very nearly a definition of marriage. Certainly, a woman who would refuse to do these things when living with a man would be far more immoral than a woman who would do these things for a man without going through any marriage ceremony.

DIVORCE AND DESERTION

The small family is a very stable group. Among marriages observed, there is no case of a separation of a couple having young children. Still, such cases are not unheard of. Adultery, though a grave matter, does not often result in breaking the marriage. A man will give his adulterous wife a thorough beating and endeavor to bring about the punishment of the man; but he is not likely to leave his wife if there are children of him. If a man commits adultery, but continues to live with his wife and treat her well, public opinion does not justify her in breaking the marriage; if she leaves him, she loses her rights in the marital property (p. 62). Three cases of marital separation occurred during the period of observation. In one case a young woman gave birth to another man's child five months after marriage; the husband secured a divorce and remarried; public opinion thought him entirely right. The girl did not remarry and, after living for a time with her mother, found escape from immediate obloquy by leaving the village and getting employment as a house servant in a nearby town. In the second instance, the wife left her husband soon after marriage for no apparent reason. Later she went off with a married man of another village as his mistress; thereupon the husband took steps to get a divorce. The third case was of an older couple; both had been married before and the children were all grown. The woman left the man, who straightway set about finding a substitute. Desertion is a woman's remedy; a man will beat his wife, or complain to her parents, but rarely desert her. Divorce, in conformity with statutory law, is a novelty; so far as it is used, it is a man's remedy; no woman is likely to take the initiative. In the cases where it was employed, the motive was probably to prevent the wife from making claims upon the divorcing husband. Second marriages without ceremony are so generally accepted as to make divorce, in order to remarry, not necessary.

GODPARENTS AND COMPADRES

Quite as important as the respect relationships established connubially, are those called into being by the institution of godparenthood. By this institution, also, those of the older generation fix for those of the younger their personal ties and kinship obligations. In selecting a wife for their son, an older couple in effect select also his parents-in-law. But this is merely the third of such acts by the parents. Shortly after the birth of the child, they select his baptismal godparents, and within the first year of his life, through the custom of hetzmek (p. 188), they establish for him another set of relationships with another adult couple, or a single individual. (By this custom the child is placed for the first time astride the hip in the position in which he will be carried until he runs about by himself, following a ritual performed by another set of godparents called upon for the purpose.) The baptismal godparents are much more important than those of the hetzmek, but these latter are also of consequence in the subsequent life of the individual. And finally special sponsors are selected to superintend the marriage and wedding; and with these sponsors also the young person establishes relations of respect, regard, and some dependence.[1]

The establishment of the godparental relationship—whether of baptism, of hetzmek, or of marriage—involves necessarily the establishment of a reciprocal relationship of respect and intimacy between the godparents and the parents of the child. This relationship is signalized by the use of the terms *compadre* or *comadre*[2] between any one parent and any one godparent. The relationship is one of respect on both sides, but it is not symmetrical, for the parent is more respectful of his son's godparent than the latter is of him. "My son treats his godparent like another father. And I treat my *compadre* like a father. Whatever he says, I do not deny. Maybe I do not like what he says, but I do not discuss it. I must treat him with much respect. It is not the same with him; he may differ with what I say." The godparent has conferred a favor upon the parents by assuming the sponsorship of the child in one of these various periods of crisis and transition, and the debt of obligation therefore runs to him from the parent and not the other way. This is expressed in the rituals (described in Chapter XI) in which the godparent is asked to assume the responsibility, or in which he is thanked for having

[1] In Maya discourse, the godparents of the baptism are called uah-mekul ("bread-carriers"). Some of the old people call the godparents of the hetzmek "hetzul," but most say simply "*padrino*," even in Maya discourse, as they do also referring to the sponsors of the marriage.
[2] In Maya discourse, "cumpal" and "cumal."

assumed it. It is the parent who petitions, who brings gifts, who kneels in respect and gratitude.

The *compadre* relationship brings into intimacy and special mutual regard older persons who may not be kin to one another. In many cases the relation of regard and intimacy comes first; then one naturally asks the other to act as godparent of his child, and the personal relationship now conforms to a pattern provided by the culture. The term "compadre" is sometimes used in an extended sense between older men who feel themselves close to one another, and yet have never actually been bound through a baptism, a hetzmek, or a wedding. On the other hand, it is common for a man to ask his father or older brother to act as godparent of his child, and in such cases the ordinary kinship terms are not abandoned for the term "compadre"—the man is first a father or brother, and then only the godparent of one's child. The use of the term announces and reaffirms the special relationship between two persons who would otherwise be at some distance from one another. If a man sees, talks and works beside his *compadre* every day, it is not natural to him constantly to address the other as "compadre." But if he meets his *compadre* only now and then, the term is naturally brought into use.

The sponsors of the baptism, both as godparents and as *compadres*, are much more important than those of the hetzmek and those of the marriage; those of the marriage have only very limited functions and importance. The baptismal godparent "should be someone who is good, and wise, and who knows how to teach and to advise." Naturally, such a person is rarely younger than the parents themselves. But if a person outside of the community is selected, as occasionally happens, youth may be outweighed by prestige, education, or reputation for wisdom. It is very common for parents to ask either pair of their own parents to act as baptismal godparents for a first or second child. The old people say that only if one is *compadre* with one's father and mother will one meet with them in heaven (*Gloria*). Ordinarily a child has both godfather and godmother; but as a person of the same sex as the child must carry him to the baptismal font, every boy must at the least have a godfather and every girl a godmother. In most cases a couple living as husband and wife are selected.

The godparent is responsible for his godchild. If the parents die or can not care for their child, the godparent will care for it. When the parents are alive, they will on occasion consult with the godparents concerning the child's welfare. If the child behaves badly, they will bring their concern to the godfather. "Here is your godchild; he is behaving badly; please punish him." The godparents commonly participate in the marriage negotiations. When the parents of a boy are seeking a wife for him, or listening to his suggestions as to a likely candidate, they will ordinarily go to the boy's godparents for advice. On the other hand, the parents of a girl whose hand has just been asked in marriage, will send word to the girl's godparents about the matter. It is usual for parents, about to carry gifts to a girl's house in petition of marriage, to ask the boy's godparents to accompany them; while the parents of a girl asked in marriage will ask her godparents to be present at the subsequent meeting of the two family groups. When the marriage takes place, the girl's baptismal godmother often gives her godchild clothes. The baptismal godparents participate in the wedding ritual that takes place after the church service; all four, if available, sit next the parents and receive the bridal party as it comes from the church; after the four parents and the two sponsors of the marriage, they receive the salutations of respect (p. 195).

On his part, the young person owes all respect to his godparent. He takes off his hat when he meets him and treats him with marked courtesy. If he has success in the hunt, he is expected to give some of the meat to his *padrino*. He listens to his advice and defers to his judgment.

The attitudes existing between a young person and his godparents of the hetzmek and those between these godparents and the parents are similar in quality to those just described for the baptismal godparents, but are much less in degree. The terms *"padrino"* and *"compadre"* are similarly used, and there is the same asymmetrical respect relationship between child and godparent and between parent and godparent. The relationship is also a serious one, and a man selects as the sponsors of the hetzmek older persons whom he respects and admires. One does not ask the first person at hand to make hetzmek, and one does not make the request casually. Not uncommonly a man may walk many miles to ask another to make hetzmek for his child, and then it is an important message that he has to deliver, and one sometimes accompanied by gifts of food. Still, the asking is not so ritualized as it is for the baptismal sponsors; there is no subsequent ceremony of acknowledgment, corresponding with the tzicil (p. 187) and these godparents have no part in the wedding ritual. The godparents of the hetzmek are not often called upon to guide or advise their godchild. Still, that possibility is always recognized, and there are cases where, parents and baptismal parents failing, the godparents of the hetzmek assumed active responsibility.

The responsibility of the *padrinos* of the wedding begins and largely ends with the marriage. As soon as the betrothal is effected the bride is supposed to be under the supervision of the woman sponsor of the marriage and the boy under that of the man. Each guardian must see that his charge can repeat correctly certain prayers. The two sponsors accompany the couple to the church, deliver solemn charges to them as to their marital responsibilities, in the presence of their families, and escort them to their new home (p. 198). After the marriage they may be called upon to compose discord between husband and wife. Thus, if the young husband is not treating his wife properly, the girl's father may call upon either the boy's father or upon the godfather of the marriage to intervene. For example, in a case of temporary abandonment that took place fifteen years after the marriage, the older male relatives of the wife called into conference the husband's older male relatives and also the male sponsor of the marriage.

STATUS

Differences in status between individuals are considerable. At public gatherings there is never any question as to who is to take the lead and assume the positions of prominence; the leaders take the center of the stage and make the arrangements, and the lowly and the inconsequential fill in the background. There are perhaps a dozen men who, it is recognized, are qualified to fill the important offices; the others are out of the question. It is, in large part, the personal qualities of character and leadership that make a man looked up to by his fellows. Wealth is connected with these qualities also; to own cattle, to have a fine house and a wife who wears several heavy gold chains is to be admired. A third important factor in determining status is the possession of knowledge enabling one to deal with the outside world: the ability to speak and to read Spanish, familiarity with the town and understanding of how to deal with officials in the city. The city person, in Chan Kom, especially the American, enjoys prestige, and some of that prestige extends to those of Chan Kom who can talk with such outsiders and interpret them to the other villagers. Yet a man may stand very high without such ability, if he has been a local leader and led a life of virtue.

Nevertheless the vertical dimension in social life is not emphasized, and such differences in status as do exist lie simply between one person and another. There are no social classes. The differences in participation outside of the folk culture of the villages are still very small; there are no terms to describe such differences in sophistication within the community and no differences in costume or occupation that might symbolize such differences in status. Furthermore, differences in status are not conferred by birth; some families are more powerful than others because the individuals separately enjoy status and because they cooperate with one another; but social superiority is not conferred by one surname rather than another. Nor are any prerogatives transmitted by inheritance or succession, except insofar as an occasional male line is noted for its h-mens—and there are no such lines in Chan Kom itself.

RACES AND CLASSES

The people of Chan Kom regard their community as racially and socially homogeneous. But they find themselves in a world in which there are racial distinctions and in which those distinctions correspond with differences in social status. The distinction is fundamentally that between Indian and White. The native calls his own Indian group *indios* or *maya*, or *"mazehua"*; he calls the White man "dzul"; the White woman, "xunan." But as in fact the people of the towns, and even of the villages in the neighborhood of Chan Kom, are obviously much mixed in blood, account must be taken of this mixture. Anyone with a Maya surname, at least so long as he lives in the village the life of the village, is one of "us"—an *indio*. Persons who live the village life, but bear Spanish surnames (such as are found in many of the neighboring villages and small towns) are "kaz dzul" ("half dzul"); they are not "genuine Indians." Such people, and townsmen with Spanish names, are also called *mestizos* and, less often, *vecinos*. But if such townsmen do not wear the folk costume, but go shod with shoes, especially if they are notably light in skin color, they will be spoken of, not as *mestizos*, but as "genuine dzules."

The term "dzul" is one implying respect. It recognizes the social superiority of Spanish name, white skin color and education. A man may be a "genuine dzul," even though his skin be dark, provided he lives the life of the city and is well educated and authoritative. "The teacher at Noh-chen is not a real xunan, because she was brought up in a little village, and she does not speak Spanish the way the *maestro* does." The city, the Spanish language and the white skin are accorded prestige.

There is, probably, a slight disposition to mix the superiority accorded the "kaz-dzul" with a modicum of contempt: he is neither the one thing nor the other. But the "genuine" dzul is a really superior and admirable creature—especially if he be blonde. Blonde men and women are admired; babies with light skins are preferred. There exists, among the older people, a myth of a blonde race, mystically kin to the Indian, for whose coming the Indian waits (p. 331).

LOCAL GOVERNMENT: THE COMISARIO

The formal government of the village represents an adjustment between traditional notions of political organization and leadership on the one hand and the provisions of recent Mexican and Yucatecan statutory law on the other. Within the uncertain limits of political authority, as defined by this compromise, there is room for much variation from time to time, depending on the personalities of the leaders who assume political office.

Before the Revolution of 1910–21, the government of the Indian villages was without statutory sanction. The villages had their traditional officers, exercising traditional authority. A local chief (batab, or tetich) led the village, with the advice of the older men, and served for life. So, when Chan Kom was still a *rancherìa* belonging to Ebtun, one man, known as the tetich, was arbiter of the settlement. He was (and is) a respected person, and all disputes were brought to him for settlement. Later a guard of two persons, a *Comandante* and a *Policía*, was created to execute orders of the tetich.

The Mexican constitution adopted in 1917 included, as one of its reforms, provisions for the creation of the "free municipality"—a rural village with its own statutorily recognized government, independent of the political domination of the State. In accordance with this provision Yucatan in 1921 adopted an organic law for the municipalities of the State,[1] and soon thereafter the authorities of the revolutionary state government set about putting its provisions into effect in the villages. But the provisions of this law are long and complicated, and some are impossible of execution in the small, poor villages; and certainly no one in Chan Kom ever read the law. Therefore, though the present government of Chan Kom in its essential outward form corresponds with the statutory provisions, in many details it does not;[2] and the *comisario*, head of the municipal government, exercises many powers not granted him by law, but vested in him by folk tradition, or simply asserted by virtue of his personal qualities of leadership.

Once a year, at some time in the Fall that is convenient to the men, all the adult males meet together and elect a *comisario* to take office on the following first

[1] "Ley orgánica de los municipios del Estado de Yucatán (con sus reformas y adiciónes)", Decreto Nùmero 368, Lic. Manuel Berzunza, Gobernador Interino (decree of the 26th Constitutional Congress of the State, December 1921).

[2] For example, the *comisario* is not appointed by the *ayuntamiento* but is elected and he receives no pay.

day of January. The meeting is informal; the old *comisario* presides; there may be some discussion, but generally it is by that time pretty well understood who ought to serve for the next year, and a conclusion is reached without any vote. At the same time a *suplente* is chosen, whom the *comisario* may call upon to help him in discharging his public duties and who will serve if mischance should befall the *comisario*. The *comisario*-elect makes a list (for this he may need assistance) of all the adult men who have not served as *comisario* or as president of the *Liga* (such are exempt). These men he groups into fours, placing in each four one older and more experienced man, known as *sargento*. These fours serve in rotation as *policía*, performing all the necessary current public tasks (see p. 78). They execute the orders of the *comisario*.

The *comisario* is not the old batab, whose wisdom and authority were made manifest for many years, but a new sort of officer, serving for one year only. His acts are shaped largely by the incumbent's personal ideas and temperamental idiosyncrasies, limited by public opinion. When matters of serious consequence are to be decided, involving public policy (as when the question was raised as to what should be done with the proceeds of a house sold by a man withdrawing from the village), the *comisario* calls a meeting of the *sargentos* and ex-*comisarios*. This brings together for deliberation all the older and more experienced men. On the other occasions, when the *comisario* wishes to announce decisions or to influence public attitude and sentiment, he calls general public meetings, which all the men in the village attend.

In Chan Kom, where public opinion is fairly well united and where the recent *comisarios* have been men of character, the *comisario* exercises whatever authority, affecting whatever matters, he and the village generally think proper. In many other villages the *comisario* merely discharges small police powers, represents the village in municipal meetings,[1] and transmits any real problem to the statutorily constituted authorities in the towns. But in Chan Kom, partly due to the social solidarity of the village and partly to the effective persistence of traditional authority from the days of the batabs, the *comisario* tends to be the leader of the village and arbiter of personal disputes. He decrees reforms and organizes the people to accomplish these. He represents his village in the government of the *municipio*. He extends the hospitality of the village; commonly before a fiesta to be held in Chan Kom, the *comisario* will go about among the neighboring settlements inviting the people to attend. Within the village he is a paternalistic judge. He lectures gossips, attempts to compose disputes, decrees the amount of and sees to the enforcement of punishment for adultery, for wife-beating (without reasonable cause), or for disorderly conduct, and imposes damages to be paid by the owner of destructive animals. Especially does he see that *fagina* (p. 78) is fulfilled; and failures to perform this public duty he punishes with imprisonment or additional toil. But in all these matters, the extent of authority exercised, and the success of its exercise, vary greatly with the personality of the *comisario*.

---

[1] The *municipio* is a group of geographically separate settlements organized in a single government centered in one of them (*cabeçera*).

STATE AND NATIONAL GOVERNMENT: LIGA AND AGRARIAN COMMITTEE

The authority of the *comisario*, although extending to the punishment of crimes that take place within the village and to the fixing of damages in compensation for private wrongs, does not mark the limits of justice and government in Chan Kom. The assertion of legal right may always be pushed beyond his authority into that of the municipal, state and national governments of which, as everyone is perfectly aware, Chan Kom is a part. Simple matters are settled by the *comisario*, but if a conflict or crisis rises to a certain level of gravity, one begins to hear people say that "the affair will have to be passed on to the authorities." *"Las autoridades"* are those representatives of the outside government that reside in the larger villages, in the towns, and in the city. In Kaua is the office of the Civil Registry, where marrying couples must go for the civil ceremony, where parents file birth certificates in order that they may present a copy to the priest when he is asked to baptize the child, and where the *comisario* files the records of deaths and changes of domicile. Cuncunul is the seat of the municipal government to which Chan Kom belongs, and Valladolid is the *cabecera* of the whole *partido*[1] of that name. Here in Valladolid are held occasional meetings of the *comisarios* of the dependent villages; for this purpose the *comisario* of Chan Kom must occasionally present himself there. Furthermore, the Cuncunul and the Valladolid authorities constitute courts of appeal for persons penalized or held civilly liable by the Chan Kom *comisario*. If such a person refuses to pay the fine or the damage which the *comisario* decrees, the latter may enforce his decision by imprisonment or sequestration of property; but recalcitrants may send word to the Cuncunul and Valladolid authorities and ask them to interfere. Such interferences are particularly likely to take place when the conflict is not merely between an individual and the village authorities, but between one village and another (or—though this happens not to have occurred recently in Chan Kom— between one faction and another in the same village). Thus, for example, in 1931, when the imposition of extra *fagina* for the new school fell heavily upon the men of Chan Kom, certain men not actually resident in Chan Kom but having their legal domicile there and therefore obliged to discharge *fagina* there, refused to perform the work demanded of them. The Chan Kom *comisario* saw these men to constitute the core of a faction resident in peripheral hamlets and opposed to Chan Kom and to the *comisario's* personal success; he therefore jailed them. The prisoners, however, were not without friends in other villages jealous of Chan Kom, and these friends sought aid in Cuncunul and brought it about that the Cuncunul *comisario*, with an armed guard, came to Chan Kom to secure the freedom of the imprisoned men. When the men of Chan Kom showed they were unanimously behind their *comisario*, the Cuncunul authorities backed down and a solution of the conflict was found in compromise. But another result of the episode was to harden the outlines of one of these divisions that are always forming and reforming, grouping one cluster of settlements against another, or one embittered faction against another.

[1] The State of Yucatan is divided into sixteen administrative units called *partidos* (sometimes called *departamentos*).

It more commonly happens that the Chan Kom *comisario* voluntarily transmits to Cuncunul civil cases that he finds it difficult to settle, as well as all serious criminal matters. Should a murder occur, for example, there would be no question but that the outside authorities would be immediately called in, whether or not the murderer was a man of the village.

What has just been said indicates how one local political institution, the *comisario*, makes Chan Kom an integral part of a formal governmental system covering the *partido*, the State of Yucatan, and ultimately the Republic. This integration, as well as the political organization of the village itself, is also accomplished by two other political institutions, the *Liga Local* and the Local Agrarian Committee. Like the *comisario* these institutions are creatures of the Revolution and have existed in Chan Kom for only a few years.

The local Agrarian Committee was organized in Chan Kom in October 1929, by a traveling representative of the *Comisión Nacional Agraria*. At this time the first President, Secretary and Treasurer were elected. New sets of officers are elected every year. The president, in fact, does the work—with the very great assistance of the school teacher, who alone is able to keep satisfactory accounts. The Committee has real and important functions, for it is the effective tax-collecting body, and through its operations money is obtained for public improvements. *Fagina* will supply labor for such purposes, but it will not buy tools or imported materials. The Committee puts into effect for Chan Kom the national law providing that every worker on land furnished by the government shall pay 8 per cent of the value of his crop to the Committee. The Committee expends these funds for the benefit of the pueblo. As soon as a man has his harvest in, the value of his crop at the current price of maize is known, and he is required to pay 8 per cent of the value to the Committee. The receipt is signed by the President and by the Treasurer, and given to the agriculturalist. One copy is retained by the Committee, and another is sent to the National Committee. In fact, 8 per cent is not collected, for the workers are allowed to set down their harvests at about half their actual value. Nevertheless, from 200 to 400 pesos is collected every year.

It is this same National Committee, with which the local Committee is affiliated, which is petitioned for lands for *ejidos*. Such a petition is one of the causes that occasionally brings the villager to Merida, where the Committee maintains an office.

The *Liga Local* is a political organization of all the adult males of the village. Like the Agrarian Committee, the *Liga* is one of the necessary elements of a pueblo organized under the laws of the revolutionary government. But it differs from the Committee in that it discharges few functions of interest or of value to the villagers. It exists, along with hundreds of other local *Ligas*, for the benefit of the political organization which controls the State of Yucatan. It represents one unit in the organization which the Socialist Government has made of the rural workers. The functions of the Chan Kom *Liga* are, therefore, in large part perfunctory, so far as the real interests of the villagers are concerned. The villagers would not be without their *Liga*, if they could, because it is a symbol of their status as a pueblo—recognized and aided by *"las autoridades."* And it does give them a claim upon the aid of these *"autoridades."* At the same time, it is something of a burden. Five officers (*Presidente*, *Secretario*, *Tesorero*, *Agente de Trabajo* and *Agente de Reclamaciónes*) are elected every year, usually on one of the last Sundays in December. As these offices carry with them small prestige and many duties, persons proposed for office often seek to excuse themselves, and the absurdity of the excuses offered makes the occasion one of hilarity rather than gravity. The village leaders insist, however, that suitable men accept their posts, and the results of the election are communicated to the *Liga Central* in Merida. Thereafter the president is obligated to go to the meetings called by the *Liga Central*, and to attend political demonstrations arranged by the central government. Summons to such demonstrations often state the minimum number of village representatives which the authorities expect to be present; and prudence suggests that such instructions be carried out.

In exchange for this political support, the *Liga Central*, or, what is the same thing, the Socialist Party of the State, distributes minor largess in the form of tools, dynamite, doors for new public buildings, clocks, maps and propaganda. It is the duty of the officers of the local *Liga* to present requests of the village for aid in public construction projects. Such requests are made of the *diputado* for the *partido* of Valladolid,[1] or of the Governor himself (who is also head of the *Liga Central*); and they are occasionally granted. Each member of the *Liga Local* pays 10 *centavos* a month dues, of which half must be transmitted to the *Liga Central*, except when the president of the local obtains permission to expend the whole sum on village improvements.

Among those burdens which participation in the State government entails is that of suffrage. The officers of the local *Liga* are required to go to Merida to assist in the naming, "in full and democratic session," of candidates for *diputados*. Such gatherings take place, of course, simply to endorse the nominations made by the small group in actual control. The subsequent election takes place in all the organized villages, including Chan Kom, under the direction of a representative sent from Valladolid. As there is only the one candidate—that of the Socialist party—and he is generally entirely unknown to the voters, the casting of ballots is an event as formal as it is unimportant.

Except as expressed through the National Agrarian Committee, Chan Kom has few relations with the national government. The Federal forestry inspector makes his rounds in order to collect 25 *centavos* for each *mecate* of public land that is being cultivated, and once in a while a stray leaf of political propaganda from the National Revolutionary Party sinks quietly to the ground in this distant village.

[1] Representative in the State legislative body.

CHAPTER VII

THE INVISIBLE WORLD

If Chan Kom differs from the typical tribal community in that it is tied into wide economic and political systems by the institutions that have just been described, on the other hand it is like all such preliterate communities in the imminence and importance of gods and spirits. The bush is close at hand, and the shadows there have shapes and names and powers to do good or evil. The organized world in which the individual moves is unseen as well as seen. There is at least as much to say about the sacred as about the secular. A man's moods and his needs are objectified in a variety of spirits, and the expression of his relationships to these spirits is institutionalized in ritual. Moreover, the ritual is communal as well as individual; the homogeneity of the community is such as to maintain collective religious activity; public festival is still largely worship.

THE SANTO

Everyone in the village has the same gods. All draw on the same sources of supernatural power. Personal experience or personal choice has little to do with determining to which spirit, or to which *santo*, an individual is bound. A man may hope to get more aid from a *santo* than does his neighbor, by burning more candles before it, or he may seek to secure the special care of the milpa-guardians by punctilious offering and prayer; but one man has the same gods as his neighbor.

The foregoing statement requires some modification. Some men—seven or eight—own individual *santos*. Most of these are heirlooms; a few were recently purchased. The ownership of an image brings with it the special tutelage of that *santo* and also involves the obligation to care for the image and to recite prayers before it on the name-day of the *santo*. If a man has such a private *santo*, he makes it the center of the domestic altar when a religious ceremony (novena or *rezo*) is held in his house. Most homes are without such domestic images and have, at most, a rude wooden cross. When a man who owns a private image is in trouble or when he wishes to express gratitude, he burns a candle to the domestic *santo*. But he also burns a candle to the patron, San Diego.

So far as there is specialization of divine protection, it is the village that has its particular guardian. The village is the important social unit. Chan Kom is separate and largely self-sufficient, and so it feels itself to be. Therefore it is the village that has its particular gods. There are thought to be four special balams (p. 113) that watch over the village. But these balams have no special names or attributes to distinguish them from the balams that watch over other villages. The Holy Cross is an important object of adoration, but it extends its beneficence over all the villages. The village patron *par excellence* is the *santo*. The *santo patron* has a special name, a special appearance, and a special reputation. Thus there can be comparison between one *santo* and another, and competition for miraculous power. The *santo* is as distinct a symbol of the village-group as would be a flag; as is the case with flags, *santos* are all different while they are all the same kind of thing.

Three *santos* represent the village at large and are housed in the *oratorio:* San Diego, the Holy Cross and the *Niño Dios*.[1] To these three, and especially to the first two, most vows are made and most candles are burned. If the village is threatened by drought or disease, the inhabitants turn first to San Diego, and then to the Holy Cross; but never to another *santo*. If an individual is in trouble, he will seek the aid of the same *santo*. Except for occasional reference to the Three Kings of Tizimin (of which one or two men in Chan Kom have chromolithograph reproductions) there is small knowledge and no concern with the various miraculous *santos* of distant towns and villages of Yucatan.

"San Diego is our *santo*." The people are fond of attesting the superior miraculousness of their patron. The evidence may take the form of a beneficence granted: A man vows a novena to the *santo* should he return safely from a journey. He comes home to find his wife ill. He fulfills his promise, and his wife recovers. But more commonly the events cited as proof of miraculous power reveal punishment dealt the neglectful or the impious: A man burns four candles to San Diego in order that nothing shall happen to some pigs he is raising. The pigs die; the man says the *santo* is no good, and that he will shoot it. Next month a fire destroys all his harvest. The men of the village discuss whether or not to omit the annual fiesta and substitute a simple and less expensive novena. One man, who has argued for the novena, while attending its celebration is seriously burned as he is engaged in discharging fireworks. The villagers plan to build a new *oratorio* for the *santo*, but are persuaded by a school inspector to begin work on a new school instead. The new school collapses during construction, killing one and injuring several.

The *santo* is closely identified with its image. It is doubtful if the saints are thought of apart from their effigies, and it is probable that two effigies of the same name are regarded as two distinct supernatural personages. On the other hand the saints' names[2] are mentioned in Maya prayers rendered by the h-men. Some of these saints are thought of, by the h-men at least, as having special functions and as forming parts of the hierarchy of gods addressed in his petitions. Saint Michael is chief of the rain gods (p. 115). San Roque, San Lazaro and the *Virgen Asunción* are appealed to in curing the sick. San Cecilio, San Gabriel and San Marcelino are guardians of the wild animals that are hunted by men. But the Maya prayers often include the names of the saints simply because it is wished to appeal to all the holy names. The Spanish prayers, being memorized from the liturgy of the Church, do not mention the names of saints, but are addressed to God the Father, to the Son, or to the Virgin. Differences in spiritual potency are often thought of as existing between effigies, rather than between saints thought of as apart from these effigies.

[1] The owner of this image sometimes keeps it in his house.

[2] Those mentioned in prayers used by the Chan Kom h-mens are: San Francisco, San Antonio, San Pedro, Santo Domingo, San Juan, San Cecilio, San Vicente, San Roque, San Isidro, San Clemente, Santa Ana, San Diego, San Miguel Arcangel, San Gabriel, *Virgen Asunción*, "Santo Cristo," "Santa Cruz Verde."

The actual images in the *oratorio* belong to particular individuals. San Diego belongs to the son of one of the founders of the village. The little figure of the *Niño Dios* belongs to another. A third man owns the chromolithograph of the Three Kings. The *Santa Cruz* is the property of a fourth. (When this man's father first came to Chan Kom as an early settler, he found two crosses at the cenote. He put them in the *oratorio*. When these wore out, his son had new ones made and blessed by the priest.) If the village should be broken up and abandoned, each of these owners would claim his property. Nevertheless San Diego, and to a lesser extent the other *santos*, are thought of as representing not their individual owners or their families, but the entire village. The festival which falls on the feast-day of San Diego is the festival of the entire village; it asserts the separateness of the village and exalts the community god. No one would think of referring to San Diego, though one man owns the image, as "the *santo* of Don X." It is the *santo* of Chan Kom. The novena of the annual fiesta is organized by any pious volunteers, not by the owner of the image. This is true also of the annual novena for the Holy Cross; and it is even approximately true of the annual novena for the *Niño Dios*, although in this case the owner of the image habitually takes the last and most important night of the novena.

When a new settlement is founded, the need is early felt for a protecting *santo*. The settlers at least make a cross of wood and house it in a little shrine. The more enterprising villages, and those nearest the towns, secure carved or plaster effigies. This they do, in most cases, by looking over the stock of a *santo*-maker in Valladolid. The village fathers listen to his account of virtues attributed to the various images and select one that presents a reputation and an appearance that attract them. The effigy has no potency, however, until a priest in the town is induced to bless the image. It is then taken to the village and received with a *novenario* and a *jarana*. A few *santos* in the region have a different sort of origin. The San Francisco of Noh-Kak was taken from the convent of Sisal when General Alvarado encouraged the Indians to destroy the images. But why destroy what had supernatural power?

One or two of the images are said to have mysterious origins; the first owners claimed to have found them hidden, perhaps in some distant cave, perhaps in the bush at the entrance of the village. It is believed in Chan Kom that the patron, San Diego, had such an origin: the founder asked some of his kinsmen to look for a *santo* for the new settlement. In a *sascabera*[1] deep in the bush these men found three *santos:* the San Antonio and Santo Cristo, which are now in a little hamlet called X-Culasi, and the San Diego of Chan Kom.

The *santo* is, then, chiefly a guardian of the village, of whom any member of the community may ask aid, and to whom are addressed many of the petitions arising from communal need. The different *santos* do not have, apparently, special functions or powers.[2] They are generally beneficent; they can grant various favors. They are not closely bound up with elements in nature, as are the pagan gods, but

[1] Pit from which is taken lime rubble for building purposes.
[2] But see p. 108.

stand apart and ready to grant any sort of miraculous aid to the pious. One turns to the saint in any sort of emergency—whether a child is sick, a horse is lost, or a harvest is threatened.

THE CROSS

The Holy Cross is a *santo*, for it is represented in definite effigy form[1] and to it is rendered the same sort of cult that is offered to other *santos*. Furthermore, there are differences in miraculous power between one cross and another, as they occur in various shrines and villages, just as one San Francisco, or one Virgin, may be more miraculous than another. To justify this statement with examples it is necessary to go outside of the immediate Chan Kom area, but it is certain that the Chan Kom people know of crosses of especial potency.

On the other hand, the Holy Cross is, in a sense, present everywhere, as God is. Any village and any individual may worship the Holy Cross. The symbol of its presence is easily created: two sticks are bound together and erected on a table. Therefore, although some one village may have a cross of exceptional power, every village has the Holy Cross and does worship it. The Holy Cross is a common religious denominator for all the villages, and its especial worship extends into the towns. The village *santo* is the patron of the local community; the Holy Cross is the patron of all.

The most extensive and the most important religious festivals are offered to the Holy Cross. Novenas may be offered to the Holy Cross at any time; but during April and May, and especially on May 3 (Day of the Discovery of the Cross), the Holy Cross is honored by novenas and *jaranas* in all the villages of the region. Also it is common for a man to offer the first fruits of his fields to the Holy Cross, as well as to the pagan gods. In Chan Kom the Holy Cross shares with San Diego the paramount position among the deities that lie in a context of Catholic ritual worship. These two receive most of the prayers. Although the native may express an opinion to the contrary, both of them rank in importance above God—who is not a *santo*, because he has no effigy.[2] The attitude is represented by the course of events in 1930 when, a drought threatening, the people organized a novena for San Diego. At its conclusion the villagers determined to begin immediately another novena to the Holy Cross, "because he might be jealous." One man then argued that God was greater than the Holy Cross, and that therefore the second novena had better be offered to Him. The weight of opinion was against this suggestion, however, and a compromise was effected whereby God received two nights of prayer and the Holy Cross nine.

Related to the Holy Cross that receives this abundant formal worship, and yet not quite the same, is the sign and form of the cross as it is used in hundreds of different situations to sanctify and to protect from evil. It is not the same, because people do not say that they put "the Holy Cross" on the forehead of a dying

[1] Many of the crosses are painted green, and in prayers the Cross is often referred to as "Santa Cruz Verde." None of the villagers has been able to give an explanation. If the present cross is a historical derivative of the yax-cheil-cab, the first, or green, tree of the world, of the ancient Maya, the people of Chan Kom are unaware of it.
[2] But *Santo Cristo* is a *santo*, and the *Niño Dios* is another.

man, but that they put "a cross" on his forehead and "two others" on his hands. Wherever the form of the cross is, there is protection from occult danger. That a lime-burning may not be spoiled by evil spirits, a cross made of a certain kind of leaves is laid upon it. A cross is set up on the mound of earth above the first ears of corn that are roasting in preparation for the new corn festival. To protect their babies from sickness, mothers will paint crosses on the children's foreheads and breasts with indigo. And the most important protective crosses of all are those four pairs of large wooden crosses that stand at the four entrances of the village. Together with the balams, who are on watch at these four points, they keep evil from entering the village. From these most explicit and persisting crosses, there are all these others that are more ephemeral and casual, down to the signs of the cross that are made by a *maestro cantor* or as well by a h-men—a minimal sanctifying formula, like the accompanying phrase, "In the name of the Father, the Son and the Holy Ghost," present at all ritual occasions, whether Catholic or pagan in form.

The shape of the cross, as a symbol of power and protection, pervades the thinking and imagery of the people so that they see crosses everywhere. The tortoise is a sacred animal (p. 207), and its sacred character is attested by the pectoral cross it wears upon its plastron—the intersection of the mid-line of articulation with the principal transverse line. Of the few constellations known by name, one is the Southern Cross. Each house (of the old Maya type) has its protecting crosses, formed by the intersection of vertical poles with horizontals, to which offerings are made (p. 147). Indeed, a home is a lacework of crosses. Even the street intersections are identified with this form, and that is why they are proper places to perform certain acts in connection with magical medicine (p. 162). One man telling how on a certain occasion he made the signs of the cross, expressed it, "I made the three crosses that are in me"—as if they were parts of his very structure.

GODS OF THE FIELD AND THE FOREST

While it is convenient here to distinguish the Catholic divinities from the pagan gods, of course no distinction on the basis of historical origin is made by the people themselves. To them the deities about to be discussed are different from the *santos*, not because one group is Indian in origin and the other group European, but because they occur in different ritual contexts and because they have different sorts of attributes. It has already been stated that the distinguishing feature of the pagan spirits is their close identification with nature. They people the woods and the fields, and hover over the village. They are, somehow, closer at hand than God and the *santos*. Alone in the bush at night a man is uneasy, not on account of the *santos*, but because the balams and the kuilob kaaxob are watching him; and they are not hard to offend. The pagan gods of the milpa and the forest take vengeance on those careless of their rights. This is the meaning of many of the ceremonies: they are advance propitiation of a deity that might become vengeful, or they offer atonement to a deity already made wrathful.

These deities represent and guard all parts of the natural world that are of most concern to men: the woods, the fields, the bees, the deer, and the cluster of houses that are the physical village. Unlike the *santos*, each pagan deity, or group of them, has one particular set of functions: each pertains to one element in nature. Certain of them watch over the milpas; others guard the pueblo; others are in control of the rain. Furthermore, in asking favors from them, one asks them to relinquish what is really theirs. It is not so much that they belong to nature as that nature belongs to them. It is their trees that are felled when a man makes a new milpa. The offering of the first fruits of the harvest gives back, in gesture, what is theirs.

The writers feel that there is much they do not yet understand about how the people of Chan Kom look upon the various gods and spirits. But it is plain that part of the confusion is in the minds of the natives. No doubt the pagan deities have been growing less distinct as the influence of European civilization has grown. Many names of deities occur in the Maya prayers that the h-men can only partly explain and that some of the laymen can not explain at all. And there is blurring in the attributes of deities; one deity is confounded with another. The prayers contain many descriptive epithets that refer, in the mind of the h-men who recites the prayer, to the chaacs or to the balams; the layman does not understand the references at all, or he assumes that some other deity is indicated. For example: A certain infrequent ceremony is held at a certain mound in order to propitiate the alux; a layman did not remember what the h-men said about the ceremony when it was last performed, and in speaking of the zip, quite another class of spirits, he associated them, and not the alux, with the mound. From the h-men's point of view, this is error; but the episode truthfully represents the average layman's state of mind. Some of the deities he distinguishes sharply; others he does not. The account that follows, though it probably underestimates the amount of special knowledge of the h-mens, probably over-systematizes the understanding of the matter by the average native of the present generation. The ordinary man encounters these nature spirits as uncanny and powerful beings, with outlines none too clear, that walk at night and that may be offended or propitiated. The following account illustrates the point:

One time I went out to the milpa, because the animals were eating the maize. I spent the night there, beating on a tin can with a stick, so as to frighten them away. All at once, at about two in the morning, while I was dozing, there came a strange whistling noise; it seemed to be all around me. The next day I persuaded a friend to come with me. That night we sat together, beating on the can with a stick. At midnight a great wind came rushing down through the bush, whistling around us. I fired my gun into the bush and ran off. Next day the old men in the village told me it was the nucuch uincob ("great men") and the yum-i-col ("lord of the milpa") coming to see what was making the noise. They told me what to do. I took five gourd dishes of zaca (corn meal in water) out to the milpa and left them there. After that the noise did not come again, nor did any animal come into the milpa to eat maize.

There are three principal groups of these pagan deities: the balams, who are guardians of the milpa and of the village; the chaacs, who are gods of the rain, and the kuilob kaaxob, who are the deities of the forest.   These three together are the recipients of offerings in most of the ceremonies which the h-men performs, and they are addressed in his prayers.   These three can be named by the average person in Chan Kom, and their functions and attributes are kept fairly distinct. To these deities the agriculturist also makes offering in those minor rituals which do not demand the services of the h-men.   The kuilob kaaxob[1] have vaguer outlines than have the other two and are not mentioned quite as often.   The trees of the forest are theirs, and one must get their permission to fell them for new milpa (p. 132).   But as felling is essential to agriculture, the kuilob kaaxob are also agricultural deities, and so offerings of new corn are made to them too.

The balams are protecting spirits of the milpa (balam-col) and of the village (balam-cah).   Men speak also of balams of the beehives (balam-cab); but this is a point of confusion, for the h-mens give special names for the gods of the bees and say they are not balams.   People commonly refer to the balams collectively by various descriptive epithets: they are the "great men" (nucuch makob, nucuch uincob), or the "lords" (yuntzilob).[2]   In the prayers the balams are invoked by various other special terms, which apparently do not occur out of the liturgical context: the balams are there referred to as the canan-cacabob, the "guardians of the village"; they are the canan-semillaob, the "guardians of the seeds"; and they are the canan-era, the "guardians of the garden plots."

The balams are thought of sometimes as spirits without definite form, and sometimes—especially those that guard the milpa—as "little people, only made of air."   Some natives have seen them in the milpa.   They appear then as small old men, with white hair, wearing sandals, sombrero, and the rest of the local costume. A favorite folktale theme is the meeting with a balam by man or boy who does not know who it is he has met, and of the consequences of the meeting.

The balams are good to men.   Provided the agriculturalist makes them the proper offerings and prayers, they watch over his cornfield and protect his maize from marauding animals.   They stand over the village to guard it from wild beasts and from evil winds.   They watch over the forest paths and set the lost traveler on his road again.   By night you may hear a high whistling sound; this is made by the balams, who are driving away evil winds or animals by shooting at them with fragments of obsidian or flint.   They do this in a certain manner (called piliz dzonkab), by holding the fragment of stone with the first finger of the right hand against the outer edge of the first finger of the left hand, between the two lower joints; the left thumb holds the right first finger steady while it skips the fragment off into the air.   These fragments (pieces of knife or lance-point of the ancient Maya) are found in the bush; then people know the balams have been shooting at the evil winds.   Therefore these fragments have magical protective power, and so when the h-men performs the Loh ceremony (p. 175) to protect the village from the evil winds, he buries toks (as these pieces are called) at each of the four

---

[1] In some of the prayers one such deity (u kuil kaax) is mentioned, but more commonly they are thought of as plural.

[2] One man asserts that the yuntzilob are the balams of the pueblo, while the balamob are the guardians of the milpa. But most do not agree. Most commonly the term "yuntzilob" is used to include all the great gods of the field and wood: chaacs, balams and kuilob kaaxob.

entrances of the village and, in some cases, when a new house is dedicated, one of these "arrows of the balam" is set above the door.

But the balams are also much to be feared. They are uncanny beings of the night. When they cry out in the darkness, it is a sign that some one is going to die. They watch over lost children, but they return only a changeling, for the balam endures on a succession of children's souls; the idiot and the feebleminded are children of the balam. The balams guard the milpa, but only if the owner gives to them the corn that is theirs and offers them the prayers they expect. If the offerings are not made, or the longer ceremonies not performed, the balams bring sickness to the owner. On the other hand, they punish trespassers in the milpa with sickness or sudden death. Many stories are told of men who stole from strange milpas and were struck dead by the balam. These stories are the real locks on the open granaries in the distant bush. The balams answer the needs of the agriculturalist for protection for his crops—a situation brought about, in turn, by the scantiness of the soil and the simplicity of the agricultural techniques. The corn must stand ripening in the far-off milpa for weeks, and thereafter too it usually remains in the fields. And the milpa is a place the native feels to be inhabited by invisible presences, as he comes upon it, suddenly, after walking through miles of bush: the planted corn, the fence, perhaps a broken calabash. It is the feeling one of us has on entering an empty house, with the table laid and the fire set.

Mention has been made of the four entrances to the village. These four entrances exist in the thinking of the native; in cold fact there are seven paths, that converge crookedly upon the village from no particular compass points. But the world, the village and the milpa are thought of as squares with four corners lying in the four cardinal points of the compass and with defined central points. It is for this reason that pairs of wooden crosses are erected at only four of the seven actual entrances to the village; these four are "the four corners" of the pueblo. Above each of these entrances hovers one of the balams that watch over the village, ready to seize upon any evil that should attempt to cross the threshold. The village is conceived of as a square, walled with supernatural protection of which the balams, the crosses and the buried toks are symbols. The center of the village is marked by the cenote; in most villages[1] it is usual to erect one cross near its edge; this marks the middle point. The most important of the balams is known as the thup—a word which stands generally for the smallest of a series, for the youngest of a number of brothers and sisters, or, still more specifically, for the little finger. He is thought of as smaller than the other balams. Some men think of him as a fifth balam, hovering over the central point of the village. But a commoner view considers him that balam which occupies the eastern position. The thup is ready to descend to the aid of any of the other balams should they struggle with animal or evil wind. "Sometimes you see bits of fur at one of the four entrances. It is where the nucuch makob have seized an animal that tried to enter the pueblo."

[1] In Chan Kom there is now no such cross at the cenote.

The same pattern of thought is expressed in the beliefs and practices as to the balams of the milpa. Four offerings are made: one dish of zaca is set in each of the four corners of the milpa, some men adding a fifth in the middle of the field.

The pattern is likewise apparent in the conceptions as to the raingods. But while the balams watch over each particular milpa and each particular village, the chaacs are gods of the whole world—or, better, of the sky. Four of them stand at the four corners of the heavens, in the four points of the compass, and are known as ek-xib-chaac, zac-xib-chaac, kan-xib-chac and chac-xib-chaac (black-, white-, yellow- and red-man-chaac). These are the chaacs who are personified by the four men who stand at the four corners of the altar in the rain ceremony (p. 143); the altar is the world itself with the heavens above it. This same fundamental notion of fourfold orientation explains the fact that, in some ceremonies that take place in a walled yard, the h-men plants crosses in each of its four corners and why offerings are hung on each of the four corners of the apiaries during ceremonies to the gods of the bees.

The chaacs are addressed in the prayers by many descriptive terms which the h-mens can not entirely explain. The understanding of the chaacs held by the shaman-priest is more complicated than in the case of the balams, and there is a wider distance between what the h-men knows and what the layman understands. Indeed, some laymen can not repeat the simple color names of the four chaacs that stand at the four corners. The chaacs are many and arranged in a hierarchical rank, which cuts across but does not interfere with the spatial positions of some of them. The chief of the chaacs is San Miguel Arcangel. His supremacy is indicated in the ceremonies by the fact that he receives the largest and most important bread—the cruz-uah, which is placed closest to the cross on the altar. Beneath him comes the kunku-chaac. He receives the bread of second importance—the noh uah. He rides with the other chaacs across the sky and acts as their leader. The other chaacs are referred to by names that describe their attributes as deities of the rain. All the chaacs generally are commonly called the Ah-hoyaob—"the sprinklers." In the prayers, and less commonly in conversation, many chaacs are mentioned by name. Ah-bolon-caan-chaac ("nine-sky-chaac"), also called Bohol-caan-chaac ("gourd-rattle-sky-chaac"), makes much thunder, but little rain. "The wise men can tell when he is coming. Then there will not be much rain." Ah-hadzen-caan-chaac ("whip-sky-chaac") makes thunder claps like the crack of a whip. Ah-lelem-caan-chaac ("flash-sky-chaac") produces the lightning. When the prayers are uttered, special invocation is directed to the chaac that makes rain fall in abundance. This is the x-thup-chaac,[1] least of the chaacs. His post is in the east. He is also referred to as Ah-bulen-caan-chaac, and sometimes as Ah-chaalen-caan-chaac ("clear water-sky-chaac"). When he passes over the milpas, the waters fall in torrents. He carries a small calabash known as zaayam-chu ("inexhaustible water-carrier"). This calabash is mysteriously connected with the cenotes. As the x-thup-chaac rides over each cenote, with a roar the water from the cenote passes up into the air to fill his calabash again.[2]

[1] The prefix "x" indicates what is less. The term x-thupil-caan-chaac also occurs. the least-heaven-chaac.
[2] Therefore, in performing the cha-chaac ceremony, the impersonator of the chaac must carry a small, not a large, calabash (p. 142).

During the dry season, the chaacs dwell in the "trunk of heaven" (chun caan), which is situated in the eastern sky. Sometimes it is thought that they assemble to receive their orders at the ruin of Coba, which lies to the east of Chan Kom. As the dry season draws to a close, they are given their directions by San Miguel Arcangel. Then they prepare to ride forth. The first thunder is heard in the east; that is to announce the coming of the chaacs. Then a small cloud appears, again in the east. It is said that on the second of June the chaacs get their orders at Coba, and on the third [1] they ride forth. They issue from the chun caan through a small round opening in the sky: the holhuntazmuyal ("doorway in the clouds"). Then the clouds sweep westward across the sky: it is the chaacs riding the heavens. The clouds spread till they cover the sky; the chaacs have taken their places at the four quarters of the heavens.

The chaacs are visualized as old men who ride on horses which are seen as clouds. Each rider holds a gourd vessel containing the waters of the rain, and brandishes a machete-like object known as lelem, which produces the lightning. The horses of the chaacs are known as *santo cangel*. These horses are of different colors, but the colors are not definitely named and the layman, at least, does not associate any particular color with any particular cardinal direction. When a black cloud first arises in the east, it is said that "the black chaac" or "*el arcangel morcillo*" is coming. When a storm comes, with much wind and rain, it is said that there rides through the sky "the sorrel-colored horse" (tzimin *santo cangel alazán*).

Also mentioned in the formal prayers, but never mentioned by the layman when he makes his offering in the milpa, are the four pahuatunob: kanpahuatun, zacpahuatun, ekpahuatun and chacpahuatun. The h-mens regard these terms as alternative names for the chaacs of the four directions. [2]

When the chaacs are invoked by the h-men in formal prayer, the Virgin is also addressed, by the phrase cichpan-colel-canan-gracia ("beautiful lady guardian of the maize") or cichpan-colel-metaan-gracia ("beautiful lady embracer of the maize"). In the more figurative and formal language of the prayers, the young maize plants are referred to as *gracia*.

GODS OF THE BEES

The animals that most concern men are the cattle, the deer and other wild food-animals, and the bees of the apiaries. Each of these groups has its supernatural protectors. But of the three, only the gods of the bees are the objects of important religious ritual. The products of the hives are used chiefly in religious practices: the bees furnish the honey for the ceremonial beer and the wax for the offertory candles.

The attitude toward the gods of the bees is much like that toward the gods of the milpa and, indeed, as has already been said, some or all of them are by some people thought to be balams. The apiaries belong to these deities; by prayer and

[1] The rains come at the end of May or beginning of June. The third of June is probably selected because of the importance of the third of May (Day of the Holy Cross).

[2] But Genet suggests (page 232 of his edition of Landa) that anciently the pahuatunob were different deities: the gods who lived in the subterranean world and supported the earth.

offering man atones to them for taking their honey, for touching their insects. This is the explanation of the custom never to take all of the honey from the comb, and of the care exercised toward the bees themselves when the honey is taken. If a bee gets into the honey, one should, it is felt, wash and dry it, and then gently blow it off one's hand. If a bee is drowned in the honey, it is wrapped in a leaf and buried.

As with the harvest, so with the honey of the hives; for each year's yield which man secures, he owes a ceremonial offering to the gods. One of the ceremonies made for the gods of the bees (u hanli cab) fulfills this obligation. The other (u hedz luumil cab, p. 146) is made when the hives are moved, or when a new hive is established.[1] If these ceremonies are not performed, the patrons of the apiaries are likely to visit the owner with sickness; then the owner will make the ceremony in atonement, so as to get well. The custom is to move the hives only on Saturday, the belief being that only on Saturdays do all the bees return at one time to the hives, to rest as men do.[2] Indeed, it is by observing the bees that one may tell that it is Saturday.

The gods of the bees take the form of large bees and dwell in the east (the chun caan) as do the rain-gods. Their number and their names are not matters of general common understanding and agreement. Some laymen speak only of the "balam-cab," or of the "noh-yum-cab" ("great lord bee"). One h-men gave the following account: The noh-yum-cab is the principal ruler; under him are all the other bees of the world. Then come a class of bees known as x-mulzen-cab.[3] These dwell in a certain place at Coba, where there is much red earth and many nests of bees (such as the wild bees make). This place is inaccessible and protected by a tiger-like animal with a long tongue, called hak-madz, who devours anyone who attempts to enter the place. It is the business of the x-mulzen-cabob to inform the noh-yum-cab of everything that happens in the apiary. Then come the bees known as bolon-hobon ("nine (?) hives"). Their task is to cure the bees who have been injured when honey is taken from the hives. If, on a Saturday a bee is reported missing, one of these bolon-hobon goes out to search for the lost one, to cure or revive him. The next class is known as balam-cabob. They remain at the beehives and keep away the evil winds. When u hedz luumil cab is made, it is to make offerings to the noh-yum-cab so that he will direct the balam-cabob to move to the new site and there continue their protection of the apiary.

GUARDIANS OF THE DEER

All the wild animals of the bush that are hunted by men are under the protection of San Gabriel, San Cecilio and San Marcelino, and to these *santos* appeal is made when a deer or other game-animal is sought for a ceremony (p. 140). In addition, the deer are guarded by certain supernatural beings called zip. They are

---

[1] Without any direct corroboration, the writers suspect that the establishment of a new site for a hive is connected with the ideas of orientation. Offerings are hung at each of the four corners of the roof that shelters the hives, and over the opening in each hive is carved a cross. It may be that moving a hive is comparable to moving a village.

[2] In fact Sunday is not strictly a day of rest (p. 86).

[3] A layman understands x-mulzen-cab to be the name of the place of red earth at Coba where the bee-gods dwell. The balam-cabob he calls balam-kanche, and he adds the name of still another god of the bees—kuna.

not gods; although appealed to in certain prayers, they occasion no ceremonies by themselves. They have nothing to do with men directly, and they do not punish men. They are present only where the deer are, out in the bush. The deer are their domestic animals (alakob); they watch over them as men do over cattle. It is part of the hunter's task to circumvent the magical power they have, and so secure his prey. If all practical care has been taken to load and fire, and still one misses, it is because of the zip. Thus the belief in the zip explains the odd mischances of the hunt. On the other hand, the fact that there are some places where deer are unusually abundant is likewise explained by the existence of the zip, because the deer are thought to follow their patrons. If one sees many deer at one place it is probably because someone has found and killed a zip, and the deer have come from all around to attend its wake.

The zip look like deer, having their bodies, their horns and their hoofs; only they are small, about the size of a dog. "One can not grasp a zip; it would be like grasping the wind." Some of them, that rank high in their number, have between their horns a wasp-nest, with a star-shaped opening. Should a hunter pursue the zip, the wasps would fly out and sting him. Only old hunters of long experience ever see the zip, and even these can not kill the zip by ordinary means; but there is one way in which it can be done. The hunter wads the powder in the cartridge with a little of the cottony fluff one finds in the hollow-tree nests of the small opossum (holil-och). Then he puts the bullets in, each marked with a cross, and some leaves, on top of all. These should be leaves of the zipche, but if this tree is not at hand, one may take any dried leaves from the path, by reaching behind one without looking. As soon as the hunter fires the gun, he must run off, or he would die too, a victim of the evil winds that surround the zip at the moment of dying. But later he may come back, to shoot the deer that have assembled for the *velorio*.

GUARDIAN OF THE CATTLE

The cattle in the corral are watched over by a very ill-defined supernatural personage known as X-Juan-Thul. The laymen, at least, are uncertain as to whether his form is that of man, or of bull. It is probable that the name is a corruption of some older term, for the older men sometimes speak of him as X-Juan-Thuyul.[1] He is not confused with the X-Juan-Thul of the rabbit tales. This X-Juan-Thul is a deity: he is spoken of as x-thupil-yuntzil, "the least of the yuntzilob." He watches the corral, keeping evil winds away. At the ceremony performed to drive the evil winds from the corral (p. 175), offerings are made to X-Juan-Thul, and the same is done, in the neighboring villages, before the *vaqueros* go to the bulls in the festal bull-fight (p. 158).

THE WINDS

With the zip, this inventory of supernatural beings leaves those that are definitely gods, with power to give affirmative aid to men, and who, in ceremonial form, are petitioned for this aid, and turns toward the beings who are merely

[1] "Thuyul" is probably "termite."

evil and dangerous, and whose evil must be warded off. The list moves away from deity in the direction of demon.

The most important and pervasive of the evil spirits are those thought of as and identified with the winds. The winds are evil and harm personified; there is scarcely an ailment that may not be caused by them and hardly a moment of crisis at which they are not present. The winds are not gods; they are mischief to be averted. As their importance lies chiefly in the bringing of sickness, discussion of them will be reserved for the chapter on that subject.

But one wind out of the many that are named and distinguished is not evil; it grants help to men and is addressed in prayers; this wind is referred to as one, the kakal-mozon-ik ("fiery whirlwind"), or as plural, the kakal-mozon-ikob. The kakal-mozon-ik is a great spiral wind that, properly besought, sweeps down upon the field made ready for burning and carries the kindled flame across the cleared milpa (p. 133). That its cooperation may be secured in obtaining a good crop, this wind is mentioned in many prayers along with the chaacs and the balams. It is not thought of as a god, but as a wind; it has no powers except to blow. When spoken of in the plural, these winds are identified with the souls of men who have had sexual intercourse with their wives' sisters (p. 96) and for this sin are condemned forever to wander through the world in this form.

THE SOULS OF THE DEAD

The dead almost never appear to people, but animals see them frequently. It is observed that when dogs howl lugubriously at night, or other animals snort with fright, it is a sign that on the next day, or maybe the following, there will be a funeral in one of the neighboring settlements. A traveler in the bush is sometimes made aware that ghosts are near, though he does not see them. He hears mysterious voices, or perhaps small stones are thrown at him from an invisible hand.

On the whole, ghosts are not among the most imminent of the supernatural beings. This is because most souls of the dead find rest in Paradise, or are bound in hell (metnal), or enter the forms of animals or the bodies of other men (p. 199). Just after death they are still near at hand; and on the Day of the Dead they return in numbers to their earthly homes (p. 202). Nevertheless, the living are long bound to the dead; this is the meaning of novenas held at intervals after the death of a relative, and of many of the candles lighted in the *oratorio*. Many of these are offered not to San Diego, but are lit in commemoration of some restless soul. Unaided by the living in their desire for peace, the dead may bring sickness to the living. "For spirits watch us, and when we neglect them, and fail to light for them even one candle, then they punish us, as it is not fair that we enjoy life while they suffer."

THE ALUX

The bush is thought to be inhabited by a small goblin people known as alux (aluxob [1]). Their uncanny and mischievous acts form the subject matter of many

---

[1] Brinton (*The Folk-lore of Yucatan*) Folk-lore Journal, London, vol. I, part VIII, pp. 1-13), derives this word from h-loxkatob, "the strong ones of clay."

stories told in the evening, as men sit together in the plaza, or as women are gathered in the kitchens. Some claim to have seen them in the bush. "They are about a foot high and look like small children, except for their beards and their crowns. These crowns go around the head; they are square in outline, and are made of clay. Inside there is a hollow, and the hollow extends through the body of the alux, so that rain enters at the top and runs out the toes." Other accounts are very similar. In figure 11 are pictures of alux drawn by men of Chan Kom (see also Plate 11*a*).

The alux are spirits that dwell in the pottery idols and incense-burners that are sometimes encountered in the bush or in excavations in the village. This is

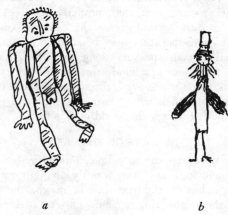

a   *b*

Fig. 11—Alux, traced from pencil drawings by two men of Chan Kom.

what makes the low mounds, that are so evidently of artificial construction, uncanny and dangerous places. It is best to avoid the sleeping alux or to destroy them. A man in Chan Kom dug a hole behind the wall that ran around his house-lot. There in the ground he found an alux lying—"even including his dishes—he was the color of clay." Quickly the man threw stones on top of him and covered the place with dirt, lest he should do some harm. Any other man in Chan Kom would have done the same.

From the many stories told about the alux, we quote enough to show the identification of the alux with the clay artifacts of the ancients, the fear of these beings and the tendency to confuse them with the balams, by attributing to them the milpa, machete and calabash of the milpa-guardians, as well as the balams' tutelary functions. Indeed, although by the large the alux are merely mischievous goblins to be avoided, it is not unknown in Chan Kom for men to offer corn-gruel to them as among the guardians of the milpa; and in one ceremony (p. 175) the h-men carries offerings to a mound where the alux are thought to dwell so as to induce them to refrain from doing evil to the pueblo. The evil is exerted, as is most evil, through the evil winds.

In the old days, in the times of the grandfather of Isidro, people used to make the alux come alive. They were only of clay, but they made them come alive. They burned copal in one, for nine days and nine nights, without sleeping at all. Then the alux came alive. They would give him his calabash, his dog, his gun, and his machete, and let him go. In gratitude, the alux would take care of the milpa of the man who thus released him. Such milpas would always be green, and a man who stole from it would get fever.

Then fathers used to forbid their sons to whistle or to shout after nightfall, because this is when the alux come out.

In Santa Maria they sometimes hear the alux hunting at night with their dogs. They hear the shouting of the alux, the bark of their dogs, and the report of their guns. The people put out gourd dishes of zaca, so that the alux may take the zaca and do no harm.

Once, about thirty years ago, there was an uprising in this region. About forty men, among them the father of Don Elut's father, were sent southward into the bush. There they lost their way. Suddenly they came upon a deserted settlement, with milpas of corn about a foot high (*caña rosa*) and watermelons. Some of the men cut a watermelon from the vine. But there arose a great rustling and shaking of the bush, together with a whistling noise. They looked around but saw no one, and some of the men cut the watermelon and began to eat it. Immediately they fell down dead. About ten died. The other thirty returned to their general. He sent a hundred men back to the deserted settlement to cut the corn and see what was hiding there. There were about a hundred *mecates* in the milpa. The men began to cut; again the trembling and whistling occurred. Suddenly an alux ran out of the bush; the men tried to kill it, some with guns, some with machetes, but to no effect. The men fled to their general. He ordered two hundred men to return and destroy the milpa. But when they tried to go back, they could not find the path; it had disappeared.

The milpa mentioned in this last story is, in the more usual thinking in Chan Kom, the milpa of the balam. But apparently, as the balam shrinks from god to goblin, it meets with the alux, and the attributes of both are mingled.

DEMON AND MONSTER

There are many sorts of dangerous and uncanny beings that have none of the qualities of deity, but are all demon. They are the subjects of fearful stories, and ideas about them express the uncanniness of the bush. These include animals that are not animals, but witches that have taken animal forms; animals that have exchanged forms with one another; huge animal monsters; and evil things in human form. The devil is one of these last; he is apt to appear as a hairy man; he has supernatural powers to sell for the souls of the tempted (p. 180). He is apt to appear on the hills made by a certain ant (mul zay); on this account, these ant hills are avoided by the nocturnal traveler. There is considerable reluctance to mention the devil by his name (cizin); it is thought better to refer to him as "the very evil one" (kakazbaal).[1]

[1] "A young man of Xocen asked for some money from his father, who was a h-men. The father promised to give it to him on the day following. The son, wishing to know where his father got his money, decided to spy on him, and followed him until he came to a mul zay, where the father gave nine leaps in the air. At once there appeared a spectre covered with hair, who inquired what his visitor wished. The h-men asked for some money, which was handed over to him without delay by the hairy phantom, which was no other than the devil himself. For this reason the son never wished to accept money from his father any more."

"Pedro Caro was a blind musician who lived in Yaxcaba. One night he had had something to drink, and felt like playing some music. So he got up from his hammock and went to a friend's house, and borrowed his fiddle and his fiddle bow. Out in the street again he felt some one take hold of his arm, and a man's voice said, 'Come along with me; we will go to your house.' So they walked on together, but farther and farther until Pedro Caro put out his hand and felt a *trinchera* (stone wall built on village outskirts)—they were at the outskirts of the village! Then he felt his companion's arm, and it was all covered with long hair. So he began crying out and beating at the Thing with his fiddle bow; but when his friends arrived there was nothing there. Who knows what it was?—a demon, perhaps."

The x-tabai, well known in Maya folklore, is one of the most prominent of these demons of the bush. She appears in the form of a beautiful young woman, dressed in a fine *huipil* with fine embroidery (*terno*), and with long hair. She induces a young man to follow her into the bush, or into some *sascabera*, and there, unless he is lucky enough to escape, she chokes him to death. In Chan Kom this belief makes its contribution to the hazards of the bush and to the forms which prudence takes. The x-tabai is identified with certain trees; especially the ceiba, but also a tree of the cashew family, known as kulinche. Therefore, in going past such a tree, especially if it be large and hollow, one is watchful; if one is on horseback there is danger that the horse may see what you do not and, in his fright, throw you off. In such trees the x-tabai lives, or into such a tree she changes her form. She is also identified with a certain snake, green and yellow with a patterned back and known as chay-i-can. Into this snake she turns, and with the tip of her tail stops up a man's nostrils. "Two months ago we were going to Valladolid to see about cattle for the cooperative, when we passed a kulinche, and in its branches we saw the snake. Don Tino was certain it was a x-tabai. We wanted to shoot at it with our pistols, but Don Tino said it would do no good; you could not kill it, and it would only come back and do us harm."

Men in the form of animals are witches, and will be treated under that heading. There are also beliefs in huge and monstrous animals, that figure in stories hunters tell about other hunters, who saw these animals, or who even shot them. Such are the boob, a large animal with long hair, looking something like a bull, the chan-ekal, a spotted animal resembling the tiger, and the hak-madz, already mentioned (p. 117). These creatures are thought of as inhabiting the more distant bush, into which hunters rarely penetrate, especially in the neighborhood of the mysterious ruins of Coba.

PROPITIATION AND PRAYER

The situations that call forth the images of the supernatural beings vary from the simple uneasiness aroused by the shadows of forest in the mind of the solitary traveler to grave crises that threaten the security of the entire village. As the danger deepens and spreads, so do the invisible beings increase in stature from demon to god, and so do the acts appropriate for the occasion change from simple magical practices to elaborate ritual and invocatory prayer. The dark comes every night; if one does not like it, one may ask a friend to come with one, or one may stay at home; it is only uneasiness anyway; nothing has really happened. So the little people of the wood, and the shadowy monsters, are merely to be avoided. At most there are amulets to carry, or simple protective acts—"secrets," the people call them. The hunter keeps away from the ancient mound where the alux dwell; the mother makes safe her child from any balams that might be looking for a changeling, by painting a cross of indigo on his breast; the x-tabai may be foiled by winding one's sandal straps from left to right. These dangers are exciting and only half-real; so they make good stories when men are gathered together; they titillate the imagination without terrifying it.

But in the troubles that are wholly real, where practical action is inadequate, the gods appear. Sickness, a lost bull, a threatened crop—these are situations that provoke the most genuine anxiety; then one turns to the *santo*, or, if the matter fall within their province, to the balams and the kuilob kaaxob. Such situations recur, not often enough to make them trivial, but often enough so that usage has conventionalized, in ritual and formal prayer, the ways of dealing with the situation. But the memory of the last situation and the anticipation of the next are present between instances of the situation themselves; and therefore prayer and offering are partly matters of routine. It is good to burn an occasional candle to the *santo;* it is well to hang out corn gruel for the balams from time to time. You may propitiate in advance, or you may atone and repay after the crisis has occurred. Some men make the Dinner-of-the-Milpa ceremony regularly every four years as it should be made, and some wait until sickness reminds them that they have not been punctilious. One man pays insurance; the other pays his losses. A third construction of the situation is made by the institution of the vow, which has a limited use in Chan Kom. Don Rosa's daughter is sick; he contracts with San Diego to make him a novena if the *santo* will grant the girl a miraculous cure.

The events in the life of the individual that occasion propitiation and prayer are illness, property loss, death and its commemoration, and those times of crisis in the agricultural cycle that come upon each cultivator singly and alone. At such times it is one man who feels the need; the rest of the village may be content, or at least occupied with humdrum matters. Therefore, one of two things is true about individual ceremonies: either they are performed privately—as is the case with the minor agricultural ceremonies—or, if other persons participate, the ritual is for these others a merely social occasion, secular, rather than sacred. The latter alternative is represented by the novena, to be discussed in a later chapter.

The private, or individual, agricultural ceremonies are few and simple, and are tending to disappear. For most such occasions practical action is adequate. When a man fells bush, sows or weeds, his practical skill alone assures him of the success of that particular act. Before the bush is burned, however, there is a prayer, because the winds are tricky and no man can be confident of a successful burning by touching his torch to the fallen trees.

The more important individual ceremonies are those performed to cure or to prevent sickness: when the gods have punished a man for his neglect of them, or when a good harvest is in and gratitude and prudence recommend the ceremony. At such times there is no practical action at hand to express the mood or answer the need. A man will fall back upon these ceremonies only after secular medicine has failed to cure him.

As has already been said (Chapter V), the important religious ceremonies are those agricultural rituals taking place at times when the moods of the individual men coincide and when practical action is not demanded. At harvest, and at times of drought, when all men are together in one deep anxiety, the important religious ceremonies are performed. Then all the tall gods are invoked in prayer. There is then no trace of averting the evil the supernatural may inflict; the demons are forgotten. Either the gods are thanked for the goodness they have given, or they are asked that they give of it to men.

One important communal ritual does not depend upon the agricultural cycle (or upon irregular, but common, needs, such as plague), and that is the fiesta of the village patron. This occurs on a fixed date. As, in Chan Kom, this date falls within the period when the crops are not yet secure from drought, this fiesta too (if held at all) is apt to partake of the prayerful qualities of the agricultural ceremonies to the pagan gods.

THE TWO RITUAL CONTEXTS

The pagan gods and those of Christian origin are distinguished by the natives, not, of course, in terms of the difference in their historical origins, but in terms of the two different ritual contexts in which lie the worship and propitiation of each group. There is San Diego, there is the Holy Cross, there is Dios—and there are the yuntzilob. Many occasions call forth the ceremonial worship of both *santo* and yuntzil, either successively or simultaneously. If a man is sick, he may burn a candle to San Diego, or he may perform a ceremony in propitiation of the chaacs and the balams, or he may do both. When the harvest is in, thankfulness is expressed to both groups of deities. The Holy Cross tastes of the new ears, and so do the yuntzilob. There are certain sorts of occasions, soon to be mentioned, where it is appropriate to use the ritual centering around the one group rather than that centering around the other, but on the whole these two sets of beings, these two kinds of ritual, are just two equally good modes of religious expression. The people are ceremonially bilingual, as it were.

The difference between the two is, then, a difference in ritual organization. Certain acts are appropriate in one context, and certain other acts are appropriate in the other; and other acts are equally appropriate in both. The relationship between these two contexts is indicated in the accompanying diagram. The one complex centers around the recitation of Latin and Spanish prayers by persons who have specialized to do this. Such a recitation before an altar, followed by the consumption by the worshippers of foods first offered to the gods, is a *rezo*, or novena. The novena is a private ceremony, but it may be, on occasion, communal. It is central to the village fiesta, which, by including the elements of folk-dance (*jarana*) and bull-fight (*toros*), becomes secular and so moves out of the sphere of religious ritual.[1] The *rezo* is peculiarly appropriate to funerals and death-commemoration, but the novena may be used, as has already been said, for all sorts of individual and communal needs, where too the pagan gods may be involved. Appropriate to this context are the use of the *oratorio;* the offering of candles to the god; the active participation of women; the numbers three and seven in ritual acts; certain flowers such as *Plumeria;*[2] and *atole* (boiled gruel of ground meal)[3] as a food offering.

[1] It is not unlikely that certain elements in the village fiesta, such as the pole-planting and the cuch ceremony, have Indian origins, not European. But if this be true, it does not affect the fact that these ritual elements belong in the novena context centering around the gods of Christian origin.

[2] In the ceremony of consecration of a new h-men (p. 76), *Plumeria* flowers are used. This is the only use we know of the flower in the other context.

[3] But *atole* of *new* corn, is, once a year, offered to the yuntzilob.

The other ritual context centers around the recitation of Maya prayers, in all important ceremonies, by the h-men. For the most important occasions the h-men is indispensable, because he alone can, by divination, interpret the will of the yuntzilob, and because he alone can recite the prayers and direct the ritual. In the case of minor rituals, however, the layman may carry out the ceremonial acts himself. In the house, for example, he arranges the three bowls of *atole* for the Holy Cross, while in his yard he places nine dishes of gruel and thirteen roasted ears for the yuntzilob. A few occasions call forth rituals of this second context only: the need to exorcise evil winds, and matters involving the beehives; also, the agricultural crises lean heavily upon this pagan ritual context, rather than on the novena and the *santo*.[1] The disposition is, generally speaking, to fall back on the h-men and the yuntzilob in a pinch.

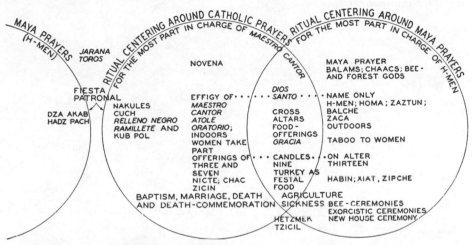

Fig. 12—Diagram indicating the two complexes of sacred ritual.

Appropriate to this second context are the conduct of ceremonies out of doors; the taboo of the ritual acts to women; the h-men's divinatory paraphernalia and the special offertory vessel (homa); the ceremonial beer (balche);[2] certain special breadstuffs made with squash seeds; certain plants (p. 207); cornmeal cooked without lime (zaca); the number thirteen in ritual acts; and—less clearly—the earth-oven.

Some elements of ritual are, so far as has been determined, equally at home in either context. The h-men uses them when he makes offerings to the yuntzilob, and the *maestro cantor* and his group of laymen employ them in their novenas for the *santos*. Such are the use of the cross, both as a gesture of sanctification and as a symbol of adoration; *Dios*; the notion of *gracia* (spiritual essence of food taken from the offerings by the gods); the use of altars; the number nine; and the turkey as a food of sacred ritual.

[1] Certain ceremonies use neither Catholic prayer nor Maya invocation to the yuntzilob; such are the hetzmek and the tzicil; these ceremonies, indeed, are only half sacred.

[2] Balche is also used in the annual fiesta of the patron, which otherwise belongs to the novena type.

With reference to the wider world, including the other villages and the towns, these two contexts have very different meanings. For while the context centering around the novena is public and open, and links Chan Kom up with the towns-people, the ceremonies of the h-men are more secluded; they are almost occult. The townsman may visit the novena and participate; this he has in common with the people of Chan Kom. But the exorcistic and agricultural ceremonies centering around the yuntzilob belong to the villager. They take place apart and their celebration is not advertised in advance. If the townsman attends, he does not really participate. One result of this is to keep them entirely sacred. It is only a real need, a genuine piety, that occasions them. The folk-dance and the gambling game, that cling to the peripheries of the novena, have no place in these other ceremonies. The pagan rituals grow dim, perhaps, but they are not secularized, let alone commercialized.

Chapter VIII

CEREMONIES OF FIELD AND HIVE

THE OFFERINGS TO THE YUNTZILOB

What man wins from nature, he takes from the gods. The woods, the maize, the honey, and the wild food-animals belong to the yuntzilob. The ceremonies which the h-men performs are to ask of the gods that they give of these to man, or they are to pay for what man has already taken. The ceremonies acknowledge and make safe the transfer of the natural yield from the yuntzilob to man. It is at the moment of separation, when the fields pass from divinity to humanity, that the ceremonial recompense must be made. The high bush is zuhuy kaax ("virgin forest"); in cutting this the permission of the guardians of the forest must be asked. But the following year, if the agriculturalist sows that same tract again, no account need be taken of the gods, because that land is already man's. Similarly, the offering of first fruits is made only by those whose harvests are taken from corn grown on milpas made from zuhuy kaax, and the u hanli col ceremony (p. 134) need be made only in payment for maize grown on new milpas.[1]

The pious think it wise to offer to the yuntzilob a part of any first-fruit. For such offerings the general word is hol-che. The first beans of a new milpa are offered to the gods, as are the first roasted ears (hol-che-pibil-nal, p. 143). When a deer is killed, it is customary to put the head, the liver and the stomach in a *sabucan* and hang this on a tree in the yard for about an hour. In this way the entire animal is symbolically offered to the zip, and to San Cecilio, San Gabriel and San Marcelino. Those who do not make such offerings are spoken of as "dzuut"—haggling or grasping. For the more important ceremonies a sort of balance sheet is kept between the gods and man. For every year that a harvest is taken (from zuhuy kaax), just so many fowl are due the yuntzilob. The principle can be illustrated from the recompense-ceremony to the gods of the bees—the u hanli cab. This ceremony is made, theoretically, every four years. It should be made in the spring months, when there are many flowers on the trees. This season (March to May) is called nic che ("tree-flower"). When the owner of the hives has taken the annual yield of honey, it is felt that he now owes the gods of the bees an offering: cu ppaxic u hanalil u cab hunppel haab ti nic che ("as he owes the dinner-of-the-bees for one year of blossom-time"). The bee-keeper may make the ceremony every year, offering one large hen with an accompanying small chicken. Or he may wait, allowing his debt to accumulate. After four years he offers four large hens and four chickens, or a turkey with two hens. If he is reminded by sickness of his failure to make one of these ceremonies, the h-men asks how long since the ceremony was performed and, in advising his patient, instructs him to offer a number of fowl corresponding to the years of accumulated debt to the gods.

[1] *I.e.*, only for chacben, not for zacab. See p. 43.

As will appear more fully in Chapter X, one of the main causes of sickness is the retribution of the gods for failure to make the compensatory offerings. The evil winds, that so often bring disease, are in many cases (but not all) sent by the yuntzilob. Wherever the yuntzilob are, there also are the evil winds. If a man crosses a path where shortly before a balam has been, it is likely that an evil wind will strike him there. In the ceremonies, after the yuntzilob have been summoned to take the food offered, there is special danger from *vientos;* therefore, when the ceremony is over, the h-men sprinkles balche to remove that danger, otherwise some child might walk over the spot and be taken sick. The holy has two inseparable aspects: the beneficent and the punitive, the bounty-yielding and the perilous.

Essentially the ceremonies consist of an offering of certain special foods and drinks to the gods. Most of them fall into three parts: an invitation to the yuntzilob to be present at some later hour to receive the offerings; the actual delivery of the prepared foods to the gods, including a solemn invocation and a short period when the men retire to allow the gods to take the spiritual essence (*gracia*) of the food; and the concluding feasting of the devotees on the food from which the *gracia* has been taken. Between the first part of the ceremony and the second there is an interval, during which the ritual foodstuffs are prepared and consecrated. This essential ritual core is surrounded with other elements of ceremony. Some, like the asperging with balche or with rum, and the recitation of fixed formal prayers, are common to all the ceremonies; others, such as the mimetic rainstorm in the cha-chaac, are peculiar to just one ceremony. But the resemblances among the different ceremonies are so great that, in describing one in detail, one describes much that occurs in many or even all of the others.

On the other hand, there are considerable differences between two performances of the same ceremony. Some variations are due to differences in the special circumstances that call forth two examples of what is regarded as the same ceremony. Thus an u hanli col performed to cure the sickness of the man who gives it includes features not present when given as one of the periodic ritual offerings of gratitude and propitiation. Other differences, often quite conspicuous, are due to contrasting practices of individual h-mens. Thus, while the same h-men in giving the same ceremony a second time will not substantially vary the prayers he uses, two different h-mens performing the same ceremony will use quite different prayers and will introduce other noticeable variations—in the exact mode of preparation of the sacred breadstuffs, for example; or one will insert a piece of ritual additional to the central body of practice to which all will adhere. For these reasons it is best to begin by describing the features that are fundamental to all ceremonies, then to indicate the elements essential to a ceremony of a given name, and finally to suggest some of the occasional variants of the same ceremony.

The offerings vary, but characteristically for the important ceremonies there are four: zaca, balche, boiled fowl prepared in a certain manner, and breadstuffs cooked in the earth-oven. Although the ingredients of this sacred cookery (with the exception of balche) are common to the secular cookery, not one of the dishes offered to the gods is a part of common fare. Zaca is maize cooked without lime, ground, and stirred into cold water. It is rarely eaten except when prepared as an offering to the yuntzilob. Balche is an intoxicating drink made by steeping the bark of the Lonchocarpus tree in water and adding honey. Although the older men remember when balche was made and drunk as a secular intoxicant, it is nowadays a purely ritual drink, always offered in gourd vessels of special form (homa).

The fowl to be sacrificed are consecrated by having balche put into their beaks just before they are strangled. The meat is boiled and served in gourd vessels. The broth is seasoned with pepper, arnotto, clove, cumin, garlic, marjoram, *epazote*, cinnamon and salt, and is thickened with cornmeal dough, that has been cooked in the pib, to make a thick soup called kol, or yacĥ. This dish is also made only as an offering. It is combined with parts of the boiled fowl, in very definitely fixed ways.

The breadstuffs are known generically as tuti-uah. Each kind of ceremony calls for definite numbers of certain classes of these breads, and each bread is dedicated to certain of the invited gods and is afterward consumed by the participants in the ceremony according to their rôles. Seven kinds of sacred breadstuffs are made in the earth-oven. With the exception of the last (nabal-uah), all are made by taking a ball of ordinary cornmeal (*masa*; zacan), putting into the center a small quantity of ground squash seed, which is spoken of as the "heart" (puczikal), and then flattening out the ball to form a large tortilla.

Noh-uah ("great bread"). A pile is made of thirteen, eleven, nine or seven large tortillas, each of which is covered on one side with a paste of zicil (ground squash seed) and water. On the topmost tortilla depressions are made with the finger and filled with zicil. The number of depressions corresponds to the number of tortillas in the pile.

Cruz-uah ("cross bread"). The same as noh-uah, except that the topmost tortilla is marked with a cross, filled with zicil.

Bolon-taz-uah ("nine-layer-bread"). A pile of six such tortillas. On the topmost, nine depressions in the form of a cross are made with the fingers and filled with zicil.

Hol-che-uah (or hoppel-uah). Precisely similar to the preceding, except that only five tortillas constitute the pile and only five depressions are made.

Yaxche-uah ("ceiba bread"; also called ba, "gopher," "because they are given to the boys who hide under the altar at the cĥa-chaac, like those animals"). Single, large, long and narrow tortillas.

Yal-uah ("divide bread"). Four tortillas, with a leaf of the plant called bob between each two, and with four holes arranged in a square and filled with zicil on the topmost.

Nabal-uah. The remaining dough is thoroughly mixed with zicil and made into large thick tortillas of diminishing size superimposed on one another to form a sort of pyramid. These breads are mixed with the broth to make the kol.

All these breads are wrapped in bob leaves, tied with strips from a hibiscus tree (hol), and are cooked in the pib.

The foods offered to the gods are special, consecrate and holy. These offerings are suitable for the gods, not simply because they are traditionally correct but because they evoke two categories of thought which on the one hand suggest the rain-giving functions of the gods and express the dominant prayer (for rain) and on the other signify the purity of that which is set apart for divinity.

Many of the foods and drinks in the native's experience, and many other elements in his environment, are regarded as belonging to one of two classes: "the cold class" (ziz u.cuch), or "the hot class" (choko cuch, or kinal cuch). "Cold" things are "cold" (ziz), not so much because their temperature is low, as because, in the case of foods, they are good for fevers and bad for chills; or because, in the case of plants and other parts of nature, they are green, fresh and suggestive of water. The ramifications of this double category into the notions of diet and of disease will be discussed in another chapter.

All the offerings made to the yuntzilob in the ceremonies belong to the "cold" class. Zaca is "cold," while *atole* is "hot." The water from zaca is a useful remedy for fevers. Balche is very "cold." So are all foods cooked in the pib. It does not matter how warm they actually are; as soon as they are cooked in the earth-oven, they are "cold." But foods cooked on the pot or on the griddle (*comal*) are "hot"; and as the broth made from the consecrated fowl is prepared in a pot, the h-men adds a little balche to it, to make it "cold."

All the plants—habin, halal and xiat—used in the ceremonies are "cold" also. These are evidently "cold" because they grow near the cenotes and remain green after other plants are dry. Xiat is the "coldest"; it is used on the altar at the cha-chaac. At the other ceremonies habin is used. All these are known as ziz-che ("cold trees"). Chac-ah belongs to this class, and of it is made the lelem (p. 142) used by the chaac impersonator. Beehives must be made of "cold" trees, or the bees will not thrive. Lands are recognized as being either "cold" or "hot." Hot lands are those that dry quickly after rain or from which rise mists at night. This mist (yoxol luum) is the heat rising from the ground. "Cold" lands are those that remain moist. In order to determine if a piece of land be "hot" or "cold" one buries in the ground a piece of habin (a "cold" plant) and if, after three days, it is found to be still green and fresh, the land is "cold." Trees grow fast, but not well, on "hot" lands; they soon turn yellow and die. On "cold" lands they grow slowly but well.

Everything at the ceremonies must be "cold," as the punishment brought by the yuntzilob is always sickness in the form of fever. The offering of "cold" things is, incidentally, an expression of the wish that fevers be not brought to men. "Cold" lands are safe from evil winds, which are associated with "hot" foods, "hot" lands, and "hot" plants. The winds, sent by the yuntzilob to punish men, bring fevers. Drought is also a punishment of the gods; it is a fever of the milpa. When the pibil-nal (p. 143) is made, zaca is offered to offset the danger of the heat of the pibs. When the fields are burned, the heat of the burning brings danger of fever. It is best to wait with the sowing till all the yoxol luum has passed out of the ground; then the maize will grow well.

The other general idea which is involved in the offerings made to the gods is expressed by the word zuhuy, which is most easily translated "virgin." It means more than the absence of sexual intercourse, although this idea is involved. A zuhuy colel is not merely a virgin—the word is used of girls who do not go out much and mix with others. The water, drawn for the cha-chaac from covered cenotes where men seldom or never come, is zuhuy ha. The animals of the zip, the deer that are kept by their supernatural owners in secluded spots in the woods, are zuhuy alakob. A hammock or a tablecloth that has never been used is zuhuy.

The high bush, distant from the homes of men, is zuhuy. The gods are there. Therefore it is thought bad to have sexual intercourse out of doors, either in the house-lot or in the bush. Even in the milpa, a man sleeps with his wife only in the little hut built there. If the yuntzilob should see sexual intercourse, they would become offended and send the kazap-ik (p. 167) to bring sickness to the couple.[1] Nor does one act boisterously, or foolishly in the bush, because it is zuhuy.

The animals offered to the gods must be zuhuy. In dedicating fowl, the h-men speaks of them as zuhuy alakob. They are alakob (domestic or tame animals) because they have been dedicated to the gods, and they are zuhuy for the same reason. It is customary to set aside turkeys or hens that are to be sacrificed, keeping them apart from other fowl. Capons are most suitable as offerings. So also are hens that have ceased to lay. Cocks are never offered, but young cockerels may be sacrificed as noox.[2] Turkeys are not castrated, but a turkey cock that is to be given to the gods is kept from others, especially hens; then it becomes zuhuy alak.

This notion of "that which is set apart" becomes almost the same as "that which is holy; that which is effective in dealing with the gods." Thus, because balche is made only by men, because it is used only for the ceremonies, and because it is "cold," it is preferred in all important ceremonies to rum. It is said: "Balche is more zuhuy than rum."

The center of ceremonial activity is the table-altar, which the h-men erects in the yard where the ceremony takes place or, in the case of the cha-chaac, in a cleared rectangular area in the bush. All the ritual foods are arranged in a definite manner on this table before they are formally delivered to the gods. The foods that are provided for the greatest gods are set nearest to the cross, which is always set up in the center of the eastern side of the altar. The altar is oriented with the points of the compass, the h-men and the other participants facing eastward as the invocation and dedication take place. That is because the gods are situated in the chun caan, in the eastern sky (p. 116).

In the prayers, the altar is often referred to as *mesa;* however, it is built not like modern tables, but tied together, as is the Maya house; and the four forked corner posts (ocom) and the horizontal posts (balo), that rest in these forks, bear the same names as do the corresponding parts of a house. To each corner-post is bound a branch of habin (except in the cha-chaac when xiat is used); and the two pairs of these branches are fastened together at the top to form arches. The symbolism of these arches is not apparent, to Maya laymen at least.

[1] The same idea is held with regard to the *santos.* The *santos* must not see sexual intercourse. Therefore most people have little cases into which they put the *santos* at night. It is remembered that "the old people" built separate shrines for their *santos.* It likewise brings sickness to expel flatulence from the rectum before a *santo.*

[2] A noox is a smaller fowl put with a larger one to complete the offering. Such a pair often makes up the gift to the gods. Generally, "noox" is something supplied to support or complete another larger than itself, in order that the latter may not fall or fail. A piece of stone or wood set under the leg of a table, to keep it from toppling, is noox. If a house-post is too short, it is completed with a noox. Every officer should have his noox (as do the organizers of the fiestas) so he will not fail. "The Governor does not fall because he has many noox."

In some ceremonies the participants move around this altar, as in others, involving the hives, they walk around the hives. Such movement takes place in a counterclockwise direction. This is thought of as going "to the right." [1] "If we should move to the left, we would be serving the devil."

The principles that have just been described are fully manifest only in the longer ceremonies held in the latter part of the agricultural year, but in order to preserve the natural order of events, the following account begins with the simple rituals which initiate the agricultural round.

MAKING THE MILPA

In the thinking of the native of Chan Kom, the felling of the bush is a matter of concern to the kuilob kaaxob, for it is they who protect the trees of the forest. No offerings are made to these deities when the felling begins—the kuilob kaaxob will be thanked at harvest-time for their part in assuring the yield—but one negative observance asserts the dependence of the practical act on supernatural sanction. If the field is being cleared for a first harvest (chacben), the agriculturalist is ordinarily careful to measure off for his milpa no more land than he is sure he will be able to clear. He cuts a narrow swathe around the proposed field, and by this act serves notice on the kuilob kaaxob that he proposes to make use of so much of the "virgin bush" (zuhuy kaax). Then when the trees ask the kuilob kaaxob if they may not do injury to the man when he begins to cut them down, the deities say no and explain to the trees that they are old and that it is good for them to be cut so that new growth may come up. But if the agriculturalist measures off more land than he later clears, then the kuilob kaaxob grow angry; for they have been deceived and have been asked to keep back the trees from doing ill when in fact the trees were not to be cut at all. Then they tell the trees to do injury to the man. Stories are told of men who returned a second year to fell bush that had been measured the previous year, and who were injured or killed by the fall of a tree or the slipping of an ax. And if such an accident occurs, it is suggested that probably the unfortunate man at some time in the past in this way offended the protectors of the forest.

When the felled bush is dry, it is ready for burning. As has been explained, this is a critical time, for the agriculturalist is torn between the disposition to defer the burning until the field is surely dry enough to burn and the fear that the rains may come and make it impossible to burn it at all. In solving this uncertainty, he is assisted by the mode of divination known as xoc kin ("day count"). This system of prognostication is attended to by the h-men. It is based upon the supposition that the weather prevailing during certain days and hours of the month of January is like weather which will prevail during each of the remaining months of the year. As recognized in Chan Kom, the correspondences of the xoc kin are in four parts: (1) Hunualak-xoc ("one turn count"), in which the twelve first days of January in their natural order predict the weather for twelve months of the year, respectively. (2) Caualak-xoc ("two turn count"),

---

[1] The right hand is considered better than the left; the right as good and the left as evil. The old people advise that one sleep not on one's right side but on one's left, so that the left hand may be held down during sleep where it can do no harm.

in which the second twelve days of January announce the weather for the twelve months of the year, but in inverse order, the thirteenth day corresponding to December, the fourteenth to November, and so on. (3) Oxualak-xoc ("three turn count"), in which each successive day from January 25 to January 30 corresponds to each of the successive pairs of months, beginning with January-February. (4) Canualak-xoc ("four turn-count"), in which each of the hours from six in the morning to six in the evening on January 31 corresponds to one of the twelve months of the year, beginning with January. The h-men remembers the weather prevailing at each of the days and hours in January involved in the prognostication and sums up, for the benefit of his consultants, the probabilities as to the weather during each of the remaining months of the year.

Once the agriculturalist has made up his mind when to fire his milpa, his worries are not over. The actual moment of firing is critical, for if the bush does not burn thoroughly to a fine ash, it will be difficult or even impossible to sow the field. One important unpredictable factor is the wind: a strong breeze from the

WHISTLE FOR THE WINDS

right direction will carry the flames swiftly across the field, even though the trees be not thoroughly dry. Therefore at the moment of kindling, the prayer is to the whirlwinds (kakal-mozon-ikob), that they may descend upon the field and sweep the flames across it. It is common for the agriculturalist to make an offering of zaca to these wind spirits, and sometimes also to the balams and to the chaacs. This is a small private ritual; the h-men is not involved; therefore there is a good deal of individual variation in the practice. The small altar of poles is erected outside of the southeast corner of the field and tangental to it. On this some men place two bowls (gourd dishes) of zaca for the kakal-mozon-ikob. Others regard one of these two bowls as an offering to the kunku-chaac. Some men offer three bowls, and still others four, "because there are four balams who guard the milpa," and at least one man adds a fifth, "for the fifth balam who is above the center of the field." One man, during the time of these observations, did not make the offerings at all, but later, after his milpa had burned, placed zaca in the field for the mozon-ikob.

Some men say nothing when they make this offering, merely scooping out a little of the gruel to each of the four directions. Others say, in Maya, "Mozon-ikob, here I hand over to you your zaca. Come and help me burn my milpa."

As the agriculturalist and his helpers run along the two sides of the field, kindling the dry bush, they make the whistle summoning the winds, ending with a shout. "Immediately the whirlwinds come, bowing down the trees and flattening the grass, and carrying the flames across the milpa."

When the men reach the ends of the field, they return to the little altar, where the zaca is divided among them and eaten.

A similar private offering to the agricultural deities is made by the older men before sowing (Plate 11, b). Like the offering made at the time of burning, there is no uniformity in the character of the ritual, and the younger men tend to neglect it entirely.[1] When the offering is made, the little altar is erected in the center of the milpa. Probably the commonest practice is to make the offering just before sowing the milpa on which the first rains have fallen, and to set out two gourd vessels of zaca—one for the kunku-chaac and one for the other agricultural deities. One man (who comes from Yaxcaba) makes the offering at any convenient time between burning and sowing. He offers five bowls, "one for each of the balams," and recites a part of the Ave Maria (as other men on the same occasion recite the Credo) as he scoops out zaca with a habin leaf, spilling it in each of the four directions.[2]

THE DINNER-OF-THE-MILPA

The ceremony of this name (u hanli col) is the most important of all agricultural rituals performed by and for the individual agriculturalist. It requires the services of the h-men; it demands the aid of a group of male friends; and it consumes several hours of time and a considerable quantity of food and drink. By performing it the agriculturalist establishes satisfactory relations with the chaacs, balams and kuilob kaaxob. The ceremony secures him wealth and health: the beneficence of the yuntzilob assures him a good harvest; and if it be omitted, they will bring sickness upon him. It is recognized that one should perform the ceremony every four years, at a time when the maize is just ripening. But many men neglect the ceremony until sickness reminds them of their remissness. Then, advised by the h-men that the cause of their sickness lies in this failure, they perform the ceremony. The ritual is thus on some occasions a therapeutic measure; on others, an expression of thanksgiving and a measure of prudence. Although the ceremony may be performed at any time of year, it is most common in August, September and October.

As in the other ceremonies, the h-men begins by clearing a piece of land 15 or 20 meters square. As this ceremony is performed at the initiative of some one man, the clearing is made in the yard of his house. The usual altar is erected, covered with habin leaves and provided with a small wooden cross. The h-men begins by offering zaca to the gods, asperging the altar with it using a leaf of habin, and reciting a prayer which invites the yuntzilob to the feast that they are about to prepare.

[1] In Piste they say, "These were things of the old people; no one does them now."
[2] In all these offerings of zaca it is customary to scoop out some of the corn gruel to each of the four directions with a leaf of habin, and afterward to drink a little of it.

The owner of the house has asked some of his friends to help him. The h-men now directs these men to prepare the earth-oven and he supervises the preparation of the sacred breadstuffs. In this work the laymen are engaged for an hour or more, mixing the meal with water, patting out the cakes, inserting the squash seed and other special ingredients and grouping them into the specified piles. This is play, not work nor prayer. The atmosphere of sanctity, manifest in the operations of the h-men and in the subdued voices of other participants, is qualified by the bustle and interest aroused by the preparation of the breads for the oven.

While the sacred breads are baking, the h-men offers balche to the gods. This has been prepared three days in advance of the ceremony, so that it may have reached the desired degree of fermentation. As is almost invariably the case in offering balche, the liquor is placed in thirteen of those vessels known as homa (p. 36), and these are placed on the altar. When this is done (and again from time to time during the rest of the ceremony) balche is sprinkled on the cross and on the altar itself with a half-folded leaf of habin employed as a scoop. This is done because balche has the quality of sanctifying and cleansing from impurity and evil anything with which it comes in contact. This is also the association that makes the intoxication of the h-men a part of the sacred developments of the ritual, although, in fact, rum is used to hasten this condition.

The h-men recites a prayer inviting the gods to come and partake of the liquor. After a pause, to allow the deities to do this, the balche is distributed among those present. No one may refuse to drink at least a little. Each recipient returns thanks in the phrase always employed in the distribution of sacred food and drink: ox tezcuntabac tech, tat ("Thrice be saluted, sir").

The second dedicatory act is the consecration and offering of fowl. As has been explained (p. 127), the number of these varies with special circumstances. In some cases the h-men directs the giver of the ceremony to hold the fowl while he consecrates them. One h-men appoints four persons, whom he calls Chaacs, each one of whom holds a leg or a wing of the fowl while it is ritually killed.[1] The consecration is accomplished by the recitation of a short prayer by the h-men while he puts balche down the victim's beak with a scoop of habin. As the prayer concludes, the assistant (or the four Chaacs) kills the fowl, the hens by wringing their necks, and the turkeys by cutting tongue or throat and allowing them to bleed to death.

These ritual acts of the h-men take place after intervals during which he is occupied in arranging the altar, in directing the preparatory activities of his assistants, and in drinking quantities of rum. At this point in the ceremonies another interval occurs, during which the laymen gather in a group to pluck and cut up the fowl. When this has been done, they carry the dismembered birds into the house, where the women (led usually by the wife of the man who is giving the ceremony) have gathered to prepare the broth (kol) which forms an essential part of all the food offerings to the gods. During the ceremonies the women must not approach the place where the h-men's activities center, but inside the house they

---

[1] This h-men explained that "in the old days it was a human being, and not a fowl, that was so held and sacrificed."

are enjoying the social pleasures incidental to the cooperative preparation of festal foods.

Meanwhile, out in the yard, the men are gossiping together and the h-men from time to time sprinkles the altar and the cross with balche, to the accompaniment of a certain spoken formula. This he does thirteen times.

The h-men is supposed to have supernatural knowledge as to when the breadstuffs in the oven are done. When he is satisfied as to this, they are removed and arranged by the h-men on the altar in a special and symmetrical arrangement.

The breadstuffs of a certain kind (nabal-uah) are broken into the clear broth prepared from the fowls, making a thick mixture referred to as kol, chocob, or yach. Four pails of these soups are distributed on the altar. On the surface of the mixture in each of the pails is placed a leg or two of the sacrificed fowls. The rest of the meat is distributed in ten gourd vessels, each one of which is placed on top of one of ten piles of sacred breadstuffs. The arrangement of the offerings, which we have seen used, is indicated in the accompanying diagram.

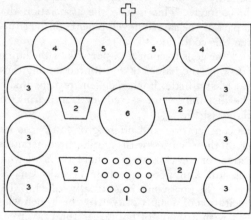

1. Thirteen homa of balche.
2. Four pails of yach.
3. Six yal-uah   ⎫   Piles of breadstuff, each sur-
4. Two bolon-taz-uah ⎬   mounted by a gourd vessel
5. Two noh-uah   ⎭   filled with fowl meat.
6. One holche-uah (largest breadstuff).

Fɪɢ. 13—Arrangement of the altar at the u hanli col ceremony.

The cumulative point of the ceremony has now arrived. The h-men lights two candles and, placing grains of incense on a dish holding live coals, incenses the altar. He then kneels in front of the altar. On each side of him kneel two special assistants (idzacob), named by him without formality from among the participants. As he kneels he recites a prayer that is the longest of those used in the ceremony. Although the texts used by different h-mens differ, the tenor of their context is the same. Using the invocatory formula, "ox tezcuntabac cu lubul in than" ("thrice be greeted, as falls my word") these prayers call upon the chaacs and the balams, one by one. They must all be summoned to partake of the offerings. The chaacs and balams of the four directions, "in the four corners of the sky, in the four corners of the clouds," are addressed by the invocatory formula, "Be thrice greeted."

Then, over and over, the h-men repeats this phrase, following it each time with the name of some place in the neighborhood of Chan Kom. Some of the places are occupied villages today; some are the sites of ruins from ancient times (Coba, Chichen and Oxkinkiuic) and some are merely *milperíos* or cenotes in uninhabited bush. But in all these places are cenotes, and it is not so much the places he is invoking, as the chaacs (and balams?) thought to reside in them.

During the prayer the two idzacs sprinkle the altar with balche. Then the h-men, with the aid of the idzacs (and sometimes of four other men), lifts the offerings from the table, one by one, and as he holds each up he recites a short prayer dedicating that breadstuff to the gods, afterward setting it again upon the altar (Plate 12*a*). Everyone then withdraws a short distance from the altar, while the gods, now present in response to the invocation, take the *gracia* of the food. At the end of this period the h-men moves the foods from the altar to an ordinary table, where he blesses them with the usual phrase "u kaba *Dios* yumbil, *Dios* mehenbil, *Dios Espíritu Santo. Amen*" ("In the name of God the Father, God the Son, and God the Holy Ghost. Amen"). The food is divided among all present, the h-men retaining the largest share, and a feast ensues.

When this is over, the h-men takes down the altar and directs the idzacs to sprinkle balche in the form of a cross, in two diagonals from altar post to altar post.

The foregoing description presents the ritual elements present in the various examples of the u hanli col included in the observations upon which this study is based. The conspicuous variations appear from a comparison of the ceremony as performed by one h-men with its performance by another. One h-men (and others agree with him in this practice) introduces an element of ritual that, judging by its form, may have been incorporated into the ceremony from the Catholic communion. Just after dedicating the separate breadstuffs to the gods, he makes use of a special homa, made in the shape of a very small calabash, and known as tzel. This he fills with balche and covers the mouth with habin leaves arranged in the form of a cross and then with a napkin on which is embroidered a cross; this cross he causes to coincide with the cross of habin leaves. The homa, so wrapped, is passed among those present, who reverently kiss the embroidered cross. The h-men then kneels by the altar with his head bent over the homa and recites a short prayer, He then unwraps the homa and drinks the contents, while the two idzacs do the same with two ordinary homas of liquor which they hold; and balche is distributed to all present. This procedure is then gone through a second time with a smaller quantity of balche in the same vessel.[1]

THE DINNER-OF-THE-THUP

A ceremony very similar to the preceding, but involving the offering of only one hen, is known as u hanli x-thup. This ceremony is offered to the smallest and most important of the chaacs (p. 115), who is regarded as the guardian of a certain

[1] *Cf.* "Ppobom-mesa," (p. 197).

sort of corn (x-thup-nal) that matures rapidly and is harvested a few weeks after planting. Persons planting such corn are supposed to make the ceremony once a year. But, as is the case with other ceremonies that have a theoretical periodicity, the obligation is often disregarded until sickness serves as a reminder; and the debt of hens is allowed to accumulate. "I plant x-thup-nal," said one man, "but I make the u hanli x-thup only when I get sick. So now it is seven years since I made the ceremony." Most of the men in Chan Kom, in part restrained by the trouble of making the offering, do not plant this variety of maize at all. "I never plant x-thup-nal," said one of the majority, "because the x-thup is so demanding of offerings that when one neglects to make them he punishes one with serious sickness." For this reason, chiefly, the ceremony did not come into the field of direct observation.

THE RAIN CEREMONY

Ritual finds its most elaborate expression in the ceremony known as cha-chaac ("bring-rain"). The reasons why this is so have already been indicated (p. 123). The cha-chaac is not the mere periodic offering that prudence impels as are, commonly, the u hanli col and the u hanli cab. Nor is it stimulated, as are those two ceremonies on many occasions, by anything so private and individual as one man's sickness. The cha-chaac is performed only in response to crucial need that strikes simultaneously at everyone: the common anxiety produced by drought. Only pestilence brings about a situation that is comparable, and to combat pestilence there is another major communal ceremony (p. 175).

Therefore the cha-chaac is a ceremony in which every man in the village participates. During the period of its celebration all ordinary masculine activities cease; the entire adult male population is gathered at the place of ceremony. Therefore, although the ritual forms used in the cha-chaac conform to the pattern represented by the u hanli col, they are cast on a larger scale. Where the other ceremonies require only a few hours, the cha-chaac demands three days; where the others demand the sacrifice of a few fowl, the cha-chaac requires dozens, with cornmeal dough in proportion. Finally, the fact that this ceremony expresses the desire of all the participants for just one particular concrete result—the coming of rain—is ritually reflected in the mimetic representation of rainstorm which forms the central feature of the cha-chaac.

During the period of these observations only one cha-chaac was performed in Chan Kom. The following account is, therefore, written in the past tense. The h-men who officiated was one who had charge of several of the variant u hanli col ceremonies just mentioned; the ritual about to be described probably includes some elements not characteristic of all cha-chaacs—notably the element of ceremonial drinking from a special homa.[1] Some of the prayers this h-men used for the cha-chaac were identical with those which he uses habitually for the u hanli col.

The summer of 1930 was unusually dry. The people of the villages saw their entire harvest threatened by a prolonged drought. This was not the only anxiety.

[1] Notes on other cha-chaacs are given on p. 143.

PLATE 11

a, Carved stone figure at X-Ceh-yaax, regarded as a portrait of an alux by people of Chan Kom.

b, Making offering of zaca to the gods of the rain and of the milpa, preparatory to sowing.

PLATE 12

a, U hanli col ceremony.   Offering the breads to the gods.

b, Cha-chaac ceremony.   Offering the breads to the gods.

The drought being merely local, much corn was growing elsewhere and the price of maize had accordingly fallen to the extraordinarily low figure of one peso a *carga*. An epizoötic was destroying the hogs. By the middle of July the number of candles burned in the *oratorio* had notably increased. People were going singly to bear their individual troubles to the *santo*. As the dry weather was prolonged, it became more and more a subject of conversation till it absorbed other interests. Individual concerns coalesced in one great communal anxiety. The first public expression of need was a *novenario* held for the patron *santo*. Rain fell thereafter, but not in sufficient quantities to save the threatened corn, now approaching ripening. The *novenario* was followed by prayers to the Holy Cross and others to the *Señor Dios*. But the drought persisted. Then at last, at the end of August, the men of Chan Kom decided to hold the cha-chaac. A h-men of repute, from a neighboring village, was already present, summoned by one agriculturalist to perform for him the u hanli col. He was asked to take the rain ceremony in charge.

Early on the morning of the first day he erected an altar, in exactly the manner described in connection with the u hanli col, in the yard back of the *cuartel* (public building). More commonly the place for the cha-chaac is at a slightly greater distance from the plaza, on the outskirts of the village. The withdrawal of the men from contact with the women, which is always a part of the ceremonies over which the h-men presides, is particularly manifest in the cha-chaac. This feeling is expressed in the first collective act involved in this ceremony. At noon on this first day all the men went with the h-men to get "virgin water" from a cenote situated in the depth of the forest some kilometers from Chan Kom. Water used in preparing the foodstuffs for the other ceremonies is customarily drawn from the village cenote, but at the first hour of dawn before it has been contaminated for ritual purposes by contact with the women who there draw water for household purposes. For the cha-chaac this precaution is not sufficient and the water must come from the sacred cenote, where women are supposed never to go. The h-men tells the others that it is to this cenote that the chaacs come to fill their calabashes when they are about to water the young maize plants. The cenote can be reached only by crawling through a dark and slippery tunnel, about 30 meters in length. The difficulty of entrance, and the snake-wise movement of the torch-lit procession enhance the awesomeness of the ritual act.

In the evening the men returned and hung their calabashes beside the altar. Many of the men now swung their hammocks near the cleared space; and here it is expected they should remain till the ceremony is concluded. Once the sacred water has been brought, no one is supposed to return home. This provision assures that during the period of the ceremony no man has intercourse with a woman, a circumstance which, the h-men assures them, would pollute the sanctity of the proceedings and render them of no avail. The men spend the hours not occupied in sleeping or in actual preparations for the ritual in conversation and story-telling.

On this particular occasion, activities were resumed a little before dawn on the second day. The h-men named two of the older men as idzacs. They received and recorded in a notebook the two kilos of zaca, one-quarter kilo of sugar, and two candles which each man contributed. When these materials had been collected, the h-men prepared part of the zaca, stirring the meal into water from the calabashes. He put a large water-jar of zaca on the altar and offered "holy cold water" to the chaacs and balams. Then the idzacs divided the zaca among those present. This was the first of six times that day that this act was performed.

At about six o'clock in the morning, the h-men prepared three jars of zaca and placed them in gourd-carries (cħuyub) hanging in a tree near the altar. These were offered to, respectively, San Gabriel, San Marcelino, San Cecilio, the guardians of the forest, and the zip (p. 117) who watch over the deer, asking them for "virgin animals." The word (alak) used in the prayer is that reserved for tamed or domesticated animals; for the deer are the domestic animals, or familiars, of these deities. The prayers ask "that the zips may not warn the deer of the approach of the hunters"—it is a prayer for success in the hunt.

After reciting it, the h-men went to the altar and consulted his zaztuns. By looking into these small bits of translucent stone or glass, the h-men professes to learn the wishes of the gods. On this occasion he announced that "by the will of *Santos* Lazaro, Jorge and Roque,[1] you will kill two deer over toward X-Cocail." The prophecy was received with shouts of delight, and the hunters made off through the bush. At about eleven o'clock they returned, sweaty and weary, and without any deer. The h-men explained that probably the zip had protected the deer, but that they would be found in the direction of Tzeal. Zaca was again offered to the yuntzilob and thereafter the hunt was resumed, this time with more success, for the hunters got a small deer in the predicted direction. The meat was cooked in an earth-oven and placed on the altar for the hunters to eat.

At three o'clock in the afternoon, at seven in the evening and twice again before two in the morning, the h-men offered zaca to the gods; as before, the meal was divided among the men and consumed. In the intervals the men amused themselves by eating toasted squash seed and telling stories.

The activities of the first two days were preliminary to the actual ceremony, which took place on the third. At dawn, after a short intermission for sleep, the h-men filled thirteen homa and two shallow gourd vessels with balche and offered it to the gods with the same prayer used on the analogous occasion in the u hanli col ceremony.

Then he called to four of the men present; these seated themselves on a bench in front of the altar and chanted a prayer to the chaacs and balams for rain. This ended, the idzacs distributed the balche among those present.

Meanwhile, inside the houses of the village, the women had been preparing the dough and the ground squash seed to be used in making the sacred breadstuffs. Morning had now come, and the idzacs received and entered in their notebooks the amounts contributed that day by each man: three kilos of dough, one-half a kilo of

---

[1] The h-men on this occasion referred to these three *santos*, but the others previously mentioned are generally regarded as the guardians of the deer.

ground squash seed, a hen, and 75 centavos with which to buy seasonings and with which to pay the h-men.

When the hens had been collected, they were sanctified and dedicated to the gods. As described in connection with the u hanli col, the h-men put balche down the beak of each, meanwhile repeating a prayer, the idzacs wringing each fowl's neck and then handing the h-men another. In this way twenty-three fowl were sacrificed. The prayer used here declares that there is offered to the chaacs (and to Saint Michael) a "holy virgin animal." The prayer is in nine parts; in each of the last eight parts the h-men counted the nine times he tossed the liquor down the bird's throat.

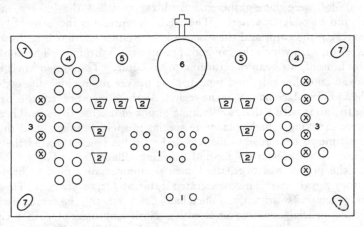

FIG. 14—Arrangement of the altar at the cha-chaac ceremony.

1. Thirteen homa and two shallow gourd dishes of balche
2. Nine pails of soup
3. Thirty-six yal-uah (those marked with a cross were surmounted by dishes of chicken-meat)
4. Two bolontaz-uah
5. Two noh-uah
6. One holche-uah
7. Four yaxche-uah

This proceeding consumed a considerable period of time. When it was over, the h-men returned to his hammock, and thereafter from time to time interrupted his rest to approach the altar and asperge the cross and the table with balche, to the accompaniment of the usual prayer. This he did thirteen times, and thirteen times the consecrated balche was distributed and consumed, the men returning the usual formula of thanks: "ox tezcuntabac tech, tat."

The morning was spent in the preparation of the sacred breadstuffs. These were the same as those prepared for the u hanli col ceremony, except that as this was a ceremony for the chaacs, many more yal-uah were made (this being the kind offered to these deities), and, in addition, four yaxche-uah ("ceiba-bread") were prepared. By the time the breads were ready, it was midday and the idzacs covered the cross on the altar with branches of habin, to protect it from the rays of the sun.[1] The breads were taken from the pib, and with the soups (prepared as

[1] To keep it "cold." See p. 130.

described for the u hanli col) and the balche, were arranged on the altar as indicated in the diagram (fig. 14).

The moment had now come to deliver the feast to the gods and to make more explicit the prayer for rain. The h-men fastened four boys under the table-altar, each tied by the right foot to one post of the altar. These were the "frogs." He then selected one of the older men to impersonate the kunku-chaac, chief of the raingods. The two idzacs and two other men lifted this man up and carried him to a specially cleared space about 8 meters east of the altar—the "Trunk of Heaven" (chun-caan), where the kunku-chaac is thought to dwell. This was done with care and reverence and in such a manner that none turned his back to the altar, for now all the yuntzilob were there gathered. An idzac supplied the impersonator with a calabash and a wooden machete. The calabash represents those used by the rain-gods in watering the corn, and the wooden knife stands for that brandished object known as lelem, with which the raingods produce the lightning. The kunku-chaac was left by himself, his bearers returning to the altar. The h-men knelt before it, with an idzac on either side, and repeated the prayer summoning the gods and invoking the various place-names of the region. As the h-men prayed, the idzacs were sprinkling the altar with balche and adding grains of incense to a small brazier; the "frogs" were croaking a particular note special to such occasions, and the kunku-chaac from time to time rose to his feet and with his voice imitated the sound of thunder, and with his lelem the flash of lightning (Plate 13a and b).

When the prayer was over, the h-men summoned four men to help him lift the food from the altar, and he consecrated it, bit by bit, to the gods. Then (as this particular h-men was wont to do in the u hanli col ceremony), he ceremonially drank balche from a special homa covered with a cloth embroidered with a cross; and caused every man to follow him in draining a homa of balche. This ended, all went some distance from the altar, keeping complete silence so as not to interrupt the feasting of the gods, now enjoying the *gracia* of the tuti-uah and the kol.

When the h-men decided that the gods had finished, he ordered four men to go with him to the kunku-chaac impersonator. When they were in his presence, the h-men poured balche on his head, saying, "In the name of God the Father, God the Son, God the Holy Ghost, once, twice, three times, four times, thirteen times in the name of God the Holy Ghost. Amen."

The impersonator of the kunku-chaac then went and sat among the "frogs," who were busy consuming the yaxche-uah. The other tuti-uah and the soups were divided among all present, and the ceremony concluded with the usual feast.

Afterward the h-men built one of the little racks used to make minor offerings, consisting of two horizontal poles bound to two vertical ones, and on this placed thirteen dishes of zaca, offering them to the deities with the prayer first used in the ceremony. Then, assisted by the idzacs, he took down the little altar and sanctified the place by sprinkling it with balche. This sprinkling of balche, so much used in all these agricultural ceremonies, is the device whereby things and persons are safely conveyed from the world of the secular to that of the sacred, and back again. The

PLATE 13

a. Cha-chaac ceremony. H-men kneeling at the altar, "frogs" seated beneath it, and Kunku in the center background.

b. Cha-chaac ceremony. At the left an idzac is sprinkling the altar with balche.

PLATE 14

a. H-men consulting his zaztun during a ceremony (u hanli col).

b, H-men performing a *santiguar.*

altar becomes a place where the gods may approach when balche is sprinkled upon it, and the fowl are consecrated to the gods by the same act. On the other hand, the place of ceremony, and the man who assumed the role of kunku-chaac, are made once more safe for the activities of ordinary life by means of this same asperging with balche.[1]

FIRST FRUIT CEREMONIES (HOL-CHE)

Of each sort of foodstuffs which the harvest yields, it is thought proper to make an offering to the gods of agriculture (see p. 112). But only in the case of maize, the staple, is the harvest ceremony one of importance and expressed in ritual of which only the h-men has command. For the other crops the simple practice is to hang gourd vessels of the new crop in the yard of the house, or in the field from which the harvest is taken. This some people do, but not all. It is common to make an offering of the first beans of the year. This little ritual does not require the h-men and it differs from all the elaborate agricultural rituals, in that the offerings are made by the women of each household. They prepare special bread-stuffs: buul-i-uah, a mixture of cornmeal and beans, and ib-uah, a mixture of white beans, cornmeal and ground squash seeds, and bake them in an earth-oven. Plain boiled beans (kabac-buul), or some of the buul-i-uah, together with thirteen tortillas and a gourd-vessel of *atole* of new corn, is hung on a tree in the yard of the house for a few hours, until the deities have taken the *gracia* of the food.

But neither beans nor any other foodstuff except maize has for the people an importance at all comparable with that of the staple crop. The first beans or cassava of the season is a trifling matter in comparison with the new corn. The harvest of maize brings to successful conclusion the effort of the year; it is the antic-ipated event which has shaped both work and prayer for a twelvemonth. Anxiety relaxes into security. Furthermore, for eleven months the people have been living on a diet of dry corn. Now, for a few weeks, they enjoy the succulent new corn, prepared either as roasted ear (pibil-nal) or as *atole* (ahza or iz ul. See p. 39). The weeks during which the new corn is brought in are devoted to feasting and visiting, to the joys of hospitality given and received. The period of pibil-nal is a cheerful orgy.

The actual ritual attendance upon these pleasures is relatively simple. The new corn ceremony is made by each separate agriculturalist,[2] as his particular milpa ripens. But these successive ripenings take place within a period of two or three weeks. The ceremony is one for which the h-men is needed. By reason of these combined circumstances, no very time-consuming ceremony is possible.

[1] At cha-chaacs observed at settlements near Chan Kom (X-Kopteil and Santa Maria) the mimetic representation of the gods of the rain was carried further by having four men impersonate the four chaacs of the cardinal directions. These men, each with a calabash and a machete, stood at the four corners of the altar. As the h-men murmured the prayers, the chaacs began a rude dance, moving nine times around the altar, brandishing their machetes. This they did when the balche was offered, again when the breadstuffs were offered. Four boys, in addition to those acting as frogs, were put in the underbrush to imitate the sounds made by chachalacas (*Ortalis vetula*)— a bird whose cry is supposed to presage rain. At the conclusion of these cha-chaacs, the h-men and the idzacs joined hands in a circle; every man present in turn passed inside it and was gently beaten with branches of habin, meanwhile turning around nine times.

According to men of Piste, at cha-chaacs performed there the four impersonators of the chaacs are present (as is also the kunku-chaac), but there is no dance around the table. The h-men officiating at Piste is accustomed to suspend a gourd dish of balche above the altar on a swinging mat (peten) of liana (see p. 37). To this object four cords of vine are attached, and as the dedicatory moment arrives, the four chaacs at the corners of the altar set the mat swinging, spilling the balche as a symbol of rainfall.

[2] Not all make the ceremony and the duty devolves only upon those whose corn is harvested from new milpas (p. 127).

The owner of the milpa invites a group of his friends to make new roasted ears. They come together in his cornfield and harvest the first ears, which they carry to some spot beside the road leading to the milpa, but outside the village. The h-men accompanies them. At this spot, just beside the path, they dig a pit for the earth-oven. When the stones have become hot, upon them are laid bark of habin and choy or of tzalam and bohom, so that the new ears will not burn. The ears of maize, wrapped in their husks, are laid upon this bark and the pib is closed, as usual, with leaves and earth. A cross is then made of corn stalks and laid on the soft earth that covers the roasting ears. It is immediately raised again to a vertical position just east of the pib, but it leaves a cross-shaped depression in the earth. "This cross gives notice to the gods of the milpa, in case of the sickness of the owner, that the sickness is not deserved, because he has made offering of pibil-nal to the kunku-chaac, the balamob and the kuilob-kaaxob who guard the milpa."

The earth-oven is made after nightfall. At about three in the morning the men gather to open it. No woman may be present. First the h-men erects behind the pib one of those small altars made of four poles already described (p. 142). The cross of corn stalks is removed from the pib and placed on this altar. Then the pib is opened. If all the bark that was put on the stones has been burned to char-coal, it is a sign that the owner of the milpa will soon suffer from a fever. The first twenty-six ears of corn that are taken from the ground are hung from the horizontal poles of the altar in thirteen pairs, the husks of each pair being tied together. The other men stand back, while the h-men recites a short prayer (the text of which has not been obtained). The thirteen pairs of ears are usually eaten then and there. Another thirteen pairs are taken for the second part of the ceremony that follows in the yard of the owner's house. The corn-stalk cross is taken to the pile of stones on that road that marks the entrance to the village and one of the four "corners" of the pueblo over which watches one of the four guardian balams.

After the men have reached the house of the milpa-owner, the h-men erects another small pole-altar in the yard, and on this he hangs the second thirteen pairs of ears. On it also he places a cross, two lighted candles, and thirteen homa of atole of new corn. This, and the young ears, he offers to the four chaacs, reciting a prayer while pouring out a little of the atole toward the east. To this performance the others pay little attention; indeed, the h-men may be the only person present; the others are now enjoying the feasting and the festal mood inside of the house.

THE DINNER-OF-THE-BEES

Parallel to the u hanli col ceremony, in both meaning and form, is a cere-mony known as u hanli cab ("dinner of the bees"). As the former ceremony is supposed to be performed at certain intervals to propitiate the gods of the milpa, so the bee ceremony is supposed to be performed every four years to propitiate the gods of the bees, and the ceremonies are alike in that they are often deferred until the sickness of the owner reminds him to perform them. Both rituals could be discussed in connection with sickness and its cure. The formal ritual is much the same: an offering of zaca, balche, consecrated fowl and special breadstuffs to the gods. But of course the deities to whom the prayers are offered are quite different and the details of ritual are not the same.

On the evening before the ceremony, the h-men invites the lords of the bees to be present next day. On the usual altar he places thirteen homa of zaca, sweetened with honey. After the invocation has been uttered,[1] the men present wait for an hour or two, till the gods shall have taken the *gracia* of the zaca. Meanwhile,

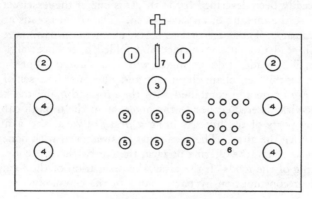

Fig. 15—Arrangement of the altar at the u hanli cab ceremony.

1. Two noh-uah, surmounted by gourd dishes containing the legs of the fowl (hub). To be given to the h-men.
2. Two bolon-taz-uah, surmounted by dishes containing other parts of the fowl (legs, or part of the breast). One to be taken by the giver of the ceremony, the other by the other idzac.
3. One cruz-uah, surmounted by a vessel containing gizzards, livers and heads. To be distributed to all.
4. Yal-uah—as many as the dough allows. Surmounted by vessels containing other parts of the meat. To be distributed to all.
5. Six pails of kol, made of the broth and of nabal-uah. To be distributed to all.
6. Thirteen homa of balche.
7. Candle.

the h-men consumes rum provided by the giver of the ceremony. When the interval has elapsed, the zaca is distributed to all.

Next morning the participants bring cornmeal to be made into the ritual breadstuffs, and the giver of the ceremony provides the fowl to be offered. The h-men puts thirteen (in some cases nine) homa of balche on the altar and offers it to the gods with a short prayer. When the breads have been taken from the pib and the kol has been made ready, the altar is arranged as in the above diagram.[2]

As in the other ceremonies, the h-men appoints two men to act as idzacs; the giver of the ceremony is usually one of these.[3] Standing between these two, the

---

[1] The text of the prayer was not secured.

[2] Although the other altar-diagrams in this chapter have been actually observed by one or the other of the writers, this one is given only from accounts of informants. The writers were unable to make satisfactory notes of the one u hanli cab they witnessed.

[3] At the u hanli cab witnessed, the giver of the ceremony was very weak with fever; he nevertheless acted as idzac; this was essential to his cure.

h-men offers the food to the gods, reciting a prayer calling upon each of the classes of bee-gods. Then the h-men and the two idzacs, carrying one homa of balche, the five large breads, two of the yal-uah, and one pail of kol, move nine times around the hives, the idzacs sprinkling balche and some of the kol on the hives, while the h-men repeats the same prayer.

FIXING-THE-PLACE-FOR-THE-HIVES

The circumstances under which this ceremony (u hedz luumil cab) takes place have already been described (p. 117). It is one of the lesser ceremonies,[1] and does not require the making of an earth-oven. The ritual breads are prepared on the griddle (*comal*). These are of two sorts: cham-cham-uah, large tortillas with ground squash seed put on one surface and folded over once; and pim-pim-uah, large thick tortillas made of dough mixed with squash seed. For each hen offered there is a pile of thirteen cham-cham-uah and one gourd vessel of zaca. Three pim-pim-uah are made and combined with the broth to make the kol.

The table-altar is erected beside the hives, as in the u hanli cab. To each of the four corner-posts of the hives is hung a *jicara* of zaca, and a fifth is hung in front of and above the altar. The zaca must be sweetened with honey. The order of the ritual is as usual: the offering of zaca, then of balche, the consecration of the fowl, the placing of the foods on the altar, the dedication of the foods to the gods, and finally their consumption by participants in the ceremony.

THE NEW HOUSE CEREMONY

Before a new house is occupied, it is felt that a ceremony should be performed to make it safe for the people who are to live in it. "Otherwise the evil winds will get in, the people will get sick, or be unable to sleep." At the present time the old ceremony (u chuyenil na) that took place on such occasions is no longer performed, principally because most new houses that are built nowadays are of masonry. The owner of such a new house summons the *mæstro cantor* and has a one-night novena to the *santo* of the house, if he has one, or to *Dios*.

The ceremony was performed in Chan Kom, and is still performed in the neighboring *rancherías*, in the following manner. Like the u hedz luumil cab, this ceremony does not require the making of a pib. No plants are used on the altar. The ceremony is exceptional in that it is not performed out of doors, but inside the house. That is because not the yuntzilob, but the house itself is the object of propitiation. The altar is erected in the middle of the room. To each of the four corner posts (ocom) the h-men suspends a gourd vessel of zaca. Then the owner of the house holds a live hen, and the h-men offers it to each of the two ocoms at one end of the house; and another hen is offered to the other two ocoms. The hens are then consecrated with rum,[2] and strangled and prepared into broth. On the altar are placed a candle, a cross, two gourd dishes containing the boiled fowl,

---

[1] The u hedz luumil cab which was observed by the writers was not satisfactory for study, as the h-men was very intoxicated and as he was apparently attempting to perform three ceremonies: a u hanli cab, a u hedz luumil cab and a loh-cab (p. 175). Discussion with informants has made clear what ritual elements are essential to each.

[2] Apparently balche need not be made for this ceremony.

two pails of kol made with nine pim-pim-uah, two small vessels of zaca, a bowl of rum, and a cloth containing twenty-five ordinary tortillas.

The h-men recites prayers and offers each of the foods successively to the poles composing the house. He begins with the ocoms, and then goes successively to the other poles in order of size. Special attention is given to the tiseras (p. 34) "because they bear the weight," and "because they have the form of crosses." In some houses three of the uinciche at each end of the house are bound together by means of a short horizontal piece, forming a very evident cross. These two crosses are given special attention and are regarded as the particular guardians of the house. Some h-mens advise that this piece be left out of new houses, because the crosses are the most demanding and would be most offended should u chuyenil na not be made. Offerings are also made to the many small crosses formed by small withes transverse to the uinciche.

Chapter IX

NOVENA AND VILLAGE FIESTA

THE NOVENA

In speaking of the ritual prayers recited in honor of *Dios* and the *santos*, the terms "novena," "*rosario*," and "*rezo*" are used almost indiscriminately. When a villager speaks of a "novena," he does not mean, necessarily, nine consecutive nights of such prayers; quite as likely he is thinking of a single session of ritual worship. Sometimes the word "*novenario*" is specially used to describe a series of nine consecutive evenings of prayer. Novenas, as held in Chan Kom, always include the recitation of a rosary, but in addition other prayers and hymns are recited or sung. In speaking of the prayers recited in repose of the souls of the dead, however (at certain intervals after death or on All Souls' Day), the word "novena" is rarely used; such occasions are simply "*rezos*." In the following discussion, this more special usage of "*rezo*" will be adopted, while "novena" will mean either one night of prayer or a full *novenario* for God or a *santo*.

Two kinds of novenas are recognized. One is called u novenai u kino kaba ("novena on the name-day"). This is given every year on the name-day of the *santo*, by the person or the community that has the *santo*; and it is thought dangerous to omit it. There are only a few novenas of this sort in Chan Kom: one corresponding to each of the different *santos* owned by persons in the community (p. 107). Until recent years, only two of these name-day novenas were full *novenarios*: that of the patron (San Diego) and that of the Holy Cross. Both were (and still are) performed by the whole village, for the common good. As is the rule with *novenarios*, these are cooperative affairs, in which responsibility for the arrangements, including the refreshments with which each evening concludes, is distributed among a group of people. The first novena in the series takes place on the eighth day before the day commemorated, and the last novena (evening of prayer), regarded as the most important, occurs on the evening of the day itself. Until recently, all the other name-day novenas were observed merely by a double prayer (vespers and matins) celebrated as a private undertaking by the owner of the *santo*. But in very recent years, some of the owners of private *santos* have expanded these two-prayer novenas to full *novenarios*, inviting their friends to participate.

The other kind of novena is known as he'-chi-novena ("open-the-mouth-novena"), or novena *de promesa*. These are held on any day in the year, at the choice of the giver. They are made in fulfilment of a vow, after a benefit has been received, or in petition for a favor asked and not yet received. They are offered sometimes to *Dios*, more often to the Holy Cross, and occasionally to one or another of the special *santos* whose images are to be found in Chan Kom. These novenas *de promesa* are very common; scores are given every year. They may be occasioned by a wide variety of circumstances; in most cases probably the occasion is a genuine need or religious impulse. Sickness is the most common initiating circumstance; a man wishes himself or his child to be relieved from an illness, or during the sickness of a member of his family he vows a novena to a *santo*, or to the Holy Cross, conditional upon recovery. A novena may even be given to secure the recovery of a sick horse or bull. Another large group of novenas springs from the ever-present concern with the milpa. The agriculturalist gives a novena to assure himself a good harvest or to express his thanks that a good crop is already safe. Especially when new corn is picked is it customary to give such novenas. Dozens are then given, each preceded and followed by the two parts of the pibil-nal ceremony (p. 143), offering *atole* of the new corn to the Holy Cross—the whole constituting a first-fruit offering. It is not apparent that novenas are ever organized merely for the social pleasures and satisfactions, although these elements contribute in some degree to every novena and may be uppermost in the minds of some organizers. Sometimes, to bring people together, a man will give a novena to the *Niño Dios*, for example, in order to organize a *novenario* to the same *santo*. In every novena it is made known to what deity the prayers are offered and what sentiment of gratitude is felt or what favor is asked.

The novena *de promesa* is usually a single short period of prayer, but in exceptional cases a man may perform a full *novenario*. The occasional novenas *de promesa* undertaken by the whole community—as in a time of drought—are, naturally, *novenarios*. Communal novenas, being offered either to San Diego, the Holy Cross, or *Dios*, are always held in the *oratorio*. Most private novenas are held in the house of the organizer, but if the individual chooses to give the novena to San Diego, he holds it in the *oratorio*,[1] for the image of the patron is of course in the public chapel. The essential fact is that the *santo* must be present at the novena. Novenas offered to the Holy Cross or to *Dios* may be held almost anywhere, because *Dios* requires no image for his presence, and sanctified crosses are easy to obtain. *Rezos*, discussed below, are invariably held in the houses of the organizers.

As has already been indicated (p. 124), there are many occasions which may give rise to either novena or ceremony to the pagan gods. Such occasions are sickness, anxiety as to the condition of the maize, gratitude for a good harvest. If the individual is in trouble, he may hold first a novena to the *santo*, and, if this is unavailing, he may call in the h-men and by his advice perform a ceremony to the deities of the milpa or of the beehives. Similarly, the entire village, if threatened by drought or disease, may perform first a *novenario* and then a pagan ceremony; the two rituals, however, are not in emergencies performed successively in the opposite order; the ceremony of pagan type is a graver matter, a last resort. On the other hand there are some occasions, such as the moving of bee-hives, that give rise only to ceremonies of the sort described in the last chapter; while there are other occasions—notably the commemoration of the death of a relative and the appeasement of the soul—of which only the *rezo* can take account.

---

[1] On one occasion, a man borrowed the image of San Diego from the *oratorio* and held a private novena for the *santo* in his house.

Aside from the obvious fact that while the ceremonies previously described are offered in the form of Maya prayers to pagan deities, and while the novena is essentially the repetition of parts of Catholic liturgy to the Christian God and the saints, the two ceremonies differ strikingly in their immediate social settings, in their full meaning and function. Where the h-men officiates, the occasion is one withdrawn from the everyday social life of the village. His knowledge and his acts are esoteric. The ceremony is entirely in the hands of the h-men; laymen merely receive and carry out his directions. The pagan rituals are performed out of doors and, on graver occasions, at a little distance removed from the village. And when the more serious ceremonies are performed, the men are separated from the women.

The novena, on the other hand, is at once a sacred and a secular institution. Prayer is its center, but social entertainment is its periphery. There is hardly a week in the year without at least one novena. The constant succession of novenas, held now in one house, now in another, provide the occasions for visiting, for relaxation, for cooperative participation in a familiar ritual pattern. They make it possible, at small expense, for first one household and then another to assume the rôle of hosts and organizers. While novenas are occasionally held in the *oratorio*, most of them take place in private houses. Here are present all members of the household, invited guests, and the relatives and the friends who know they are welcome to attend. Both men and women are there, and both men and women participate. The male head of the household ordinarily organizes the novena and arranges for the *maestro cantor;* the woman and her friends prepare the foods; husband and wife together arrange the table altar. The ritual of the novena is not in the least esoteric. Everybody knows some parts of the prayers, and those who can read can study them in printed versions. The worshippers are themselves the performers of the ritual, in that the prayers and hymns involve the repetition of frequent responses. The main body of the prayers is recited by a *maestro cantor*, who is occasionally accompanied, in singing the hymns, by some woman from among those participating. For this person, it is an opportunity to display his or her superior knowledge of the texts. But all the ritual, spoken and acted, is exoteric.

The novena is, in a word, a party. The recital of the prayers does not interrupt the preparation of festal foods nor prevent the participants from enjoying social pleasures unrelated to the occasion that is being recognized. The *rezos* commemorative of the dead are little less enjoyable than those held to express rejoicing for a successful harvest. The women engaged in making tortillas to be served at the end of the ritual make their responses from beside the hearth and griddle. The older people are grave, but the girls smile and giggle by themselves and the young fellows may be off in a corner playing cards. When the prayers are over, there is eating and conversation. The *atole*[1] on the altar is distributed to all; and after eating, everyone gives thanks to the host and hostess as he leaves.

The rosary is the central and unvarying nucleus of the body of prayers recited and hymns sung at a novena. The other prayers used vary with the character of

---

[1] The usual refreshment served at novenas is *atole* sweetened with sugar. But at some novenas, and on the last nights of full *novenarios*, more substantial food is served, usually boiled fowl.

the occasion celebrated: whether it be a novena offered as a sign of gratitude, as a prayer for recovery from illness, or a *rezo* in commemoration of the dead. For each of these classes of occasions the *maestros cantores* know, either through oral tradition or by reference to printed booklets, prayers of especial appropriateness. Within any one class of occasions the prayers used do not vary. Thus, the novena about to be described in detail employed the prayers always used on occasions where gratitude is expressed to God—whether the gratitude be for the good condition of a milpa, a child, or a horse. The hymns, on the other hand, are not reserved for special occasions; they vary simply·with the interest and knowledge of the *maestro cantor*.

A description of the ritual[1] employed at one characteristic novena will illustrate the features that have just been mentioned. In the early part of July 1930, Don Madal determined to offer a novena to God as an expression of his gratitude for the luxuriant growth of his milpa, and to invoke His aid to secure the full development of the maize plants. Don Madal asked Don Guillermo, a *maestro cantor*, to recite the prayers. The women of his household prepared the altar and the offerings. On an ordinary table, they placed a small wooden cross, a plaster image of the *Niño Dios* (which Don Madal owned), two gourd vessels of cooked fowl, a plate of tortillas, five gourd dishes of maize *atole*, and five lighted candles. When Don Guillermo arrived, at about three o'clock in the afternoon, several friends and relatives were gathered, seated on chairs or small wooden benches. The women of the household were making tortillas at the end of the room distant from the table. Don Guillermo knelt, made the sign of the cross and began reciting the prayers. *"Por la señal de la Santa Cruz, de nuestros enemigos libranos, Señor Dios nuestro. En el nombre del Padre, del Hijo, del Espíritu Santo. Amen."* Without pausing he continued, reciting an "act of contrition" or "act of sorrow for sin." This took several minutes. He then began a recital of a rosary, in which the others present joined him. After the first twenty words of the first "Our Father" he seated himself, and the congregation continued the prayer: *"—el pan nuestro de cada día, danoslo hoy, perdona a nuestros deudores[2] y no nos dejes caer en tentación, libranos de todo mal, Amen."* Don Guillermo then began a Hail Mary, which the congregation similarly completed. In this antiphonal fashion was completed a rosary of five groups, each of one "Our Father," ten "Hail Marys," and one "Gloria." After each group was interpolated a sung strophe and antistrophe—the *sanctus* of the mass—Don Guillermo and his son (also a *maestro cantor*) singing: *"Santo, santo, santo, santo, Señor Dios de los ejercitos, Llenos estan los cielos y la tierra, de vuestra Gloria."* To which the others sang the customary response: *"Gloria al Padre, Gloria al Hijo, Gloria al Espíritu Santo."*

In order to keep count of the ten decades of the rosary, with their proper component parts, Don Guillermo used the beads of an actual rosary.[3]

When this group of prayers had been concluded, Don Guillermo recited the anthem "Salve Regina" (like the preceding prayers and anthem, in Spanish).

[1] Father T. L. Riggs kindly helped us identify the prayers and hymns used.
[2] *Sic.*
[3] This is called, not a *rosario*, but a *misterio*, probably because the rosary is supposed to be recited while meditating on one of three sets of five "mysteries" (Father Riggs).

Don Guillermo repeated the verses in praise of the Virgin, to each of which the congregation gave the customary reply: "*Santa María, Madre de Dios, ruega, Señora, por nosotros pecadores, ahora y en la hora de nuestra muerte. Amen.*" The leader then recited the Apostles' Creed, and the congregation repeated it after him. After this Don Guillermo recited the Litany of the Blessed Virgin,[1] the litany being in Latin. After each line of the fifty or more praising Mary, the chorus repeated "*Ora pro nobis,*" and this took many minutes to complete. When it was over Don Guillermo recited a prayer to God the Father in which the others took no part; they occupied themselves meanwhile with subdued conversation on mundane topics.

In the last part of the novena Don Guillermo and his son sang four vernacular hymns,[2] three to the Sacred Heart and one to Jesus.

The last chant concluded, all present stood up, and with hands folded together at the breast, and heads bowed, they sang:

> *Sea bendito, alabado por toda la eternidad,*
> *El divino sacramento sacrosanto del altar,*
> *Y María concebida sin pecado original.*
> *Amen, Jesús y María, Jesús, María y José.*
> *Así sea, por los siglos de los siglos. Amen.*

Don Guillermo then said "*Gloria al Padre, Gloria al Hijo, al Espíritu Santo. Amen.*"

Immediately the people wished each other a good night, the women making tortillas leaving their work to join the others and do this. Then Don Madal and his wife took the dishes of food from the table and served those present; eating and conversation became general; some food was sent to houses of neighbors. As soon as the food was consumed, all persons not members of the household took their leave, saying—as is always said on such occasions—"*Dios* bootic tech, tat" ("God reward you, sir").

PRAYERS FOR THE DEAD

The description given earlier in this chapter of the general social functions of the novena has included also the *rezos* commemorative of the dead, because in respect to these characteristics there is little difference between novena and *rezo*. They differ in that the *rezo* is held in commemoration of the death of a member of the family. Theoretically, one should be held on each of the following occasions: seven days, seven weeks, seven months and one year after the death; and on each occasion (or at least at the anniversary) the prayers should be recited at the hour at which the death occurred. The prayers recited include a rosary and litanies for the dead: if for an adult, *Oid Mortales; Perdón, O Dios Mio;* and *Adios, Jesús del Cielo;* if for a child, then only the *Sube, Sube.* Instead of *atole,* which is appropriate for a novena, chocolate is served at a *rezo.* But at the more important *rezos* (seven months and anniversary), boiled fowl may be served. The anniversary (*cabo del*

---

[1] Of Sixteenth Century origin, probably (Father Riggs).
[2] Probably not earlier than the Nineteenth Century (Father Riggs).

año) is often the occasion for making breads in the earth-oven (pibil-uah) and some make pibil-uah at the *rezo* of the seven months.

These commemorative *rezos* are, of course, never communal, but always familial. The meaning of the ritual will be discussed in Chapter XI. The *rezos* are, in a way, repetitions of the funeral ritual and will be taken up in that connection, where also will be found an account of the annual services for the dead held on All Souls' Day (*Los Finados*).

THE VILLAGE FIESTA

At many places in these pages mention has been made of "the village fiesta." This, as in other Catholic countries, is the annual celebration held on the name-day of the patron saint of the village. The celebration is in part worship of the *santo*, and in very large part play. Its ritual core is a *novenario* held in honor of the *santo*. To this central sacred ritual adheres a variable cluster of secular elements. These elements vary with the traditions of the particular village and with the special circumstances of the year in which the fiesta is held. An account of the essential patterns of the village fiesta, as understood by the native of Chan Kom, can not be based simply on the fiesta as held in Chan Kom. In the first place during the past three years the fiesta has not been held there (a simple *novenario* to the *santo* has been substituted); in the second place the native's ideas of such fiestas are formed by the many fiestas which he attends in neighboring villages. It has already been remarked that the annual fiesta is in many cases the only occasion which brings a Chan Kom family to some of these villages. Everybody goes to a good fiesta and, once there, becomes a part of it.

To add concreteness to a general statement, a description[1] of one particular fiesta will first be given. This fiesta took place in X-Kalakdzonot on April 30, 1930. Its celebration involved all the features most frequently encountered in such fiestas.

It is four o'clock in the afternoon. After four hours of travel by a narrow and rocky path, I have arrived at X-Kalakdzonot. The teacher tells me that X-Kalakdzonot is a *pueblo*, but in truth it can hardly be called a *ranchería*. In the center of a clearing which forms the plaza is erected the kax-che—a rude enclosure of sticks and vines. At one side, on a little eminence, is the school. There are no streets; small paths lead crookedly to the ten or twelve houses hidden in the foliage.

The place has a holiday appearance. People come and go by the little paths. Everyone is talking and laughing excessively. Some men are pouring rum out of a bottle into their stomachs. From the schoolhouse, where I sit, I hear distant shouting. In a moment appear a number of half-drunk and sweating men, their faces contorted by happy shouts; they are carrying on their shoulders the great trunk of a ceiba tree. This is made firm in the center of the kax-che; it will serve to tie the bulls to. By the shouting and clamor which the act occasions one can tell that the bringing of this tree from the bush to the enclosure is an interesting and important part of the fiesta.

My attention is drawn to the house of the *cargador*, the principal organizer of the fiesta. It is the principal center of activity. There are a number of women are preparing tortillas and cooking the *atole*, amid a loud and cheerful babble, precursor of greater joys. In the patio some men are grinding *nixtamal* on little handmills. From time to time they divert themselves with drinks of rum.

[1] Written by Alfonso Villa.

Near this house has been erected the *enramada,* a roof of palm-leaves sheltering the dancing place. Two houses nearby have been evacuated by their owners to provide a shelter for the visiting dancers.

Evening is coming. The excitement increases. Every moment one sees little lights coming down the paths; these are the dancers and other celebrants who are arriving on foot or on horseback from the surrounding *rancherías.* With hardly a pause, rockets shatter into space. Every family has brought a dozen or more of these rockets which they set off when it pleases them.

In the house of the *cargador* a supper has just been served. Everyone present has been fed. One table is reserved for the visiting teachers and merchants—*los principales,* the people call them.

From the supper the people move in a procession to a little *oratorio.* There they celebrate the last night of a *novenario* held in honor of the Holy Cross. A *maestro cantor* is in charge; he recites the prayers, and the congregation make the responses.

During the novena the men have withdrawn a little from the women. Now the men of X-Kalakdzonot, accompanied by a few male friends, go to the house of the man who has promised to be *cargador* next year. The future *cargador* asks the help of those present to organize the next fiesta, and offers them cigarettes and rum.

The sacred ritual is over; next the Holy Cross will be honored with a dance. The *cargadores,* present and future, go over to the *oratorio.* They are followed by the crowd, and their passage takes place to a great burst of rockets, the playing of music by the little orchestra, and the shouts of the people. The *cargadores* take the Holy Cross from its place on the altar and carry it to a special hut erected in front of the *enramada.* The *santo* is now present at the dance arranged in its honor.

Hours pass before the dancing actually begins. Two kerosene lamps shed a feeble light. Round about the *enramada* people are selling candies, chocolate, bread, drinks, and even ice brought from Valladolid, 65 kilometers away. At about ten o'clock the dancers begin to arrive at the *enramada.* Groups of young fellows excited by alcohol, move about shouting, "Yauti! Yauti! Palalee-ee-eex!" (Hurray, Hurray, boys!) Thus many of them pass the night, walking about the *enramada,* drinking and shouting.

The girls take seats under the *enramada.* They do not dance—not yet. They remain grave, immutable. One would say that they are not enjoying it. On the contrary it is the moment they have been dreaming of all year. At last the brassy notes of the cornet arouse them to activity. The drums begin their stirring beat; the first couple is led out on to the wooden platforms; these resound with the heel-taps of the dancers. The *jarana* has begun.

* * * * * *

Dawn comes, and with the crowing of the cocks mingle the last notes of the *torito*— that air with which *jaranas* always end. The last couples leave the dance-platform. Many of the dancers, overcome with fatigue, are already sleeping in hammocks tied to trees, out in the open—for the shelters here are not enough to give lodging to all.

Their repose is brief. At eight o'clock in the morning there is a bustle of activity at the house of the *cargador.* His two assistants, the kulelob, take no rest at all. Now they are busy distributing plates of turkey seasoned with toasted chili (*relleno negro*) to the various groups into which the celebrants have gathered. Gourd dishes of *atole* pass from group to group. With insatiable appetite, the young boys consume whatever is left in any dish. The musicians are given special attention and offered the best of the food.

At noon the present *cargador,* together with his wife and his associate organizers, the nakulob, go to the house of the future *cargador,* whom he thereupon invites to his house, that he may deliver to him the *carga,* or cuch. This is the essential part of the fiesta and gives its name (cuch) to the whole. On a table the kulelob place a cross, a clay vessel containing the cooked head of a pig, a pile of tortillas, several bottles of rum, and on a little plate some cigarettes.   The present *cargador* carries the cuch: a decorated pole from which hang many-colored paper streamers, packages of cigarettes, cloth dolls and loaves of wheat bread made in the form of an eagle.   He addresses the *cargador* of the fiesta to be celebrated next year, saying:

"In the name of the Father, the Son and the Holy Ghost, I deliver to you this charge (cuch), and that which is upon this table, so that next year you may make your fiesta to the Holy Cross."

To this the other replies: "Thanks, sir; if the Lord God gives us life and health, I promise to do this."

Then he tells three nakulob (who are to help him with the future fiesta) to take what is on the table.   Lifting up the various objects, these men move around the table, turning about as they go, and dancing a slow dance, with little leaps, while the musicians play the air of an old Spanish song—"La Carbonerita."   Afterward the bread, chocolate, cigarettes and other objects forming the cuch are divided among the nakulob, who must return, the following year, twice what they receive.

The crowd then moves off to the kax-che, where the bull-fights begin.   The bulls are rented or loaned; therefore they must not be injured.   A number of youths with red cloths enter the enclosure; they show the greatest agility at the slightest movement of the bull's horns.   One man only, from Ebtun, executes in a recognizable manner the steps employed in the real bull-ring.   His devotion to the art has caused him to buy the green trunks, yellow jacket, stockings and leather shoes of the professional; these, at times of fiesta, he wears in place of his rustic shirt, apron and sandals.   The crowd surrounding the enclosure breaks into stentorian cries each time that a *torero* is upset, or when, in excess of caution, one runs off at great speed, with the bull unaware of it.

The sun, with its fiery rays, moves along its path unnoticed by the crowd, who for the moment have shaken off their habitual melancholy.   Under a tree the musicians sit forgotten, playing *jaranas*.   Explosive rockets increase the din.   Moments of excitement, for long periods of hereafter to be the themes of talk for old and young!   Moments to become nostalgic recollection for young women, keeping their finery in a trunk not soon to be opened!

The *corrida* has ended, and with it the fiesta.   The costumed enthusiast has been mangled by a bull; he will be back next year, nevertheless.

The people begin to leave.   On the paths one sees groups returning home on foot or on horse-back.   I set my feet in the narrow path back to Chan Kom.

This fiesta of X-Kalakdzonot is typical of the fiestas held in honor of *santos* in the region in which Chan Kom lies, in the sense that it presents all the features characteristic of the older folk custom.   But there are many small differences of local tradition, and besides these, great differences in such fiestas depending upon the extent to which the community has been affected by modern civilization.   The native of Chan Kom does not expect to find the same kind of fiesta in the towns on the railroad as he does in the villages of the southern hinterland.   Indeed, in Chan Kom itself the "cuch" element has not been present in any annual fiesta for several years and it may never be included again.

The essential features of the village fiesta are the *novenario* and *jarana*.   Both are offerings to the *santo*.   The *jarana* must take place where the *santo* can watch it; it is therefore held at the door of the *oratorio*, or else the image is moved to a place where the dance may be more conveniently held.   But the *novenario* is worship, while the *jarana* is secular play.[1] It is the *jarana* that makes the occasion a fiesta; a *novenario* is not a fiesta. A *jarana* is a social dance; an opportunity for youths and girls to enjoy rhythmic, complementary, stylized activity; to let music enter and stir the blood, to wear festal attire, to excel in a form of play that is also art. For the unmarried the *jarana* is a prelude to marriage, a chance to choose and to be chosen.

The *jarana* is not dependent upon the village fiesta. A *jarana* may be given to celebrate any occasion—the dedication of a school, for example, or the presence of a distinguished visitor. But it is always a part of the village fiesta. If the fiesta attracts enough people and if the funds of the community permit, the fiesta may last several days, with a new *jarana* every night.

The *jarana* is a complex of interdependent elements that occur together: the characteristic dance-step and accompanying posture; the wooden dancing platform (usually), the palmleaf shelter (*enramada*), the appropriate musical airs, certain etiquette of the dance-floor, special steps and tunes with which the *jarana* is brought to a close. In the more sophisticated communities, to these elements are added the recital, by a dancer when challenged to do so, of humorous quatrains (*bombas*).

There are other invariable elements of the fiesta that, like the *jarana*, occur also in many other festal settings. Such are the discharge of explosive rockets (*voladores*), the consumption, by men, of large quantities of rum, and the distribution to all comers, by the organizers of the fiesta, of festal foods. These foods, at village fiestas in the region, are almost always tortillas and *relleno negro*.

The rustic bull-fight (*toros*) forms a frequent but not essential element of the village fiesta. The feature is included if the organizers of the fiesta have the necessary enterprise and funds. *Toros* enliven and prolong the fiesta; a really good fiesta offers them. But the feature requires bulls, or money to rent bulls, and is enhanced by the presence of someone with some pretense of knowledge of tauromachy. *Toros* offer to men who attend the fiesta another opportunity to participate and excel, either by skill in the "ring" or by entering as proud owner a particularly fierce and intractable bull. The accessory elements of this particular complex are the building of the kax-che, the semi-ritual securing and erection of the ceiba-tree, the rustic simulation of the bullfighter's art, and the accompanying music.

The organization of the fiesta by special volunteers and their selected assistants, and the handing over of this responsibility, to be discharged the following year, to another man or group of men, by some conventional symbolic act performed toward the end of the fiesta, are also characteristics generally present. These features provide for a self-perpetuating administrative machinery that will keep up the fiesta, year after year. But these are the features that vary most, depending on whether the community is a hinterland pueblo preserving the older folk culture, or whether it is a more modern village or town. In the X-Kalakdzonot fiesta, the form and the meaning of the festal organization are typical of the fiesta of the backward village. There, as in other villages of the sort, the name of the fiesta (cuch) has reference to its essential meaning: a charge, or burden, voluntarily assumed as

---

[1] But sometimes a *vaquera* dances a *jarana* as an offering to the *santo*, in fulfillment of a vow.

an act of piety. The organizer of the fiesta in such a village assumes more than the responsibility for a popular success. He takes, for a year, the solemn charge to render to the *santo* his fiesta. The organizer may expend the equivalent of a year's income. His only recompense is in the form of special divine protection by the *santo*.

This concept is symbolized in the handing-over of the decorated pole (*ramillete*) from the organizer of this year to the organizer of next year. The promise which the recipient makes is one of great solemnity; it is believed that death is likely to follow its breach. This grave sanction provides for the continuity of the festal organization and also for the perpetual assertion of the corporate personality of the village and of the special relationship between the village and its patron *santo*.

It is, in such villages, the principal organizer (*cargador*) who gives the fiesta. He arranges for the musicians, sees to it that enough food is provided for the guests, serves a meal at his house, and furnishes shelter to visitors. The *enramada* is erected beside his house, and there the saint comes to watch the dancing. When the new *cargador* is chosen and the cuch transferred, the pious burden has shifted to new shoulders. But each *cargador* gives the fiesta not merely as a personal act of piety, but also as the official representative of the community, which through an endless succession of individual members expresses its perpetual devotion.

The *cargador* delegates part of his responsibility to two (or more) nakulob, who are selected by each *cargador* immediately after his own selection. The expenses of the fiesta are distributed among *cargador* and nakulob, the *cargador* taking a larger share, the nakulob sharing equally. The nakulob help in making the arrangements and in providing hospitality.[1] In taking their share of the objects hanging from the decorated pole, they make, in effect, a pledge like that of the *cargador*, and bind themselves in all solemnity to share his pious responsibility.

In villages where the ways of the city have exerted more influence, and in the towns on the railroad where there are markets and merchants and opportunities to make a crowd the occasion of pecuniary profit, the religious significance of the village fiesta disappears. The organizers, in such places, are not even called by the same name: they are *diputados* ("deputies"), mere officials, not persons under solemn charge. They organize the fiesta as a mere matter of popular entertainment and, not being motivated by devotion and piety, they see to it that the celebration pays expenses—or better. In some of the towns *jarana* and *toros* are placed on a paying basis, by means of admission fees. In Tizimin, and perhaps in some of the other larger towns where there are *santos* of such especial miraculousness that great crowds are attracted to the fiestas, the annual fiesta is a very profitable matter and the post of *diputado* has become a political prize. In such completely secularized fiestas there are modern dances and gambling games. Then the religious exercises are formal masses in the churches by priests from the city; the sacred ritual is no longer in the hands of the people.

In such fiestas of the town and modernized village, the ritual of delivery of the cuch, with the delivery of the pig's head (kub-pol) and the dance of the nakulob, is not present. In such fiestas there is no meaning for these acts to express. The

---

[1] The food is distributed at the festal meal by two functionaries (kulelob; *kuleles*) chosen for this particular purpose.

fiesta is then not held at the house of the *cargador*, but in one of the public buildings of the town. For, as they say, "the fiesta is not cuch, but merely an undertaking." The holy burden has disappeared.

DZA AKAB AND HADZ PACH

In most of the villages of the Chan Kom region, as for example in X-Kopteil and X-Kalakdzonot, two related ceremonies are practiced which assert the sacred character of the annual fiesta and connect it with the semi-esoteric rites of the h-men.

The first of these rituals (dza akab) takes account of the perilous meeting of man and bull in the rustic bull-fight. Although not every fiesta includes *toros*, the dancing and the *corridas* are closely associated. The young men who both dance the *jarana* and go out to bring in the bulls are *vaqueros;* the girls who dance, by putting on men's hats for certain of the *jaranas*, become *vaqueras;* the dance itself is referred to as a *vaquería*; and it always concludes with a special dance (the *torito*) in which the girl, striving to cause the man who dances opposite her to lose his balance and step off the platform, represents the bull-fighter, while he is the bull.

It has been explained (p. 118) that the cattle are thought to be under a supernatural protector known as X-Juan-Thul. This protector is occasionally given offerings, else the cattle weaken and die. Like the other supernatural beings, X-Juan-Thul has the power of sending evil winds. X-Juan-Thul puts winds into the bulls. That is what makes them so fierce (*bravo*), but that is also what makes them so dangerous to the *vaqueros*. The time of the *corrida* is a critical one: the *vaqueros* are to test their strength against the bulls of X-Juan-Thul.

In the villages of the region, the annual fiesta usually includes four *jaranas*, each undertaken by a *cargador*. The actual conduct of these *jaranas* is in charge of two functionaries known as the nohoch mayol and (his assistant) the chan mayol. These men direct the musicians and lead the dancers on to the dancing-floor. The nohoch mayol gets two h-mens to come to his house on the night of the last *jarana*. In the yard of this house these h-mens offer two gourd-vessels of zaca to the yuntzilob of the village and to X-Juan-Thul. The balams are asked to be present that night to protect the *vaqueros* and the *vaqueras* from the evil winds.

The night when ends the last *jarana* is the night before the *corrida de toros*. When the *jarana* is over, the *vaqueros* accompany the nohoch mayol to attend the offering of zaca to the yuntzilob. They spend the rest of the night in the company of one another, without sleeping and under the supervision of the nohoch mayol. This is "vigil" (ppix-ich). The remainder of the night is spent in more or less equal parts in the houses of the four *cargadores*. These houses are visited in the order in which occurred the *jaranas* for which each is respectively responsible. At each house a bottle of rum and a package of cigarettes await the men, and more of both are furnished from time to time, so that as they go from house to house there is apt to be a good deal of shouting and uproar.

The h-mens tell them that they must not sleep, because "the yuntzilob are present," and above all that they must not go home to sleep with their wives. If the *vaqueros* return to their homes at all during the night and day of the *corrida*, they leave their lassos outside the door, because they are filled with evil winds, which it would be dangerous to bring into the house. They always keep their ropes with them. The spending of the night in this way is referred to as dza akab ti lazo dzuytal zuun yoklal ma u thoocol tumen *toros* ("give the night to the lasso, twisting it thick so that it will not break on account of the bulls").

The ceremony known as hadz pach ("strike the back") takes place after the *corrida* ends. At the first *jarana* the girl-dancers wear men's hats; at the remaining three, they do not. But after the *corrida* there takes place that night a short *jarana*, spoken of as "half a night"—"to finish off with."[1] No *cargador* is responsible for this *jarana*. At this dance the girls wear hats again. When it is over, *vaqueros* and *vaqueras* go to the house of the nohoch mayol, where a table is arranged, with a bottle of rum, cigarettes and leaves of zipche. At the table sit the nohoch mayol and the two h-mens. The *vaqueros* place their lassos under the table. Each *vaquero* brings the nohoch mayol a *medida* of rum.

Each *vaquera* is brought to the table, and the chan mayol begins striking her back with a rope made by twisting together three of the large handkerchiefs such as are used by the men and as are employed in the *torito* dance. Because sometimes the men are drunk and the mayol may hit rather hard, a *vaquero* may volunteer to substitute for a *vaquera* and receive the beating instead. After the strokes have been administered, the girl (or her substitute) passes to the h-mens. One gives her a drink of rum, while the other strokes her head with zipche, praying to expel the evil winds. The h-men first moves the zipche in a clockwise direction; then he gives a smaller drink and moves the zipche in a counterclockwise direction. Then the second h-men takes rum in his mouth and blows some on the girl's head.

"It is because they have danced so long and have slept so little that the evil winds are about them. The h-men does this to make them sleep well. So that they will not have bad dreams, he sometimes puts in their eyes a mixture of water and rum, into which tancaz-che bark has been scraped. If hadz pach is not made, then later, when the *vaqueras* marry and have children, their children will die."

It is the abnormal physical and mental conditions of excitement and of fatigue, and especially the unusual association of the sexes in the dance, that is objectified in the thought of evil winds; hadz pach is lustration and restoration to the normal and the ordinary.

After the *vaqueras* have been cleansed of the evil winds, the h-mens again offer zaca to X-Juan-Thul and the greater yuntzilob, to tell them that hadz pach has been made.

[1] *Cf.* the ppobom custom (p. 197). This *jarana* is called *elección*, because after it the *cargadores* for the following year are chosen.

Chapter X

SICKNESS AND ITS CURE

In Chan Kom ideas and practices with regard to disease are of the sort usually called "primitive"; that is, sickness is not commonly thought of as due to mere functional disturbances or lesions within the sufferer's natural organism. In most cases of illness, especially those of any gravity, an explanation—at least a more ultimate explanation—is found in the intervention of some cause from outside the body of the person afflicted; and such outside causes are not characteristically thought of as operating on the sick person through mechanical or chemical means. These outside influences are exerted directly, "supernaturally," as we say. To the native the mechanisms of their action are not ordinarily matters of consideration; or, if thought of at all, rest upon assumptions as to cause-and-effect strikingly inconsistent with the considered observations of modern civilized men. Furthermore, among these outside causes the mere volition of god, spirit or human being is a very important element. People get sick, roughly speaking, because an evil influence was involuntarily communicated from an outside source to the sufferer, or because somebody wished it so.

None of these remarks serve to distinguish the ideas as to disease prevalent in Chan Kom from the ideas found among many other non-civilized peoples. A distinction begins to be made when we state the most important concepts of causation in which the general ideas take form. These concepts are, in Chan Kom, possession by semi-personified "winds," the evil eye and kindred influences, punishment by god or spirit, witchcraft and certain mythical birds that carry disease or death.

It would be a misrepresentation to assert any detailed consistency or system or rules governing native thinking on these matters. All that can be done is to state the ideas that are paramount and indicate some of the extensions of these ideas into various classes of situations. The categories are blurred and run into one another. One example will indicate the difficulty. *Ojo-mac* is the evil influence exerted, wittingly or unwittingly, by certain classes of persons, especially upon children, through looking at them or fondling them. There is also a belief in personified winds, who enter into the bodies of people, causing sickness. *Ojo-mac* is exercised by certain persons born with this evil power; but it may also be exerted by any person who, when fatigued or after exertion, fondles a child. The reason for this lies in the belief that at times of physical exertion evil winds cling to the person and may be transmitted to others who are susceptible, especially to children. In such a case the recommended cure follows, in general, the pattern for evil eye (*ojo*-mac). But the trouble could as well be called *ojo*-ik, a name for the evil wind and its effects. This particular situation lends itself to classification in two categories that ramify in divergent directions of thought; the native probably does not feel that he has to select one category rather than the other.

"COLD" AND "HOT"

In qualification of what was said at the beginning of this chapter, it should be stated that there is one important concept which enters into the ideas of disease and its treatment that does not involve the intervention of the supernatural, but constitutes a sort of physiological principle of the folk. This concept is the distinction between things "cold" and things "hot," already mentioned in another connection (p. 130).

Many—perhaps all—foods are recognized as being more or less "hot" or "cold." Very "hot" foods are honey, coffee, beef (especially from a bull) and *pinole*. Foods that are very "cold" are peccary, wild turkey, rice, boiled eggs (chacbil-he), papaya, limes, Lima beans, pork, *jícama*, squash, lard, two bananas known as x-box-haaz and *bárbaro*-haaz, the meat of the large deer and all foods cooked in the earth-oven. Foods that are thought of as intermediate ("half-cold") are oranges, chachalaca, anona, cassava, sweet potato, domestic fowl, pineapple, *chayote*, tomatoes, pigeon, cane sugar, beans, *atole*, chocolate, tortillas, two bananas known as *manzana*-haaz and *plátano*, eggs cooked in the ashes (mucbil-he) and the meat of the small deer (yuk). "Cold" things are made less "cold" by adding other edibles that are "hot." Thus, adding *epazote*, marjoram or garlic (which are "hot") to a cold food, such as peccary or Lima beans, makes it only "half cold"; and beans may be made more suitable for a weak person by cooking them with *epazote*. On the other hand, beef may be made less "hot" by putting lime juice on it; sweet orange juice would not have the same effect. And the effects of two examples of the same category are cumulative—coffee with honey is a very "hot" drink.

It will be seen from the lists just given, how little consideration of temperature in the foods themselves has to do with the allocation of a comestible to one class rather than to the other. The notion of heat or cold in connection with these classes of foods has meaning in connection with the appropriateness of foods of one class for persons whose supposed temperature is of the opposite class. A person with a fever should not eat "hot" things, should most particularly eat "cold" things, and may eat things that are "half cold." But a person with a chill, or merely weakened by sickness or childbirth, should not eat "cold" things, but is especially advised to eat "hot" and some "half-cold" things. The good or bad effects of the foods are dependent upon the condition of the person who eats them. In general, "cold" foods are thought to "require more cooking in the body" than are "hot" foods; one may therefore more safely partake of them in the morning when "there is more time for them to be cooked."

The categories are invoked, therefore, partly in the prescription of medicine and diet to persons suffering from sickness or chill; partly, also, they are involved in the explanation of the cause of sickness. For a fever may be attributed to the fact that the sufferer ate too many "hot" foods; and the eating of too many "cold" foods produces debility and especially sterility. It is regarded as especially risky to eat of "cold" foods when one is actually hot. The "cold" drink, which might be the recommended remedy to a person suffering from a fever, is dangerous to a person who is warm from exercise or work. Women who have just been ironing, or bending over the fire, are careful not to bathe immediately, or to go out in the wind, or to drink *pozole* or eat oranges. Yet the practical difficulties of this limitation are met in various ways; it is said that if one continues to work no harm comes from partaking of something "cold"; it is also said that one is protected if a little salt is taken at the same time. This idea that it is risky to mix both "cold" and "hot" is also represented in the belief that a person who has drunk any warmed potion of which honey—"hottest" of all foods—is an ingredient, should not drink plain water—which is "cold"—for three days.

The contact with something "cold" when one is warm is the chief cause of that physical disability known as being *pasmada* ("chilled" or "numbed"). Any weakness, anemia, loss of appetite or other low physical condition, especially such as occurs in a woman, is apt to be described by this phrase. As is the case with many sicknesses, evil winds often enter here too as the sole or as a contributing cause, but the contact with cold is usually emphasized. Sterility in women is commonly regarded as *pasmo*. It is also believed that a fit of anger may arrest a woman's menstruation; this is also *pasmo*. If *pasmo* is thought to be the result of these "natural" causes, and no evil wind is involved, the h-men is ordinarily not summoned and the woman's close kinsmen treat her with "hot" baths and drinks.

To a person in normal condition and good health, all foods are suitable, if not eaten to excess. Of the "cold" foods, limes are considered the most powerful. They are thought to be very effective in reducing fevers, but their use involves danger; one may go too far. Thus, there are in Chan Kom two cases of lameness which are explained by the fact that in each a sufferer from fever was washed in an infusion of lime-leaves which was "too strong." Just to step on a lime with bare feet is enough to act on one as a powerful purge; and to a woman in child-bed lime juice is little short of poison.[1]

A disease known as x-holom-xal occurring in women, usually after child-birth, is regarded as caused by taking too many "cold" things. It is this danger that makes the midwife advise only foods and drinks that are safely "hot"; for example, she recommends that honey be used instead of sugar. The disease is recognized by pallor, loss of appetite and irregularities of menstruation. It is treated with the usual "hot" drinks and baths, and especially with an herb that has the same name as the disease.

One of the chief responsibilities of the h-men, in diagnosing and treating sickness, is to determine whether the patient is in a condition in which "hot" or "cold" foods and medicines are indicated. If the decision is not easily made from the apparent state of the patient (fever, chill or weakness), he sometimes makes use of a method of blood-testing. Using his bleeding-knife (p. 172), the h-men draws a little blood from the patient and puts a drop in each of a number of bits of corn-husk. Then he tests these drops by putting into some a small quantity of a substance belonging to the "cold" category, and into others substances belonging to the "hot" category.

---

[1] These cases, incidentally, also show that a "cold" substance is not necessarily one cold in temperature. The medicinal bath became too "cold" because the water in which the lime leaves were steeped had heated too much. Baths are "hot" or "cold" almost irrespective of their temperature. Salt in the water makes the bath "hot." Orange or lime leaves make it "cold." A "cold" bath is not heated on the flames, however, but by the use of the zintun: nine small stones taken from the cross-roads, heated on the hearth and then put in the water. But the water may, in fact, be quite hot.

Thus, he puts in a drop or two of sour orange juice and stirs it about with a stick. If the blood turns a clear red color, it means that the orange juice is suitable to that blood and therefore the patient may take foods that are "half-cold." Cold water may be used instead of orange juice. If the blood turns black when orange juice is put into it, it means that the patient should take "hot" things. The h-men may put a little wood-ash, mixed with water, into the blood. This is "hot," and therefore if the blood in this case turns red, "hot" things are indicated; if black, "cold" things. The h-men may carry this principle of testing beyond the "hot" and "cold" categories. If, when a little rum is put into the blood, it turns black or "to pus," the person should not drink rum.

The treatment prescribed is, of course, in accordance with the diagnosis. Baths and medicines are advised which will counteract the condition of the patient. A person suffering from fever, for example, will be bathed in the clear water from zaca (yalil) and be made to drink some of it. The patient may first be required to lie in his hammock without any sheet, so as to become cold before the "cold" bath continues the treatment.

Although the discussion is carried outside of the subject of disease and its treatment, mention may be made here of other extensions of the double category of "hot" and "cold." There exists the idea that all persons belong to one of two groups: those with "hot hands" (choko kab) and "hot blood" (choko kik), and those with "cold hands" (ziz kab) and "cold blood" (ziz kik). Women with "cold" hands are more apt to be unsuccessful in cookery, and men known to have "cold" hands are expected to refrain from participating in the preparation of the foods for the earth-oven, or from opening the oven. It is regarded as bad for a "hot" man to marry a "cold" woman, and vice versa. One or the other spouse will get sick. Most spouses are regarded as having blood of about equal quality, but if, after marriage, one spouse grows weak and thin, it is apt to be said that the bloods of the two are very unequal: one must be very "cold" and the other very "hot." The same classification is applied to domestic animals. Small horses of a certain kind are "cold" in blood, while mules, burros and large stallions are "hot." Cattle are likewise "hot" (the fat of a steer is a powerful "hot" medicine). A man who attempts to raise small horses and finds them dying under his care will conclude that he has "hot" blood and will sell the small horses and buy burros and mules.

It is also said if a person fails in raising bees or cattle, or in caring for fowl, that "he has a pain (kinam) in his hand." Kinam means more than an ordinary pain; "it does not hurt," they say; it is an evil in the body, that produces misfortunes of the kind indicated, or it may be responsible for sickness. In some manner it is identified with or connected with the actual pain from an illness. Thus it is unsafe for a wounded person to attend a wake, for the "pain" (kinam) with which the person died might enter the other's wound and cause his death.

At any rate, these ideas of "hot" and "cold" and of "kinam" are regarded, more or less, as "natural" physiological principles. They do not involve the will of man or of supernatural being, as do, in so many cases, the illnesses discussed under the headings that follow. The h-men recognizes the difference plainly enough:

in bleeding and cupping a patient, he makes the incision in the form of a cross if the trouble is caused by the evil winds, because the evil winds must be exorcised; but if it is only a "kinam," several small scattered punctate incisons are made. If, after bleeding, the wound swells, it is proof the patient has a kinam in him.

THE EVIL WINDS

This phrase (vientos maléficos) is that used in Spanish discourse to describe what is probably the most frequently mentioned cause of disease, operating in some cases by itself and in others conjointly with other causes. In Maya the corresponding phrase is ojo-ik, "evil wind" and also "wind-evil"; but this word is also used to refer to one particular wind. Although sometimes it is as if there is but one general "wind"—"a cuch yikal," "he is loaded with wind," a man will say— yet everyone recognizes that there are many special winds, each with its particular disease-bringing characteristics.

In very large part these winds are identified with actual winds that blow, and these, especially some of these, people try to avoid. Thus, when the wind blows just before a rain, people call their children indoors lest a wind should strike them. The kan-lacay (?) blows when the sky is yellow or dark in color, as sometimes happens in the evening. This wind brings colds and fevers to children; therefore at such times children are not allowed to be out of doors, and some parents then make a cross with ashes on the ground. The wind-eddies that one sees running down the road in little spirals of dust are especially dangerous. If such a wind (mozon-ik)[1] comes toward a person, he usually gets out of the way. One reason why children are sick more frequently than adults is because they do not know enough to avoid such winds, although, of course, their parents are on the watch for them. Any little unusual agitation of the air suggests the presence of dangerous winds. It is dangerous to put one's eye close to a crack in a wall or a hole in a door. It is not safe to sweep under a hammock when some one is lying in it, for evil winds may be stirred up to enter the person resting there. The old people advise against building a house in the space between two hillocks (calap) because the evil winds pass through such places. So houses and bee-hives are placed on slight rises of ground.

The winds that blow from the water are the winds that are apt to bring sickness. In Yucatan, water appears in just three forms: the sea, the cenotes and the rain. When winds come from any one of these, they are evil winds. This is a notion recognized by everyone; the details of belief vary from individual to individual and are not sharply defined by anyone. "The wind that blows from the clouds" (ojo-ik-muyal)—from the clouds, that is, that threaten rain—is one such dangerous wind. Ojo-ik-ha is the name given to the wind that blows from the water just before the rain comes. There is, in fact, an idea that it is water which causes wind; that winds arise only from the water. In proof of this it was pointed out that the

---

[1] "One day the comisario of Kancabdzonot was sitting with five other men. They saw a mozon-ik coming toward them. All but the comisario got out of the way; the others shouted to him to stand aside, but he went at the mozon-ik, making as if to catch it with his hat. That night he began to have pains in his chest and the next night he was dead." One man speaks of these small wind-eddies as x-bohton-ik.

leaves of the plants growing on the sides of the cenote are in motion when everything else is quiet. The cenotes are the doors to the sea, or at least to the source of all the evil winds. The word "chun," which means "trunk" or "source," is used in reference to this ultimate watery origin-place. When the h-men drives the evil winds from the body of a person whom they have come to occupy, he induces them to enter dishes of food, which he then empties some distance from the house, in order that the evil winds may return to the sea—to the source from which they have come. The north and the west winds are thought of as blowing from the sea more directly than does the east wind (or, of course, the south wind). The mozon-ikob are likewise thought to come from the water, for they are small whirlwinds, similar to the great whirlwinds (the kakal-mozon-ikob that kindle the milpa), and all such whirlwinds issue from the cenotes. Even a dry cave (actun) is a source of evil winds; one may feel the cool air blowing as one nears the mouth; and it is thought that somehow behind its walls the waters lie.

Though closely associated with actual winds, nevertheless the *vientos maléficos* are personified, sometimes vaguely, sometimes quite explicitly. The ritual medicine employed to cure diseases caused by them treats them as persons—imploring, cajoling, tricking them. They are sometimes seen, moving and dancing about one. "They look like many little lively children playing." They are distinguished by individual names. In getting rid of the disease-bearing representatives of their class, the h-men sometimes appeals for aid to ak-than-ik, "the wind that drives forth," and to dzan-che-ik, "the wind that tramples." Sometimes the evil winds are completely anthropomorphized and thought of as little people, with hats and other garments; at this point they merge with the alux. Then they are conceived of as performing any sort of mischief—coming into people's yards at night, throwing pebbles, rattling the dishes, and the like. Some people mention the kazap-tun-ik ("nuisance" or "fright"-wind) as the author of such annoyances. It is commonly said that three certain evil winds are wont to go about together in the forms of little people. These three are *ojo*-ik (in this context used as the name for a special wind), coc-ik ("asthma wind") and coc-tancaz-ik ("asthma-seizure-wind"). Children's sicknesses, especially intestinal troubles, are often attributed to the malevolence of these three supernatural persons. But such a triad of small evil supernatural personages is an element of belief in contexts where the notion of winds is not present. Thus whooping-cough is regarded as brought to a house or village by three similar small personages known as u-yumil-x-thuhub ("lords of the whooping-cough") and it is common to hang out dishes of zaca to propitiate them. On such occasions the dogs are tied up, lest they bite these visitors and annoy them into reprisals.[1]

The winds are distinguished from one another partly, as has already been explained, in terms of their supposed sources and forms, and partly also in terms of the kinds of ailments they bring. This is a matter concerning which there is no great consistency between the account of one person and that of another. Some

---

[1] It is also thought that smallpox and measles have their similar "lords," but these are usually ignored. Yet one individual or another may put out zaca, or thirteen of the breads known as pim-pim-uah, when any sickness, even of the domestic fowl, is present in the village.

winds (*ojo*-ik; mozon-ik; kazap-ik) are very generally known and associated with particular ailments, while others are mentioned only by the h-mens or by particularly interested older persons. The details of the topic are matters for the h-men, who professes to determine not only if an illness has been caused by the evil winds, but also which particular wind has brought the ailment. This he does partly by divination (p. 170) and partly by referring to the sufferer's symptoms. Some of these winds are to the layman no more than the names of beings which he hears the h-men, in his exorcistic rites, beg to depart. And two h-mens gave two quite different lists, with the ailments each was said to cause:[1]

I

Ojo-ik ("evil wind").

Coc-ik ("asthma wind").

Coc-tancaz-ik ("asthma-seizure-wind").

(The above three cause fever and "green diarrhea" in children).

Loopob-coc-ik ("asthma-wind-that-doubles-one-up"). Causes pain in the side.

Hul-ne-coc-ik ("pierce-?-asthma wind"). Severe stinging pains. Attacks especially horses and cattle.

Nak-tan-coc-ik ("sticks-to-the-chest-wind"). Pneumonia.

Buyul-tun-ik ("vertigo-wind"). Weakness and vertigo.

Kan-pepen-coc-ik ("yellow-butterfly-asthma-wind"). Malaria.

II

Zuhuy-ik ("virgin wind"). Cardiac weakness and chills.

Balam-tun-hol-ik ("jaguar-entrance-wind"). Headache.

Uayak-tun-ik ("dream-stone (?)-wind"). Delirium.

Mamuk-ik ("weakness-wind"). General weakness.

Hol-mek-ik ("suddenly-embracing-wind?"). Chills.

Kazap-tun-ik ("injury-stone (?)-wind"). Any serious sickness.

Dzanche-ik ("trampling-wind?"). Rheumatism.

Winds mentioned by other people in Chan Kom are: Uenel-tancaz-ik ("sleep-seizure-wind"), which causes people to be unnaturally drowsy or sleepy. Ol-xe-ik ("wants-to-vomit-wind") makes one feel like vomiting, but one can not. Kakaz-ik ("very-bad-wind") makes swellings on the body. This wind get into trees also and produces the large swellings one sees on the trunks. When a person ceases to wish to eat, it is said that it is ma-hanal-ik-tancazob ("not-eating-wind-attacks"). When one can not sleep, the trouble is referred to ma-uenel-ik ("not-sleep-wind").

The word "tancaz"[2] has reference to the condition of faintness, shock, or swoon—"One is without light," "one is as if dead." But tancaz is also spoken of as if it were a substance or object put into the person. It is closely associated with the wind. "Every wind has its tancaz." The effects of the wind, in itself, are the opposite of those produced by the tancaz: trembling, shivering, restlessness, excitement. The tancaz is "faintness" (buy-chal); the wind produces "trembling" (cicil ancil). It is the spots dancing before the eyes that are identified as the

---

[1] There is probably a feeling that there should be *nine* of these evil winds.

[2] Tamacaz. Envaramiento, o pasmo, gota coral, o enfermedad de frenesí que enmudece, entontece, y ensordece al que tiene tamacaz (Motul Dictionary).

actual forms of the winds themselves. But the tancaz is just blackness; it can come about without the agency of the wind. Thus, of a person made dizzy and faint by the sun, it was said that it was because of "tancaz of the sun" (u tancaz kin). The tancaz is not itself personified, as are the winds.

However definitely each separate wind be thought of, and however much they are imagined as like men or like ordinary winds, generally and collectively they constitute an ever-present and pervasive danger. It is chiefly against the evil winds that a man must protect his child, his horse and himself. It is *ojo*-ik that makes dangerous the first hours of morning and the sudden cool shadow that falls across the village before the rain. It is chiefly against the evil winds that the balams stand guard at the four entrances of the pueblo. It is, in large part, by means of the evil winds that the deities of the village and the cornfield punish those who fail to make the proper ritual offerings. Thus, they constrain toward piety. The worst of the winds, it is said, is kazap-ik, and the older people say that this wind appears when a woman goes out to have intercourse with a man in the bush; in this way the conception operates to enforce moral rule, for such surreptitious intercourse is, in most cases, extra-marital. The kazap-ik is the wind that above others strikes the village or the herd in the form of pestilence. Then the winds have entered, and prayer and formula are shaped so as to drive them out.

For the winds take possession of those whose sufferings they cause. It is probably not clear to the native just how the winds occupy his body. One man said that they diluted his blood. Recovery is dependent upon getting them to leave the patient's body by prayer and spell, or by mere ritual washing and stroking. The essential idea is manifest in the phrases used by the h-men: "break the wind" (paabal yikal); "sweep away the wind" (miztal yikal); "fan away the wind" (piktal yikal); "unwind the wind" (uachal yikal).

The efficacy of the zipche plant, and of balche, lies largely in their power to waft or to wash away the evil winds. Furthermore, the winds may pass from one person to another and carry sickness with them; they constitute a kind of contamination. This is the explanation of the feeling that it is a wise precaution— although one by no means always followed—never to lie in a new hammock before tumbling a small wooden stool (kanche) about in it. For when the henequen fiber is twisted into cord, it is rolled by the worker on his thigh, and this rolling and stroking against his person strokes away from him and into the cord the evil winds that cling about him; and from the hammock they would enter the new owner and cause him back-ache if he did not first get them off and on to the stool. Similarly, a person who seeks to visit a new-born child and its mother is—unless excluded entirely as too great a danger—requested to sit quietly outside for a little while until the evil winds have left him.

Apparently the danger that a person will succumb to evil winds is partly dependent upon his immediate circumstances. Childbirth is a time of crisis, when the dangers of the evil winds are multiplied. The celebration of an important ceremony to the chaacs and the balams is also a critical occasion; when the gods are present, then also is there danger of evil winds.   Then balche and zipche keep the place of ceremony pure and protect the participants from the winds.   It is also believed that evil winds are especially present about the person after exercise, when the body is hot and moist with sweat, or at the time of sexual intercourse.[1]   Especially is the traveler likely to meet with evil winds on the trail, for by that road balam or alux may recently have passed.   As one cools off, the evil winds depart.   So a man who has just come from traveling in the bush, or working in the milpa, is a greater danger than one who has not.   Nevertheless, the danger would not keep him from ordinary associations, but he might refrain from picking up and handling an ailing child, or from visiting a woman just after she had borne a child.

OJO

It is this aspect of the evil-wind concept—the notion of transmission of sickness-producing evil from one person to another—that merges with another complex of ideas: that known as *ojo*.   By its name and by many details of belief this concept is easily identified (historically) with the Evil Eye of the Old World; but its ramifications extend far into the customary ways of thinking of Chan Kom.   The connection with the name is made in two ways: some of the people who cause *ojo* do it by merely looking at others; and a diagnostic symptom of the disease is that one eye of the sick person diminishes in size.   But, as already said, the term *ojo* is more widely used to refer to any communicable malignity.   Thus the evil brought by the winds is one kind of *ojo* (*ojo*-ik), although a baleful glance has no part in it.

If a man causes the sickness by merely looking, or by fondling a child, or by his mere presence, it is *ojo*-mac ("man-evil").   But animals can cause it too; there is "dog-evil" (*ojo*-pek), "fowl evil" (*ojo*-cax), etc.   It is those animals that stare fixedly at one that have the power of *ojo:* the domestic fowl, the parrot and the owl. Persons with this evil power are those born on Tuesday or on Friday.   There is a belief that they may be recognized by some small mark between the eyebrows; a mole or a conspicuous vein.   It is dangerous to cross such persons; if, for example, they are refused the purchase of a cow or horse, they may cause its death by merely gazing at it.

The other classes of persons who may cause sickness are those whose physical state is abnormal in one of various ways.   Thus, it is dangerous for children to be looked at not only by people born on Friday or Tuesday, but equally by persons who are drunk or crazy.   Diarrhea and fever are caused in children if they are caressed by persons who are hungry, or thirsty, or merely tired.   And here the notion of evil winds enters once more; about people in such conditions cling the evil winds.

The underlying idea of contagious evil extends along the connection indicated by belief in the perilousness of unusual physical conditions into ideas of danger and sickness that would probably not be called *ojo* at all.   Thus a menstruating woman is dangerous, not to anyone under any circumstances, but to a man with a wound or to a new-born child.[2]   If she passes near the former, his wound begins to ache.

---

[1] See also, with reference to the danger of evil winds after dancing, p. 159.

[2] For this particular danger the following preventive is recognized: Around the wound is put a mixture of honey, ground garlic and the soft terminal leaves of the anona (yoyolni).   Then the "kinam" can not enter.

And a corpse is likewise dangerous to a person with a wound (p. 163). The latter belief represents the conception that openings in the body are the entrance-points for any contagious evil. Thus, evil winds are apt to enter a new-born child through the navel.[1] Finally, women are always dangerous when certain of men's affairs are critical. Their presence would defile the sacredness of the important agricultural ceremonies, and they are not welcome around a lime-burning. Anyone can spoil a lime-burning by tossing a woman's garment or a fragment of domestic pottery on it.

For all sorts of *ojo* in which the presence or gaze of a person in any of these dangerous conditions is regarded as the instrument of sickness, the cure tends to take a form which might be called "counter-inoculation." Different people know of or practice different remedies, all falling into this general pattern. One recommends that the person who causes diarrhea in a child be asked to take the child's finger in his mouth, or to rub a little of his saliva on the child's mouth. Another says that the former should give the child nine little blows, saying, "Go away, diarrhea," or else that the sick child be bathed in water in which the other has bathed. A third has the child drink water from a glass from which the person who brought about the sickness has already drunk. "We did this with you. Because a while ago when you came back from Sahcabchen, you brought *ojo*-mac to Gabol. Don't you remember that as soon as you got back you began to play with him? Well, a little while after that he got sick with vomiting and diarrhea. Then, without saying anything to you, we used the water you had been drinking of, to cure him. That is a very sure way, because in a little while Gabol had nothing the matter with him."[2]

NOCTURNAL BIRDS

Among the causes of death must be mentioned two mythical birds, known respectively as moo-tancaz ("parrot-seizure") and tzitz-moo-tancaz ("purple parrot-seizure"); they are thought of as dark blue or purple in color. Tzitz-moo-tancaz attacks all children. Both cry at night, like babies. They bring death to children, as they fly over houses and vomit a substance, which, dropped into a sleeper's mouth, causes death; for this reason mothers are careful that their children do not sleep face upward, especially with the mouth open. The soul of an unbaptized child becomes a moo-tancaz. The bird then flies over other unbaptized children, trying to kill one. If it succeeds, the child passes to Glory (Heaven) and the other child's soul takes its place. The blue or purple color of these birds is related to ideas of both diagnosis and cure. Babies who die from cardiac difficulties and are blue in the face or lips, have become the victims of these birds; on the other hand, blue dye is used in amulets and is painted on children's wrists and breasts, partly to ward off danger from the tzitz-moo-tancaz.

[1] One man said—and he was not corroborated by others—that zuhuy-ik ("virgin wind") comes from women who have never experienced sexual intercourse, that it appears at the first menstruation, and that if such a woman comes into the presence of a young child, this wind may cause it illness, "even to making the navel burst."

[2] Besides the use of herbal medicine, which is utilized for all sorts of ailments brought about by all sorts of causes, it is said that a mother may keep a child from *ojo* by chewing leaves of rue and rubbing them on the child's eyelids, but that the child, when it grows up, will cause *ojo* to others.

DIVINATION

The techniques of divination, of which the h-men is in command, are used chiefly to find out the cause of sickness. This discovery is of course essential, because the treatment corresponds with the cause. If it be found that the patient's illness is a retribution of the gods, then a propitiatory ceremony will effect a cure. If the evil winds are involved, they must be driven out or enticed to leave. If the ailment has been brought upon the sufferer by the neglected soul of a dead relative, a novena for the rest of that soul is indicated. If there has been witchcraft, still another course of action must be taken. In making these determinations the h-men makes use of two principal methods of divination: crystal-gazing and counting with grains of corn. Besides using these in connection with sickness, they are employed in other connections. Especially does the h-men consult his crystal to discover the will of the gods in all ceremonies of the fields and hives (Plate 14a) to learn if the offerings are acceptable to them, to find out if the breadstuffs in the earth-oven are ready, or to locate deer for hunters (p. 140).

Divination with the zaztun ("stone of light" or "clear stone") is referred to as ilmah ("to look"). The zaztun is a translucent stone or, more commonly, a bit of glass—for example, a bottle-stopper. Every h-men has one or more of these, which he usually keeps in a small leather bag. They are sacred objects, which he does not permit to be casually handled. It is sometimes said by the h-men that he finds such objects on the paths leading into the pueblo, where the balams have placed them for him, but the ordinary layman is skeptical. Before using a zaztun, the h-men often plunges it into a bowl of balche (or rum) "to cleanse it of evil winds," or "to awaken its power." He consults it, ordinarily, only in the light of a candle. The reflected glow of the flame the h-men calls the *lucero;* in it he reads the will of the gods, or sees the cause of the sickness.

Divination with grains of corn is called xixte ("to cleanse, to separate good from bad") or cħapach-*cuenta* ("divining-count"). The h-men takes thirty grains, separates from these an indeterminate number, and proceeds to put these segregated kernels into piles of four; the favorability or the unfavorability of the response depends on two factors: whether the completed groups of four kernels are even or uneven in number, and whether the kernels remaining after the last four are found to be even or uneven in number. If both piles of kernels are even, the response is favorable or the answer to a specific question is affirmative; if both are uneven, the outlook is unfavorable or the answer to the question is negative. If one is even and the other is uneven, then the outcome is in doubt, "there are two words in it" (yan cappel than ichil).

Before beginning this divination the h-men asks that the information wanted be granted him. There is apparently no set formula, the words varying with the circumstances. The phrase "u hahil than" ("the truth of the word") is usually included. For example, in diagnosing the cause of an illness on a certain occasion, the h-men asked whether its cause lay in the sick man's failure to perform the u hanli col ceremony or in the effect of some evil wind, and assigned one cause to one outcome of the corn-grain divination and the other cause to the other. He addressed the grains as follows:

Hunppel, cappel, oxppel, canppel, hoppel, in kati
One,   two,   three, four,   five,   I wish
u hahil than alac ten
the truth of the word be shown me,
u hahil than   ua u hanli col
the truth of the word   whether the dinner-of-the-milpa
uaix ik u tal
or a wind that comes.

If the result is indeterminate, the h-men asks for a second opportunity to know
the truth. On this occasion he said:

Ya be *ora* xan cin katic u hahil than
         now also I ask the truth of the word
caten xan yumen, u kaba *dios* yumbil, *dios* mehenbil,
twice also, Lord (?), in the name of the God the Father, God the Son,
dios espíritu santo. Amen.
God the Holy Ghost, amen.

TREATMENT OF DISEASE

In Chan Kom today the local lore is not the only guide for medical treatment.
It has become usual for sick persons to visit the free clinic maintained by Carnegie
Institution of Washington at Chichen Itza.[1] Almost everyone in the village is
disposed to turn to this clinic for help. Moreover members of the community, more
familiar with the ways of the towns and cities, make considerable use of drugstore
medicine. Nevertheless there is no person in the community who does not apply
traditional medicine and who does not ask the h-men to diagnose and to treat his
ailment or that of his child. The individual differences are merely matters of emphasis: the less sophisticated will go to Chichen only if urged and if the case is
desperate; the more sophisticated will try the outsider's medicine first and fall back
on the h-men when matters become more grave.

The traditional medicine is a great body of remedies and therapeutic practices
in which purely ritual elements form an inseparable part. The herbal lore alone is
enormous.[2] It is plain that this knowledge is very unevenly distributed. Some
men know much more than others about it; women, in general, know more than
men, and h-mens know most of all. Some plants, such as rue, yucca and the
prickly-ash (tancaz-che), are familiar remedies to everyone. Certain h-mens know
hundreds more and the ailments for which they are employed. These plants are
administered either internally in the form of boiled infusions, or the patient is
washed in the infusion. Many elements of domestic cookery enter into medical
compounds: honey, coffee, garlic and chili-pepper, for example. There are many
other ingredients that are not herbal, such as the water in which a woman's gold

[1] Closed in 1932.
[2] As we have made no systematic collection of this lore, and as there are many published works containing data on the subject (see
Paul C. Standley, *Flora of Yucatan*, Field Museum of Natural History, Botanical Series ,vol. II, No. 3 (1930), Ralph L. Roys, *The Ethno-
botany of the Maya*, Tulane University, Middle American Research Series, Publication No. 2 (1931), and bibliographies there cited), we
do not go into the subject in this report.

chains have been boiled or—as in the case of a remedy for difficult respiration—an infusion of the ants' larvæ found inside the thorns of the bull-acacia. The administration of medicine is usually in part ritualistic—before opening a boil, one strokes it nine times with the blade to be used; the nine-fold repetition of some act, dose or treatment is a persistent feature. The characteristic mixture of dosing and ritual is illustrated by the following statement, in which a man tells what he knows about veterinary medicine.

When a horse can not work, does not want to eat, and when it drinks sometimes the water comes through its nose, then it has "little mucus" (*moquillo*). Then I bleed the horse. This I do just as the h-men bleeds people, but I do it longer. First the blood runs black; when it comes red, it is time to stop bleeding. Afterward, it is good to put a little vinegar in a bag (*sabucan*) and let the horse smell it. Morning and evening one should mix fat with chili-pepper and burn it under the horse's nose; this will help to clear away the catarrh. There are two kinds of *moquillo*; *moquillo blanco*, which is easily cured, and *moquillo amarillo* when the horse's neck swells up. This kind can not be cured.

Haba is another trouble horses have: the roof of the mouth swells up and a sort of phlegm appears. I cut this off with a heated *machete*. The horse's tongue is fastened down with a stick, so it won't get burned.

When the horse is attacked in the belly, and has pains, then it suffers from x-bohton-ik. That is because the horse's path and that of the wind have crossed at some road intersection. Then one picks up nine small stones,[1] one at each of nine road-crossings; one wraps them in the horse-blanket and shakes them up; then with them in the blanket one gives the horse two blows on each side of the belly. This is repeated in one hour. This drives out the wind. Afterward one makes the horse drink coffee, rum and tancaz-che (prickly-ash) bark, all boiled together.

If the horse is constipated, I give it castor-oil. If it can not urinate, the trouble is kal-uix ("urine-closure"). Then the cure is to take some bedbugs, such as one finds in hammocks, and burst them in the horse's teeth.

When a horse runs neighing with its tail straight up, it has been attacked by the wind x-hul-ne-ik. Then one cuts the tip of the tail in the form of a cross, and puts in six drops of 3-H (a patent medicine) and one makes the horse drink twenty-five drops of this. It is good to use the nine stones too, to drive out the wind. If a horse suffers a rope-bruise, or a cut, one puts warm fat and chili in the wound.

The therapeutic techniques of massage, bleeding and cupping are largely, but not entirely, in the control of specialists. The bone-setter (kax-baac—who, as has been indicated on p. 73 is in many cases not a h-men) practices a kind of massage called hiikab,[2] in which the motions are downward along the limbs; then the limbs and back are separately stretched. Ordinary commercial vegetable oil is employed as a lubricant. The bone-setter sets bones and applies splints. In the case of injured bones that are difficult to manipulate, such as the ribs at juncture with the sternum, he uses cupping, which "by absorption makes the bone take its normal position."

The h-men—who is such because he discharges priestly and ritual magic functions—may also make use of massage and cupping, and frequently employs bleeding. Most h-mens draw blood by means of an instrument (tok) made by

[1] Cf. footnote, p. 162.
[2] The midwives make much use of this massage in attending women during pregnancy and at delivery. It requires special knowledge, being distinguished from yoth—the simple rubbing of an ailing part of the body.

fixing a small fragment of glass, flint, or obsidian in a small split stick at right angles to it; and some use the fangs of a rattlesnake. The blood is drawn from the part of the body that seems to be affected. "The first blood is black; afterward it comes red; then one is all right." Bleeding is resorted to in ridding the body of evil winds. In such a case the h-men may make scores of punctures all over the body, that the blood may wash out the winds. It is common for a h-men to cup the wound after bleeding, using a homa, or an ordinary glass tumbler, and burning a little cotton in the receptacle to make it stick to the flesh.

THERAPEUTIC CEREMONIES

The curing functions of the h-men also include the performance of special ceremonies. Because of the connection between neglect of the agricultural deities and disease, many performances of field and hive ceremonies are in meaning therapeutic (Chapter VIII). But there are also two ceremonies which are solely therapeutic and which do not take the form of offerings to the yuntzilob, but are cleansing and purificatory rites. One of these is known as *santiguar*, or as *santiguada* ("be sanctified"), and the other as kex ("exchange").

The *santiguar* depends on the effectiveness of certain plants to cleanse of evil winds. The most generally used plant for this purpose is zipche, but the h-mens also employ tancaz-che, sucure-ic, cedar, xul, and—in very serious cases—tobacco.[1] When the h-men arrives to treat a person afflicted with the winds, he is given rum to drink, and he then directs the members of the household to bring certain of the plants just mentioned. Zipche is apparently always one of these. No altar is prepared for the ceremony, because no foods are to be offered. If the sick person is able, he sits on a little bench beside the h-men. The plants to be used are sometimes spread out on a little table. If the patient can not sit, the h-men goes to his hammock. He prays, asking the aid of San Lazaro, San Roque and the *Virgin Asunción*, and ordering the winds to depart. Meanwhile he brushes the sick person with zipche (Plate 14 *b*). He may take into his mouth some rum and spray a little around the hammock or on the head and in the eyes of the patient. Then he brushes the hammock and the house-posts with the zipche. The herbs that he has used he then takes some distance from the house and throws them all away. The winds have now been cast out and, to prevent their return, he tosses after them, in a motion that makes the sign of the cross, a little rum. On re-entering the house, he says "Good afternoon" (or evening, etc.). The sick person's clothing is changed and carried out to the washing-table.

Santiguar is the remedy commonly applied when by divination the h-men learns that the illness is not the result of the failure to make a ceremony, but is due simply to an accidental encounter with the winds. It is also very frequently performed as an adjunct to other ritual medicine, as for example in concluding an u hanli col or an u hanli cab made to alleviate a sickness. It may be performed in

---

[1] At the kex ceremony the h-men sometimes smokes a cigarette, and blows the smoke around the patient. This smoke is called by the same name as incense (ppuluth), and the act of incensing with smoke by the same verb (ppultah). When the h-mens wish to catch a snake (for medicine, or for the fangs), they "put a cigarette between the toes, and allow the smoke to pass over the snake, which falls asleep."

any case where there is danger of evil winds. Thus a *santiguar* is often performed at the end of a cha-chaac; and the hadz pach (p. 159) in effect includes a *santiguar*.

In more serious cases of illness, where no breach of ritual duty is involved, the h-men performs kex. Commonly, if *santiguar* does not bring relief, he hangs out a vessel of zaca, asking permission of the winds and the three *santos* previously mentioned, to offer them their dinner at some future day named. This day is nearly always Friday, for on this day the winds go abroad. When the dish of zaca is taken down, particles of corn (puczikal ixim, "heart of the maize") are seen to have risen to the surface. If these particles are distributed in pairs, the outlook for the patient is favorable; if uneven, it is unfavorable.

The kex is a promise of a return to be made to the winds if they abandon their victim, the patient. If the patient recovers, the winds have fulfilled their part of the bargain, and it is then necessary to make kex. If he does not get better, it is not necessary; but it may be made anyway.

The ceremony takes place, ordinarily, at midnight. The h-men comes Friday evening. The owner of the house has prepared three *cuartillos* of maize and a *cuartillo* of ground squash seed, and a turkey or other fowl. In the early part of the evening the h-men offers the fowl to the winds. This he does by holding it over the head of the sick person while praying an offertory prayer. If the sick person is a man, a pullet must be used; if a woman, a cockerel. It is usual to strangle the fowl as it is being held over the patient's head.

The other people of the house are busy securing the plants that the h-men requires: always zipche, sometimes hunchich, iximche, zuputh, kaxab-yuk, and the roots of xul. It is also necessary to get thirteen small fruits of the kax tree. These are hard, like nuts, and those must be found from which the birds or rodents have eaten the centers, leaving them hollow. For these little cups are to be the homa of the winds.

At midnight the table of food is offered. On top of the table are placed the offerings for the three *santos:* two dishes each containing a boiled fowl (one of these is to be eaten by the sick person and the members of the family, and the other by the h-men), two napkins, each containing thirteen cham-cham-uah (p. 146), and two dishes of kol, and branches of zipche. Underneath the table is placed the special food for the winds—that which is to be exchanged for the sick person. These foods are a dish containing the viscera, beak, comb, claws and feathers of the fowl earlier offered to the winds, the thirteen kax fruits, each containing a little zaca mixed with rum (this is called yach-kazap-ha, "bad-mixture-water"), and a bottle of rum with a glass.

The h-men prays, delivering the table to the three saints and to the winds. Then the articles under the table are carried outside the house and some distance from it and thrown away. The h-men says that thereby the winds, that have come for their dinner, are returned again to the sea (kanab). Before returning to the house the h-men tosses the rum after the other articles. This is called kal pach ("shutting the door on the back"). The h-men repeats this process twice, once about a *mecate* from the house and once just at the door. This is called "making two locks" (kalal). On entering the house, the h-men says, "Good evening." The food on top of the table is distributed and consumed. After this a *santiguar* is performed, to get rid of any winds that may remain.

The loh ("redeem," "free") ceremony, known to all the people of Chan Kom, is much more elaborate than these, but also has for its purpose the driving out of evil winds. The ceremony is not a common one, however, and the information available is scanty. The ceremony is performed over the bee-hives when the honey is scanty, in the cattle-pens when the cattle are sick or when cattle are brought back to an old corral, and especially in the village itself when epidemic or unusual sudden deaths have occurred.[1] The loh ceremony is therefore apt to be not a private or familial matter,[2] but a communal act, comparable in significance and in seriousness to the cha-chaac. Like the agricultural ceremonies, and those offered to the gods of the bees, the loh ceremony includes familiar ritual elements: offerings of balche, consecrated fowl and special breadstuffs. But the meaning of the loh is propitiation and exorcism of evil spirits. Partly the offerings are made to the balams, that they may keep the evil winds away, but partly they are given to the evil spirits themselves. As loh-corral used to be performed, it was customary to bury in the cattle-yard a calf or even one or more bulls, to appease the evil winds and the alux. In making loh-cah, the h-men buries at the four entrances to the village, where stand the crosses and the balams, objects which prevent the entrance of the winds: tancaz-che, rum, and flakes of obsidian (tok. See p. 172).

A loh-cahtali ("redemption of a settlement") performed in 1929 at the *milperío* of Sahcabchen was occasioned by epizootic among the animals of the *milperos* who were wont to stay at this place while working in their fields. The h-men announced that the evil winds had been brought to the place by the alux, whose presence was evident from the existence nearby of mounds containing ancient ruins. He therefore erected a large altar for the protecting balams and a small one for the ill-natured alux. Ritual breads were prepared, fowls consecrated and kol made, as in the u hanli col, cha-chaac and u hanli cab. On the large altar the h-men placed most of the ritual breads, the large pots of kol and thirteen homa of balche. On the smaller altar he put one noh-uah and thirteen shells of the wine-palm filled with balche. These foods were offered to the balams and to the alux. By consulting his zaztun, the h-men determined where the alux were to be found. Most of the night he consumed in repeating the prayers, in drinking rum, and in repeatedly consulting the zaztun. At last he learned where the final offering was to be made. At dawn all the men present, carrying candles, followed the h-men to a small mound which, by reason of the hewn stones forming a stairway in one of its faces, must have been a temple-structure in ancient times. The h-men explained that in this mound the alux were hidden. Bidding the others remain at a little distance, the h-men alone ascended the steps, carrying the noh-uah and the little shells of balche. In a short while he returned to his followers without them and announced that he had calmed

---

[1] Correspondingly it is called loh-cab, loh-corral, or loh-cah.
[2] With exceptions hereinafter noted.

the anger of the alux. Satisfied, all returned to the altars, where, just as the sun rose, began the feasting with which all ceremonies conclude.

In the previous year an unusual amount of sickness in Chan Kom itself was the occasion of another loh ceremony. The h-men in charge was a famous practitioner from Tixcacaltuyu. He required each man of the village to furnish an *almud* of corn, a *cuarto* of rum and a hen. Under his direction, thirteen large crosses were made of xul wood. He selected thirteen men who could best recite Catholic prayers. When the h-men had erected the usual table-altar, he had these thirteen men carry the image of San Diego from the *oratorio* and place it on the table-altar in place of the usual cross. He then had the thirteen men recite the Lord's prayer, and after this he himself offered prayers in Maya. Then all the participants went together to each of the four "entrances" of the village in turn, and at each, the h-men buried in the road, the usual preventives against the evil winds: a piece of obsidian (tok), a cross made of tancaz-che, another of halalche, and a little salt. All then returned to the altar, and the h-men prayed again. After this all went to the cenote from which the village draws its water, and the h-men had the men throw into it the thirteen crosses of xul wood, "so that the winds would not come out of it again." He also poured in rum, and threw in the intestines of the hens that had been offered. He explained that this was done to satisfy the hunger of the winds—hunger evidenced by the circumstance that several animals had recently fallen into the cenote. When all had returned to the table-altar, he had the thirteen *cantores* carry the *santo* back to the *oratorio*, singing hymns as they went. Then he lectured them on their responsibility to give good care to the *santo* thereafter. The ceremony ended with the usual distribution of the offered foods.[1]

Another kind of loh ceremony is known. As explained in an earlier chapter (p. 114), strayed children are taken and cared for by the balams. If, however, the lost child is not found within a day or two, a loh may be made, to offer food to the balams to "redeem" the lost child and cause the yuntzilob to put him on the path to home. Such a child returns bereft of sense or speechless, because the balams do not want him to tell of what he has seen. A *santiguar* may be performed to cure him.[2]

AMULETS

The fact that sickness and death strike children more often than adults is sometimes explained by pointing out that they are not able and experienced enough to avoid the evil winds and other kinds of *ojo*. An adult may exercise judgment and take care of himself. If he is sick, in many cases he has only himself to blame: he has offended the deities, or the souls of his relatives; or else black magic is in operation against him. But children do not make enemies.

The special need of children is met by the wearing of amulets. They may be worn constantly, or else at times when unusual danger threatens them. Thus, mothers will put amulets on their children if there is much sickness about. Or they

---

[2] This ceremony (which neither of the writers witnessed) is the only one of those performed by a h-men in which Catholic prayers and the effigy of the *santo* formed a part.

[2] From information furnished in other communities in the Chan Kom region, it is probable that a loh ceremony is sometimes performed for those who have had the misfortune to see a balam. Such an accident is thought to cause sickness or death.

will put them on a child when they are about to take him through the bush; for the amulet will prevent a balam from making a changeling out of a laggard child (p. 114). So also are amulets used during the Days of the Dead, when some returning soul might enter the body of an unprotected child (p. 202).

But chiefly the amulets are used to keep off the evil winds and other sorts of *ojo*. The ordinary amulet (such as that illustrated in Plate 17*a*) is a collection of small objects tied together with thread. The thread should be dyed blue with juice from the choh plant (indigo), the same blue dye that is used to paint the nails of persons in imminent danger of death from sickness and that keeps away the tzitz-moo-tancaz. Necklaces and bracelets are made from such a thread and various small seeds, bones and shells. Small oyster and snail shells have protective power. So also has the bark of the tancaz-che (prickly-ash); from it cross-shaped pieces are prepared. From the coc-ac, or plastron of the tortoise, is cut that part on which appears a little cross. This is especially a preventive of whooping-cough, asthma and other respiratory afflictions. Sometimes a patient suffering from such an ailment is given to drink the water in which this bone has been boiled. A necklace made of the seeds of a plant called oxol also protects from these illnesses, and sick people are bathed with an infusion of leaves of the same plant. When the seeds which form the necklace change color and split into pieces, it shows that they have absorbed the evil winds that were troubling the sufferer. Sometimes such a necklace is made from the fruits of the chac-molon-che.

Amulets often include a small bone from an agouti's head. This is known as ppuc tzub (agouti's cheek). Beside keeping evil winds away, this charm gives the child ability easily to find sweet potatoes and other root crops, when he comes to harvest them. Other common protective charms are the horn or the hoof of a deer, cleaned and polished, and known as *sucure*-baac;[1] a little bone called *jiga*,[2] found in the backbone of some fishes; and the seed-stones of the wine-palm.

WITCHCRAFT

Although black magic is generally recognized, and although death from sorcery is a not uncommon allegation, witchcraft is not one of the leading causes of sickness and death. The evil winds, either as a punishment sent by the yuntzilob or encountered accidentally, are easily paramount. "Is it the dinner-of-the-milpa, or a wind that comes?" runs the divinatory phrase of the h-men. Sickness is either an unfortunate accident or the result of a lapse from piety. The fear of sickness is a constraint to right conduct and conformity to ritual. Even the failure to observe the prayers in commemoration of the death of a relative may bring illness. At any rate, witchcraft is not apt to be the first explanation given. Characteristically, it is a prolonged sickness, a growing debility, that suggests to the sick man that he is being bewitched. After two months of illness, and using up many hens in making the various ceremonies to the gods of the milpa and the hives and to appease the evil winds, "then," said one such sufferer, "I began to suspect the *hechiceros*" (p. 227).

[1] From *socorro*, "succour?"
[2] No doubt from *higa*, "amulet."

To the man who spoke thus, the suggestion came more easily because he knew he had enemies. He had secured the arrest of certain persons whom he believed to have shot a steer of his. These facts were also known to the h-mens whom the sick man summoned to cure him, and when their treatments brought no relief, they told him it was because those enemies were using witchcraft against him. One of his enemies was himself a h-men, and that made it easier for the sick man to form his suspicions. For, although (as has already been indicated in Chapter V) suspicion of witchcraft dims the priestly prestige of the h-men, and although the most famous wizards are not h-mens, nevertheless the h-men's powers are all occult and evil is easily mixed with good. They are in a position to sell their souls to the devil, although the best of them withstand the temptation.

The sorcerer "sends the enchantment into" the afflicted person. There are at least three ways in which this may be done. One is by control over the evil winds; the sorcerer knows the invocatory formula which sends the winds into his victims. Another is by making a beeswax image of the sick person and burying it, or cutting, or piercing it. The third way is most often mentioned. The sorcerer sends the sickness by one of the multitude of small living creatures that he controls. One such is a small green night-flying homopterous insect (maz); therefore, if such an insect flies into the house people are quick to crush it or burn it. Another insect (akab dzunuun), that makes a humming noise as it flies, brushes against the body of the victim and in the dust from its wings leaves the sickness. Then sores break out at the affected part, and if the sores come on the abdomen, death results. Still a third insect (chapat) is believed to lay its eggs in a vessel of water or of rum. The victim drinks the water and becomes sick or dies. Sometimes a sorcerer brings sickness to a woman by sending a certain sort of fly (chuc-muc) to lay its eggs out in the yard where the woman goes to urinate. Then the eggs get into the victim when she goes there. (To cure this sickness, the h-men gives her a gourd dish of rum; when the woman has urinated into this, the h-men burns it and so destroys the eggs.) Snakes are also carriers of sicknesses sent by the sorcerers. One such, golden-yellow in color, is called hoonob; if it crawls over one's hat or sandal, death results when the garment is later put on.

All these animal carriers of sickness or death are referred to as the "domestic animals," "personal pets" (alakob) of the sorcerer. They come from the underworld (metnal), a dark place filled with these evil creatures, from which the h-men summons them. In a vague way they are thought of as emerging from metnal through the cenotes, which are the doorways to the underworld. These are also the doorways through which must pass the sorcerers themselves when they come to die; for to metnal they must all go in the end.

Distinguished from the alak, which is a small creature which does the bidding of the sorcerer, is the uay, the familiar, the animal into which the sorcerer transforms himself at pleasure. The uay is, therefore, the sorcerer himself when he takes that shape. These shapes are usually those of the ordinary domestic animals of the barnyard: dog (uay pek), cat (uay miz), and cow or bull (uay uacax). Again it may be a h-men that is suspected of having this power of transformation, but also it is knowledge that any person can acquire, if he wishes to traffic with evil. Any old person, especially if of solitary or peculiar habits, is likely to be the object of these suspicions. Stories about witches form a large part of the narrative material in conversation; they are exciting, and at least mildly terrible. Some such stories are told of other years and other places; others are matters of current gossip and alarm—an eccentric old person, a girl suffering from a wasting illness, may start the winds of evil gossip blowing across the settlements, and the excitement may rise to such a point as to bring about the terrified evacuation of a settlement preyed upon by some witch in animal form.

The stories tell of a man who follows his wife through nocturnal exploits, seeing her change into the form of a cow and mingle with a herd of bulls, or a wife who sees her husband become a dog and dig up the graves in the cemetery to feed on human flesh, of midnight *jaranas* at which dancers, musicians and other participants are all in animal form, or who turn into animal form when day breaks. The stories include frequent references to the ritual whereby the transformations are achieved, and include instructions as to how to frustrate the witches. It is said that two witches at least must be involved in the transformation. Each gives nine somersaults backward and jumps nine times over his companion. These acts are performed in reverse order when the witches re-assume human form. Salt is the great preventive of witches in animal form. When the transformed witch leaves his house, he hides his human head somewhere; if one can find this and put salt on it, he can not regain human form. Or, if one captures a witch, one may prevent his escape by tying his foot to an onion plant. There is no public procedure against witches; the remedies are private and covert.

The evil conduct of which all these witches are suspected is especially that of illicit or unnatural sexual intercourse. Therefore, they are often distinguished, not in terms of the particular animal whose form is taken, but in terms of the animal's (and witch's) sex, male (uay xib) or female (uay x-chup). The former visits girls sleeping in their hammocks, and the latter pollutes the repose of youths. The uay xib is described as using its tongue as its instrument of lubricity. Young persons who believe themselves to have such nocturnal visitors may prevent their coming by sleeping with clothing wrong side out; the youth may turn his sandals upside down on the floor. When a girl grows pale and loses her strength, people often begin to say that a uay-xib is visiting her. Then if after nightfall, some unusually large or unnatural appearing animal is seen near some house where lives an old or eccentric person, the links of cause and effect are joined.

One kind of witch is the uay-cot[1] (Plate 15b), that turns himself into a creature with wings of straw-mats and breaks into houses or stores at night to steal goods or children. The uay-cot is the subject of stories with which adults frighten children, or excite and alarm one another; and occasionally it is said of some unpopular and unreasonably successful merchant of the towns, "that he must be a uay-cot."

---

[1] The older people sometimes say "uay-pop" ("straw-mat-witch"), which is doubtless the older form, rather than "uay-cot" ("stone-wall-witch").

All these supernatural and indecent powers are bought at the price of one's soul. The uay has made his pact with the devil, and in the end he will follow his alakob to metnal. A man may win a woman by black magic—by putting the rattles of a rattlesnake into his guitar when he plays to her, or by rubbing her hand with the powdered ashes of a humming-bird. Or a woman may escape the tedious hours of practice necessary to proficiency in the arts of embroidery, and magically master both the cross-stitch and the simpler stitch, by stroking nine times the back of a rattlesnake. But such persons are "half-damned." "Better," says the older man, "to let your father ask for her in marriage." "Better," says the older woman to the younger, "practice at embroidery in patience."

CHAPTER XI

FROM BIRTH TO DEATH

BIRTH [1]

To the critical moments in the life cycle of the individual, especially to birth, attach especially those dangers generally described in the preceding chapter: the winds, evil eye and the effects of "cold." The new-born child and the recent mother must be guarded from the various communicable evils, and at the time of birth "hot" foods and medicines are essential.

A woman usually bears her first child within a year or two after marriage.[2] Sterility is explained by "cold." Women work as usual during their menses,[3] but avoid getting chilled. They use only a little water in bathing, and are careful not to get caught in the rain—if rain threatens, a menstruating woman will put off a journey. For if she "gets a cold (ziz)" in her abdomen, she may be prevented from bearing a child. If a woman fails to bear children, it may also be because she has eaten too much "cold" food. "There was a woman here some years ago; she did not want to have children. She was a great dancer, and liked dancing better than having children. So she ate cold things, especially lime juice. She didn't have any children. But she made herself sick."

Except for the feeling that it is not good to have intercourse with a woman during her menstruation, and aside from the religious restriction during certain ceremonies (p. 139), a man has intercourse with his wife at any time. It is thought that gestation of a male child takes ten months, and of a female child nine. If a man's blood "is the stronger," the child will be a male.

That one's neighbor is pregnant is, of course, interesting, and such a fact is not long in becoming part of the village gossip. People see the midwife making her calls in the house where the baby is expected. Mothers vary in their observation of pre-natal care, but it is advised that the midwife begin her treatments in the third month of pregnancy. Once a month she gives the expectant mother massage. The purpose of this is to keep the child in the correct position. The pregnant woman goes out as she pleases and eats what foods she will.

At the time of delivery the mother is secluded from everyone except the midwife and her husband.[4] It is regarded as positively advisable that the father of the child should remain and assist. One end of the house is partitioned off with a curtain (cancel) formerly of palm-leaves, now often of cloth. This is the only time

---

[1] The presence of unessential persons during the delivery of a child is strongly discouraged in Chan Kom, and therefore neither of the authors has been present on such an occasion. The information presented was obtained from mothers and fathers—the midwife of the village at the time, was a very uncommunicative person. Miss Katheryn MacKay has generously allowed us to supplement these data with her much fuller information obtained in neighboring villages and towns.

[2] The average age of twenty-three mothers at the birth of the first child was sixteen years. Of the twenty-five married women for whom data were secured, all but one had the first child within the first two years of marriage. This one, after seven years of marriage, is still childless.

[3] "It is good for women to live out here in the bush where there are many trees, because the resin (yitz che) comes out of the trees, and therefore there is less menstrual flow in women."

[4] If the husband is not available, some female relative of the woman may attend.

such a partition is set up in the house; its presence indicates a recent or an impending birth.   After labor has begun, and up to the moment of birth, the midwife from time to time resumes her massage, the mother reclining in her hammock.   The midwife may administer "hot" drinks, or warm the mother's body with a fire, for cold, at this moment of crisis, is very dangerous.   If the birth is delayed, various herbal or magical remedies may be employed; one such is made of the soft interior of the flower stalk of the wild pinguin (chom).   Or the woman may drink water in which her gold chains have been washed.

Delivery takes place with the mother either kneeling or in a standing position, supporting herself by a rope under the armpits, or resting her arms upon the shoulders of her husband.   The midwife usually kneels on the floor, where she has ready warmed clothing.   The cord is not cut until after the discharge of the placenta.   The midwife measures two fingers' width from the navel and ties the cord with a cotton string.   She cuts the cord with a sharpened edge of a piece of cane (halal).   "It is bad for the baby to cut it with a knife."   The cord is singed over a candle flame and is dressed with oil and a cloth that has been heated to singeing; this cloth is secured in place by a bandage around the abdomen.

The new-born child is washed in warm water, dressed in a short cotton shirt, and wrapped in a large square cloth.   A folded cloth may serve as a diaper at first, but very commonly babies are not diapered.   Before clothing is put on a very young baby, it is warmed.   The baby is put to the breast soon after birth and bath.

The afterbirth is either burned or buried; the preferred place in which to dispose of it is under the hearthstones of deserted houses.   This practice, also, is a preventive of the danger of "cold," for under such an old hearth "there are many ashes, and if the afterbirth is buried there, the mother is thus warmed."   The same feeling is present if the afterbirth is burned.   Sometimes the ashes that result from burning the afterbirth are used to wash the mother's hair; this is supposed to be a preventive of the frontal baldness from which many Maya women suffer.

The cord is oiled until it drops off, "usually on the third day."   Persons who are careful of such matters take the separated piece of cord and put it under one of the crosses that stand at the four entrances of the village.   If an animal should eat the cord, the child would become timid and cowardly; therefore the cord is placed well inside the pile of stones which the cross surmounts, and under the direct protection of a balam, so that the animals can not get at it.

The child and its mother are protected from the sickness-bearing winds and from all persons whose special circumstances make them the carriers of contagious evil.   Travelers who have passed through the bush may bring evil winds upon their persons; they are not allowed to enter the house where the woman lies during the first week, or are required to remain quietly outside until, as their bodies cool and the sweat evaporates, they become harmless.   "If a wind enters, the mother's limbs are likely to swell."   Persons who are hungry or thirsty should not visit the mother and child; if they do, the child is likely to suffer from diarrhea.   Pregnant

PLATE 15

a, Amulet.

b, Uaycot.

(From a wall-painting in a house in Uayma. Photograph by Morris Steggerda)

PLATE 16

a, A burial.

b, Eustaquio Ceme.

women, not members of the household, are especially dangerous. If such a visitor does enter, sickness is apt to fall upon the new-born child in the form of a swelling or infection of the navel (called pit i tuch, "blow out the navel")[1] which causes the child to utter a little grunting cry (acan). The protrusion of the navel may be cured by using the saliva of the woman who caused the trouble; a little is rubbed on the child's navel. If a menstruating woman comes within the first three days, the umbilical cord will bleed again. Care is taken to keep away persons known to have the evil eye; the child is covered with a cloth in the presence of such a person, or carried from the room.

Soon after the birth takes place, the mother is bathed in warm water and a bandage fastened around her abdomen. The bath is repeated and the bandage bound again by the midwife every day for several days thereafter. All her foods and drinks must be "hot." If she experiences pain, she may be given a hot drink made of mint, honey and aniseed. A mother is confined to her room for some days after birth. "She must stay in her hammock for a week, remain quiet for two, and after three weeks she may go out on the street." In fact this strictness is not observed. For some days the midwife administers massage.

A child born on Tuesday or on Friday is apt to be sickly or die. The first seven days of the child's life are referred to as "the seven sacraments." If the child dies within this time, it is a sign that the mother will not die for a long time. But if the child is sick, and the sickness extends beyond the first seven days, it is felt that the child and the mother will both live.[2]

The birth of twins is regarded, for practical reasons, as something of an unfortunate occurrence. It is thought unwise to make fun of twins, lest one himself become the parent of twins. The old people speak of twins as "god children" (mehen kuob), and treat them with especial respect. If a twin of any age, comes to the house of an older person, he may give the twin some little present.

Children are commonly nursed for about two years, or until lactation is interrupted. Nevertheless, in many cases a child will be allowed, occasionally, to drink from the breast as late as the fifth or sixth year, when its diet is in other respects the same as that of an adult. A remedy to expedite the flow of milk is *atole* prepared with ground squash seeds. There is considerable individual variation with regard to infant feeding. Most people begin to give *atole* to the child within the first few months, or at least in the first year; some now prefer oatmeal or rice. A mother usually does not give tortillas to her child until it has the first few teeth, but soon thereafter the infant's diet becomes the same as that of the adults. If the mother dies, the child is given to some other woman in lactation to nurse, or it is fed on condensed milk. There is no attempt to feed nursing children regularly.

NAMES

The given name of the child is taken from one of the saint's names appearing in the church calendar opposite the day on which the birth occurs. No exceptions

---

[1] Umbilical hernia?

[2] A related idea is that although a man may outlive six wives, the seventh will surely outlive him.

to this have appeared. A natural reply to the question: "What is the name of the child?" is "It isn't known yet; they haven't looked in the calendar."

But children born after noon take their names from the names of the saints appropriate to the following calendar day. This is because "tomorrow" is regarded as beginning at noon "today." Thus Monday beguns at noon Sunday. It is for this reason that some men go out to do half a day's work on Sunday afternoon. Sunday begins at noon Saturday. By noon on Saturday all the bees, they say, have returned to the hives, and at noon on Saturday the waves of the sea have become quiet.

There is, however, sometimes uncertainty among the people themselves as to the baptismal names of children, even of their own,[1] partly because not uncommonly parents fall into the habit of applying to the child a name other than that by which it was baptized, and partly because the full baptismal names are rarely used in referring to or addressing either adults or children. The short abbreviations used conceal the real names, so that they may be forgotten. Thus a man or boy called "Eus" or "Us" may have been baptized Eustaquio, Eulalio or Eusebio.

The surnames are all Maya (*i. e.* none are Spanish), and only thirty-one are represented in the population of two hundred and fifty. The uncertainty as to given names is equalled by the uncertainty as to surnames. This is because many unions have not been solemnized by either church or state, and in such cases the children may be known either by the mother's name or by the father's. The father's name is entered in the Civil Registry if the father acknowledges the child and himself files the record of its birth. But the people themselves apply to the child the father's name if the couple live together as man and wife, whether they be legally married or not, and whether or not the father has legally acknowledged the child. At the same time they recognize the fact of illegitimacy, and so may refer to the child sometimes by the one surname and sometimes by the other— "She is Pastora Cen and she is also Pastora Puc."

BAPTISM

Baptism is a matter of extreme importance; unbaptized children, except the very young, do not exist in Chan Kom. It is a great sorrow to the parents if their child dies unbaptized. A baptized child goes straight to *Gloria;* young children, in the language of the rituals, are referred to as "angels." An unbaptized child wanders between the worlds in the form of the death-dealing nocturnal bird (p. 169).

In most cases the child is brought to the priest in Valladolid for baptism. But if an unbaptized child is likely to die, some layman in a nearby town, or the teacher, may be asked to administer the sacrament. As the baptismal act itself is performed by an outsider, a priest of the town, the form of the ritual is something with which the folk have no concern. Often the parents do not attend, and the meal served by the parents to the *compadres* immediately after the baptism is a simple dinner of boiled fowl, served without ceremony. The important rituals are two: that in which the *compadre* relationship is pledged, before the baptism,

---

[1] A case is that of a young girl known to her playmates as Paula, who asserted her name was Claudia, was called Paula by her mother, and Claudia or Paula indifferently by her father, and had been actually baptized Paula.

and that in which the parents, after the baptism, acknowledge their gratitude to their *compadres*.

These rituals are performed when the godparents are not members of the family. Like those attending marriage, they have a theoretically perfect form which is realized in varying degrees in actual cases. That is to say, the older people and the more conservative, retain the details of ceremony: the delivery of set traditional speeches in formal Maya—what is called "sweet speech" (cħuhuc than), the ceremonious and courteous entrances, presentations and departures, and the bowing and kissing of hands. It should be understood that the following descriptions conform to the ideal type of ritual and, in many contemporary instances, elements of formality are omitted.

When parents of a recently born child request another couple to carry it to baptism, they go to ask a great favor and to propose the establishment between the two couples of the significant and unbreakable relationship of *compadre*. Such solemn petitions, in the thinking of the people, should not be delivered directly, but through an intermediary. The father of the child therefore asks, to accompany him and his wife to the house of the other, some friend, a respected man of mature years. When they together enter the house, the friend, the father and the mother successively kiss the hand of the godfather-elect. The latter places his thumb over his first finger, forming a cross; and this the others kiss, bowing as they do so. The friend then addresses the owner of the house in the following words:

> He cen bix tu pahta ca yumi ti *Dios* yetel
> Here then as it is established by the Lord God and
>
> colebil zuhuy Maria u chan dzocbezah u chan dzabal
> the Holy Virgin Mary to fulfill, to give
>
> mehen *ángeles* utial chan ocac, tat, kuchoon uaye
> little children for baptism, sir, we come here
>
> tuux u boyi beix mech cichcelem yumi, yoklal katic
> where is the shade which I ask of (?) the Holy Lord, so as to ask
>
> ti a tzicbenil ua uchac a betic u yaabal utz
> of your respected person if you can do a good thing
>
> ti bin ectata(?), a chan dzic le chan *ángel*
> for this *señor*, (that is) give the small child
>
> utial *santo* oca.
> to holy baptism.

If the other is willing to act as godfather, he replies as follows:

> *Pues*, tat, ezac ua yetel u yaabal u *voluntade*
> Well, sir, if it appears that with much will
>
> u thanicenob, ua *igual* u tuculobe, *pues*,
> they address me, or your thoughts are the same, well,
>
> cimac in uoli, he in chan dzocbezic tun tiobe.
> I am willing, I am going to fulfill them (their wishes).

When this consent has been received, the father withdraws and returns to his house or to some other place where he has already made ready the offering, acceptance of which is to seal the agreement. The accompanying friend provides a table, and upon this are placed four *reales* of wheat bread, ten tablets of chocolate, one *kilo* of sugar, two bottles of rum (or soft drink substitute), a package of cigarettes and two candles. The table is carried into the house of the godparents. One of the candles is lighted. The friend and the father of the child then stand and the godfather does likewise. The friend kisses first the hand of the father and then that of the godfather, and delivers the table with the following speech:

Pues, tat, he cen bix dzoci u yantal a dzaic
Well, sir, as has been accomplished that which you gave

a *voluntad*, utial a ualic a dzocbezic le *santo bautismo*,
your willingness to say that you would fulfill the holy baptism,

he tu hunppit chan cimac olal, chan yacunah tamba,
here is a little good-wishes, a little love-each-other,

chan *festejo*, cu dzaic tu cumpaleex.
a little feast, which your *compadres* give.

The godfather accepts the gift, saying:

Maalob, tat, ua yan u *voluntad* tiob, *pues*,
Very well, sir, if they have the wish, then

cin kamoltic hach cimac in uoli.
I receive it very content.

The friend again kisses the hand of each, and all are seated. The godfather-designate directs his wife to take the gifts from the table and to make chocolate with the tablets provided. There is general conversation, and the chocolate and bread are served, and the rum or other liquid refreshment drunk. After this, the godfather puts back on the table the napkin in which the bread was brought, and the empty bottles. He kisses the hand of the friend, and with another short, formal speech, delivers these articles back to his visitor.

The father then takes the napkin and the bottles, and bidding the others good-night, leaves with his wife and his friend.

The godparents fix the day of the baptism and, in preparation for this day, the godmother makes ready the clothing the child is to wear. (If there is no godmother, as occasionally happens, the child's own mother prepares the clothes.) The clothes provided include two shirts, two diapers, a cap, and—if the child be a girl—a small pair of earrings. It used to be customary to give also a little chain, but it is not usual now. The earrings may be put into the ears before or after the baptism. But, if they are put into the ears before baptism, they are taken out for that occasion. The godfather makes the arrangements with the priest and pays him his fee—twenty *reales* (Pesos 2.50). It is also customary for the godfather to give the child twenty-five centavos worth of soap, to provide for washing the clothes that are given.[1]

---

[1] The midwife does not have any part in the baptism.

THE HAND-WASHING CEREMONY

About a year after the birth of the child, and after the baptism, is held a ceremony in which the parents acknowledge their gratitude to their *compadres*. The ceremony is known as tzicil ("to pay respects"), or is referred to as "the washing of the *compadre's* hand" (u poc u kabo u cumpale). It is preferably held on some afternoon in the spring months, when the *Plumeria* flowers are in bloom, most suitably on Saturday of Holy Week; but the Day of the Cross (May third), or any Sunday, is suitable.

The parents make ready their house for the coming of their *compadres*. They place four chairs beside a table. On the table are placed a cross, two candles—to each of which are bound a *Plumeria* (nicte) flower and a leaf of tabasco pepper, and one of which is lighted—and a gourd dish containing water and flowers. This last is for "the washing of the hands" (x-ppobom-kab). To each of the posts which form the outer edges of the backs of the chairs is fastened a *Plumeria* flower with a leaf of tabasco pepper.

The godfather finds a friend to accompany him. On this occasion this friend is known as the chapach. These two men and their wives are seated in the chairs and the parents, first the man and then the woman, kneel in front of these, kissing the hand of each and saying, "Cici thantabac cichcelem yum, tat (colel)," "Sweetly (respectfully) be addressed, fair sir (madam)." Then each parent washes the hands of each of the other four, using the water with the flowers. The vessel is then passed to any others present, who dip their hands in it.

Usually, then, someone named as kuleb—functionary to distribute refreshments at a fiesta—offers rum and cigarettes to all. On some occasions a meal is served.

Then is placed on a table the offering to the godparents. This is always a turkey (usually cooked in the manner known as *mechado*),[1] some tortillas, some cigarettes, and four candles. The kuleb kisses the hands of the godparents and of the chapach and his wife, and delivers the table with the following speech:

U kaba cichcelem yum ca yumil ti *Dios* yetel
The name of the holy lord, Lord God, and

colelbil zuhuy Maria yetel San Diego yetel ......[2]
the holy Virgin Mary and San Diego and ......

he cen bix tu thanaheex a cumpaleex utiala uaye
here then as you have been invited by your *compadres* in order here

dzocbezeex a tzicbenileex le *santo bautismo*
to fulfill your esteemed persons for the holy baptism

ti chan *ángel*, tat; *pues*, hach yan u *voluntadi* tiobe;
of the small child, sir; well, very willing are they;

he bin hunppel noh tzicil yacunah tambali cu chan
here is a great and proper cherishing of one another, which

tibiolcob ti a *santo* tzicbenileex.
they are pleased to make to your respected persons.

---

[1] In former years, this turkey was placed in a kix-lac, as at weddings (p. 36).
[2] Other saints may be mentioned.

As the kuleb speaks for the parents, so the chapach speaks for the godparents.
The chapach now says:

Bey, c-uyic tun baax cu tibioltico u tzicbenilob
So, we hear then what their respected persons wish to do

tiob u cumpale yetel u cumale, tat; hach yaabal cimac yolob
for them, their *compadre* and their *comadre*, sir; very happy are they

u talob utialob u kamoltob.   Cichcelem hahal *Dios*
to come in order to receive (it).   Holy True God

yetel colelbil Maria, ca yanac u toholalob yetel u
and the Virgin Mary, may there be health for you and for your

chan *ahijado*.
small godson.

The godfather then says:

Pues, he cen bix yan u chan yacunahil tiobe,
Well, as here there is love,

cu chan dzaico toon, hunppel noh tzicila, tat;
as their little gift, a great festivity, sir;

pues, hach cimac in uoli.   Chen baax cin ualic teche,
well, very happy I am.   One little thing I ask, that you

nombrad oxtul maax tial chan bizic tin *posada*.
name three persons to carry it to my house.

The kuleb accordingly names three men to carry the table to the house of the
godfather.   But before the table with its gifts is removed, the godfather turns
over a small plate already standing upside down on the table, and places in it
three pesos, one of which the chapach furnishes and two of which he supplies himself.   He then addresses the two parents, in no set words, but in substance offering
them the money as "the redemption of the table" (u lohol *mesa*), and charging
his *compadres* to love one another and to care for their godchild.[1]   The godchild
then embraces his godparents if old enough, or is placed for a moment in their
arms.   It is customary for the godfather to give ten or twenty *centavos* to each
brother or sister of the godchild.   The wife of the chapach gives a small present
of sugar, chocolate and bread to the godchild—a gift usually received by the
child's mother.   The godparents carry away with them in person the four candles,
which, during the last part of the ceremony, have been standing lighted at the
four corners of the table.   They take these candle ends and burn them before the
patron saint of the village.

HETZMEK

Up to the age of three or four months[2] infants are carried lying across the
mother's arm.   Thereafter, and until the child walks well enough to keep up

[1] At villages where rum is more generally drunk, the gifts on the table include a bottle of *anis* with nicte (*Plumeria*) flowers stuck in its mouth; and at this point all drink of this rum.
[2] The ceremony is performed when the child is three months of age if it is a girl, and at four months if it is a boy, "because the hearth has three stones, and the milpa has four corners."   But not everyone can give this reason.

with adults, it is carried astride the left hip of its mother or older sister, whose left arm supports it in this position. The first time the child is placed in this position is the occasion of a domestic ceremony known by the phrase describing this manner of carrying a child: "to make hetzmek" (hetzmek tah). In Chan Kom the custom is as universally performed as is baptism, and—as has been already explained (p. 100)—is like baptism in that it involves the selection of godparents and the establishment of *compadre* relationship. The ritual is supposed to awaken the physical and intellectual faculties of the child and make him useful for the future. By spreading his legs on the hip of her who carries him, he is made ready to walk long distances. The rest of the ceremony assures his competence at the tasks that life will demand of him.

Usually two persons, man and wife, act as sponsors of the hetzmek, but sometimes only one takes part: a man, if the child be a boy; a woman, if it be a girl. These sponsors bring a shirt and diaper for the baby. The ceremony is a family matter; outsiders are rarely asked to be present. The persons present take seats around a table. On this have been placed nine objects which are likely to have great use in the future life of the child. These objects are not always the same and they vary with the sex of the child, but a characteristic list follows: A book, a pencil, a notebook, a catechism, a hammer, a hatchet, five pieces of bread,[1] a plate of boiled fowl, and a piece of money.[2] Underneath the table, on the ground, are placed a *sabucan*, a *mecapal*, a gourd vessel of water, or other objects of daily use.

The father hands his child to the godfather and says, "Here is the child, so you may do it the favor of making hetzmek, sir." The godfather takes the child and puts it astride his hip. He then goes nine times around the table, at each circuit taking one of the objects from the table and putting it into the hand of the child while he utters an admonishment according to the character of the object. Thus, on the first trip around the table he takes up the book, and says, "Here you have a book. Take it so that you may learn to read" (He yantech hunppel *libroe*. Chae utial a canic xoc). Thus he does with each object—the pencil and the notebook, so the child may learn to write; the catechism, so he may learn to pray; the hammer, that he may learn to work; the hatchet, that he may learn to fell bush; the bread, that he may "learn to eat everything"; the boiled fowl, that he may learn to eat "good food"; the coins, that he may learn to earn money. He then hands the child to the godmother, telling her to make hetzmek with it; and she does as he has already done. It is also customary for the godmother, on each of the trips around the table, to eat one of nine squash seeds which have been placed on the table.[3] "As the squash seed is opened to expose its soft interior, so will the mind of the child be opened." When the squash seeds are used up, the godmother has finished her task; she returns the child to the godfather, saying, "Well, here is the child. Now I have done that which they have asked us to do" (*Pues*, he le chan palo. Dzoci in dzocbezic letie baax ca ualic toon ti metic). The god-

---

[1] These five breads are tortillas made of cornmeal mixed with ground chay leaves. This bread is very poor fare, and here symbolizes humility.

[2] Sometimes a gun is substituted for one of these articles, if the child be a boy. If it is a girl, needle and thread are used instead of hammer and hatchet.

[3] The godfather sometimes keeps count of his trips around the table by taking from it, on each circuit, one of nine grains of corn.

father receives the child and hands it over to the father, to whom he says, "Well, just as you asked us to, *compadre*, that we make the hetzmek of this child, so we have done it" (*Pues*, he bix ta mahantoon, cumpale, utial hetzmektic le chan palo, dzoc dzocbezic). The parents then fall on their knees before the godparents in sign of their gratitude. A kuleb distributes rum and the boiled fowl and bread.

CHILDHOOD

The relations of children one to another and to their elders have not been studied by the writers; certainly they are not obviously patterned. The infant is cared for by its mother, often with the help of older sisters; the father often holds or fondles his child, but rarely feeds or bathes it. The techniques of eating are so simple—to hold a tortilla in which, perhaps, other food has been placed, and to drink out of a gourd dish—that they are mastered very early, often before the child has ceased entirely to suckle. Little or no attempt is made to control the child's habits of urination until it is walking about; then it may be lifted from the room, or admonished with a reproof of a slap.[1] Occasional slaps from elders are common, but formal punishment is not, although occasionally, for more serious offenses, a father will whip his child. The tradition persists from earlier generations of turning the erring child over to formalized authority for chastisement; the teacher may be asked occasionally to deliver a beating to a child, as in the memory of the fathers of the present time they were themselves whipped by judge or cacique. An observer from our own culture is impressed with the patience of the older people toward the children—as when a child having taken and lost the only large needle in the village, his parents, his grandfather and several uncles searched for an hour in the dust and dusk, without once uttering a reproof. On the other hand, parents and older brothers and sisters begin very early to ask the child to perform small services; a habit of obedience is generally acquired, and departures from it are very exceptional. The duty of obedience to and respect for one's elders is implicit in conduct and conversation. The family is a hierarchy: the parents expecting obedience from their children, and older brothers and sisters expecting it from those younger than they. The custom of handing over the second youngest child, upon the birth of a junior, to an older brother or sister, to be carried on the hip, establishes the dependence upon the senior in the series of siblings.

The boy is permitted and encouraged to accompany the father to the milpa as soon as he can walk distances, and early begins to help in carrying wood and then in the tasks of the cornfield. The separateness of the man's tasks from the woman's is reflected in the customs of play, for from the earliest years boys play with boys and girls with girls. The playmates are the neighbors—indeed, all the other children of the same sex that there are in the small village—and the play group has substantially the same personnel as has the group with which the

---

[1] Certain remedies are recommended for children who persistently urinate in the hammock, but we have never seen any of them employed. It is said that the navel of such a child should be anointed with the resin of the catzim tree (the common firewood). This resin must be collected from the end of a stick of this wood, while the other end is on fire. Others say that a similar application should be made of powder made of a black cricket, toasted and ground.

individual, when grown, will be associated. Much of the play is an imitation
of the elders' activities: the boys play at lassoing bulls, the girls at making tortillas,
for example. Until the school in very recent years introduced ball games and
other games involving "teams," there were, in Chan Kom, no competitive games,
not even races, jackstones, or marbles. Until the coming of the school, there
were in the village no activities in which a victor was contrasted with a vanquished,
or in which one child's superiority to another was formally measured. The toys
that exist do not involve competition with fixed rules. Every boy has his rubber
sling-shot, and it is also common to make small slings (yuntun) of henequen
fiber, with which small stones are hurled. Men use these also, to drive birds from
the milpa. Pellet guns are made in two forms. In one, a stem of a plant called
tzah is hollowed out and a sliding piston fitted into one end. The other kind is
made of cane (halal): a bent vine provides a spring, caught by a trigger, which
drives the pellet through the hollow tube. A sort of trumpet is made by rolling
palm leaves into a cone, or by hollowing the shoots of the pomolche. This last
plant makes a sudsy liquid with which bubbles are blown through a tube. Small
whistles are made of the cane called zit. Tops are carved of wood, and small
kites made of tissue paper.

It is regarded as unwise and improper to explain matters of sex and procreation
to children, and no deliberate instruction in the subject is given. All the older
people think it best that children should remain ignorant of the changes of puberty,
of sexual intercourse, pregnancy and childbirth until they actually experience these
phenomena in their own persons. A phrase often used is, "Children ought not
to be where the grown-ups are," and sexual matters are before them covered with
veils of silence and secrecy. Among themselves, men find jokes dealing with
sexual experiences, defecation and urination vastly amusing. The *double entendre*
is common in anecdote and in riddle. Between the sexes such jesting is poor
taste or worse, but men and women will seriously discuss sexual matters together.
The sexes are careful to keep apart when urinating or defecating; indeed, because
of the absence of special facilities women habituate themselves as far as possible to
nocturnal visits to the patio.

Nevertheless, this policy of secrecy with regard to the young people is impossible of exercise in the intimacy and simplicity of the village life. Both girls and
boys, at nine and ten years of age, begin to learn and make use of phrases and
stories of double meaning or illicit suggestion.[1] Many, probably most, young
children have understanding of the nature of sexual intercourse. This knowledge
depends upon individual circumstances. One or two young girls of the village
had no knowledge of the sexual act before their marriage, except for the vague
explanations of their mothers just before the marriages took place.[2] But in most
cases, in spite of the policy of secrecy, because they sleep beside their married
brothers, children come early to know something of the nature of sexual inter-

[1] For example, a child in school upon reading a story with the title "Why is it Done at Night?" volunteered an answer to the question
as he understood it: "Because it would be seen during the daytime."

[2] "I didn't know anything about it till I married. Then my mother explained it all to me. She said I had to sleep with Doso, because
now I was a grown woman; and she said I shouldn't tell anyone what was going to happen to me. But I didn't understand well what my
mother wanted to tell me, until after I was married."

course, and will sometimes joke with or ask questions of their married elders with a view to embarrass them. It is also true that in the context of animal husbandry sexual matters are subject to scarcely any taboo. An entire family will gather to watch with satisfaction the impregnation of a sow by a boar rented for the purpose.

While as a rule children reach adolescence with a strong interest in and usually a fair knowledge of sexual intercourse, they know next to nothing about the changes of puberty or of pregnancy and parturition. The first menstruation comes to the girl as a surprise attended with fear. In the cases known to us the girl secreted herself in alarm or even terror, until found by some older woman who explained the meaning of her soiled garments, and instructed her not to speak of it to anyone. So little do young people know of the course of child-bearing that in many cases the young husband, as well as the wife, will fail to suspect the first pregnancy in its early stages for what it is. Then the girl's mother or some older person will instruct her, or will turn her over to the care of the midwife.

MARRIAGE

The ritual of the marriage ceremony is an expression of the fundamental aspect of the marriage relation: a contractual undertaking between two groups of kin. Behind the bride and the bridegroom stand first their own parents, then their godparents and then the godparents (sponsors) of the wedding, and behind these the brothers of the bride and of the groom, and the more distant relatives of each. Both sets of godparents are linked with both sets of parents in the intimate and trustful relationship of *compadre;* all are interested in the maintenance of the marriage of which these subsidiary relationships between the elders are aspects. "Our kind of marriage ceremony is a good kind, because the *novios* know that all those people there will be angry if anything goes wrong."

The completion of the changes of puberty indicates to the young person's parents that they are now faced with the responsibility to make secure their child's future by means of a prudent marriage. Speaking of their son, the parents will say, "Now he needs a woman to serve him." The initiative lies wholly on the side of the boy and his parents. The girl, by her industry, health and charm can do no more than attract the attention of the parents of an eligible boy and of the boy himself. Not infrequently a boy communicates to his parents the fact that he has been attracted by some particular girl, but in many of these cases he has hardly exchanged a word with her. And more often the initial suggestion comes not from the boy but from his parents. The girl's part in making the match is even more passive; she may hardly know the boy at all when the petition is presented.

When the boy's parents have decided on a suitable wife for their son, they make formal request of her parents for her hand in marriage. Always they go in person, but ordinarily, as has already been indicated (p. 73), the actual negotiations are entrusted to the *casamentero* of the village. But the parents may go with the boy's godfather, or they may go unattended to the house of the girl's parents. This visit, and the succeeding calls, are made with as much secrecy as possible; the party sets out by night, on some ostensible errand and endeavoring to conceal the rum, cigarettes, chocolate and bread which they carry. The late hour, if nothing else, announces to the girl's parents the nature of the visit; nevertheless, conversation is long maintained on other topics before the real subject at hand is mentioned by the visitors. If the parents of the girl return an immediate negative, the callers withdraw, taking with them their *sabucan* of food. But if the reply is of a temporizing nature, the owners of the house suggesting that their visitors return after an interval to give them an opportunity to think the matter over, then it is understood that the petition is favorably entertained, and therefore the gifts of food are brought out and served to all. When the visitors take leave, another date is fixed for their return, "for these are things that must be well considered."

A second and a third visit are made, similar to the first. On each occasion the visitors bring rum, cigarettes, chocolate and bread; on each occasion the proposed marriage is mentioned only after much preliminary conversation; the girl, usually, remains asleep in her hammock. If her parents offer objections to the marriage, the *casamentero*, or the boy's parents themselves, present what arguments they can to overcome them. By the third meeting it is recognized that a marriage is to be effected, and on this occasion the parents of the girl let the *casamentero* know just what they will expect their daughter to receive from the bridegroom's family; if those demands are too great, the *casamentero* may have to bargain, enlarging upon the virtues of the boy he represents. This marriage gift is known as muhul. Its amount and quality vary with the economic condition of the two families. Ordinarily it includes a gold chain "of two loops," two rings of specified quality, two hair ribbons, one silk handkerchief, several meters of cotton cloth, two or three silver pesos, rum, bread, chocolate and cigarettes. The articles first mentioned will (with the bridal dress still to be furnished) equip the bride with her wedding clothes; the refreshments will be served at the fourth visit of the boy's parents to the house of the girl. The gold chain is the central feature of the muhul. It may be selected from a wide range of values, and it symbolizes and fixes the status of the newly married couple more definitely than any other object. These chains— often added to by the husband after marriage—become the storehouse of the family fortunes; they display the wealth and dignity of the couple; if called upon to give security, a man will pledge his wife's gold chains.

The third visit brings to a close the negotiations, and at the fourth the betrothal is signalized by formal delivery of the muhul. This occasion is less private than the first three; relatives are often invited to be present, and commonly the bridegroom is there also, but as a passive spectator. The bride is not present. The marriage contract is being made between two families, not between two individuals.

The delivery of the muhul is always accomplished with a degree of formality, although not to the extent which characterized the muhul-deliveries of a generation ago. Then the godparents of both girl and boy had also to be present, and all ate together before the gifts were handed over. Today, as before, the chain, rings, handkerchief, ribbons, money and food are placed on a table on which rests also a small wooden cross. A generation ago the food consisted of a gourd dish of x-taan chucua (p. 40) and a cooked fowl (box hanal) placed in a special clay vessel (see p. 36) with four holes in the rim, into which were inserted two withes forming arches ornamented with flowers.

Whatever be on the table, it is formally offered to the girl's parents by the *casamentero*. The words he uses are not fixed, but vary within small conventional limits. On one occasion he said:

"Fulfilling the words of the *Señor Dios*, who says that every man must take a woman in marriage, the *compadres* (indicating the parents of the boy) offer you what is on the table, as a sign of gratitude and in satisfaction of the coming union of their son with your daughter."

To this the father of the girl replies. On this same occasion he said:

"Hila (his wife) and I give you thanks for everything that you have brought us. May the *Señor Dios* return to you the expenses which you have incurred."

After the muhul has been offered and accepted, the marriage agreement is theoretically inviolable. In rare cases where the marriage does not thereafter take place, the parents of the boy may bring their complaint before the *comisario* and recover the muhul.

After the ceremonial delivery of this marriage-gift, a discussion immediately follows which results in fixing the date and nature of the marriage ceremony. Nowadays this ceremony is always the civil ceremony fixed by law before the *Registro Civil* in Kaua. In some cases this is followed by a church ceremony before a priest. The older relatives often urge that the church ceremony be performed; it was usual in their day, but is much less common now. Almost all first marriages are solemnized by the civil ceremony of signing the register, whether or not the church ceremony follows. But second marriages, the occasional concubinal union, and the rare runaway match of young lovers, get along without the sanction of any ritual, whether of church, of state, or of familial ceremonial.

From the day of the delivery of the muhul until the day of the wedding, the bride is supposed to be under the care of the *madrina* (sponsor) of the wedding, and the boy under that of the *padrino*. These two, usually a married couple, are selected by the boy's parents. The *padrino* must see to it that his charge can recite correctly five prayers: *Señor, Jesu Cristo; Yo Pecador; Creo en Dios Padre; Padre Nuestro;* and *El Pan Nuestro (sic);* and the *madrina* must do the same for the bride. The *madrina* sees to it that the clothes of the bride are ironed for the *asiento* and again for the wedding. All the expenses of the wedding, including the fee of the church, are defrayed by the boy's parents, but it is customary for the godfather of the marriage to give the boy a handkerchief and pomade for his hair, while the godmother gives the girl powder and a hair ribbon.

These sponsors often act as the witnesses required by law at the civil wedding, and they may attend the *asiento:* the declaration of intention to marry required by law. On this day the boy and his parents, and the girl and her parents, go separately to the office of the *Registro Civil* and there meet. This is often the first time that the boy and girl have conversed together, at least in public. Ordinarily on this day all go together to Valladolid to select the *terno:* the long dress of fine cloth, ornamented with embroidery and often lace insertions, which forms a part of the offering made by the boy's parents and which the bride will wear on her wedding day. Her *rebozo* is bought at the same time.

The same persons make up the party that returns to the town for the actual wedding ceremony, eighteen days later: the bridal couple, the parents of both, the sponsors of the wedding, often three additional witnesses and, if the wedding is done with all the formality that tradition authorizes, the baptismal godparents.

Following the civil ceremony and that of the church—or following the civil ceremony only—takes place a ritual solemnization of the marriage which signalizes the new familial bonds which have been brought into being. This ritual takes place either in the house of the boy's parents or, if the wedding party has had to go far from home to secure the services of a priest, in some house in that town. This is one of those rituals that are performed with varying degrees of completeness. Among the less conservative its traditional formal elements are not fully observed and the occasion tends to be a mere wedding-party, without important ritual elements. It will be described here in its full form, as it still takes place where the marriage is between two persons belonging to well-organized conservative families, and under the assumption that the couple have just been married by a priest in the church of the town.

The parents of the boy and those of the girl do not go to the church. The couple are accompanied only by the two sponsors of the marriage and three witnesses. When the ceremony in the church is over, one of the witnesses goes ahead to tell those waiting in the boy's house that the bridal party is coming. Then he returns to the bridal party. The boy's parents, inside the house, place seven chairs in a row on one side of the door, and they and the girl's parents sit opposite these in four other chairs. It is usual to invite also the four god-parents of the baptism (those of the bride, and those of the groom); and if these are present, they sit next to the parents. The party from the church proceeds to the house in single file, in this order: the bride, the bridegroom, the godmother (sponsor), the godfather, and the three witnesses. The bride-groom walks behind the bride to show "that the man is going to command." Arrived at the house, the bride kneels in the doorway on a mat prepared for her. Immediately the four parents rise. The bridegroom's father first takes her hand. She inclines her head, and says, "*Buenos días, tata.*" She has now called him "father," for the first time. Then her own father takes her hand and she salutes him similarly, and then her mother, and finally the groom's mother, who says as she takes the bride's hand, "The name of God the Father, God the Son, God the Holy Ghost," and helps the girl to rise. The bride then takes one of the seven empty chairs. Then the bridegroom kneels in the doorway and does as did the bride, but takes the hand of each in the following order: the girl's father, his own father, his own mother, the bride's mother. Then the *madrina* of the marriage enters; she does not kneel, but takes the hand of each of the same four, in this order: the boy's father, the girl's father, the boy's mother, the girl's mother. Finally the *padrino* does the same, taking the hand of each in the same order as that followed by the *madrina*. The orders followed in these salutations indicate the varying degrees of respect due to each of the persons saluted. Men are always given precedence to women. The sponsors salute the boy's father before they salute the girl's father, and his mother before her mother, for the same reason. Each spouse, however, owes respect to his or her father-in-law ahead of the actual father, but shows respect to the actual mother before the mother-in-law. After saluting the four parents, each member of the bridal party takes the hand successively of all the other persons present, beginning with the godparents of the baptism.

All now seat themselves. The father of the bridegroom, who is providing the feast and the hospitality on this occasion, summons someone present to act as kuleb. Standing on a table are a bottle of rum, a plate of cigarettes, a glass and a lighted candle. At the direction of the host, the kuleb offers rum and cigarettes to all. Everyone must take a drink and everyone must accept a cigarette; the men light theirs at the candle proffered by the kuleb; the women put theirs in their handkerchiefs to give later to their husbands. The rum and the cigarettes are offered first to the *padrino* of the wedding, then to the *madrina*, then to the girl's father, then to the girl's mother, and then to the baptismal godparents. This is the order in which respect is owed to these persons by the bridegroom's father.

Then the *padrino* of the marriage stands up, and one by one he calls upon the father of the bridegroom, the father of the bride, the mother of the bridegroom, and the mother of the bride. As each name is mentioned, its owner stands. The bride and groom then stand. The *padrino* shakes hands again with each of the four parents, in the same order. He then addresses the four parents, using words that vary with the speaker. The substance of his remarks is as follows:

"*Compadres* and *comadres*, here we are all gathered in this, your house, that we (the *padrinos*) may hand over to you (the parents) my godchild and my goddaughter whom you had us bear to marriage, and who have received the mass in the holy church, and have taken the thirteen *reales* which served as *aras*, and have put on the dzibitcab; and they have taken each other's hands and received the chain, and have fulfilled everything."[1]

When the *padrino* has said this, the four parents successively take his hand again and thank him. Then all are seated once more and the boy's father directs the kuleb to deliver to the sponsors of the marriage a table on which are placed a bottle of rum and a plate of cigarettes. The *padrino* accepts this, and directs the kuleb to distribute the rum and cigarettes. When the rum has been entirely consumed, the kuleb lays the bottle on its side to indicate this fact, and similarly indicates the consuming of the cigarettes by turning the plate upside down.

[1] In the marriage service held in the church before the priest, a double ring ceremony is used. The wedding-ring is known as dzibitcab. When the rings have been exchanged, the sacristan pours from a plate known as *ara*, into the hand of the bridegroom, 13 coins (or 13 *reales*) furnished by the *padrino*; these coins the groom then puts into the bride's hands. Afterward both kneel at the altar, and—although this last custom is no longer generally followed—the gold chain of the muhul is placed over the shoulders of both.

Thereupon, again at the direction of the bridegroom's father, the kuleb offers and then distributes half a bottle of rum and a smaller quantity of cigarettes. This is known as ppobom-*mesa*, "to clean the table."

Now the kuleb brings in from the kitchen a turkey, prepared at the expense of the boy's father. Until recently it was customary to put this turkey (prepared as *escabeche*) in a large clay vessel with an edge ornamented with small points, or fluting, known as kix-lak. Over the vessel were arched two intersecting pieces of vine covered with flowers or colored paper. This vessel, or a simple more modern substitute, is placed on the table together with two piles of tortillas (each containing thirteen), a bottle of rum, and two candles. Flowers are tied to each candle. With a short, formal speech, as before, the kuleb delivers this to the bride's father, on behalf of the boy's father. The bride's father accepts it and directs that it be carried to his house. There follows another ppobom-*mesa*, accepted by the bride's father.

In the same manner another turkey (usually a hen, because this gift may not be just the same as that offered to the bride's father) is brought in and presented, again through the kuleb, by the boy's father to the *padrino* of the marriage. In this case only half a bottle of rum accompanies the turkey. These things are accepted and carried to the recipient's house, and again there is a ppobom-*mesa*.

The father of the groom has now discharged his obligations. Dinner—turkey or other fowl—is now brought in and served to everyone, and there is general conversation.

When dinner is over, the father and the mother of the bride ask the *padrino* of the marriage to explain to the bride and groom their marital duties and responsibilities. It is the parents of the bride, and not those of the groom, that ask this, because "naturally they are more afraid that perhaps later the bridegroom will go off with some other girl and leave their daughter. The parents of the bride have fulfilled their duty in bringing up their daughter to understand her obligations." Speaking together, the bride's father and mother say:

Mixbaal, cumpale, c-chan katic tian tzicbenile
Nothing, *compadre*, we ask of your respected persons

ca chan tzol u xicnob ua a ualmah thanticob
but that you set before the ears or advise

u palalilob cu chan dzocbez u yahcunah
the children that they fulfill their love

thanbalilob tac tu xul u cuxtalob
spoken of till the end of their lives

yoklal u mankin tiob hebix tu yalahob
so that they pass their days as they said

cat chunbezah u tzicbalil ca dzocpahac,
when they began to speak so that it be fulfilled,

yoklal beyo hach cimacol yacunticob.
that they may be happy loving one another.

Then the *padrino* arises and addresses the bridegroom. He charges the boy in words that are not fixed, but that carry the following sense:

You (naming the boy), as you have expressed your wish before the *Registro* and before the priest, that it is your great desire to devote yourself to the love of my god-daughter, therefore you must perform, get, bring and buy everything that she may need, and not mistrust her or give her cause for jealousy; you must fulfill her everything. If the day should come when you would cease to cherish one another, then we will intervene to demand the reasons why you do not fulfill your promise to cherish one another.

He then charges the bride in similar language. This done, the father and mother of the bride ask the *padrino* to take the bride and groom to the bride's house to get her clothes. The *padrinos*, the parents of the bride, and the bride and groom then go to the house of the bride's father, and the bride collects her clothes. While she is so occupied, the bride's father distributes to the others the rum sent him from the house of the groom's father. When the bride is ready, her father and mother take leave of her. Each takes her hand and blesses her, saying: "Pahteneex u *bendición* yum hahal *Dios* yetel a uicham, ca kinmanac kinteex utz" ("May great God let his blessing fall on you and your husband, that all your days may be good").

Then the *padrinos* alone escort the bride and groom to the house of the bride-groom. In marriages of the old style at which the full ritual here described is employed, the usual custom is for the bride and groom to begin their married life in the house of the husband's parents. Arrived at this house, the *padrinos* direct the couple to take off their wedding finery and put on the attire of everyday life. By this act the bride and groom show that they have passed from the control and care of the *padrinos* and are beginning life together.

THE DYING AND THE DEAD

The rituals that attend the dying express the wish to speed the soul safely on its heavenward journey, that it may be quit of earth and not remain below to trouble the living.

A good man goes to *Gloria* when he dies. *Gloria* lies behind and above the clouds. At its great gate stands Saint Peter, with the keys. Outside the gates of *Gloria*, but still beyond the clouds, is the region of the angels. To this place are instantly transported the souls of those who die in the innocence of childhood. The dead soul passes through the host of the angels before he reaches the gates; and if, on earth, that person was not kind to children, they will tell Saint Peter and he will not admit the soul.

The teachings that have been the source of these beliefs are summarized by one as follows:

"The man who goes to *Gloria* is one who does not lie with a woman till he marries, and then only with his wife; who does not mistreat animals; who obeys his father and his mother; who does not swear; who does not think evil of another; who does not want another to present him with the things the other has; who learns prayers every Saturday and Sunday; who says a prayer and gives the sign of the cross (dzib-ich) when he is about to go to sleep; and who does not beat his wife or child."

Other souls go to Purgatory, there to be burned white, that they may then go to *Gloria*. Souls of the very bad go directly to metnal, which is the home of the demons and lies beneath the earth. All sorcerers go there, for they have made a pact with the devil and have sold him their souls for their special black art. Those that know love philters, or can change themselves into animals, those that can send evil magic into others, and all those that have uncanny ability at any-thing—prestidigitation, bull-fighting, or even needlework—have made the dreadful pact. Suicides go straight to metnal, and therefore some advise that they be buried face downward, looking toward metnal.

Some sinful souls are turned into frogs, and are condemned to live as such for long years, shut up in stones or in trees, until some hand opens their prison and releases them to go at last to *Gloria*. Those who have intercourse with their wives' sisters are transformed into the whirlwinds that quicken the fires at the time of burning the fields. A person who dies leaving money buried, without hav-ing told anyone of the fact, can not go to *Gloria*, until, on some day of the Holy Cross, he communicates the fact to someone on earth. Those who die leaving their debts unpaid may be changed into a deer or wild turkey. Their creditor then encounters the animal in the wood and shoots it, thus, by selling the meat, recover-ing the amount of his debt. And the released soul then passes to *Gloria*.

After long periods all souls return to earth again, reincarnated in new-born children. "God has not enough souls to keep forever repopulating the earth." If a child is born with teeth, much hair, or other signs of precocity—if, for example, its eyes are unusually clear and alert—it is because it has been born with the soul of one who lived on earth before. "It has been given the eyes of the old people" (yiche uchben macob dzabti). And the same is said of a person whose hair turns prematurely grey.

The time of death is a time of struggle, the soul seeking to leave and yet to remain, the forces of evil contending with Heaven for his soul. Nothing must be done to hinder its passage. For the unfortunate dead remain about the place where they died. Men seldom see them, but dogs do, when they howl at night, or horses when they snort and rear.

When it is thought that death is sure, the *maestro cantor* is summoned to recite the prayers for the dying (these are the Sacred Viaticum in Maya, and the *Sube*, *Sube* and *Santo Dios* in Latin and Spanish). The recitation of these prayers releases the soul from the body and confounds the demons of metnal. These demons are known as the "soul-robbers" (ocol pixan); they crowd around the doorway of the house, ready to seize the soul. Sometimes the dying man sees them, grimacing and beckoning to him, silently, with eye and hand and lip. Then he shrieks and cries aloud. But the prayers recited by the *maestro cantor* defeat these demons; the dying man sees them shrink and shrivel.

To assure the soul's safe passage to *Gloria*, it is customary to make a round opening in the thatch above the hammock of the dying man, kept open with a ring of twisted vine. The old people, seeing now the construction of houses of masonry, advise that a small window for the same purpose be put in one end near the ceiling.

When a man is dying, he sometimes speaks wisely, telling of heaven and of the life hereafter. That is because when he is dying the soul makes a first trip to see what *Gloria* and what Purgatory are like; then it returns. It is noted that even as much as several days before a death, a man soon to die will preach wisdom to those around him.

It is bad to weep as death approaches, for then the soul may be stayed. Especially is this true if it is a child that is dying, for every child is a *voto* for the parents in *Gloria*, and by that child the parent may be saved. If the parents cry, then the soul will not be received in *Gloria;* it will be sent back to its weeping parents. If one weeps, whether for child or adult, the soul will be delayed. "Your tears," they say, "are wetting the road to *Gloria*." But as a child reaches Heaven quickly, it is safe to cry after the first days have elapsed.[1]

In some cases the soul has such difficulty in getting free from the body that the dying person is whipped with a rope, to bring the soul's release.

When the end is imminent, all seed corn, and any other seeds reserved for planting are removed from the house, else would their "hearts" die also and they would not sprout. It is customary to remove all clocks, sewing-machines or phonographs; else would their power of movement cease with the owner's death.

When death comes, it is announced to the village by the ringing of the bell of the *oratorio*. The immediate relatives do not prepare the body for burial; they ask friends to perform this task. Usually the body is shrouded in a sheet. Upon the body of a child is placed a cape-like garment (the *palma*), made of paper, with wings of paper attached, to indicate its identity with the angels. A crown of paper flowers is placed on the head, and in the folded hands is placed a small stick with colored papers attached (the *ramillete*). An adult is not so equipped, but to the belt or waist is fastened a cord of candle-wick, with fifty knots in it, corresponding to the number of Ave Marias in the Rosary; with this cord the soul, arrived in the presence of God, will receive a whipping for sins committed on earth.

When once the body has been shrouded, it is placed on a table, but not covered. At each end two wax candles are lighted, and the wake (ppix ich) begins. The friends and neighbors of the deceased attend this vigil, bringing candles, food and coffee. The younger people amuse themselves telling stories, drinking and playing cards. The older people comport themselves somewhat more seriously and some continue to recite the prayers for the dead.

Interment takes place twenty-four hours after death. The bells of the *oratorio* ring again and the clothing last worn by the deceased is placed on the bier, together with a rosary and the gourd dish from which the dead person last drank on earth. (When it is thought that a person is dying, in some cases those attending him furnish him with a new *jícara*, in anticipation of this need.) If a child is to be buried, a bunch of flowers is laid with the body; and if the parents have another child already in *Gloria*, a second bunch is added. When the new angel arrives beyond the clouds, the other angels come out to meet it, and the

---

[1] The same feeling is present at all partings. One should not weep. If you weep when someone dear to you leaves, then he will become sad or sick—"your tears will wet his heart." When men were taken away to be soldiers during the revolution, this was said to wives and children: "then they did not cry, but only smiled."

brother or sister steps forward to receive the flowers. Sometimes, if the body is that of a woman, needle and thread are added.

Before the body is lifted from the bier, the relatives scatter corn to the barnyard fowls and break bread for the dogs, as a last kindness of the departed. Then the body is placed in a wooden coffin—red for a child, black for an adult—together with the various objects mentioned, and carried to the cemetery. Those who go along carry lighted candles and sing the songs for the dead: *Santo Dios* and *Despedida* for an adult, and the *Sube, Sube* for a child. There are also two chants known as *Adios, Reina del Cielo*, one of which is used for adults and the other for children.

If the death takes place in some *rancheria* that uses the Chan Kom cemetery, one member of the party scatters corn along the way, so that the soul, when it has ended the visit it will make to the house and people that it knew in life, will find its way to the place of burial and from there to *Gloria*. On some occasions, so as to cause the soul to follow the body, and not to remain wandering about the home of the living, they speak the name of the dead in a loud voice, bidding him "hear mass" in the place of burial.

Arrived at the cemetery, the coffin is placed in the small thatched structure which stands at the back of the burying-ground, while the grave is dug. Then the men present enter the little structure and stand beside the coffin while the *maestro cantor* again recites the prayers for the dead. The body is lowered into the grave without ceremony (Plate 16a); if holy water is available it is sprinkled into the grave. A candle is lighted at the grave and a small wooden cross set at its head.

On the day following the death, begin the prayers which assure the repose of the soul and its separation from the homes of the living. It is usual to begin a series of nine days of prayer. On the third and seventh days after death the prayer is held at the hour at which the death occurred. The prayer held on the third day is thought to reveal to the soul its incorporeal state. When the soul learns of this, it returns again on this third day and remains near its old home till the seventh day. During this period the house must not be swept. This is because the soul leaves the body at the moment of death perfectly clean, but must return again to get its sins and carry them to Judgment. These sins have been left in the dirt of the dead man's body, and in the clothes, and in the hammock. Because the soul must gather up its sins from this dirt, the house is not swept, but the prayer offered on the seventh day delivers the soul to God; and as soon as it is over, the house is given a thorough sweeping.

The departed is commemorated in the *rezos* performed at fixed intervals after the death (p. 152) and on All Souls' Day of each year, but there is little formal mourning. To the direct question, a villager will say that for seven months at least, or a year, the close female relatives should put off jewelry. In fact, however, there is rarely any alteration in the woman's costume, and never any in the case of the men; and the activities of life go on as usual. If a new embroidery is to be purchased by a woman recently bereaved, she will select one of black;

but, with little exception, mourning costume exists only in theory. For children, of course, who become angels at death, colored decorations are suitable, and it is also common to use colored tissue papers to decorate the bier of an adult.

THE DAYS OF THE DEAD

On the thirty-first of October and the first of November all the souls of the dead return to earth for an annual visit and depart again one week thereafter. On these occasions food is set out for them and they are bidden to eat. The festival is known as *Finados* ("the dead"), or as hanal pixan ("dinner of the souls"). It is a domestic ritual, in which each family recalls and propitiates its own dead; and most families are careful to observe it, for then the dead do not trouble the living. But, as with the other ceremonies, its performance does not always include all the details of ritual mentioned in the following description.

Preparations begin the evening of the thirtieth of October. The foods that are to be offered are made ready and the flowers that will be used are gathered. At midnight the people of the house get up and arrange the table, because at midnight the souls of the dead begin to arrive. The table is adorned with the flowers of the tez-*abanico* and with the blossoms of the silk-cotton tree (known as flowers of San Diego, or as flowers of San Juan). Sometimes use is made also of the flowers of the plant known as *tempora* and those called chic-mul. The same flowers are fastened around the doorway of the house, as an invitation to the souls to enter. On the table are placed chocolate, bread and several lighted candles. The number of *jícaras* of chocolate, of candles, and of *reales* worth of bread vary with inclination and ability; but these numbers (and those of objects offered on the table prepared later in the day) must in every case be even, not odd. One *jícara* of chocolate, one piece of bread, and one lighted candle are set in the doorway, for any souls who may not have living kinsmen to care for them this night and who may not be expressly bidden to the feast.

When the table is ready, the *maestro cantor* is summoned and friends may be invited. The *maestro* recites one of the prayers for the dead, and then another table of chocolate and bread is brought in and delivered to the *maestro*. Then all eat of the food on this and on the other table. Now the dead souls have been given breakfast. Later in the day they are offered dinner. The table for this dinner is spread with a cloth used for the first time: a "zuhuy *mantel*." For the dinner two hens are boiled, and the meat is cut and divided equally among an even number of those small clay vessels known as lac (p. 36). The fowl must be put in these vessels, and never in *jícaras* or in modern dishes. Pains are taken that each vessel contains an equal quantity of the same parts of the fowl. To each lac is added a little of the broth and small equal quantities of whatever other food has been prepared—squash, *chayote*, pork, rice, macaroni. The fowl cooked are always hens, "for roosters would crow and frighten away the souls." On the table are placed also an even number of *jícaras* of *atole* and another filled with water and flowers. This last is the "hand-washing" (x-ppo-kab), the water which the souls of the dead will use, as do the living, to dip their hands in before and after eating. Beside it is placed a new napkin.

When all is ready, the *maestro cantor* comes again, and kneeling on a blanket, prays. This first day is that on which the souls of dead children return: the day of the "angels," "the great day of the dinner of the child souls" (noh kin u hanal mehcn pixanob). So, after he has recited a rosary, the *maestro* recites the *Sube, Sube*—the prayer appropriate for child dead—and concludes with an "Our Father." When he finishes all say, "Good afternoon," as at a *rosario*, or novena.

Another table is now brought in, with more cooked food; often this is more boiled fowl. This is a secular table; it is provided merely so that everyone will have something to eat; the fowl may be rooster, the cloth is an old one, and china plates may be used. The food on both tables is divided and eaten.

The following day is "the great day of the dinner of the big souls" (ninoh k u hanal nucuch pixanob)—the day of the adult dead. The same ritual is followed, except that the prayers recited are those appropriate to adult dead: *Señor, Dios Mio; Salve Regina; Oid, Mortales; Perdón, Dios Mio; Adios, Jesús*. And the candles, if the ceremony is carefully followed, are black.

A week later (the octave) these rituals are repeated, except that the food offered is kol (broth of fowl into which breads are broken). The bread especially appropriate to this day is chachac-uah—bread colored red with arnotto and baked in the earth oven. It is common also to cook other foods in the pib on these two days of the octave.

On the day after the first day of the adult dead (November second) the people of the households where the hanal pixan has been made go to the cemetery, carrying half of the candle-ends that have been used at the ceremony. These they set alight on the graves of their dead, and place there also the flowers used to decorate the tables. On the day following the octave, they go again to the cemetery to remove the wilted flowers from the graves.

The week between the first two days of hanal pixan and the octave of the festival is the time proper for taking from the graves the bones of any relatives who were interred two or three years before. In the shallow soil of the country, this practice is necessary, to make room for new interments. The occasion is one of ceremony, much resembling in its form the *rosarios* held at the wake.

Two fowl are boiled and *atole* is prepared. In the afternoon two or three men go to the cemetery and take out the bones. When the grave is opened, a little holy water is sprinkled on the bones and they are blessed. The bones are placed on a piece of new cloth and cleaned. Another piece of cloth is put in a small box; the cleansed bones are laid therein and again sanctified with holy water. The box is closed and carried to the little shelter in the cemetery, where a *Pater Noster* is said over them. Then the box is carried back to the village and into the house and placed on a little stand under a table, on which the food is set out. The *maestro cantor* recites the prayers used at the wake. The table of food is then offered to the *maestro cantor*. Another table of food is brought in and served to those present.   At night chocolate is set out, another series of the same prayers recited, and the dead person called by name.   The chocolate is served.   Holy water is again sprinkled on the box, and that night it is taken to the house in the cemetery and left there.

This occasion is one of sadness and mourning.   It is not a cheerful occasion, as is the wake, when people often play and laugh.   For now the soul is safely out of the world of the living, and the lamentation, that had then to be withheld, may now be given expression.

Chapter XII

THE MEANING OF NATURE

OUTLINES OF THE UNIVERSE

The sky covers the flat earth like a bowl, and in it the stars are fixed. Beyond the clouds are the gates of heaven. Just outside these gates is the realm of the angels, and inside dwell the souls of the saved. Metnal, where the damned dwell, lies beneath the earth. The chaacs and the balams are not in heaven; they move invisible through the air or across the sky. Unseen, the balams hover over the bush or at the four entrance-ways of the village. The chaacs are wherever water is; they are, of course, in the rain and they are also in every cenote. The waters of the cenote are mysteriously connected with the waters of the sea, and from these waters arise the winds, evil and good. The cenotes, indeed, have various connotations of the sacred and the dangerous. They are residing places of the rain-gods; they are sources of evil winds; and they are the mouths of hell. When the h-men summons the rain-gods, he utters the names of the cenotes. When he appeases the evil winds, he may put offerings to them into the cenote (p. 176). And the unfortunate who, fascinated by the deep waters of the cenote, hurls himself to destruction in them, passes through the bottom of the cenote directly into hell (p. 199).

The milpa, the village and the earth exist in space with reference to the four cardinal directions—"the four winds." The east wind and the north wind bring the rain. The east is paramount; in the prayers it is always referred to as "the great east" (noh lakin). Here dwell the chaacs during the dry season, and from the distant Trunk of Heaven (p. 116) in the east emerge sun, moon, stars, clouds and rain. Therefore all altars face the east, and to the east prayers to the rain-gods are directed. In the east lie Coba and the home of the bee-gods, and in the eastern forests roam the strange animals of which hunters tell (p. 122).

SUN, MOON AND STARS

The sun is spoken of by the older people as "lord sun" (yum kin), and the moon as "lady moon" (colel *luna*[1]), but they do not enter into religious beliefs or practices. The new moon is called chichan *luna* ("very small moon"), or is referred to as mun *luna* ("green, or unripe, moon"). A moon not yet full is simply tun chan nohochta *luna*, "a moon neither large nor small." The full moon is uncun *luna* ("full pot moon?"). Maize may be planted at any time of the moon, but fruit trees and root crops are best planted just after the moon is full. If one wants a gourd vine to produce small gourds, one plants it when the moon is new. But for good crops of large fruits or roots, one plants three days after the full moon. From the full moon the days are counted; hu' muc *luna*,

[1] The same terms that were used until recently in addressing persons, where now are used "Don" and "Doña."

ca muc *luna*, ox muc *luna*, and so on. One waits until the third day (ox muc *luna*) to plant, because then the full moon "has been in the ground for three days"—that is, the moon, that has theretofore ridden the sky all night, now rises late, having spent some time "in the ground."

The morning stars are apparently not distinguished and each is referred to as puk za, "dissolve *atole*," because "when it rises the woman must get up to make *atole*." A falling star is spoken of as *cabo* chamal yum, "the cigarette butt of the Lord." The Milky Way is "white road" (zac be)—the same name given to the stone roadways built by the ancient people. The constellation of the Great Bear is called either *los siete sacramentos* or *noria* ek, "the water wheel star." Scorpio is known by its Maya equivalent: zinaan. The Southern Cross is the "cross star" (*cruz* ek). "It rises over Jerusalem"; but where Jerusalem is, no one knows. The Pleiades bear the name of the rattlesnake's rattles (tzab), and the evening star, whatever it may be, is "the fire of the tzab" (u kak tzab). The constellation Gemini is "the turtle" (ac); the three stars in the middle lying in a straight line are "the intestines" (choch). Three stars below and to the right of this constellation are "the little dove" (chan mucuy). "It has two eggs in its nest."

The rainbow (chel) is spoken of as "the flatulence of the demons" (u ciz cizinob), because it is thought to arise out of dry wells (x-lah-chen), and these are, as it were, the ani of metnal. From these wells the rainbow spreads across the sky.

ECLIPSES

Some of the people of the village begin to regard an eclipse as brought about by the motions of sun and moon. One suggests that the moon hits against the sun, knocking out its light; another says that every eighteen years the moon passes under the sun covering the earth with its shadow; a third proposes that there is probably a hole in the sun through which the moon has to pass at certain intervals. But these speculations have not seriously affected the general belief that periodically some evil animal seeks to devour the heavenly luminaries and that eclipses are occasions of great danger for mankind.

The name for eclipse is "chibal kin" ("biting the sun"), or "chibal *luna*." Many can not specify the animal which seeks to eat sun or moon, saying merely that it is "a very bad thing" (kakazbaal); but several say that it is certain ants, either certain evil-smelling ants of a red color, or else the "king of the leaf-cutting ants." "That is why one so often sees the ants carrying bits of leaf: as fodder for the ant king's horse." But one or two of the older men say that it is no ant, but an animal like a tiger that seeks to devour sun or moon. "That is what the ancients taught by carving on the stones at Chichen Itza a disk representing the sun and two tigers coming to eat it." [1]

The moment of eclipse is one of threatened calamity, because, it is believed, should the sun or moon fail to reappear, then all the furniture and other objects with which people are surrounded would be changed into devils or beasts that

[1] A reference to the frieze on the Temple of the Jaguars at the Ball Court.

would devour all living things.[1] So the villagers strive to avert the cataclysm.
They seek to frighten away the devouring animal by making as much noise as
possible, beating on drums, cans and pails, and firing guns. If the danger of
complete extinction appears imminent, they may also go to the *oratorio* and there
begin a novena to San Diego.

PLANTS AND ANIMALS

As with all folk peoples, long adjusted to their habitat, those of Chan Kom
name and know the uses of hundreds of plants and animals. This tree is a source
of building material, this plant a medicine, that animal a source of food or a danger
to the maize plants. Some of these many practical meanings have been mentioned
in the foregoing pages. But beyond and beside significances for practical action,
the plants and animals have magical and religious meanings. The ceiba tree is
to be avoided after nightfall, because it is the haunt of the x-tabai. Little girls
should not play with the fruits of the ceiba or of the cħoy, lest their breasts grow
too large. If a woman's breasts are large, people say, "She has cħoy breasts"
(cħoy im). The flowers that are appropriate as offerings to the *santos* are flowers
set apart; the older people would rebuke a young person should he wear a *Plumeria*
(nicte) flower just for personal adornment. *Plumeria* plants and chac zicin, also
used in decorating altars, are planted in the house-yards and, when colonists form
a new settlement, some of these plants are taken along. The plants used in the
ceremonies conducted by the h-men are quite different. In these rites flowers are
not used, but the leaves of certain "cold" plants (p. 130): habin, xiat, and halal.
These plants symbolize rain; as they grow near the cenotes, they are the plants
of the chaacs.

As plants that grow at the cenotes are sacred, so are the animals that dwell
there the creatures of the rain-gods and the harbingers of rain. The frog, the toad
and the tortoise are to be found in cenotes or in caves, where also the chaacs go.
So too are the bats the creatures of the yuntzilob, for they are to be found in
dry caves (actunob). These animals, the h-men advises, should never be killed.
Especially is the tortoise respected, even revered. For the tortoise is bound to
man by a curious sympathy. When the woods are wet and the earth is moist,
then the tortoise is not seen. But when drought has dried the water-holes and
the land is thirsty and the maize may fail, then the tortoise walks abroad. He
takes the paths that men take, and the villager meets him on his road to the milpa.
All have thus encountered him, pausing in the burning sun, his shell dry and hot,
but his eyes filled with tears. The tortoise weeps for men, and it is said that his
tears draw the rain. The hunters know that it is a good omen thus to encounter
him when they set out. When the bush is kindled at the time of burning, the
pious agriculturalist does not fail to call out, "Save yourselves, tortoises! Here
comes the fire!" (Hoceneex acob! He cu tal le kake!) Many mothers, wishing to
protect their children from sickness, hang around their children's necks the miraculous cross that the tortoise carries on his breast.[2] Some say that when a tortoise

---

[1] One says that the omen of this calamity will appear when some one breaks a chaya leaf and from the broken edge comes out blood.
[2] They are bought in the markets or taken from the shells of tortoises found dead.

bites one who has injured him, he does not release his hold till the skies are cleft with lightning.   He who injures a tortoise is thereafter accursed; he is fatally drawn to water and one day he will hurl himself into the cenote.   At its bottom a tortoise of enormous size blocks passage through a deep hole, spiral like a snail-shell. Through this the suicide must pass until he reaches a place where an old man and an old woman rest under a bower of *chayote*.   When these two see the new arrival, they hasten to capture him, substituting for him a banana sprout, which, assuming the likeness of the accursed one, on the third day rises to the surface of the water.   Meanwhile the damned man suffers cruel torments.   When he grows fat devils devour him, leaving only a skeleton that time and again puts forth new flesh that is in turn devoured.

Similarly, certain birds that frequent the milpas and yet appear to take little from them are the creatures (alakob) of the balams; the white-winged dove (zac pacal), the white-fronted dove (tzuytzuy), and the red-billed pigeon (x-cucut-cib). The small hawk known as cħuy is spoken of as "the guardian of the milpa" (canan-col), for when the blackbirds enter to steal the corn, he mounts a tree and cries aloud, frightening them off.   The baacen-chulul are the poultry of the balams. One should not imitate their clear whistling note, for if one does, they become angry and fly around one.   "It is not good to mock the birds of the balams."   The sweet-voiced bird called x-kol sings in the milpa so that the maize-plants will be happy.   There is a little blue bird known as "the bird that stretches the maize plants" (u cħicħil u zadzic nal).   It jumps from maize plant to tree, then from tree to maize-plant, jumping and singing, and urging the maize-plants to grow. When the ears form on the stalks, then these birds go, for their work is done. Another bird, called "horse-catcher" (chuc-tzimin), whistles to summon the horses the chaacs ride when they make the rain.   All these are animals of the yuntzilob, and it is bad to kill them or to drive them away.

Other animals are uncanny or evil, and the omens of misfortune.   The insects and snakes mentioned in a previous chapter (p. 178) are the creatures of the sorcerers, the bearers of sickness.   But it is notable that the toad is not one of these; it has no associations with evil, sickness or witchcraft.   It is the night-flying insects and the reptiles that enter the yards and houses that carry black magic.

Many animals are not what they seem.   There are the solitary nocturnal bulls, dogs and cats that are to be avoided, as witches in animal forms (p. 178).   There are also the fairy animals that the hunter follows in vain: the deer and agouti that become snakes and slip down little holes to escape the pursuer's bullet.   Such eerie misadventures form a large part of tales told wherever men are gathered. It is generally believed that during the month of September, all animals of certain kinds change their forms into those of other animals.   In September the deer are in heat and act boldly and strangely, sometimes entering the villages.   It is believed that at this season the deer turn into snakes, and the snakes into deer. The *tepezcuinte* (Mexican agouti) does not so slip away as a serpent, but if the hunter kills one of these false *tepezcuintes*, its flesh, even after it is cooked, will change into small snakes if a little honey is put with it.   The rattlesnake turns into a peccary, and the peccary into a rattlesnake. Certain worms (zadz) that occur on the *flor de mayo* turn into the butterflies known as x-mahan-nai, or into hummingbirds. Other smaller worms turn into flies, and the ants get wings, but only for the month of September. The mouse turns into a bat, the armadillo into a vulture and the tortoise into a parrot; and each of these transformations takes place also in the opposite direction. Large black ants (hoocħ) become wasps (xanah-chac), and vice versa. But when September ends, all these creatures resume their proper forms. Hunters expect to be deceived in September. Sometimes they go to hunt partridge (nom, tinamou); they think they hear the birds whistling, but when they get there they find only zahcabtunich—a weathered limestone with moss growing on it. This stone whistles after nightfall, especially in September.

Then there are the animals that are seen only by other men, never by one's self, or that are heard moving in the darkness. Hunters tell of the great bulllike boob and of the spotted chan ekal. These are thought to inhabit the forest to the east (p. 122). Deep under the floors of houses burrows an animal known as chokol-och; making a noise like a chocolate-beater it digs its way to metnal and the sound of its subterranean progress is an augury of death.

MAN'S OWN BODY

Understanding of physiology varies considerably among members of the community. Some, who have received instruction in school or who have been influenced by educational leaflets sent out by the Government, have, for example, some idea of the nature of the circulatory system. Such persons suppose that the blood, impelled by each breath that is taken, courses through the veins, "just as the gasoline does in the lamp." The function of the circulation is to make the organism grow strong. When the blood is adulterated, the person grows weak or dies. One must guard it, and see that it is not diluted by the evil winds. Others know nothing of the circulatory system. One, for example, supposes that in breathing, air is drawn to the heart from where it is distributed to the trunk and limbs. Yet most regard the heart as the principal organ of the body. "It is shut up in something like a little box, being very delicate." Aided by the brain and the eyes, it generates man's psychic qualities. The beats of the pulse are caused by the air that passes through the body every time one breathes. The location of the internal organs is not understood; a man will indicate his abdomen as the seat of his heart and, having an abdominal pain, will say, "My heart aches." Digestion, it is recognized, takes place in the stomach or the intestines; these are aided by the liver and "the other things we have inside." There the food is cooked until it is soft, "and can be sucked up by the flesh. If this does not happen, the food sours, and we have a pain."

It is generally understood that in the sexual act the man plants in the woman the seed of the future offspring, but of the development of the embryo next to nothing is known. As they breed cattle and select corn, so the people regard healthy parentage as a guaranty of strong children, and attribute the mental deficiency of certain children to the poor health of their father: The most vigorous fathers are thought to procreate sons rather than daughters. "There are men of such good seed that almost all of their children are sons."

OMENS AND DREAMS

The behavior of the animals, plants and weather, and of the sun and the moon, and dreams, have meanings for men that the older people can interpret and that they explain to the others. From the point of view of the native, these natural phenomena make evident the ways of the gods, or announce to man the events of the future that most concern him: the wetness or dryness of the coming season; the imminence of calamity. Expressed in terms of human behavior, it is the wishes and fears of the native that are reflected back to him, clothed in the garments of his natural environment: the cries of birds, the passage of the clouds, the movements of the ants.

Many of these passing events are evil omens, and for such the general term is "tamax chi." Among tamax chi are the cackling of hens at night, the snorting of mules or stallions, and the howling of dogs. All these are signs that sickness or death is near. When all the dogs howl at night, it is a sign that pestilence is to come to the village. To see some snakes (but not all) is tamax chi. The coral snake (oonam) is a very bad sign. If one sees a small snake of this sort, it is a sign that a child will die; to see a large one presages the death of an adult. The long bright green snake known as yax kablai is another evil omen. To see snakes fighting is the worst of tamax chi. Eclipses, as has already been explained, are very bad omens: if the sun is eclipsed in the west, many men will die; if the moon is eclipsed, many women will die. If an owl cries at night, it is tamax chi; so it is when the bird called x-nuuc strikes against the roof at night; when the night-jar (puhuy) cries, "making the sound of vomiting"; when another bird, the ya, makes its harsh cry, or when a vulture walks close to the door of a house. If the orange trees drop small green fruit, many children will die that year; if large green fruit fall, then many adults will die. If, when corn is being taken from the cob, a cob happens to stand upright on the floor, it is a sign that someone is going to be sick.

The *milpero*, always anxious for the safety of the next harvest, reads in the behavior of nature predictions as to the weather and finds there guides to his own action and resolution of his uncertainties. "The old people need no books to tell them when to burn their fields and when to sow. They can tell by watching the sky." They say, "It does not matter if the almanac says it will rain in May; the signs are not that way."

If it is very cold at night, it is a sign that the next day the sun will be very hot. If the wind blows hard for several days, they say it is "buth-caan" (the sky is "full"), and it will rain hard for several days; then men go to plant their milpas. If the sun burns very hot and no wind stirs at all, then it will rain soon. When there are many stars in the sky, it is a sign of rain; when there are few, sunny weather will continue. When the Pleiades appear to be "half lying-down," it is a sign of rain, or when there is a ring around the sun or the moon. When the ceiba, plums and other fruit-trees bear much fruit, then one knows that the maize harvest will be good. When the large black butterflies come into the houses, it is a sign of rain. They are called "house-borrowers" (x-mahan nai) because they borrow the houses of men as shelter from the coming rain. If the turkeys take dust baths, or if the soot (yaabac na) drops from the ceiling, rain is coming. When the leaf-cutting ants are seen to be carrying many bits of leaf into their houses, or when they move their houses to higher ground, then the season will be rainy. Another sign of a rainy season is given when the gophers build their houses on hillocks, or when the oriole (yuyum) builds its nest of green leaves, or makes the nest very long, or when the frogs sing loud and steadily. Then the *milpero* cuts only hub-che, for the dry season will not last long enough to dry out the bush cut from high woods.

Dreams are omens of the future, usually of misfortune or calamity. To dream of many pigs, or of many cats, is a sign that there will be fighting, or other misfortunes. To dream of sapotes, or of the small banana, is a sign that one is going to be sad. To dream of happy, laughing people is a sign of sad things to come; but to dream of weeping people is a sign of good fortune ahead. But to dream of darkness is a bad sign; while of light, a good sign. When a h-men is treating for sickness, he often enquires into the dreams of his patient to make the prognosis. If the sick man dreams of light, he is advised that he will get well. Tomatoes in a dream mean the lighted candles of a coming wake; guns mean the same candles, not yet lighted. In an instance observed, when the patient dreamed of guns, the h-men gave the case up as hopeless. To dream of burning houses or milpas indicates a coming fever. Snakes mean the ropes of a coffin, or lashes that one is going to receive. To dream of red things is bad; it means blood. Doña Cef dreamt three times that she saw her husband dancing with a red handkerchief around his neck; two weeks later he was killed by machete blows in the neck. It is said that it is not uncommon to dream that the sky is falling; several dreamt this before the school fell. If one dreams he is digging sweet potatoes, it means he will help at a burial. To dream of the loss of a hat or other personal property means that one is to lose a member of the family by death. If one dreams he loses a small tooth, some child is going to die; loss of a molar means that an adult will die. To dream one is being married is the worst of possible dreams; that surely means one's death. If the old people dream this, they begin to give away their things and compose themselves for the end. To dream one is naked is a sign of one's coming illness. To dream of vultures, or black bulls or horses is a sign of a coming funeral. To dream of full granaries is a sign one is to have good health. It is also good to dream of young maize plants. To dream of much corn in the house is a sign of wealth coming.

Chapter XIII

A VILLAGE LEADER

The men and women who are the carriers of the culture described in the foregoing pages could be described to the reader one by one. From such an account would appear the various types of personality that compose any simple community. Beneath any culture, in a sense, are the same people one has always known. There are always the shy and the bold, the excitable and the phlegmatic, the intelligent and the stupid, the leaders and the led. The document which makes up the body of this chapter is included because, besides representing personality and human nature, it portrays the Chan Kom culture. In it a man sets forth a point of view, with regard to good conduct and the standards of success, that is characteristic of his group.

In Chan Kom there are three recognized leaders, and of these one is paramount. These three are sometimes spoken of as the *principales* of the village. Other men may hold office, but one or more of these three exerts an influence over all important secular matters. There are, besides, the spiritual leaders: the h-mens, whose respectful treatment nowadays conflicts with occasional suspicion or even contempt; and the village marriage-negotiator and principal *maestro cantor*, a man aloof, inscrutable, the ultimate authority on all moral or religious matters. But neither this man nor the h-mens concern themselves with leadership in mundane affairs.

Of the three *principales* one is the village patriarch, a man not yet old, but the principal survivor of those pioneers who founded the settlement, and the head of the largest and most powerful great-family in Chan Kom. He is a man mild in character and wise in judgment, slow in speech and inclined to let others put themselves forward in times of crisis.

The second exceeds his neighbors in his familiarity with the ways of the city and with Spanish, for he alone has lived in Merida. He brought to the village the mason's art, and this he taught to his neighbors while he set them an example of unflagging industry and zeal for public improvement and for communal enterprise. But an eccentric temperament and a judgment more eager than considered have limited his gifts as a leader.

The third man combines in his character all the qualities essential for leadership. He is a nephew of the first of the three men mentioned, and exhibits to a marked degree the stability of character and the superior intellectual qualities of this man's family. Furthermore, there burns in him a conviction of the superior destiny of his people and of his ability to lead them. This conviction stops short of fanaticism, but it is deeply and emotionally rooted. He has built his life around the development of his village; his career and that of Chan Kom form a single body of motives and ideals. Most of his hours are spent in making plans for himself or for the community, and in carrying them into execution. So occupied, going about to urge this man to industry, or to settle that dispute, sitting down to compose an exhortation to be delivered at a public meeting, or writing a letter to some official, he forgets, at times, to eat or sleep, and even neglects his milpa.

Close personal acquaintance with him, and his own autobiographic statements, allow us to see some of the circumstances which have shaped his character. He was brought up in the old-fashioned educational atmosphere which demanded complete obedience of a son to his father, a peon to his master, and a citizen to the authorities of his state. His conception of his relations to the people of the village is formed on this pattern: he is the wise father; they are the dutiful children. "So also we in this village," he said in one of his discourses, "are like boys who each one in his house recognizes as governor in office, his father in the house. So ought we all to understand that the authorities will fulfill their duty of helping you all with the laws and with the giving of judgments and you also should help and cooperate that we may work freely in this very beautiful village."

But just as he was entering upon a man's activities, there broke over Yucatan the sanguinary and exciting events of the social revolution. He listened to the propagandists of the new order, and heard them exhort him and other Indians to liberty and to assertion of their rights to land and economic independence. He heard Felipe Carrillo speak. He remained, moreover, so far from the city that the cynicism and disillusion with the revolution and its leaders, which came to characterize many of the more sophisticated, touched him but little; and he carried away a zeal for reform and an ideology of progress. To work, to improve, to construct, became his ambition.

A factional dispute in his village, Ebtun, gave rise to that colonizing movement which founded Chan Kom; and in this pioneer enterprise his kinsmen took the lead. To the enthusiasm of the times was added the optimism and initiative of a frontier environment. Temperamentally adapted to leadership, he was furnished the opportunity by the trend of circumstances. He came to conceive of Chan Kom as an independent and self-sufficient village of industrious and sober men and women, free of idleness and vice, the admiration of distinguished visitors.

Behind these influences one detects others, deeper and less definite. This man's thought and action have surely been guided by the vague belief of his people that one day the "Good Times" will come again, or at least that the land of Yucatan will one day belong again to the Maya and not to the dzul. He himself tells how deeply he was impressed as a boy to hear certain old people tell him that somewhere there was a race of "Red Men," men of skill and industry, the "brothers in work" of the Maya, and that one day this race would be with the mazehua again. The prestige of the Americans, who were seen to bring about conspicuous accomplishments at Chichen Itza, and were more amazingly figured in newspaper supplements, has probably been helped by these myths. He could not help drawing a parallel between these foreigners and the red builders described in mythology. The language he employs in his exordiums to the villagers is drawn partly from that of official documents and compositions of political propaganda, and partly from sermons, but it is not without phrases and figures of speech from the legends of his people.

It was this man's recognition of the part his life had played in the development of his village, and his pride in Chan Kom, that induced him, at our suggestion, to write (in Spanish) the short autobiography that follows. He is the only person in the village sufficiently literate to compose such a document. It is presented here in literal translation; we have added only the phrases set in parentheses that were necessary to complete the writer's thought.

It is the story of a successful man. The account is not, of course, objective; that is why it is interesting. It presents a career. It is entirely truthful, in the sense that there are no untruths; but the episodes selected and emphasized are those which put the author, before the world, in the light in which he would be seen. As his world is that of Chan Kom, we read in his self-history the standards of conduct which, in the village, win a man the approval and admiration of his fellows. His solidarity with his paternal relatives, his knowledge of Spanish and of writing, his winning his wife away from a boy of another family, his industry in the milpa, his honorable acquisition of property in cattle, pigs and jewelry, his conspicuous rôle as chief of a fiesta, his defiance of the h-mens, his notable success as a breeder of fierce bulls, his prowess as a military chieftain, and then as a founder and civic leader—these achievements almost exhaust the list of the ways in which a youth might at this period distinguish himself in the villages of southeastern Yucatan. These are the ways in which all men might cause themselves to be respected and admired. In this sense the document contributes to a knowledge of the culture of Chan Kom.

MY STORY SINCE I WAS SIX YEARS OLD
By Eustaquio Ceme

I was born in a village called Pixoy.[1] My father was Señor Don Diego Ceme. My mother was named Doña Petrona Pech. They were both citizens (*vecinos*) of Pixoy, and married. My mother died in Pixoy. I was living with my mother when she died; my age was six years. (Thereafter) I was under my father's orders; he taught me how to get his meals. He was the *comisario* of that village. All at once his brothers moved to Ebtun:[2] Don Epifanio Ceme, Don Felipe Ceme and Don Vicente Ceme. He finished his term and was wont to go and visit his brothers in that place. There he arranged to give a fiesta, and there one day he went to get my stepmother. He came back to Pixoy with his brothers and said to me: "Say goodbye to your grandmother and to your aunts and likewise to the village; now we are going to Ebtun together with your uncles." Then I got ready to make our journey on foot. I was very happy. The only thing I said to my uncles was that I would surely get tired on the way. My uncle, Don Epifanio, promised to carry me on the road. Then soon we arrived at that place (Ebtun); I said to him, "I am thirsty." He answered, "Go ask in that house that they give you a little water." I went and saw that my uncles and my aunts[3] were living in that house. They said, "Come in, here is your house, with your uncles." I stayed, very happy. In a little while my father came with my uncles and said to me, "Here we stay."

[1] Just northwest of Valladolid.
[2] Southwest of Valladolid.
[3] His father's brothers and their wives.

After a few days he told me we were to move to the house of my stepmother. I felt very badly to leave my uncles and my aunts because they cared for me a great deal. After a few days my father went to a *rancheria* to find or to earn our living; it was called Chan Kom. There he liked to make his milpa. There he devoted himself to making milpa. He came back and said to me, "As you are now seven years old, I deliver you to the school of this place, to study here; I am going to Chan Kom to make milpa." Willingly I agreed to study. I studied six years in the school of Ebtun; during my time of study I liked to play, to read and write a little, and to learn a little Spanish, and I liked all the boys of the school, going into their houses when they asked me, sometimes eating there, and even sleeping in their houses, as I did not have a house. Yes, there was the house of a brother of my stepmother; my father left me in that house but I didn't like the customs of the ladies there; they made me grind *nixtamal* on a stone called ka (metate), and as I saw this continue, well, I ventured to run away from the house.[1] I thought I would go to the house of a friend of mine named Magdaleno Noh. His father was Luciano Noh and his mother was Ulvana Kuyoc. They kindly gave me shelter, food, drink, clothing, and washed my clothes, treating me like their own son. For a week I was under the orders of Don Luciano, but he was half deaf. In the house I had left there was a son of my stepmother, named Anacleto Dzul, seven years old. He went to Cham Kom where my father was living with my stepmother. He arrived there and he told them, "Now he is settled in another house, my brother Eustaquio." My father, informed of everything I was doing, came immediately to Ebtun and brought very good clothes, hat, sandals, and everything I would need on the day when the examinations would be.[2] After my father arrived he made an agreement with the *comisario*, Antonio Pat C. Señor Pat ordered the police to summon Señor Luciano to come with them so we should make our appearances in the *comisaria*. We went in obedience to the summons. We arrived, and the judge said, "You get four days of work as your punishment, Lus Noh. And, Eustaquio Ceme, come to my house." And I went there with a sergeant and the judge and my father. When we reached the house I said good day to the grown people of the house, and I sat down. The judge said to me, "You have failed in the duty to your father." I said, "Perhaps." "Your punishment is twenty-five blows," and he ordered the sergeant to get two pieces of vine.[3] They brought (the kind called) uaymak. The judge told me to kneel before a Holy Cross and I knelt, feeling much shame, in view of the fact that the judge had a daughter who was sad to see how heavy was my punishment. But before I came I knew something would happen to me, and I had bought two silk handkerchiefs, one yellow and one pink, at a cost of eighty centavos. When I knelt the judge said, "Make the sign of the cross with your fingers; make a cross on your forehead."

I began praying and making the signs of the crosses that there are in my body, from my forehead to my breast. They were all sad. My father said, "Son, thanks be that you have not forgotten what I taught you."[4]

"Never in my life can I forget."

"All right. Are you ready for the punishment?"

"I don't know," I said.

But they ordered them to begin and the sergeant began with much force to beat me with the vines, both held in one hand. It began to hurt a lot when I had received five blows. I took out of my trousers pocket my yellow handkerchief so as to bandage my eyes. (But) when my tears began, it got wet right away. Immediately the judge saw it and told the sergeant to take away the handkerchief. He ordered them to take it away so I could not bandage my eyes. He said, "Ask pardon."

[1] Grinding corn is woman's work, and it is very unusual to ask even a small boy to do it.
[2] Examinations in the schools are quarterly, and are formal, semipublic occasions.
[3] Twenty-five years ago corporal punishment, especially for disobedience of a son or servant, was common.
[4] *i.e.* to make the signs of the cross.

"But that isn't possible."

I felt very badly and I took out of my pocket the other handkerchief, the pink one, and I bandaged my eyes again. My father would not let them take it away again. I asked pardon of all who were punishing me, and it ended with twelve pairs (of blows), and one pair besides. Some one took my hand and said, "Get up." I said, "*Buenos días*, zaaten zipil";[1] I kissed their hands and asked pardon of all till all were half-crying. When I stood up my father said, "I will forgive you, son, and ask the Lord God that you do good, so that you act as well brought up. Say goodbye to the *señor* judge and to everybody, so you can go to your stepmother's house. There ask her to get an orange and put a little salt on it, and with the rind anoint all your back as if it were a salad." It hurt where the scars were till the blood ran. Afterward my stepmother gave me something to eat. I said to her, "I don't eat anything."

In a little while my father came and said to me, "Why don't you eat? Eat, son. When you see that I am dead, do everything you want, even to dancing on my grave, but while I live I have to bring you up, because you are here with me."

"Well, how long, Papa?"

He answered me, "Until you learn to do right, to love much, to respect the right, to respect your betters, and besides to learn to read and write and (to speak) Spanish." And my father told me to stay and study again. And he went together (with some others) to his milpa in Chan Kom.

This happened to me when I was ten years old, and I continued to stay in Ebtun. One time I received word from my father saying to us—to me and Anacleto—that we should ask permission to go to Chan Kom to see mama[2] who was very sick. But the teacher did not give us permission. In a few days I received another message from my father saying that now our mama was dead. And we went to see her in Chan Kom, but we did not find her; she was already buried in the pueblo of Kaua. And we arrived at Chan Kom and met our father, and he told us, "Your poor mother is dead, of a serious illness. Stay here in our house under my orders. There is nearly everything you need."

My father had more than seven hundred *canastros* of corn on the ear; we children were five, including one girl; and also he had chickens and pigs. One day he told us that we should go to the village of Ebtun to continue studying. My little brothers and my sister remained there, and my aunts also kindly cared for them, because our house was (only) thirty-five meters from the house of my uncles.

After a few days all at once I received a message sent to us saying that his (my father's) health was bad. In a few days my uncles received a message telling us to come see our father who was already dead. We asked permission from the teacher, and we came. Well, in Kaua we met my uncles. They said, "There in the cemetery you see the grave of your poor father." I began to cry because I did not see him as I had seen him before. Afterwards we all went to Chan Kom, and there began the *trajin*[3] of his three days. After his three days, my uncle Don Fano said to me, "Stay here with us, in my house; this was the testament my poor brother said to me."[4]

Well, and then I saw a young lady named Hilaria Pat. Her father was Don Asunción Pat, and he and my father were together all the time. They were comrades, for my father bore Don Elut (son of Don Asunción) to baptism. They were together all the time, and if my father had any meat, he would give some to Don Asunción. Never was there any trouble between them.[5] When I arrived in Chan Kom from Ebtun, then all at once I saw the young lady coming with a dish of dinner, as we always give to one who has just

---

[1] *I.e.* he asked pardon.
[2] His stepmother.
[3] The wake and prayers following a death.
[4] It is customary for a dying widower to give the custody of his children to a close relative, commonly a brother. See p. 63.
[5] See p. 99.

come. And I began to look at her, and I half-thought, "If only my father were still alive, I would ask him to arrange it." Then I thought I would tell my uncles to go and ask her mother and her brothers so that I could get married to her. But her mother said that this was not possible because there was a woman who was trying to get her son married and this woman had agreed to hand over her son to the mother of the young lady I was interested in.[1] But it did not turn out this way. I didn't know about her being promised to someone else, but then when my uncles knew it they stopped doing anything about it. But then I thought I would come out first with the young lady by honorable means. So my uncles went to talk it over with the brothers of the young lady. They urged Don Tino and Don Madal[2] to accept me for their sister. They pointed out that Don Fano worked very hard, and that furthermore my father had cleared more than two hundred mecates of *monte*, and they said that in view of this it was not possible to calculate that I should turn out to be lazy. The brothers of the young lady said that the father of the other boy was going to deliver him as son-in-law,[3] but my uncles said that this other boy did not know how to read, and that his father was a drunkard, and died poor.

Finally the mother said to my uncles that she should have six months to decide whether she would accept me or not. Then that time came to an end. My uncles went back again to the house of the mother of the young lady to come to an agreement. They took half a bottle of rum made with honey so that they could talk things over with the brothers of the young lady, Don Elut, Don Madal, and Don Tino, and with the mother, who was named Doña Sofia Caamal. Don Madal and Don Tino listened to what my uncles Don Fano, Don Guillermo and my aunt Doña Maria said in asking for the young lady, "as the wife of my nephew," said Don Fano, "and I promise as is right to hand over the things which one should give at a well-conducted wedding." The brothers said, "Mama, what do you say?" She said, "What do you think?" Don Madal and Don Tino approved and the agreement was made. The first time they gave three flasks or nine bottles of *aguardiente*. The second time the same, and the third time the same. The fourth time they gave the *muhul*. In the *muhul* they gave three flasks of rum made with honey, a little wheat bread, cakes of chocolate, sugar, cigarettes, a couple of sets of clothing, a handkerchief and four *reales*. A poor wedding was mine![4] When the proper time had gone by, we went to the registry office and at the end of eighteen days all the business with the priest and the Civil Registry was over with. We had a dinner of turkey and that was all. For ten months after my marriage we stayed in the house of my uncle Don Fano. Then we finished making a new house of thatch and my uncle and my two little brothers moved there and stayed there. And I stayed there separate from them in a hut that was just about to fall down. And there I thought I would make my milpa, and I made two hundred *mecates*[5] and I had the luck to get a very good harvest, five hundred baskets of ears of corn or a hundred and twenty-five loads of shelled corn. And I bought two small pigs and I began to feed them up until they got fat. I sold one and one I exchanged for a *cadena corchada* and a pair of earrings, and I was very well pleased.

With one set of chain and earrings which her mother had given her, my wife had two chains and two pairs of earrings, and we lived very happily.[6] With the money for the other pig I had sold I had thirty pesos and I took ten pesos and I bought four little pigs and with the rest of the money I bought a good *terno*, or wife's dress, and a silk *rebozo* costing five pesos and some shoes. And I bought my good clothes, sandals, and a hat, and two silk handkerchiefs and a little bottle of perfume which cost three pesos and a half. And

[1] That is, the parents of the other boy had begun the four visits to the house of the girl's parents. See p. 193.
[2] The girl's father being dead, her older brothers share with their mother the responsibility of these negotiations.
[3] *I.e.* the marriage proposed by the parents of the other boy was one of haan-cab, whereby the boy goes to live for a year with his prospective parents-in-law, working for them until the marriage is consummated (see p. 87).
[4] Because no chains, earrings or rings were included. See p. 193.
[5] This is a large milpa. He is boasting.
[6] His wife's lack of these things had been causing him shame.

I sold sixteen loads of corn at two pesos the load which made thirty-two pesos and we began to enjoy *jaranas* and fiestas.   There my good friends asked me for money which I gave to them so that they would clear land for me the next year.   And this time my milpa was in all three hundred *mecates* and thanks to God I had a very good harvest.   I sold the four pigs because they were now very fat.   One I exchanged for a bull-calf weighing forty *kilos* and the three others I sold for one hundred and twenty pesos.   I took sixty pesos and I went and got a friend to go with me and some other friends from Ebtun who had sent word to me that I should go with them to the village of Yaxcaba to buy bulls to bring to our village of Ebtun because it was only three months before the fiesta would be celebrated.   On this journey my friends bought two bulls and I bought a young bull-calf for fifty pesos and we returned.   When we got to our little hamlet of Chan Kom my wife and I invited my friends to have a meal in our hut.   We were all very tired and some one said, "I am going to get a bottle of *aguardiente* to rid us of our tiredness."   A little later he came with a bottle of *anis* and we began to pass it around, all very happy. It is a distance of fourteen leagues to San Felipe where we bought the bulls.   And I got out a bottle and I shared it among them and we talked of various matters, about our good friendships and about how we would have a lively fiesta.   Then we ate and afterward said goodbye and some went to a little place called Dzonot Aban.   These were named Rodesindo Can, Nicolas Kuyoc, and Isabel Uc.   Others went to Dzucmuc and they were called Juan Bautista Kuyoc, Isidro Kuyoc, and Manuel Kuyoc.   All at once arrived the day of the fiesta of Ebtun, which is my second pueblo, and I went with my wife and took two bulls for the *jaripeo* and they turned out to be very fierce.   I was the head of the *vaqueros* and *vaqueras*,[1] I was the chief of the whole fiesta who directed the *vaquerías* of the *jefe* of the plaza.   When the former heads saw that everyone interested in the fiesta was very well satisfied with me they began to bother me.   A certain Siforiano Uc began to strike me and this really did bother me and I wrestled with him and lifted him right off the ground like a child.   Then he got over it and we started having a lot to drink, both of us.   And then all at once, at dawn, I met someone else who began to insult me so that we began to fight, and the pure truth is that I won.   The *hechiceros* talked ill of me because I didn't use them to make the dza-akab ti *lasso* dzuytal zuun yoklal ma u thoocol tumen *toros*.[2]

I didn't recognize this custom because it seemed to me just a way for the *hechiceros* to get drunk, because they never tire of asking for *aguardiente* along with the people who hang around them during the preparations (*trajines*) and the whole of the fiesta.   This is the custom in the whole *Departamento* of Valladolid and that is why all the villages and their people are getting so poor, because of the many *hechiceros* who ask for *aguardiente* on every occasion.   But during the fiesta that I directed, nothing had happened to me in all that time, nor to my *vaqueros* or *vaqueras*.   And I didn't order them to do hadz-pach because to do this the h-men asks for half a bottle of *aguardiente* from every *vaquero*. Sometimes there are thirty *vaqueros* or more.   I just said to them that whoever wanted to, should buy one candle to burn before the apostle, before the *santo*, to our Lord God. We said goodbye, both of us, in the name of God, and so it ended.   And then I returned with my wife and my two bulls to my *ranchería* of Chan Kom and I continued working on my milpa.

All at once I decided to sell my two bulls for two hundred pesos to people of Valladolid, and those of this place were very much surprised because here there were no cattle, and I decided to buy two more and I went with my uncle, Don Fano, to the *Departamento* of Izamal and there my uncle bought two very fierce bulls for one hundred and seventy pesos, the two of them.   Then we went to the *hacienda* of San Isidro and there I bought two, for

---

[1] The young men and girls who take part in the dancing; the young men are also those who bring the bulls to the bull-fight.
[2] These customs are explained on p. 158.

one hundred and fifty pesos, and one of them was so fierce that he had to have his eyes covered with a cloth (of agave), and one of my uncle's was the same.

Again came the twenty-fourth of August, the day of the fiesta (of Ebtun) and I took my bull and he turned out very bold so that four bull-fighters were almost killed. One man from Tekom, called Ursulo Canul, died two weeks later. He was a fine bugle player in the plaza and he entered to try his luck. His mother caught hold of him by the ear and said to him, "Don't go in to the bull ring to fight," but he disobeyed her and he entered the ring and soon after he fell down half-dead. Many offered to give me one hundred and fifty pesos for that bull but I did not sell him, and I returned again to Chan Kom. A short four months afterward my uncle's bull ran away and was lost for good, and five months after my bull also ran away to Yaxcaba, where because of politics things were in a bad way. There they shot (the cattle) and divided the meat among themselves and then the leaders ordered them to set up defenses against the owner of the cattle. My uncle Don Fano and one of my nephews and I went just with our lassos (to look for the bull) and when we were four kilometers away we saw many women with their children and old men too old to do anything going eastward from the village to take refuge in their milpas because the villages there had been destroyed by those thieving politicians, people of Sotuta.[1] The names of the leaders were Cico Perea, a certain Emilio Lugo, Bernadino Poot, Tomas Rodríguez, who was the President of the Liberals, and his crony Loreto Bak and still others who came from Sotuta. Everyone we talked to on the road said to us that he who is of the party of the Socialist Government is treated badly, he is made a prisoner and his punishment is to be beaten with barbed wire. We saw on the road some who showed us their wounds where they had received their beating from the hands of the Liberals of this village. Some told us, very much afraid, that they were even killing and throwing into the cenotes the poor people who believe in the Socialist Government. A kilometer and a half farther on we came to where there is this great barricade in the entrance to the village of Yaxcaba and I saw that we were very pale and I said to my uncle, Don Fano, that it is better that we go back to Chan Kom. We should not sell our lives for one hundred and fifty pesos, for while we live we can always make more money, and that is better than going in and running the risk of sacrificing ourselves, because really we have seen how these poor people are who are flying to take shelter in the settlements where their milpas are and we have seen the little villages like Kancabdzonot, Yaxuna, and yet others, all burned up. So right away we decided to go back, and we returned to Chan Kom quite satisfied. There were two bulls more and we decided to kill them. First my uncle killed his bull and afterward he did the same with mine. Later on I had it arranged with Sr. Juan Mex to buy two cows at one hundred and forty-five pesos, but I got sick so I left it to my uncle to make the arrangements at the same price. When I was better again I went to Cuncunul to buy from Don Tacio two young bulls. I bought the two of them for sixty pesos, and I brought them back to my own land; but a few days after I was harvesting sugar-cane and one of my bulls drank the sweet water of the sugar-cane, and I saw that he was going to die, so I killed him and sold the meat for four pesos only. At this time I had much corn and thirty pigs, twenty of them for sale. At this time every day there were arriving in Chan Kom people from different villages of the *Departamento* of Sotuta, some of them wounded with bullets by the Liberals of that place; and many told how people disappeared forever in the cenotes and that the assassins said to them, to my friends, the authorities who were arriving on my land—for many came from different villages of our *Departamento*—I said to them, the day that those assassins from the west come in to destroy our settlements and lands in this region of Valladolid, at that time we will summon together the authorities of the villages and their inhabitants to make a plan for our emergency (and to form) a resolution to confront

1 On the ancient feud between Ebtun and Sotuta, see p. 22.

those assassins who aren't willing to work, so that we may die facing them and not wait to die in our houses, as they have done to those others.   They all answered "That's right, that's right.   Summon us, summon us, and we will come."   (I answered) "Thank you very much, comrades.   God grant that nothing happens, because it is better to work, for here are much corn and animals and my wish is that we prosper here and don't have to forsake the village.   But if it so happens that it is necessary, I will let you know so that you may come.   There is food in this place enough for four years.   I bid you goodbye.   I shall be in this place at your service."   "We think the same, comrade, well, goodbye," and they went to their villages.   It is true that when corn is scarce Chan Kom sometimes has two hundred laborers from different villages who work in our milpas.

The tenth of June my wife and I went to Ebtun to enjoy four *vaquerías*, to which I was invited by the organizers, and I had promised to bring with me ten *vaqueras* for the dance on the thirteenth, the day of the fiesta of San Antonio.   On the twelfth there came word from the assistant *comisario* at Chan Kom informing the *comisario* of Ebtun that four people of X-Kopteil had been attacked, that they had their guns taken away and barely escaped from the assassins.   I sent word to Chan Kom and Chan Kom sent word to many neighboring settlements later on the same day.   X-Kopteil escaped; they did not enter there.   Three inhabitants of Chan Kom who had milpas in the west came and said that the hamlet of Zacbacikan had been attacked and that the bandits stole eighteen horses and money and the gold chains from the poor women, money, chains, and earrings up to the value of a thousand pesos, and seven men they carried away to throw into the cenote of Yaxuna.   The three people of Chan Kom going to get their corn (of the sort called) bekech-bacal[1] for seed, at this place met the assassins just as they had finished throwing the poor men into the cenote and they (the assassins) fired their thirty-thirties at the three of them.   At once one fell half-dead and when the evildoers saw it they stabbed him with a knife in his abdomen.   He was called Juan B. Hu.   And his life ceased.   The other two ran away but one succeeded in firing two shots at them.   He wounded one of the assassins.   I did not see this but it really happened so, according to what he said. When the two came to Chan Kom they told us that the villages of Kancabdzonot and Yaxuna had been burned, some of the furniture was thrown into the cenote and the rest burned, even much corn.   On this day I was in Ebtun and I went to see the *comisario* to have a conference with him, for from this moment on my plans changed and I left off thinking about dancing with the girls.   Most of my mind was a revolutionary struggle against those who had started (the trouble) because I judged it my duty to be firm in carrying out my promises since the occasion showed that action was needed.   The *comisario* said to me, "Let us go and talk to the *Comandante* of the troops."   So we went and saw him and he said to us that after the *vaquerías* we should summon the people.   Both of us, the *comisario* and I, agreed to name twenty men to go to Chan Kom and even to Yaxuna where our comrade had fallen dead.   Right away a sergeant named Benito Un left for Chan Kom, which was the place for getting together and making our plan.   There he found many people armed and waiting for his orders.   They came from the settlements around about.   Immediately all set out for the place where had taken place the killing of that man Juan Hu, and in passing through the large hamlet of Zacbacikan they saw women and little ones crying because they did not know what had happened to their fathers, (who had been) carried away by the assassins to be thrown into the cenote of Yaxuna. When the people came to this place they saw in the trees around about the cenote a large flock of buzzards attracted by the corpses which were floating on the water and by the bloody traces left where the men had tried to escape from the assassins.   The people went and found the dead man half a block from the plaza on the road to Kancabdzonot.   There where he was found on the ground the people acted like commissioners (coroner's jury)

---

[1] Bekech, thin, bacal, corncob.   The grains of these ears are preferred for seed because they are larger than the others.

and examined the body. They saw the holes made by the bullets and where he had been knifed, and then the father of the dead man, Valentin Hu, bade farewell to his son and they buried him in this same place and then all returned to Chan Kom together to send a report of what had happened to Ebtun and to Valladolid. On the thirteenth I was still in Ebtun with the *comisario*, because the *comisario* was Florentino Pat, my brother-in-law, and they (his family) live in Chan Kom, and we agreed to go to Cuncunul to have a conference with the *Presidente* to ask him if he could hold an audience on the eighteenth of this same month to talk over what had taken place in Yaxcaba and in Sotuta. He and the other members of the *Ayuntamiento* said that this would be agreed to on condition that it (the audience) should take place after the twenty-fourth, which is the day of the fiesta of the Apostle San Juan of Cuncunul.[1] So it was fixed. We returned to Ebtun, and on arriving at the *cuartel* we met Sergeant Un with his soldiers; he gave us the report of the commission on Chan Kom, Zacbacikan and Yaxuna, the place where our countryman lost his life at the hands of the assassins. On the fourteenth we left Ebtun to go and stay in the settlement where we lived, Chan Kom. On the fifteenth there was a gathering of all the principal men of this place, the *comisario*, Florentino Pat, Epifanio Ceme, Eustaquio Ceme, Guillermo Tamay, Magdaleno Pat, Eleuterio Pat, Anacleto Dzul, and Patricio Mac, director of the school. Of the men whose names are given only two did not attend, Florentino Pat and Patricio Mac, because they were entrenched (keeping watch behind barricades) outside. At this meeting it was agreed to send word to the villages which were very friendly to Chan Kom, in Tinum to the *comisario* Santiago Beana and to Santiago Cupul, in Piste to Lorenzo Barrera and to the fighting cock Aniceto Moreno. They had an understanding with the other neighboring villages north of Chan Kom. On the east (we would send word) to comrade Filomeno Pat of Tekom, and in Cuncunul to comrade Primitivo Escamilla. On the south (we would send word) to the settlements of Xanla, Tzeal, X-Kalakdzonot, and the other two nearby settlements. The official notice sent on the sixteenth to Tinum and Piste said as follows: "To Comrades Santiago Beana and Cupul, *Presidentes* of Tinum. According to the agreement which we made before and on order of Citizen Revolutionary Chief, José Ma. I. Traconis[2] of this *Departamento*, please to order armed men and buglers to assist in putting down the disturbances which are occasioning the abandonment of many settlements because of the Liberal robbers of Yaxcaba and Sotuta. Meeting and making of plans on the eighteenth of this month, and no excuses allowed. Chan Kom, the sixteenth of June, from the *comisario* Florentino Pat, Guillermo Tamay, Epifanio Ceme, Eustaquio Ceme P." Official notices of like import were sent to the other villages. At once I set out with the *comisario*. On the sixteenth we went to Valladolid to consult our revolutionary leaders, distinguished Sr. José Ma. I. Traconis and others, and thanks to him they gave us energetic orders, support, and official instructions to improve the situation. On the seventeenth on our return home, we slept in Cuncunul. When the eighteenth dawned we left for Chan Kom and arrived there about two in the afternoon. Before we got there, Don Madal met us and there were two more at the entrance to Chan Kom, well armed and with red cockades in their hats. They told us that since yesterday, the seventeenth, people had begun to arrive well armed. "Everything is all right; that's all that has happened." We heard their guns fired off and bugles and we entered the little plaza by the school. We saw many people like soldiers with cartridge belts crossed on their breasts, machetes, and thirty-thirties in their hands, calabashes with water and their *sabucanes* where they had their food, and even their slingshots. They were all yelling. We got down from our horses with the carbines we had received and then right off everyone gathered together and we

---

[1] The war had to wait till after the fiesta of the patron saint.

[2] José Ma. Iturralde Traconis was from Valladolid, a member of one of the principal families of that town. He took active part in the political campaign between Socialists and Liberals, finally becoming Governor. He was much loved by the Indians.

greeted each other very enthusiastically. "Comrades," we said to them, "in a moment we will speak to your leaders and to you." I saw that at the school there was a guard with a bugle, and there were the people from Tinum headed by Cupul and Paulino. I saw the chapel with a bugler as guard; there were the people of Piste headed by Anis (Aniceto Moreno) and Sergeant Valentin Pech. The people from the small settlements were in the houses and in the little paths around them, armed just like the others. Order reigned. In these days the women day and night were preparing provisions. At half past three, after discussing official matters with the sergeants of both groups (Tinum and Piste) we ordered two bugle calls for gathering together in front of the school, and we began to direct the formation into three lines, one that of Piste, one that of Tinum, and one of ourselves with the small settlements, and we ordered that each line be counted. Tinum and Piste had ninety and we had one hundred and twenty-eight. We began to divide up the people into sections of ten men with a sergeant at the head, and in a notebook which I had I wrote down their names and the lists of the sections and after that we ordered a counting of everyone again and the total came out two hundred and eighteen in the ranks the same as in the lists. We gave instructions to the buglers to use five bugle calls, first, that of entering and attacking; second, the retreat; third, the rally together; fourth, mess; fifth, the march of triumph. And then we read official letters from the other villages, Tekom and Cuncunul, which said that the people would be ready on the fifth of July, after the fiestas of San Juan and San Pedro. The leader Moreno said, "The second in command, comrades, is Comrade Eustaquio Ceme." "We wish it to be so," everyone said. They began to play marches of triumph but I asked them to be quiet and I said to them, "Comrades, already you know from the mouths of those who are here how the Liberals of Yaxcaba and Sotuta, the enemies of the workers and of the Government, are throwing men into the cenotes and are robbing and killing. Therefore now is the time to defend our rights as citizens of Liberty and to take our stand against them. Tomorrow at five o'clock after we have had breakfast we shall leave here so as easily to reach the plaza (of Yaxcaba) to help put an end to things. God will not allow anything bad to happen to us because we are workers. Now you can prepare with your sergeants to take your mess, and goodbye." Right off the bugle blew for mess. Anis did not know how to speak or read Spanish; he was only brave. During the three days in which the people stayed here (in Chan Kom) they were well taken care of, with meals of pork and beans, and coffee made in big pots. At five in the morning with the bugler blowing the march we marched off, saying goodbye to Chan Kom. We went through Zacbacikan and Yaxuna and there was no one there except buzzards on account of the dead, and we got more and more aroused and continued on to Yaxcaba and arrived at the ranch of San José de los Diaz. There we rested, at about three in the afternoon; there we had our supper, drinking *atole*. Immediately Moreno sent secret messages to the Socialists of Tacdzibichen and to D. Yama to tell them to come and join the revolution. He answered that he did not believe in it. At two in the morning we set out and entered all the streets of Yaxcaba and occupied the church in sections and one bugler remained at our command in the plaza and the other at the entrance to the road from Sotuta. Then the firing began. I heard it heavy through all the village. Immediately the sentinel struck three (A. M.) on the bell of the *cuartel* and the soldiers in the *cuartel* came out and occupied (took their positions behind) the pillars. Our section was placed near the *cuartel*, about 40 meters to the east. Immediately the firing of the guard became heavy upon our people. For half an hour we had been in position with our guns resting on the wall of the church aiming at the *cuartel*, about 40 meters away. When I saw them (come out) this way, I gave orders to open fire and (gave) the call for attack and (for the) church bell to be rung while we were shouting, "Long live the Supreme Socialist Government of the Nation and of the State! Long live liberty of the downtrodden workers and death to Liberal assassins who do not wish to work! Now, with plenty of noise, Down with them! Let them die!" There were calls to the attack both from the bugler in the plaza and from the one on the road to Sotuta. It lasted two hours, the men of the *cuartel* fighting against our men, and then we heard the voice of the guardsman waving his white sheet like a flag and asking peace from our bullets. They said they were federal troops belonging to the Government and we, judging that it was not necessary to take the *cuartel*, ceased firing from the plaza, among bugle calls and ringing of bells and yelling. At nine (in the morning) I ordered the retreat sounded, at the hour when Yama arrived with the people of Tacdzibichen. At the head of the road which goes to the Díaz ranch, I gave a command for the summon-together to be sounded, and most of them did assemble and it appeared that none of our men had been killed, and only one man, Fernando Dzul, had been wounded, but he not seriously. I did not see him because he had already gone back (home). We discussed various plans, in case anything should come up again, and we said goodbye and each group went off toward its own village, and we ordered the last call for retreat sounded. This is what really took place. Many say that there were people killed, but I didn't see them, because I didn't leave my position in the plaza. We came back to Chan Kom and we were all very well satisfied. Three days later in the morning I went to Valladolid with Don Madal to have a conference with Don José Ma. Iturralde Traconis. He treated us very well. Two hours we spent going about with him in his car, and we discussed many affairs. I went to Cuncunul and we enjoyed the fiesta and another at Tekom and I bought my horse to ride on, with a saddle, my boots, my pistol and my two lassos.

Later, having promised to take part in the August fiesta, I went to Ebtun, and there I paid for a *corrida* of bulls, spending two hundred pesos. Then my uncle Don Fano became *comisario* of Ebtun, and Don Tino was made *suplente*, and I became treasurer. We agreed to finish building the church. We set about this task till it was finished, although not all the people helped. Then we asked the Government to build a *cuartel* 20 meters long; and when only the floor was yet to be made, we abandoned Ebtun.

Then we began to promote the development of (*fomentar*) Chan Kom. We all decided to ask the valuable aid of the Government of Don Felipe Carrillo P. In this way we began to make a pueblo. First Don Fano was *comisario*, and the trees were cut down in the plaza, just the way one makes milpa; and it was ordered that we should build low stone walls; but the streets were just paths.

When Don Fano's term was over, Don Tino was elected *comisario*, and Don Guillermo Tamay was chosen *suplente*, and I was president of the Local Agrarian Committee and treasurer of the *Liga*. I began my work with all enthusiasm and in agreement with the other directors (of the *Liga*). We decided to hold a meeting, and I suggested to the *comisario* that he summon the men (*ejidatarios*) on a certain date to an assembly in the school. (At this meeting) I explained to them my wish to comply faithfully with my duty to distribute lands to everyone who wished to build his house on firm foundations in accordance with the laws about house lots, and (to construct) both streets and houses like those of civilized cities: "Whoever needs land, let him call upon me to measure it off; this I tell you now so as to safeguard my responsibility for the future. Because in truth my wish is to know that each one of you is working with goodwill; and I have faith in what you think and what you do, because our efforts in this place are not lost. Let us work in an orderly way, and soon the time will come, my companions, when Chan Kom will be a beautiful pueblo."

All listened, well satisfied. The *comisario* told them how they should fulfill their *faginas*,[1] and (gave) other orders, and this finished, we retired. The next authorities accomplished no more than this during their term; it was the same as the previous one. And I continued to serve in both régimes, but I saw that the people gave more credence to the municipal authorities in agrarian matters, so I half stopped carrying out the laws and submitted myself to these authorities.

One time I heard that the pueblos of Yaxcaba and Kancabdzonot were suffering great injury at the hands of the Liberals of Sotuta, and I went off with Don Madal and five other men, all well armed with our thirty-thirties. We found women and children

[1] See p. 78.

and old people gathered in the abandoned church of Santa Maria. Families they were from the pueblos I have mentioned, fleeing from the assassins—so they told us. I asked them where were their husbands, and they said they were at the bulwarks at Kancabdzonot. We said goodbye to them and went off to that pueblo. We arrived there at three in the afternoon and in the plaza we found many men, well armed. Immediately the leaders ordered the bugle to blow assembly, everybody came together and I spoke to them as follows: "Comrades, we had the news at Chan Kom that you were suffering much at the hands of the enemies of Liberty and Socialism, and then we saw your wives and children suffering greatly in the bush near here. Well, we come in the name of all the comrades of my pueblo to let you know that we are ready to help you to get into the condition (of well-being) in which you wish to be, and (to invite you) to come to our village; there (in Chan Kom) there is nothing such as has happened to you, (but) only work and happiness. Another service that we may render you, is (to help you) to compose a signed petition to be carried to Valladolid to be mailed there, because the Government does not know your situation, (and if it did) it would give you protection. And so, comrades, tomorrow we take leave of you."

Then three of their people replied, saying, "What our comrade says is very good; tomorrow we will go with them, because now we are tired of suffering so in every change the politicians make."

And thus came the families Díaz, Coyi and some others. They were much surprised to see so many people settled at Chan Kom. Don Tino, the *comisario* and the other chief men decided to make houses for the new settlers from Yaxcaba; at the time of his administration people made their house on hillocks and (by) little paths.

I decided to go to Merida to ask the Governor for tools. We all went, my wife, my son Talo, my brother-in-law, Don Elut, his wife, Antonia, together with the teacher, Don Candelario. We set out from here for Chichen and Dzitas, and in the railway station we met six of the officials from Ebtun. They began to annoy us, threatening to attack and burn Chan Kom, which so exasperated me that I struck them, at the same time explaining my act to the gentlemen present, saying that these individuals were planning to destroy a new village which we were developing with the aid of the Government. The affair went no further. We entered the train, and arriving in Merida we took an automobile and went to the *barrio* of the *Centenario* to sleep.

Next day we went to the *Delegación* to take up matters connected with the *ejido* of our pueblo. The delegate showed us the provisional survey and other documents that were to be delivered to us at a later date, saying further: "Who does not respect the agrarian laws, with fifty federal soldiers we make him respect them; and the same (we do) with pueblos that fail to respect your *ejidos*." "Very well, sir," I replied. We said goodbye, and going out from the office we met the men of Ebtun who renewed their threats against Chan Kom.

(From that time on) this pueblo was separate from Ebtun. But in truth this trip cost much money; the cost of sending the tools alone was eighteen pesos to me and to the chief men—Don Fano, Don Tino, Don Guillermo Tamay, Don Elut, Don Madal, Don Anal, Don Tacio Dzul, and Don Felipe Ceme.

Continuing the account of my mission: After going out from the *Delegación* we went to the palace of the Governor, but on that day we didn't get to speak. The next day we went to the palace but we couldn't all get in because it was filled with so many people; however, I alone got in.

But the Governor Don Pepe[1] was not there, only his secretary-general, Licenciado Don Antonio Cual García. I began to explain my mission in the name of Chan Kom and of all the comrades, and it came out very well. I succeeded in getting the gift of four

[1] José Ma. Iturralde.

boxes of dynamite, fuses and caps, for blasting plaza and streets, two augers, two mallets, two picks, two wheelbarrows, two hammers, one National flag of silk, one carbide lantern worth fourteen pesos. To assure us that all would be sent, he had it all written down to be sent to Dzitas. I said many thanks to him for his kind attention and praised his adminis-tration, saying: "Señor Licenciado, you will excuse me if I take the (shipping) receipt with me." Right away he gave a written order to take to the chief of the Government warehouse. Next day we went to the warehouse and I delivered the order to the chief, who carried it out only with difficulty because he was busy getting drunk with his friends. He opened the warehouse and I went in with him and collected everything mentioned on the list, and so stayed there a few minutes; and as he was waiting to go to his friends he shut the warehouse and I remained inside. Don Candelario and Don Elut began to tell him, "Open up, so our comrade may come out." So said all the others to him. But as the chief was drunk, he did not do so, and I stayed in there for a quarter of an hour, and when (at last) I got out, I saw he was quarreling with his friends. I left, saying many thanks for their bad attention, and directly called a wagon and paid three pesos to have (the tools) brought to the central station. I alone went with it (the cart). My wife, Don Elut, and Don Candel waited for me in the big plaza. I deposited the tools at the station, and obtained the receipt, which cost seven pesos and twenty-five centavos, with which to get them at Dzitas. Then we went for a walk.

Next day we said goodbye to Merida, going to Dzitas, where we collected everything; I paid eight pesos for an automobile to carry us to Chichen. We arrived at Chan Kom, everyone well satisfied. This was in the month of September. We all were thankful to Lic. Cual García.

In November I had the luck to be elected *comisario*. I entered office the first of January with my greatest enthusiasm and exerted myself to make Chan Kom prosper like a clean and civilized pueblo. Well, during the year of my administration I cleared many plum and uayam trees from the plaza; and I ordered that the walls be raised and aligned, forming new streets 8 meters wide; I ordered them to cut down trees where new streets were to go; I ordered them to make their houses in the regular form (they have in cities) each with its wings;[1] some streets to be made diagonally. I determined the house lots, walls and fences, according to fixed measure. Likewise I ordered them to white-wash their properties and to level the contours of the plaza. I summoned the people to explain the advantages of cattle-raising, and to urge them to devote themselves to it. I made a *ripio*[2] for the *comisaría*, and a jail. My *suplente* Anastacio Dzul died four months after my term began. I was succeeded by Don Eleuterio Mukul as *comisario*, and Isidro Hu as *suplente*.

My place as *comisario* was then taken by Don Eleuterio Mukul, and Isidro Hu became *comisario suplente*. I was then *ex-autoridad*,[3] but I continued to be at the disposition of the people. And I devoted myself to work, making milpa and caring for my cattle. Then all at once I received a communication from Don Filomeno Puc of Tekom, calling upon us to come to his village and unite ourselves with him in leadership of a revolution which, with the solid support of five other villages, he had resolved to start against the arbitrary authorities and against the rum monopoly of this *Departamento*.[4] We answered Comrade Puc (asking) that he come personally among us at this place so as to talk with us and explain his reasons. Soon he arrived with his companion. Meetings were held, and he said to us: "Comrades, the reason why I have decided to launch a movement of rebellion is that a number of police officers, sent by the *Presidente* of this *Departamento* came to

---

[1] Flaring walls connecting the wall of the house-lot with doorway.
[2] Building with masonry walls and thatched roof.
[3] One who has been *comisario* or President of the *Liga*, and is therefore exempt from duty as *guardia*.
[4] This "revolution" was in fact the resistance offered by Filomeno Puc's personal followers to official interference with an illicit still that Puc had been operating at Tekom.

loot my house; they came well armed, in an automobile, with an *alambiquero;*[1] and they carried off the dishes and furniture and money that I had in the house, without any reason. Now I, and all my companions, in agreement with the representatives of the other villages, have approved the following course of action: First, take steps to communicate with the Señor Diputado Lic. Tito Patron Villamil, so as to have him arrange peacefully that these persecutions not continue; and second, make secure the peace and liberty and tranquillity of the village of Tekom, as well as of Don Filo's person."

Thanks to the intervention of the Señor Licenciado, who gave full protection, all remained in peace; and Don Filo continued to stay in Chan Kom. Don Madal and Don Guillermo took up with him the matter of building two masonry houses. After these were built we went to Merida—Don Filo, the teacher A. Villa and I—to discuss matters with Don Bartolomé García. There we saw Don Tito, who offered Don Filo a horse, and also gave us a pass (on the railroad) so we might go to Campeche to talk with Carlos Barragan, the representative of the *Secretaría de Agricultura y Fomento*, and ask him for a permit to cut wood for railway ties. There we met Señor Rabachol,[2] with whom we had a few drinks in the saloon "Venus," in front of the state government building. We continued to enjoy ourselves, celebrating the fiestas of the fifteenth and sixteenth of September. Afterward we returned to Merida and went back to Chan Kom.

A few days later we accompanied Don Filo to Tekom, and when we arrived there we were received by all the people with music and flourishes (played by the band). In the evening (there was) a *vaquería* and a supper, a token of the admiration and affection (held) for all the people of Chan Kom. And we returned to our village. And I got a young lady, one Antonia of Tekom, to work in my house. But soon there was a difficulty with my wife, and I found myself obliged to go with the girl to Merida. I was there six days in a hotel and ten days in the house of Don Dolores Presuel. I went with the girl to talk with the *Liga Central*, and they gave me assurances, and transportation to return to my village. As I was *comisario*, I took my post in the *comisaría* and entered upon some public improvements. Also I learned that during my absence one of my bulls had been shot and killed by people of San Pedro—Maximo Canul, Pedro, Eusebio and Jacinto Can— father, son, and grandson. Having received a communication from the *Presidente Municipal* of Cuncunul in which he summoned me to appear in connection with a complaint lodged against me by my mother-in-law and my wife, I answered the *Presidente:* "Tell my mother-in-law and my wife that I am working at home as before, and that until the end of my life I will continue to live properly with my wife, but in case any action is taken against me, I will sign nothing in the matter. I send a mule for her to use in returning, in charge of the bearer, whom I have paid. Acknowledging your action, I remain sincerely, the *comisario municipal*, Eustaquio Ceme P."

After this I gave attention to the matter of my steer. There came one Fernando Caamal who told me that those who shot the steer were Maximo and Pedro, Eusebio and Jacinto Can—father, son and grandson; and the man swore that this was true. Immediately I communicated with the *Presidente*, and when I saw that after four days he had not replied I gave orders to summon the people. They assembled, and I gave them the facts, and afterward, in view of the fact that it was on our *ejido* that the steer was shot, I ordered a sergeant to go explore the land and look for traces, and for the bones. Directly twenty-five men went out under the command of a sergeant, and in the bush they seized the men already mentioned; and in that very place they confessed that it was true that it was they who stole the meat of the steer. We demanded that they pay a hundred and forty pesos, and they delivered a mule as a pledge. But while payment was being made, they were brought here as prisoners. Then I sent notices to four villages that their officials might

---

[1] Literally, "distiller." He means the *rematador de licores;* the officer concerned with liquor taxes.
[2] An official of the time of Felipe Carrillo Puerto.

come to take charge of the investigations.   In the presence of these (officials) the prisoners made their statements, saying that it was true that they had shot the steer, in order to prevent the development of cattle-raising, because they did not want to fence their corn fields.   Before the authorities of the *comisaría* of this and the other villages they promised to make the payment, and so the matter stood.   But afterward they refused to pay and, aroused by certain others, these men started a great quarrel, on account of which I had to go to Merida to arrange the matter so that I won out.

The *Señor Presidente*, Don Aureliano Centeno, offered us two boxes of dynamite so that the people might improve their house-lots.   A little after this I fell sick of a terrible illness; after I had been sick for three months I began to buy medicines.   I spent two months using them and found no relief.   Then I began to summon the h-mens; and all replied to me that I was being bewitched by those men who ate my steer, for one of these, named Pedro, was himself a h-men.   I had recourse to about a dozen h-mens, and all told me the same.   Although I had spent so much on rum, money and gifts for the h-mens, I did not find relief.   They kept telling me that I should wait, without worrying about my hens, that were being used up in making so many kex, u-hanli-col, u-hanli-cab, u-chuyen-na, loh-cah-talil, u-hetz-luum-cab, and u-hanli-thup.[1]

Others told me that I could be cured by massage (hiikab).   They all exploited me, but nobody helped me.   Others advised me to take blood from my veins with rattlesnake's fangs and from my head with flint (or obsidian) tok,[2] and from my hands with pieces of bottles.   The sickness from which I suffered consisted principally in pains in all my body, especially in my stomach and in my legs, and in much vomiting.   As a last resort I called in a great h-men from Tixcacaltuyu.   My brothers[3] arranged for him to cure me for forty-five pesos.   He told me to puncture all my body with tok; in my legs alone were made two hundred and fifty punctures, through which I lost much blood.   After four days there was no relief.   Then he told me I would be cured by cupping, but I did not find relief. For food (the h-men) gave me three times (a day) a drink of egg beaten up in hot water. Now I was tired of suffering; I could not work; I could do nothing but lie about day and night waiting for relief; but I did not find it.

Really, the h-mens are exploiters of the working man.   Everyone concerned, in all the New World[4] ought to study a way, with greater determination and discipline,[5] to do away with the numerous h-mens, who are the worst enemies of all the workers of the world.   My plain and simple opinion is that the First Magistrate of every nation ought to send doctors or sanitary (experts) who understand hygiene; (it would be) best to send them to each village that includes other villages in its neighborhood and is a center of the federal schools, like Chan Kom, (which) needs a main clinic (*sanitorio*); (there) they should be installed with a case of drugs, and they would inspect everything that would fall under their jurisdiction, as is understood in the offices of the Civil Registry of the villages.   This could be done with just a small tax, or a little intelligence.

(Eustaquio recounted the episode of his sickness more fully in an oral statement some weeks before he wrote his autobiography.   This statement is interpolated here, together with quotations from a notebook Eustaquio was keeping during the period.

---

[1] The ceremonies—all requiring the consumption of one or more fowl—of which Don Eus here makes mention are respectively: ceremony of exorcism of evil winds from an individual; of offerings to the guardians of the milpa; of offerings to the guardians of the apiary; the ceremony performed to the patron crosses of the dwelling; of exorcism of evil spirits from a dwelling; the ceremony performed when the bee-hives are moved; and that propitiatory of the small (fifth) rain-god.   Failure to perform any one of these may be a cause of sickness. See Chapters VIII and X.

[2] The name given to the instrument, originally of obsidian, used in bloodletting.

[3] Actually, his paternal uncle's son-in-law and his paternal aunt's son (cousin).   Both relatives were younger than he; he refers to them as *hermanitos*, and does not hesitate to ask them to run errands for him.   See p. 94.

[4] "*A quien corresponda*," "*en todo el Nuevo Mundo*"—phrases Don Eus has probably gleaned from the newspapers and from official documents.

[5] More such phrases.   These high-sounding borrowed terms continue through the remaining paragraphs.

His acquiescence in the diagnosis of witchcraft made by the h-men, and his plan to revenge himself, he omits as unworthy of his conception of himself from the later more formal self-portrait of the autobiography.)

"Two years ago I fell sick. For three months, for four months, I was sick; it hurt and it hurt; I vomited and there were winds making noises in my stomach—who knows what it was? The h-men came and looked in his zaztun and told me that the sickness had been sent into me by a man named Pedro Canul, who lived in San Pedro. That was Don Balbino who treated me, but it did no good, and I sent my two nephews[1] to Tixcacaltuyu to speak with Lino Xec. Lino Xec gave seven tok to Maco and Emiliano and told them what they were to do."

(On their return Don Eus wrote as follows in his notebook: On the day of the 19th of December, 1928, my nephews, Maximo Uicab and Emiliano Tamay arrived from a journey which they had made to the village of Tixcacaltuyu in order to interview a witch doctor, Don José Lino Xec; and my two nephews explained to this man if it is certain that he knows how to cure sicknesses. Yes, this man answered, according to whatever one suffers from. Then they arranged with this man to cure me, as I was suffering much from a sickness which had been made to fall upon me by C. Pedro Canul, because he is a man of the devil to send sicknesses over a Christian of God.)

"Maco did what the h-men said to do, and with the tok he bled me here, over this eye, and here over this eye, and in the inner side of each elbow joint."

(Don Eus recorded the event as follows:

Arrangement with Mr. Lino Xec for 45 pesos in silver in order to cure me: On the 19th of December I received 7 tok with pieces of bottles, and my holy blood gushed forth and fell on the floor and afterward my eyes received a very painful medicine; with much effort I succeeded in opening my eyes once more to see the light of God.

As a Christian son of God do not let me die in the hands of the half-Christians who hand over their spirits or souls to the demons of the devil.

I trust my health to the Lord God.)

"But I did not get better, and as I lay in my hammock I thought of my dreadful state, and I made up my mind that unless I could stop Pedro Canul from sending the witchcraft into me, I would die. One time I thought I would escape if I should go away as far as Merida. But then I thought, that if I did that I would not see my children any more; it would be better to die here where there are granaries. Better die here in resignation like Jesus Christ.

"Then after a while I decided to kill Pedro Canul. My friends came to see me while I was sick, and many of them told me of other men who were sick because of sorcerers, and some of them had even died. X-Kalakdzonot, Santa Maria, Xanla—in all villages and rancherías the sorcerers were working evil, sending their alak[2] out to bring sickness to unfortunates. So I wrote a letter to the authorities in Valladolid telling them about what the sorcerers were doing and that I was going to kill Pedro Canul. I began by saying that in view of the fact that I was suffering from this serious sickness, and had used six witch doctors without having yet been cured, and that they all told me that it was because Pedro Canul was sending the witchcraft at me, and that many other people in this region were sick or dead because of what the sorcerers were doing, therefore it was

---

[1] Whom elsewhere he refers to as "younger brothers."

[2] Certain snakes and insects, thought to come up from metnal (the inferior regions) at the command of the sorcerers to carry disease and death to their victims. See p. 178.

probably true that Pedro Canul was doing this to me. Then I told them that this was why I was going to commit this crime. I told them that there were many sorcerers throughout the *Departamento* doing these things, that they were endangering the laws of the state and the nation, and I called upon the authorities to take measures in the matter.

"I decided to make twenty-eight copies of this letter and to send one to each of the twenty-eight villages of the *Departamento*, so as to arouse the villages to action.

"I thought that as I was going to commit this crime I would probably myself be killed, or at least put in jail, so I wrote my will, and I told what to do with all my goods, except two cattle, which I told my uncle to keep to pay the fine if there should also be a fine."

(The will is as follows:

I hand over all my possessions to my uncle *compadre* Don Epifanio Ceme—one masonry house with a building plot, 165 *mecates* of milpa with the use of the harvest, 13 heads of cattle, and including eight sons and daughters of my wife, granting them both, in fulfilment of my testamentary wish, the right to live on the premises of the property, one mule and some pigs are at their disposition. And I solemnly sign,

EUSTAQUIO CEME)

Chan Kom, January 20, 1929.

"But I did not send these letters after all, because I thought of a way of killing Pedro Canul without anybody hearing about it. I thought that he would come to a fiesta at Kaua, and I would meet him there, and then I would ask him to walk with me along the road to Cuncunul, and when we came past the cenote at the edge of the road, I would push him in.

"At this time we were busy making Chan Kom a pueblo, and I went to Merida with Don Nas to see the authorities in the Liga. At Dzitas I met a bookseller, and he wanted to sell me a book. Then I remembered that ——— when he had got half in trouble[1] told me about a book he had bought and read that had got him out of trouble. So I told the bookseller this, and asked him how much such a book would cost. He told me such a book would cost four pesos, and I asked if there was not a soiled book I could have for less, and finally I bought this book[2] for two pesos. The bookseller told me that with this book I could manage Chan Kom very well. I read the book all through, and when I read it, my mind was changed about killing Pedro Canul. There are some very good things in it—that about he who lives by the knife, dies by the knife, and other things; and this part about the woman who was an adulteress. It is a very good book; it tells what the ancients (*los antiguos*) used to do."

The autobiography continued:

"Many times I reflect that although our race is very fierce in battle, making triumph our leaders of the Revolution, for just laws and for liberty, nevertheless it seems that we do not enjoy its fruits. We ought to laugh with our leaders, with those who live in the cities, but up to now we have not achieved what we sought, although it has cost the lives of many of our race. If the plan of the revolutionary laws has triumphed, the country ought to know it. (The Revolution) which was made, and which cost the lives of many in humble villages in all this countryside, ought to bring its benefits especially upon these. It is plain to the whole general public that the villages of our sort are without doctors or sanitary aid (*sanidad*). Only sometimes they are visited by the priests, or by (public) officials, or by armed police, that come to exact payments; but (meanwhile) the people die with sickness, or are sickly from childhood, without having any doctors. This happens even to those who know how to read, sometimes even to the teachers, while they are

[1] Charged with cutting to pieces several policemen sent to arrest him.
[2] A battered New Testament.

fulfilling their mission in the villages. (It is true that there arrive) notices explaining hygiene, but (we are) far from (being able to) buy the materials, the medicine. The way quickly to improve the humble villages far from the cities—would that it might be possible! —(would be) to have, even for (no more than) a week, a doctor or a hygiene officer to inspect the village and to point out the sources of harm which cause the sicknesses, and to explain this in general assemblies. Only in this way can our land be made to prosper and flourish. In truth, the customs and ambitions of today are something like those of the time of the dictatorship and of *caciquismo*.[1] In the time of General Don Salvador Alvarado,[2] who brought liberty, law, and justice, all were occupied in work from the humblest to the highest class; ambition and its vices disappeared or were forgotten. The (military) forces of public safety went from village to village. One heard music and flourishes of the band. Today these villages lack music; but they have a right to music. Chan Kom, for example, hasn't any, and we have to go long distances to the cities to hear it.

Another thing which happens in the villages, and to which those concerned ought to give strict attention in watching over the villages, even to those out in the bush with their respective properties (*predios*), (is that although) there are plenty of lands (*predios*), there is not enough food; principally (are lacking) such things as fruit trees. In these lands there are just weeds and useless (*perjudiciales*, "harmful") trees. Often it happens that there are people who do not have garden lots (*predios*); the lands are monopolized by others. In all these matters those concerned should take measures. Another thing that happens is that many villages lack playgrounds (*parques*); in this village there is no playground.[3] There are other very urgent needs in all the villages that are far from the cities. All those who work with energy, (who are) defenders of the proletarian class, ought to give enthusiastic aid in the opening of roads to the villages. When we go to the cities, we see with pleasure the paved streets, and sometimes even airplanes; but it is just that for us too should come a time for improving our streets by which we go out to obey the orders of, or to receive, our superiors.

I took office as *comisario* January 1, 1931. On the tenth of January I gave orders to clean the streets and to whitewash the walls, within a period of fifteen days after the day I made my speech at a general assembly. Thanks to the obedience given my order, the village became very pretty.

The comrades began to receive instruction in general meetings organized by the teacher Don Alfonso Villa, who is an intelligent teacher, with diploma (*titulado*), and who is improving his profession through study. He enjoys good friendship with the honorable American gentlemen of the Carnegie Institution at Chichen Itza. I too began to explain to all the inhabitants of all this region the desirability of welcoming the honorable and famous gentlemen of the Carnegie, and of treating them all like brothers, and of opening our arms to receive them in Chan Kom, and of giving the best facilities for their studies of Chan Kom, when they should need them. The first who came to visit us was the *señorita* Catita Mis Nakey,[4] and then (came) the *señor* Doctor Don Robert Redfield, and his wife, and afterward the *señor* Doctor Stigue[5] and his wife. I, with my wife and all my family were great friends with them, offering our house as their house, and attending them during their visits. Then other visitors began to come, to whom during my administration we offered dances (*vaquerías*) and general assemblies as a sign of our affection and respect. They on their part shared in the general cultural meetings, with instructive lectures. And so it has gone on till today, when my village, with its new school, has become beautiful.

[1] The time of Porfirio Díaz.
[2] Who led the revolution in Yucatan.
[3] The people of the village have since built one.
[4] Katheryn MacKay.
[5] Morris Steggerda.

INDEX